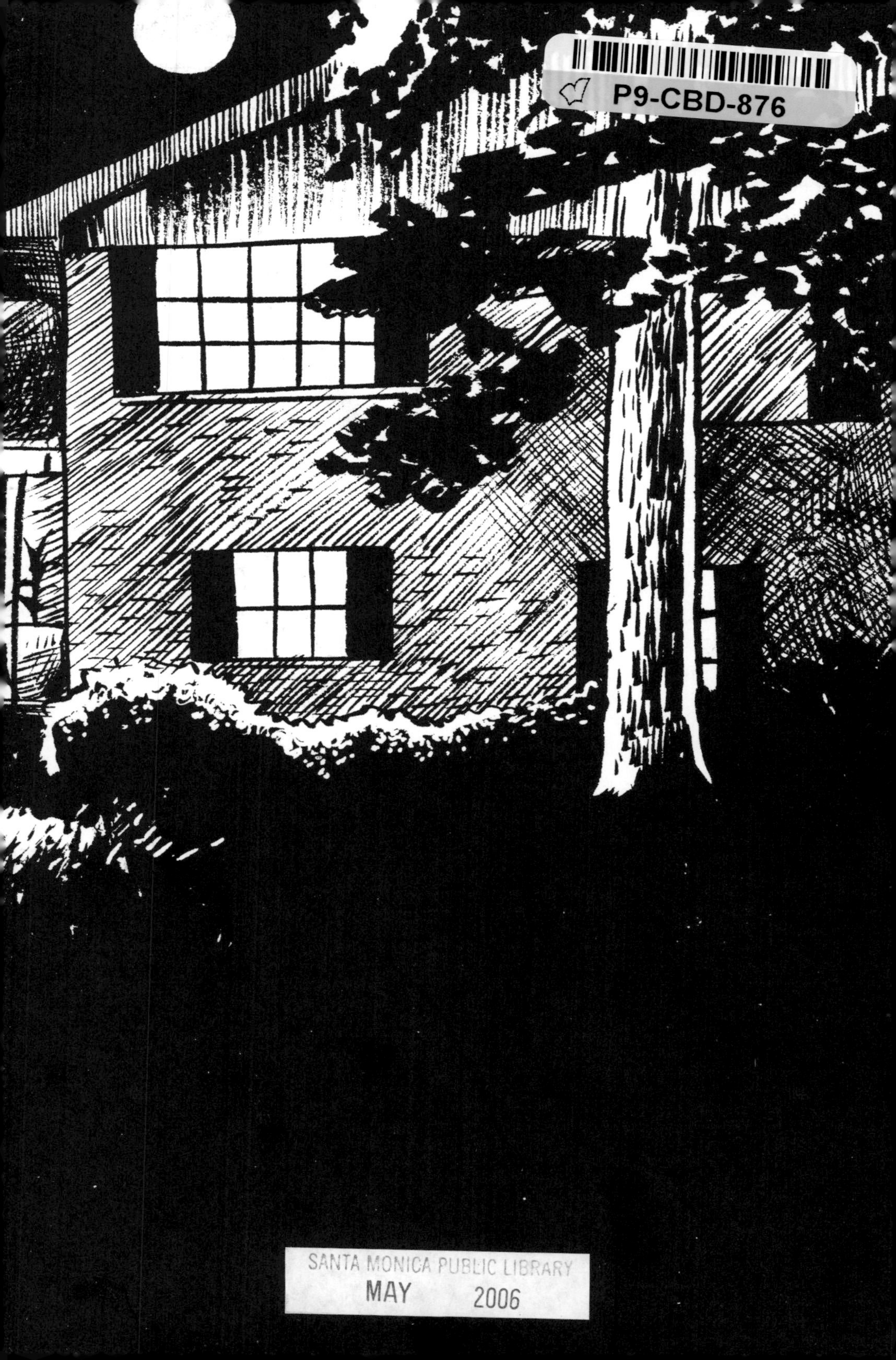

TRAILERS

Also available:
North Country, $13.95
Lucifer's Garden of Verses
in 4 volumes, $15.95 cloth, $8.95 paper

Add $3 P&H first item $1 each additional.

Write for our complete catalog
of over 200 graphic novels:
NBM
555 8th Ave., Suite 1202
New York, NY 10018
www.nbmpublishing.com

NORTH COUNTRY
SHANE WHITE

LUCIFER'S GARDEN OF VERSES
VOLUME TWO
darlin' Niki
Lance Tooks

LUCIFER'S GARDEN OF VERSES
VOLUME THREE
The Student
(Or Nude Descending a Staircase... Head First)
Lance Tooks
A Graphic Novel

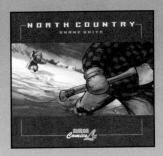

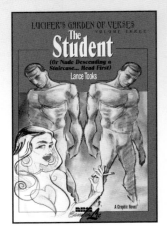

TRAILERS

MARK KNEECE
JULIE COLLINS-
ROUSSEAU

ISBN 10: 1-56163-441-7, hc.
ISBN 10: 1-56163-445-X, pb.
ISBN 13: 978-1-56163-441-5, hc.
ISBN 13: 978-1-56163-445-3, pb.
© 2005 Mark Kneece and Julie Collins-Rousseau
printed in Singapore

3   2   1

Library of Congress Cataloging-in-Publication Data

Kneece, Mark.
  Trailers / Mark Kneece, Julie Collins.
    p. cm.
ISBN 1-56163-441-7 (alk. paper) -- ISBN 1-56163-445-X (pbk. : alk. paper)
  1. Graphic novels. I. Collins, Julie, 1978- ill. II. Title.

PN6727.K635T73 2005
741.5'973--dc22

                                                              2005050524

Comicslit is an imprint
and trademark of

NANTIER · BEALL · MINOUSTCHINE
Publishing inc.
new york

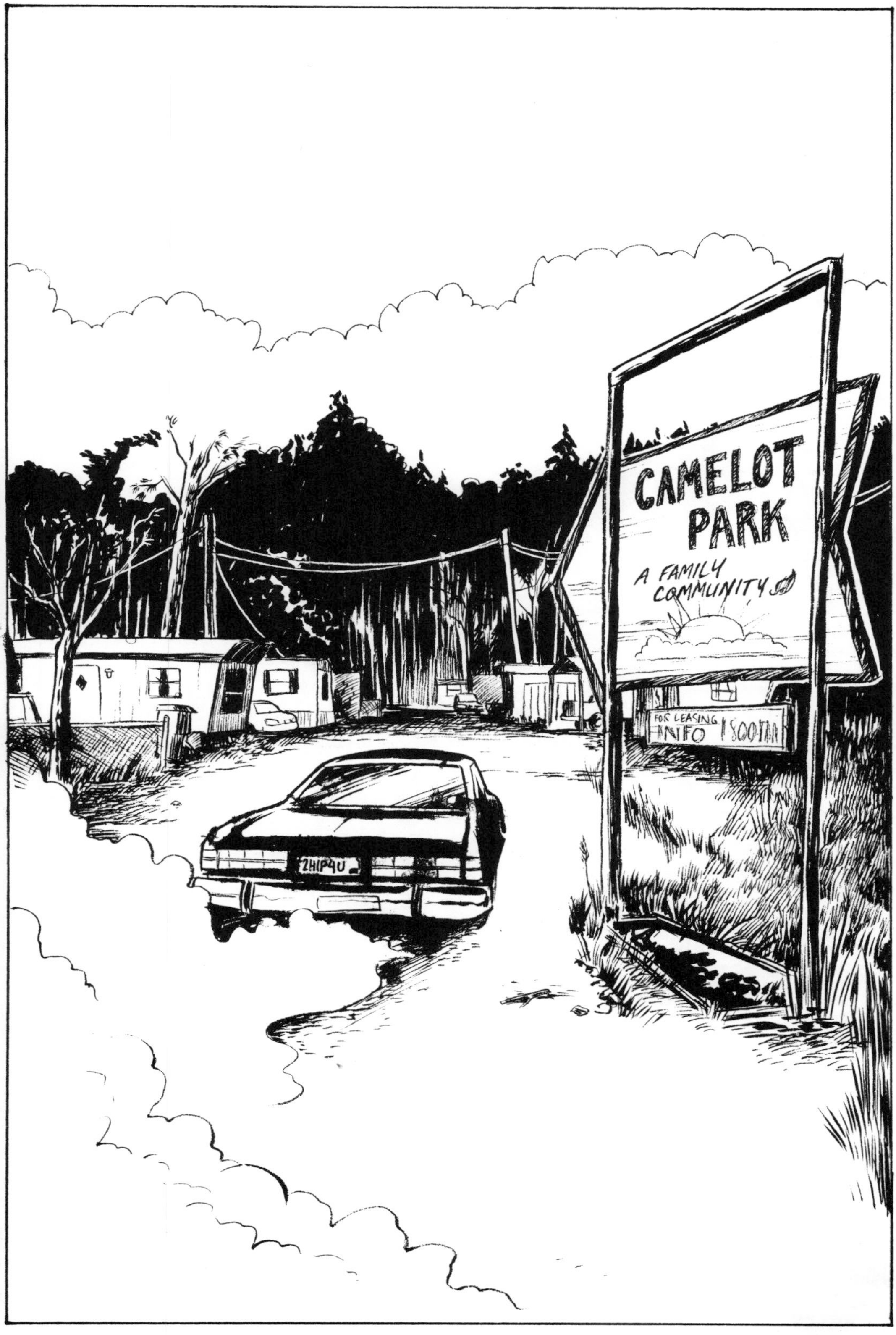
CAMELOT PARK
A FAMILY COMMUNITY
FOR LEASING INFO
2HIP4U

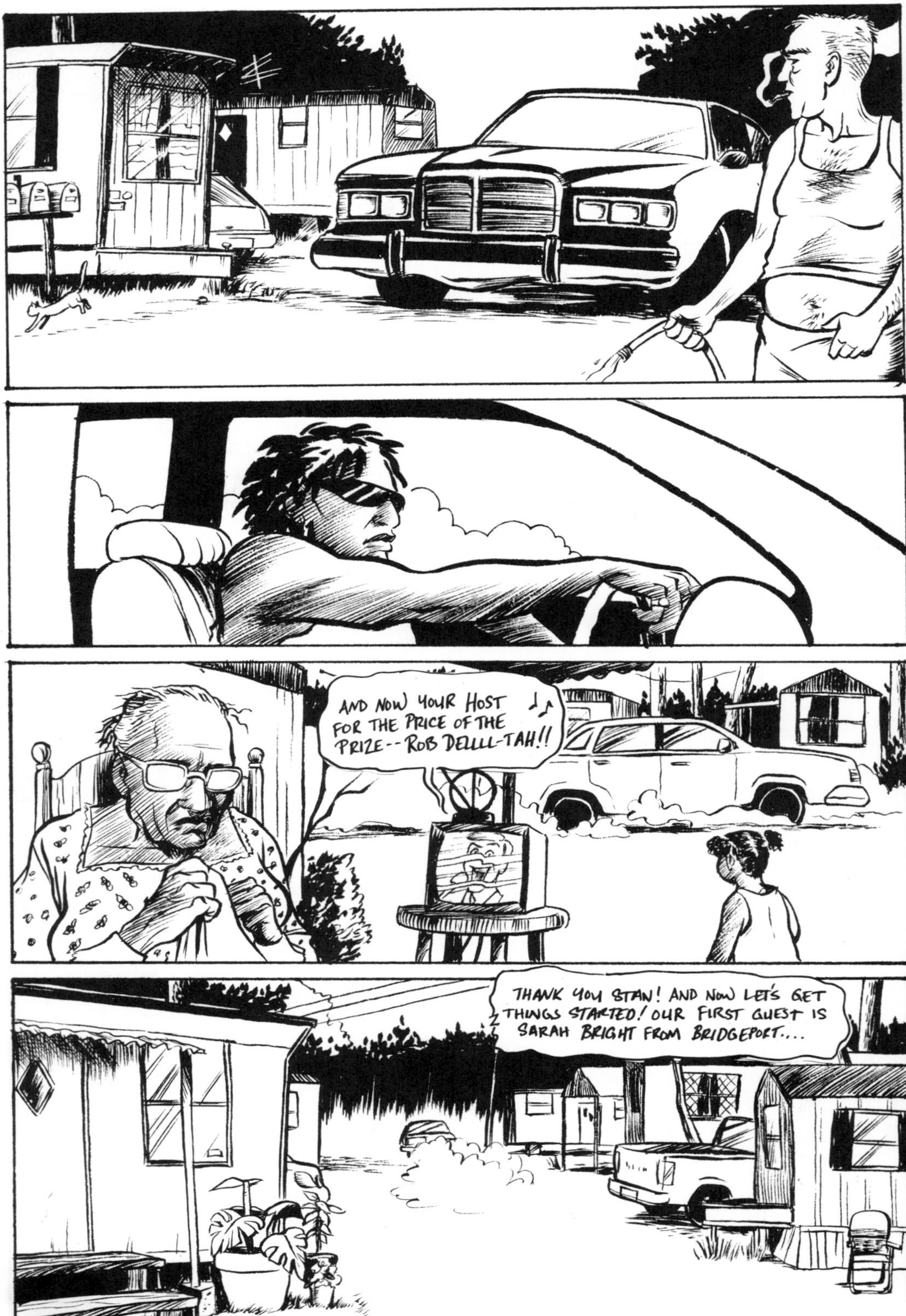
AND NOW YOUR HOST FOR THE PRICE OF THE PRIZE--ROB DELLLL-TAH!!
THANK YOU STAN! AND NOW LET'S GET THINGS STARTED! OUR FIRST GUEST IS SARAH BRIGHT FROM BRIDGEPORT....

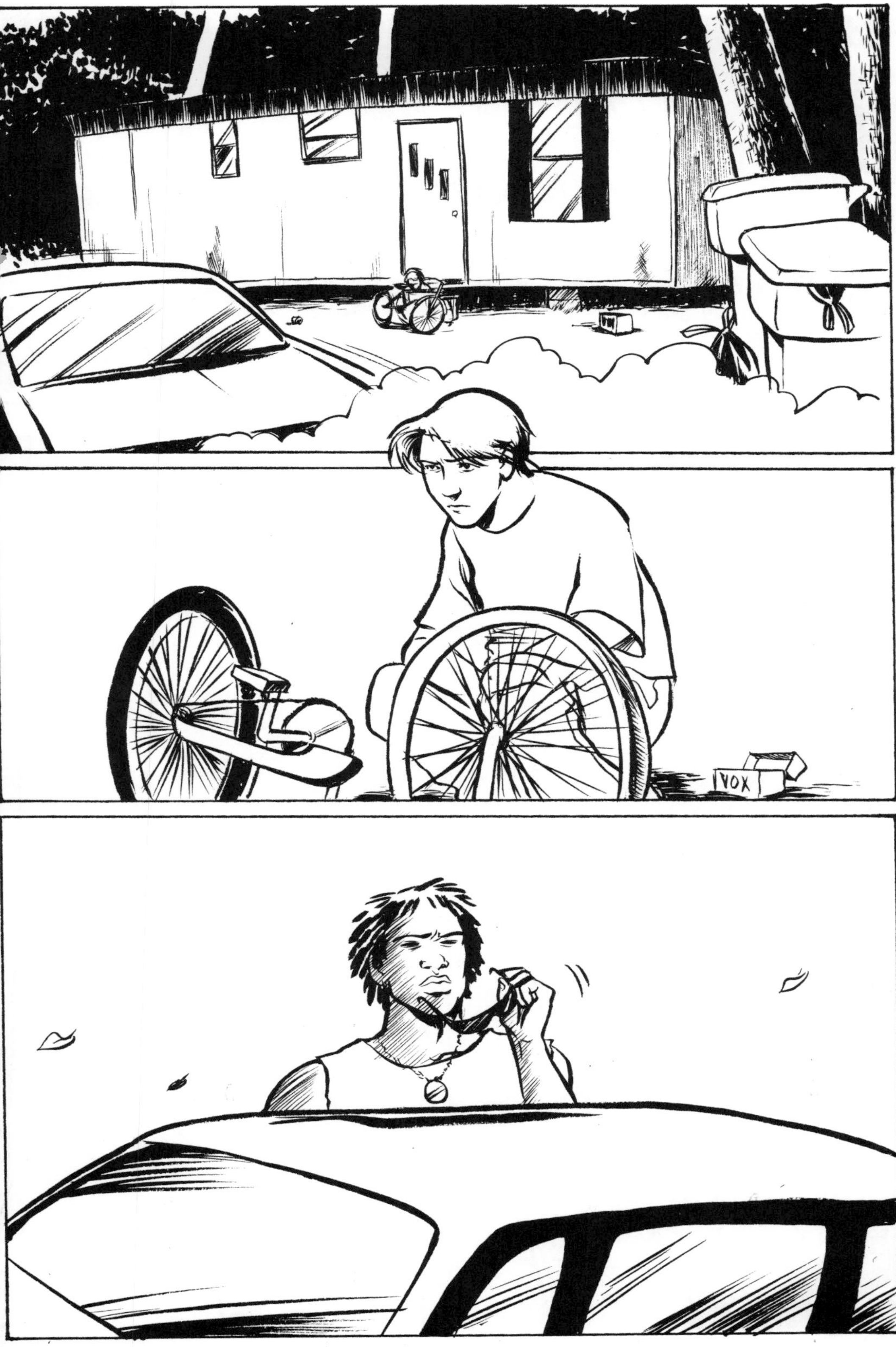
VOX

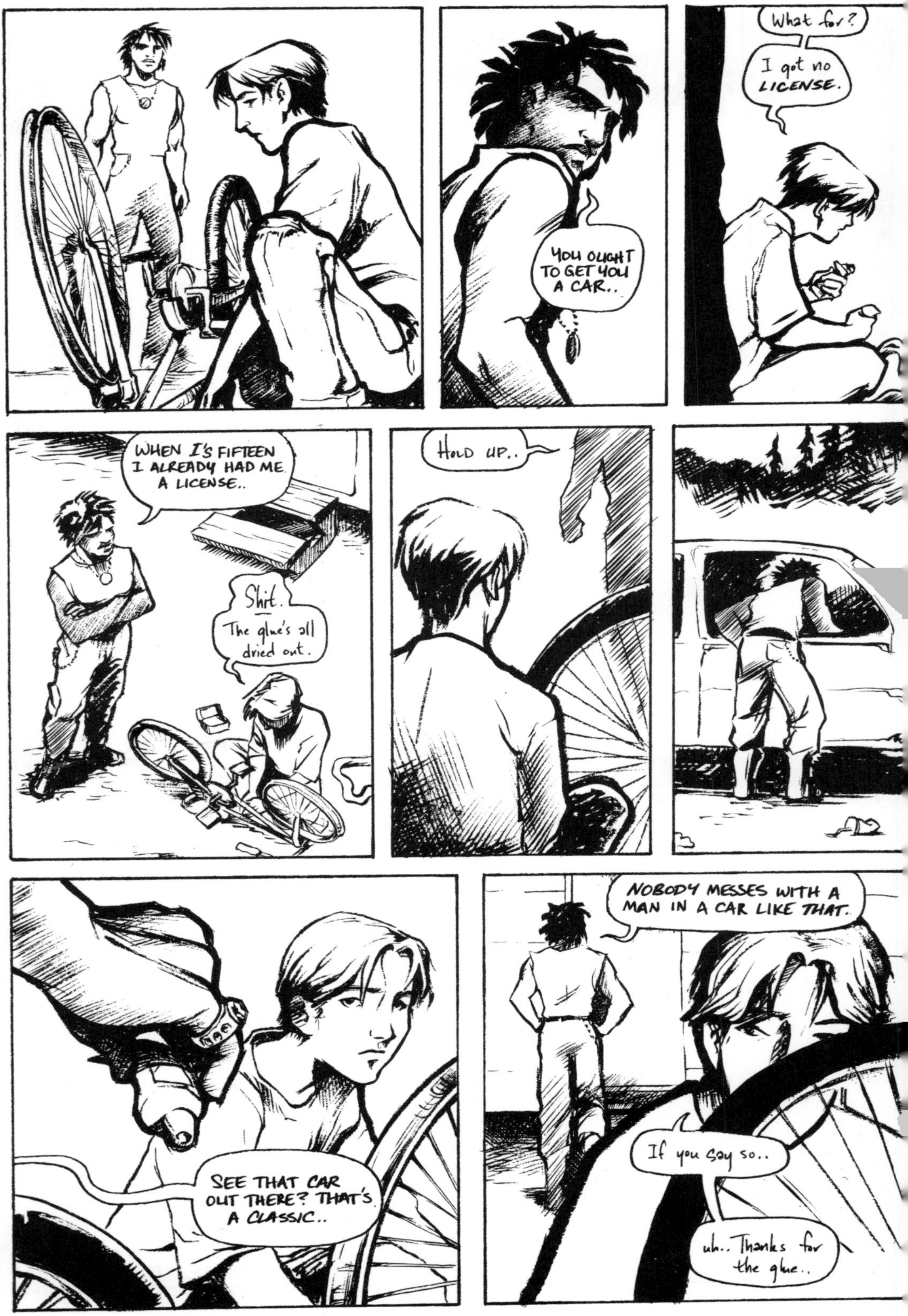
YOU OUGHT TO GET YOU A CAR..
What for?
I got no LICENSE.
WHEN I'S FIFTEEN I ALREADY HAD ME A LICENSE..
Shit.
The glue's all dried out.
HOLD UP..
SEE THAT CAR OUT THERE? THAT'S A CLASSIC..
NOBODY MESSES WITH A MAN IN A CAR LIKE THAT.
If you say so..
uh.. Thanks for the glue..

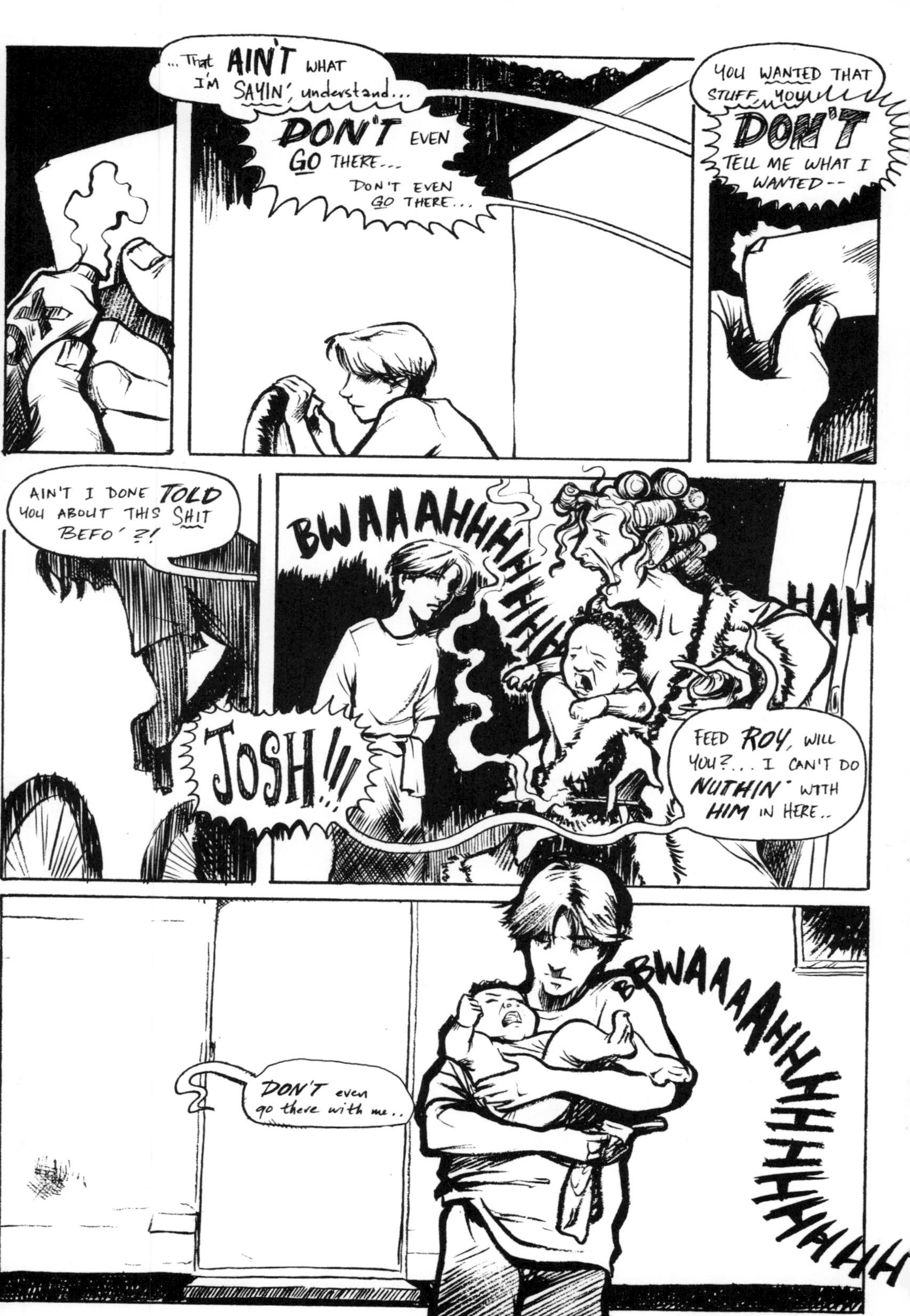
...That AIN'T WHAT I'M SAYIN', understand...
DON'T EVEN GO THERE...
DON'T EVEN GO THERE...
YOU WANTED THAT STUFF, YOU--
DON'T TELL ME WHAT I WANTED--
AIN'T I DONE TOLD YOU ABOUT THIS SHIT BEFO'?!
BWAAAHHHHHHH
HAH
JOSH!!!
FEED ROY, WILL YOU?... I CAN'T DO NUTHIN' WITH HIM IN HERE..
DON'T even go there with me..
BBWAAAAAHHHHHHHHAHAHH

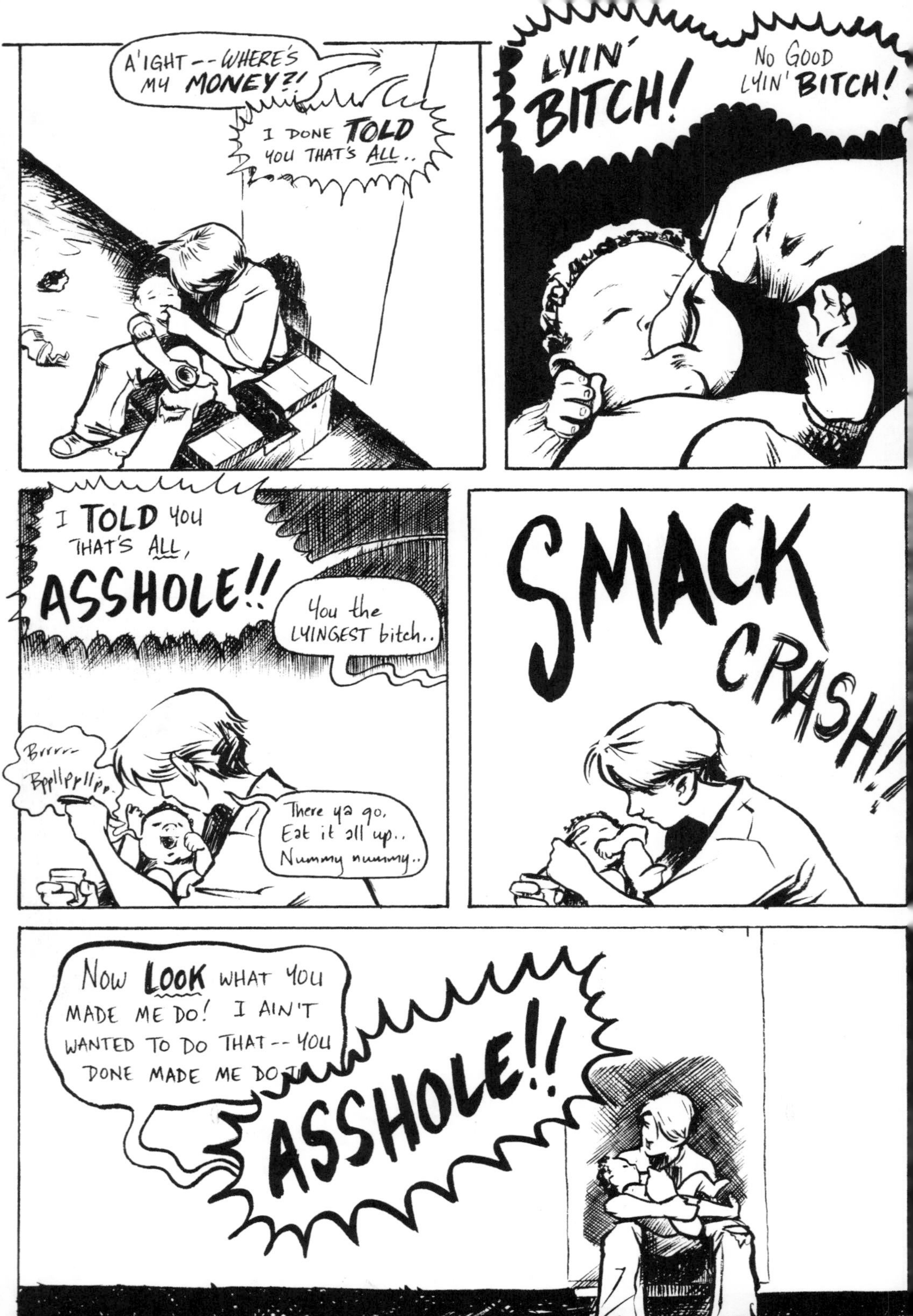
A'IGHT -- WHERE'S MY MONEY?!
I DONE TOLD YOU THAT'S ALL..
LYIN' BITCH!
NO GOOD LYIN' BITCH!
I TOLD YOU THAT'S ALL, ASSHOLE!!
You the LYINGEST bitch..
Brrrr-- Bppllppllpp..
There ya go, Eat it all up.. Nummy nummy..
SMACK
CRASH!!
Now LOOK WHAT YOU MADE ME DO! I AIN'T WANTED TO DO THAT -- YOU DONE MADE ME DO IT
ASSHOLE!!

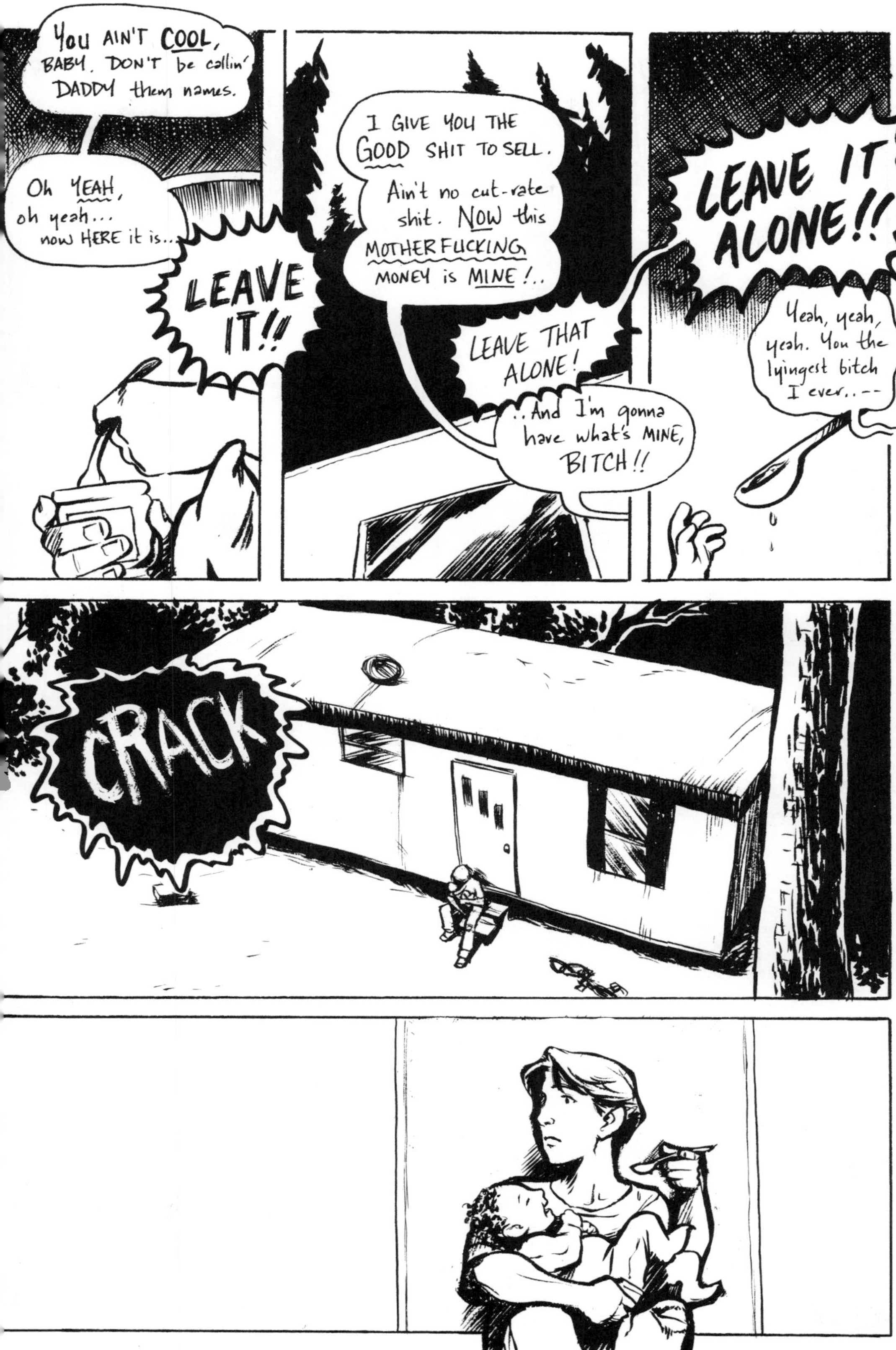
You AIN'T COOL, BABY. DON'T be callin' DADDY them names.
Oh YEAH, oh yeah... now HERE it is...
LEAVE IT!!
I GIVE YOU THE GOOD SHIT TO SELL.
Ain't no cut-rate shit. NOW this MOTHERFUCKING MONEY is MINE!..
LEAVE THAT ALONE!
..And I'm gonna have what's MINE, BITCH!!
LEAVE IT ALONE!!
Yeah, yeah, yeah. You the lyingest bitch I ever..--
CRACK

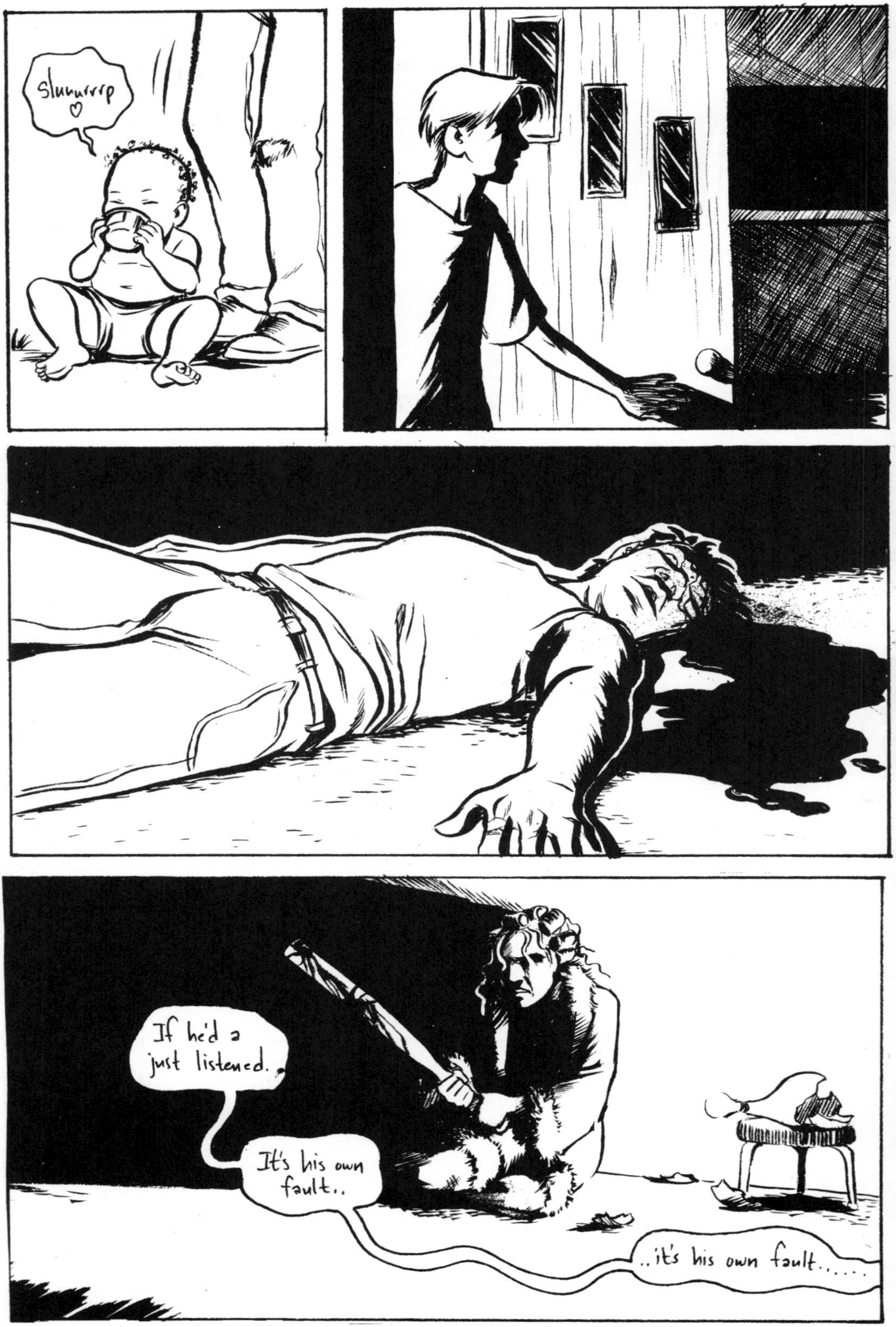
sluuurrrp ♡
If he'd a just listened.
It's his own fault..
..it's his own fault......

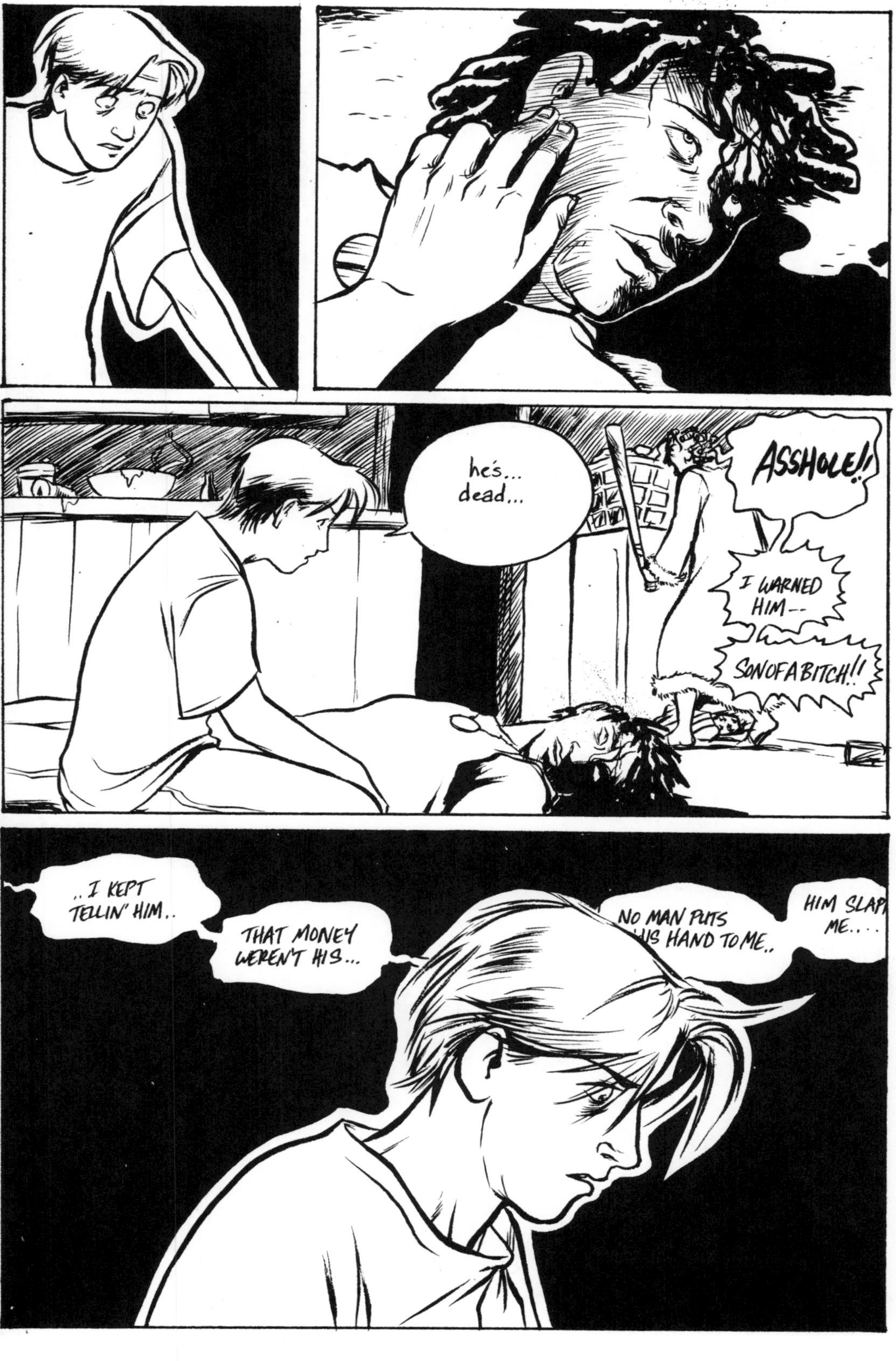
he's... dead...
ASSHOLE!!
I WARNED HIM--
SONOFABITCH!!
.. I KEPT TELLIN' HIM..
THAT MONEY WEREN'T HIS...
NO MAN PUTS HIS HAND TO ME..
HIM SLAP ME....

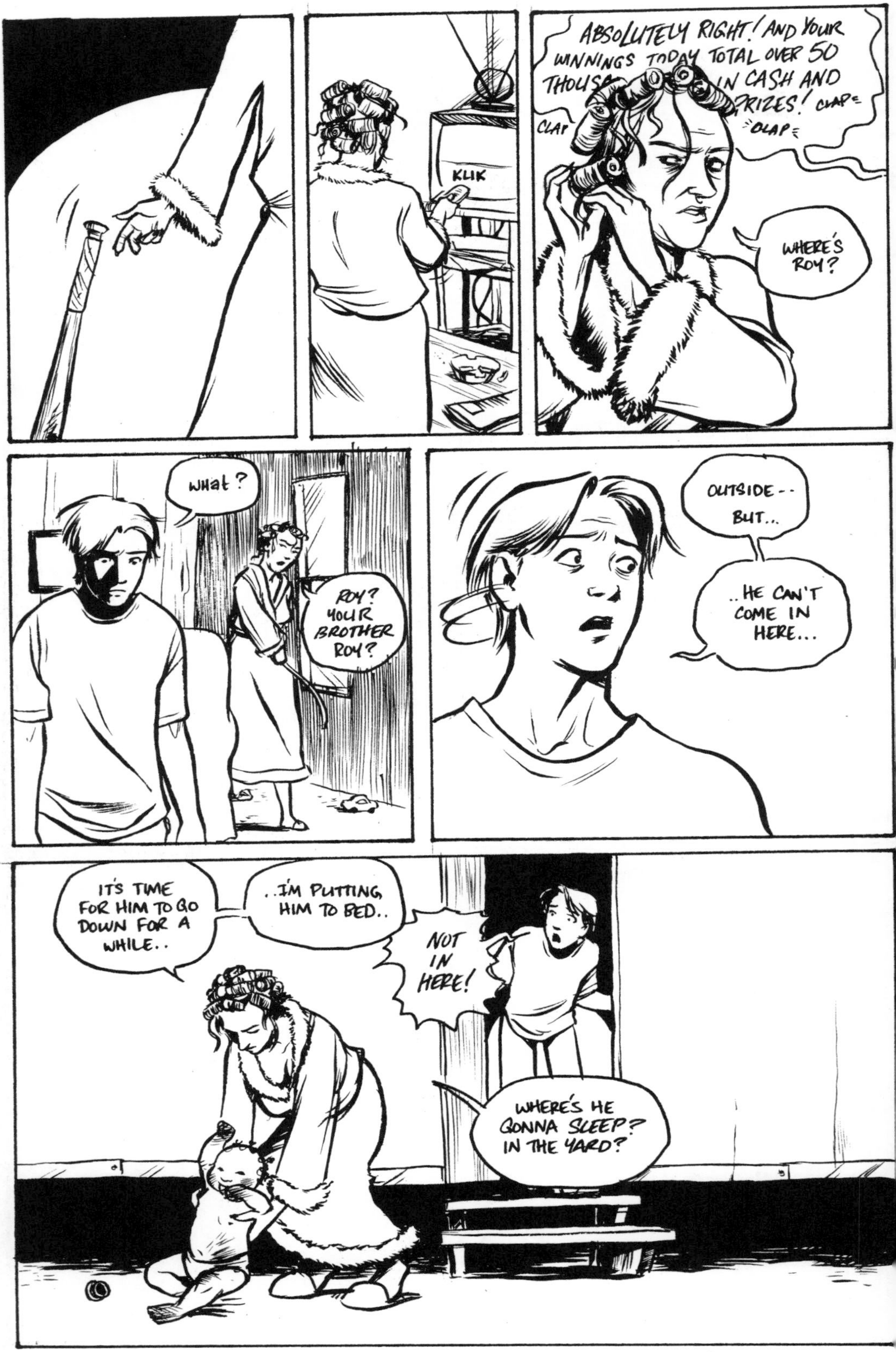
KLIK
ABSOLUTELY RIGHT! AND YOUR WINNINGS TODAY TOTAL OVER 50 THOUSA IN CASH AND PRIZES!
CLAP
CLAP
CLAP
WHERE'S ROY?
what?
ROY? YOUR BROTHER ROY?
OUTSIDE-- BUT...
..HE CAN'T COME IN HERE...
IT'S TIME FOR HIM TO GO DOWN FOR A WHILE..
..I'M PUTTING HIM TO BED..
NOT IN HERE!
WHERE'S HE GONNA SLEEP? IN THE YARD?

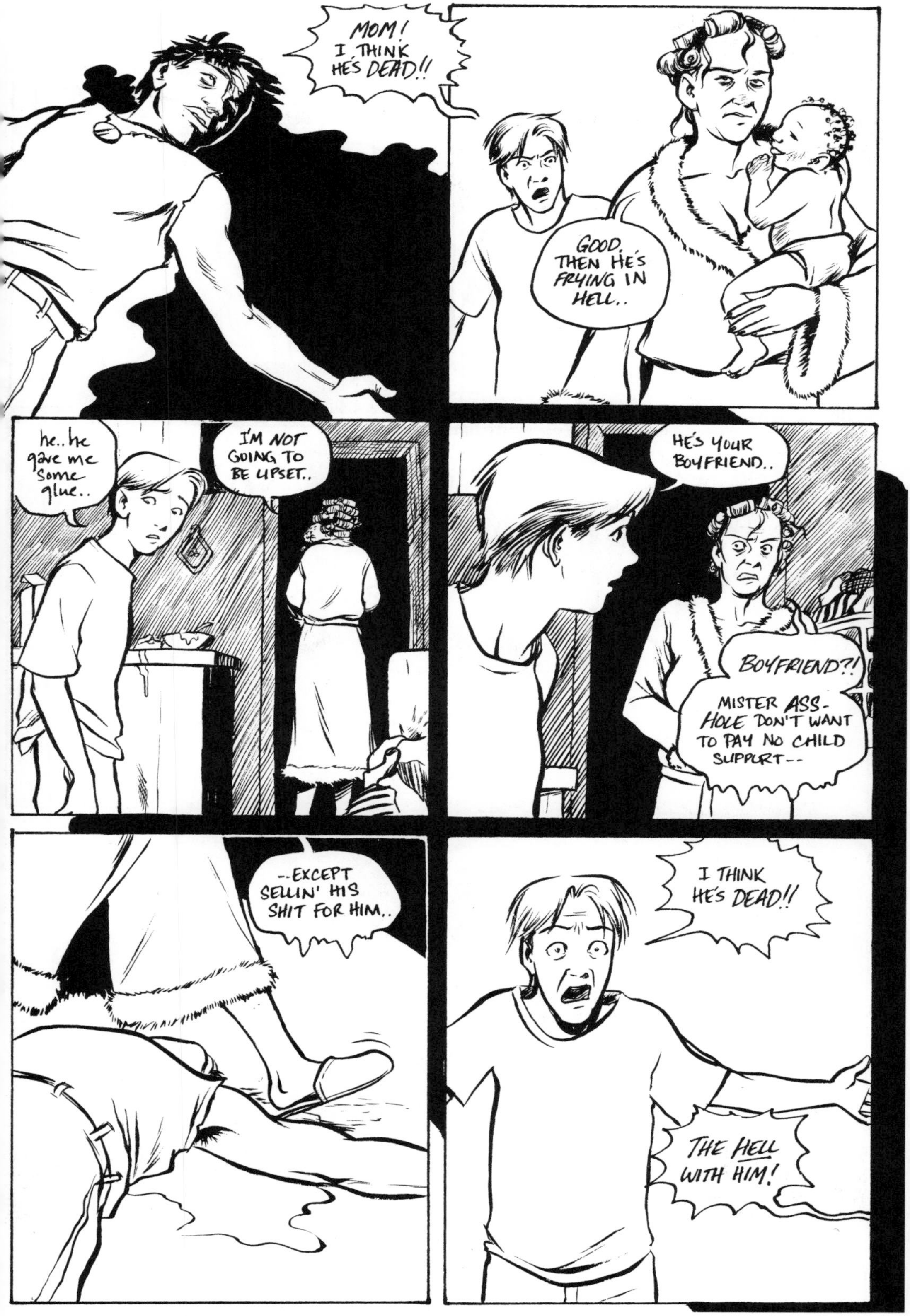
MOM! I THINK HE'S DEAD!!
GOOD. THEN HE'S FRYING IN HELL..
he..he gave me some glue..
I'M NOT GOING TO BE UPSET..
HE'S YOUR BOYFRIEND..
BOYFRIEND?!
MISTER ASS-HOLE DON'T WANT TO PAY NO CHILD SUPPORT--
--EXCEPT SELLIN' HIS SHIT FOR HIM..
I THINK HE'S DEAD!!
THE HELL WITH HIM!

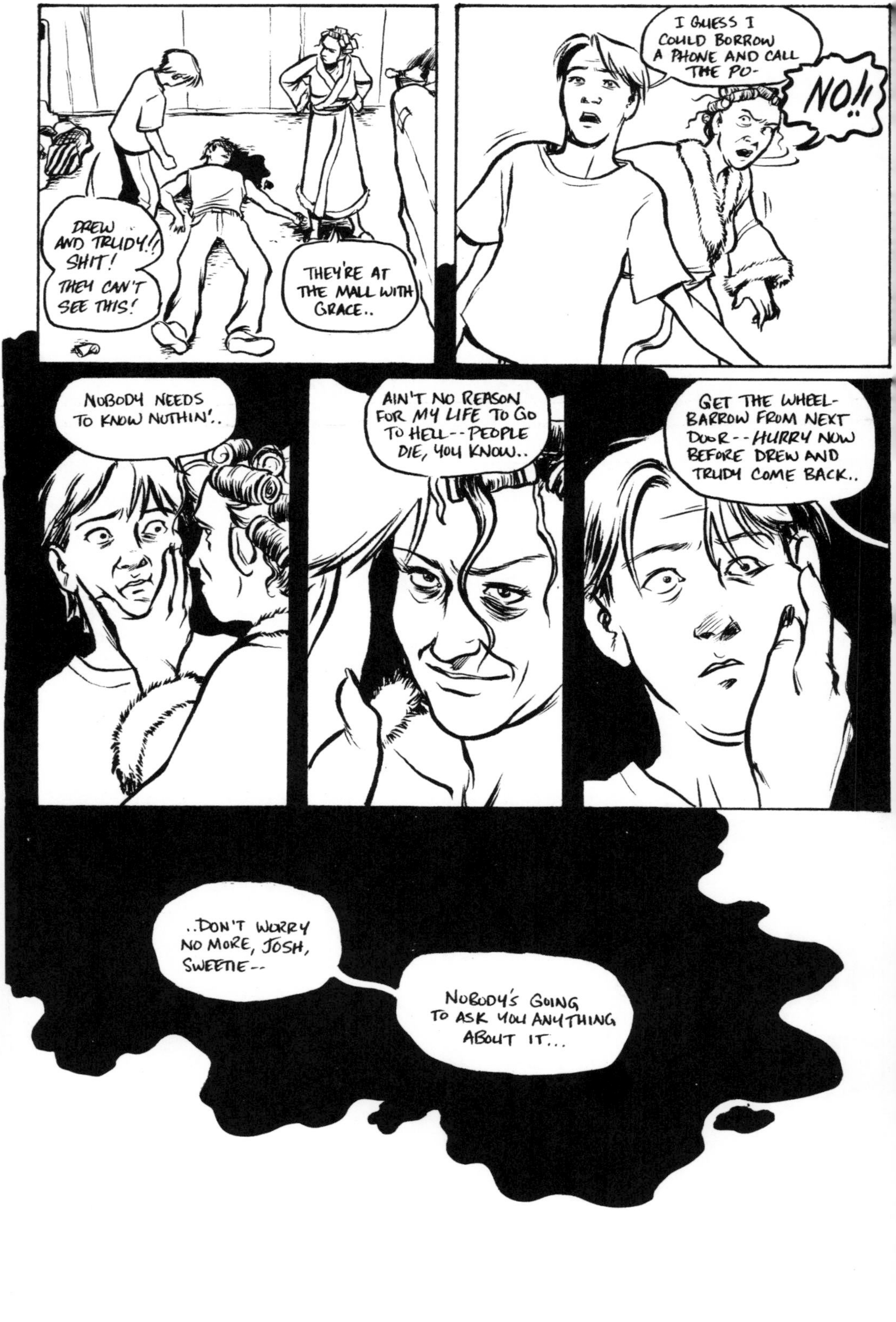
DREW AND TRUDY!! SHIT! THEY CAN'T SEE THIS!
THEY'RE AT THE MALL WITH GRACE..
I GUESS I COULD BORROW A PHONE AND CALL THE PO-
NO!!
NOBODY NEEDS TO KNOW NUTHIN'..
AIN'T NO REASON FOR MY LIFE TO GO TO HELL--PEOPLE DIE, YOU KNOW..
GET THE WHEEL-BARROW FROM NEXT DOOR--HURRY NOW BEFORE DREW AND TRUDY COME BACK..
..DON'T WORRY NO MORE, JOSH, SWEETIE--
NOBODY'S GOING TO ASK YOU ANYTHING ABOUT IT...

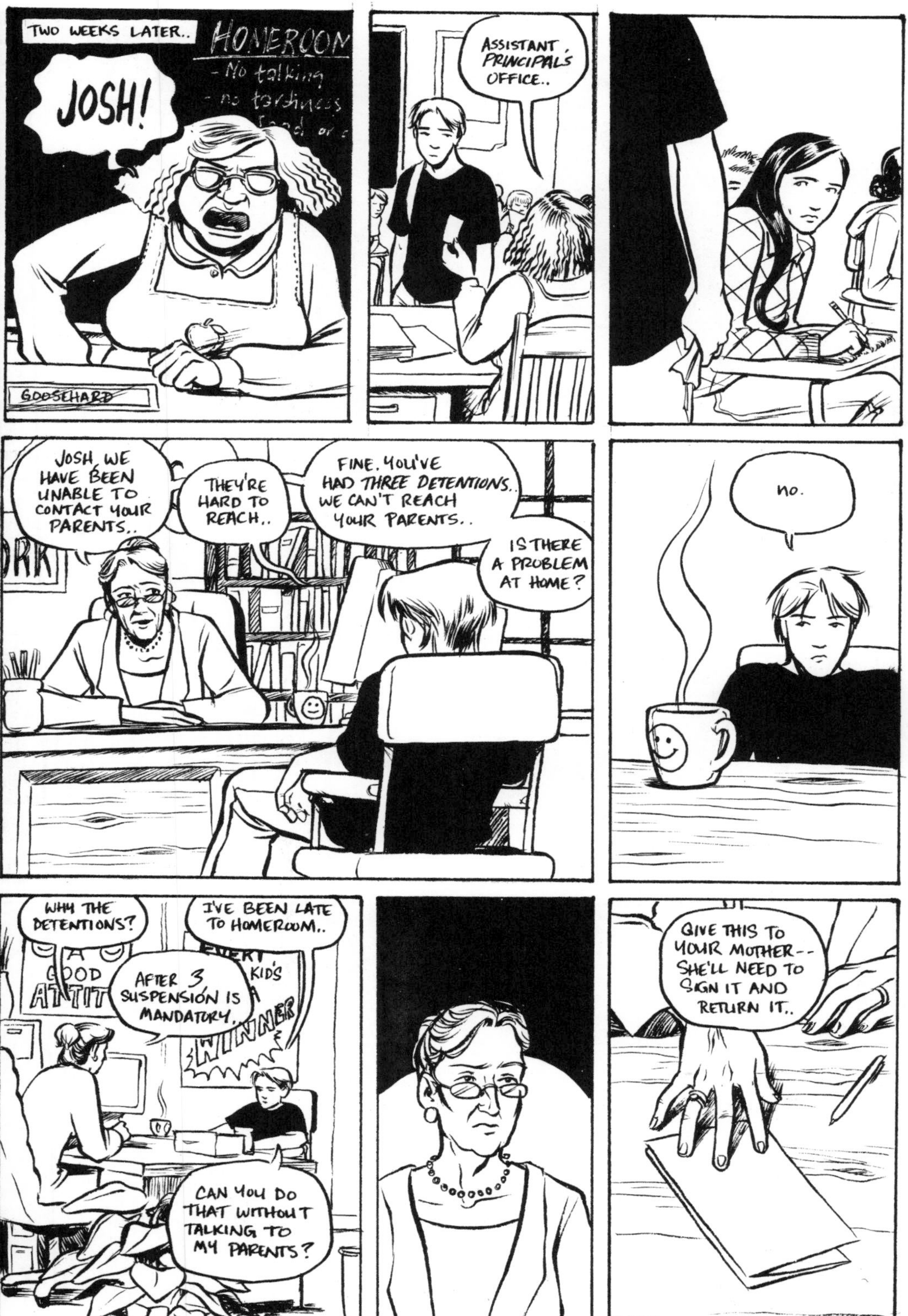

TWO WEEKS LATER..
HOMEROOM
- No talking
- no tardiness
JOSH!
GOOSEHARD
ASSISTANT PRINCIPAL'S OFFICE..
JOSH, WE HAVE BEEN UNABLE TO CONTACT YOUR PARENTS..
THEY'RE HARD TO REACH..
FINE. YOU'VE HAD THREE DETENTIONS.. WE CAN'T REACH YOUR PARENTS..
IS THERE A PROBLEM AT HOME?
no.
WHY THE DETENTIONS?
I'VE BEEN LATE TO HOMEROOM..
AFTER 3 SUSPENSION IS MANDATORY.
GOOD ATTIT
EVERY KID'S A WINNER
CAN YOU DO THAT WITHOUT TALKING TO MY PARENTS?
GIVE THIS TO YOUR MOTHER-- SHE'LL NEED TO SIGN IT AND RETURN IT..

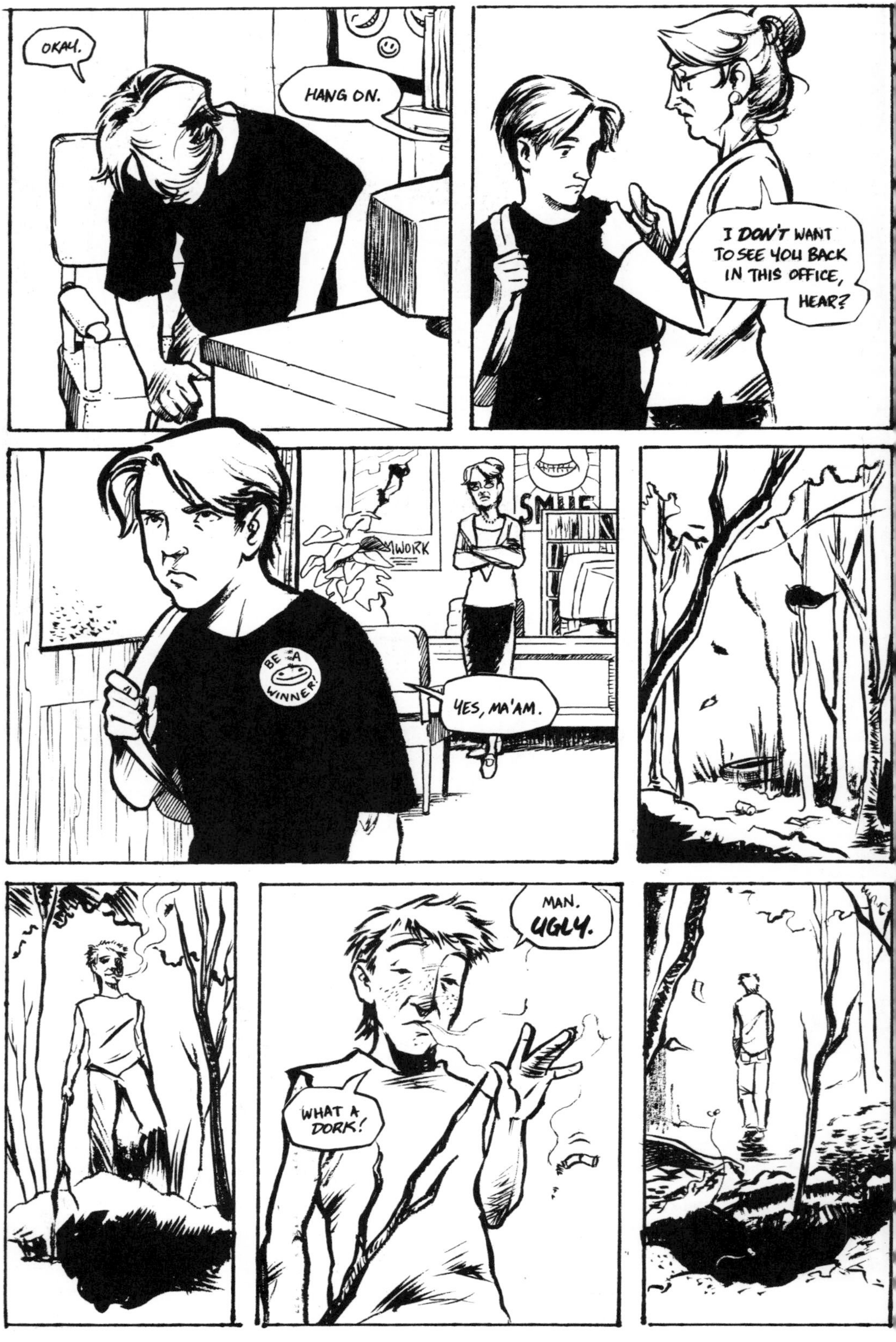
OKAY.
HANG ON.
I DON'T WANT TO SEE YOU BACK IN THIS OFFICE, HEAR?
SMILE
WORK
BE A WINNER!
YES, MA'AM.
MAN. UGLY.
WHAT A DORK!

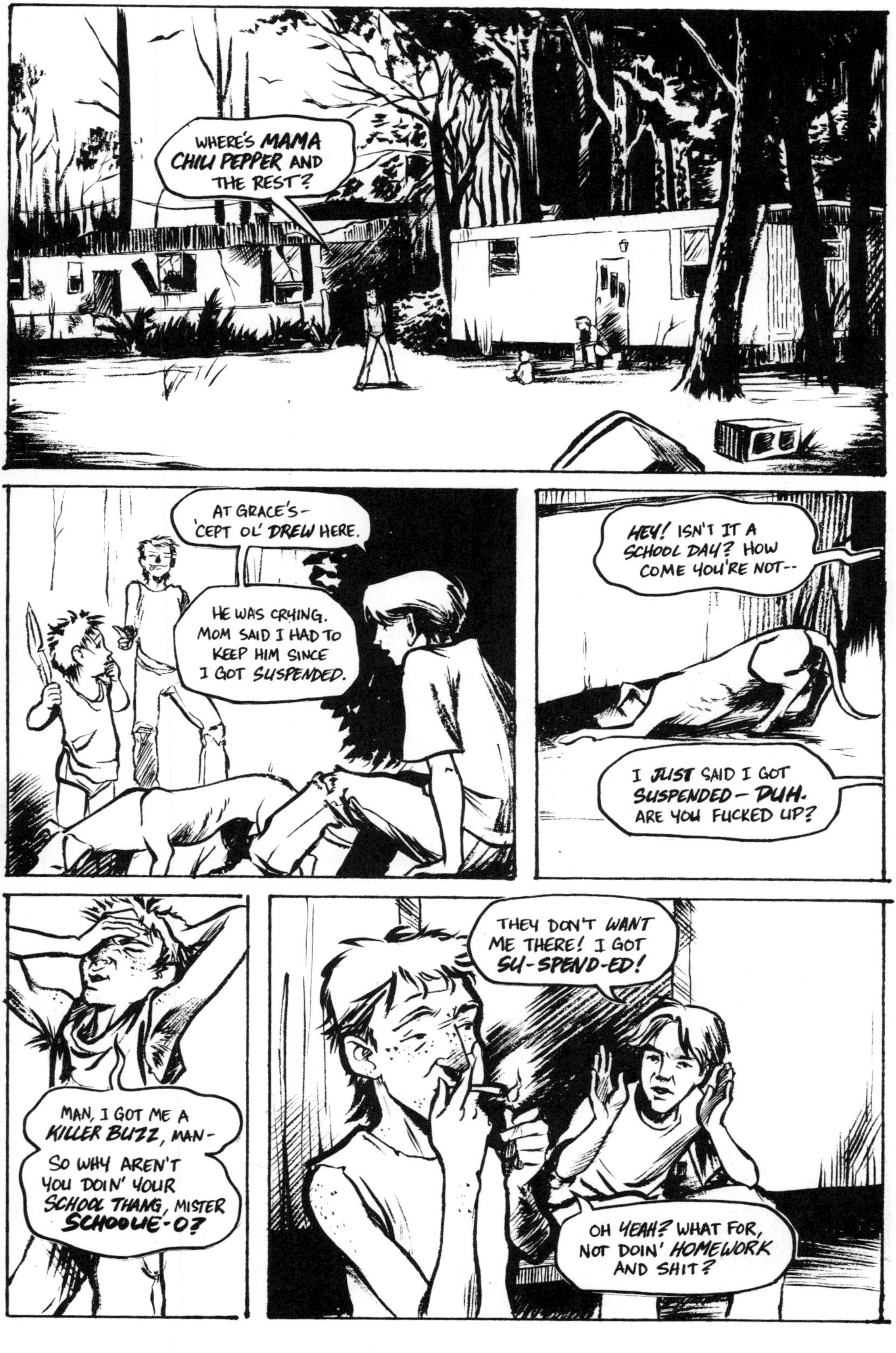
WHERE'S MAMA CHILI PEPPER AND THE REST?
AT GRACE'S- 'CEPT OL' DREW HERE.
HE WAS CRYING. MOM SAID I HAD TO KEEP HIM SINCE I GOT SUSPENDED.
HEY! ISN'T IT A SCHOOL DAY? HOW COME YOU'RE NOT--
I JUST SAID I GOT SUSPENDED - DUH. ARE YOU FUCKED UP?
MAN, I GOT ME A KILLER BUZZ, MAN-
SO WHY AREN'T YOU DOIN' YOUR SCHOOL THANG, MISTER SCHOOLIE-O?
THEY DON'T WANT ME THERE! I GOT SU-SPEND-ED!
OH YEAH? WHAT FOR, NOT DOIN' HOMEWORK AND SHIT?

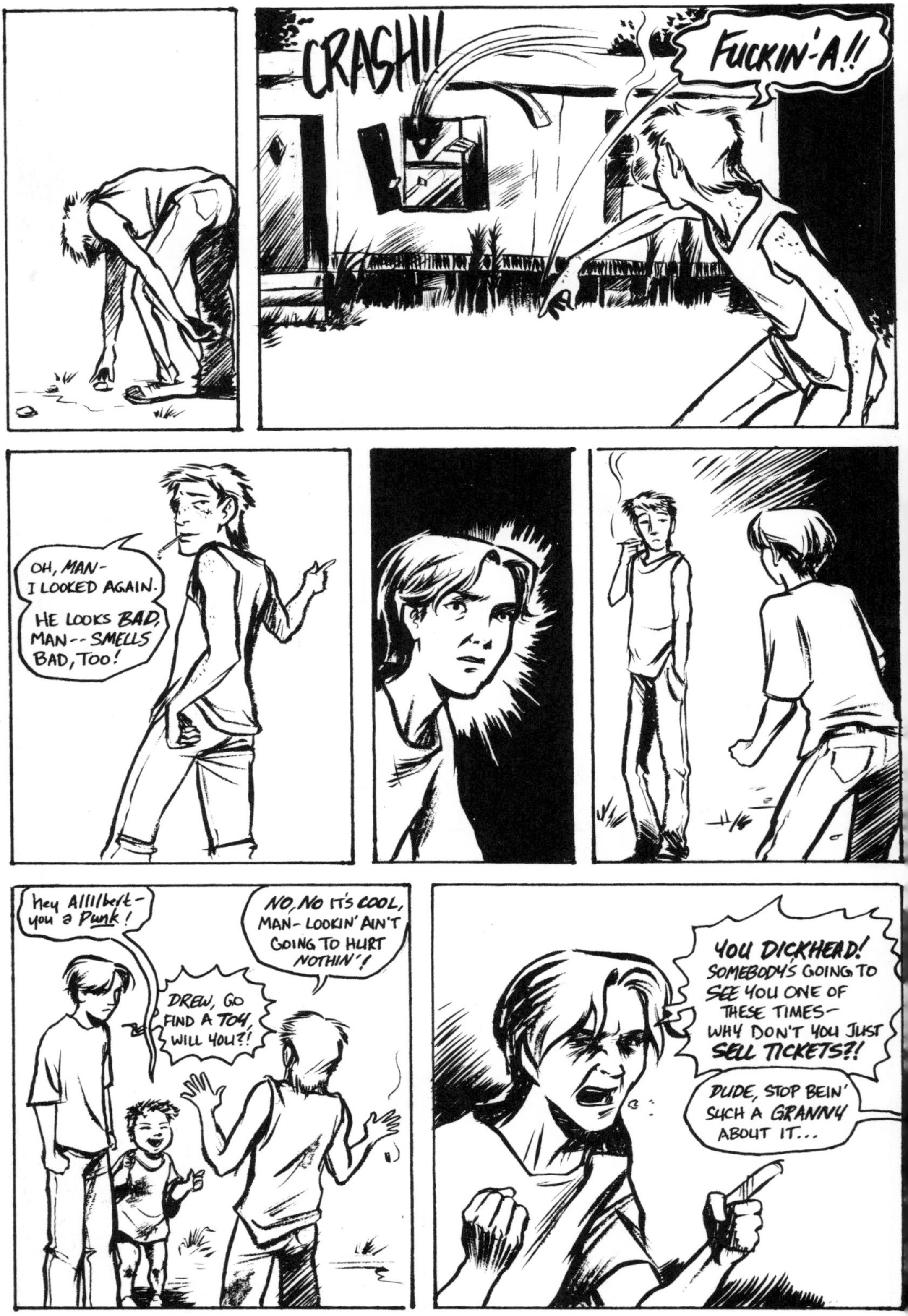
CRASH!!
FUCKIN'-A!!
OH, MAN- I LOOKED AGAIN.
HE LOOKS BAD, MAN--SMELLS BAD, TOO!
hey Alllllbert- you a Punk!
NO, NO IT'S COOL, MAN- LOOKIN' AIN'T GOING TO HURT NOTHIN'!
DREW, GO FIND A TOY, WILL YOU?!
YOU DICKHEAD! SOMEBODY'S GOING TO SEE YOU ONE OF THESE TIMES- WHY DON'T YOU JUST SELL TICKETS?!
DUDE, STOP BEIN' SUCH A GRANNY ABOUT IT...

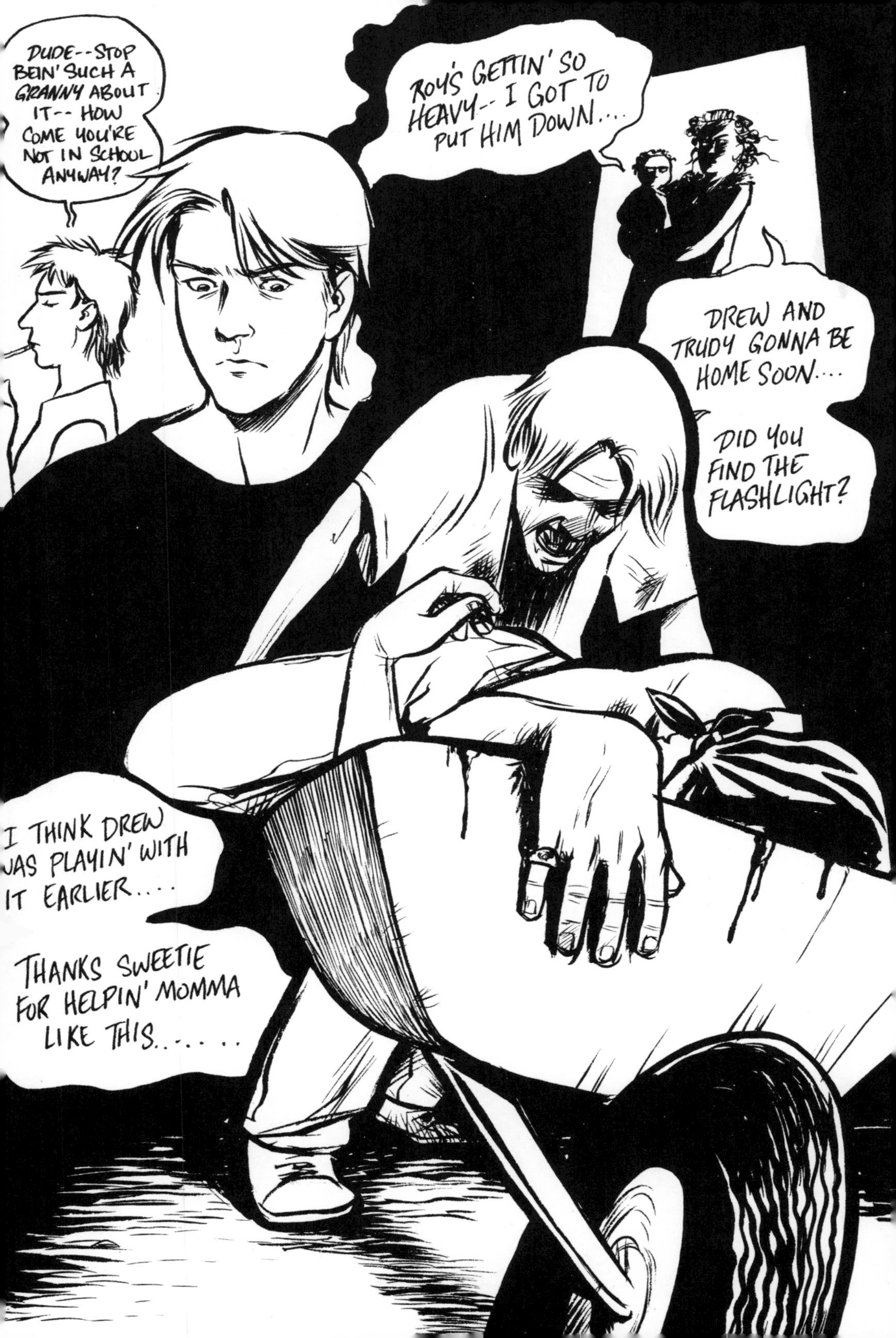
DUDE--STOP BEIN' SUCH A GRANNY ABOUT IT-- HOW COME YOU'RE NOT IN SCHOOL ANYWAY?
ROY'S GETTIN' SO HEAVY-- I GOT TO PUT HIM DOWN....
DREW AND TRUDY GONNA BE HOME SOON....
DID YOU FIND THE FLASHLIGHT?
I THINK DREW WAS PLAYIN' WITH IT EARLIER....
THANKS SWEETIE FOR HELPIN' MOMMA LIKE THIS......

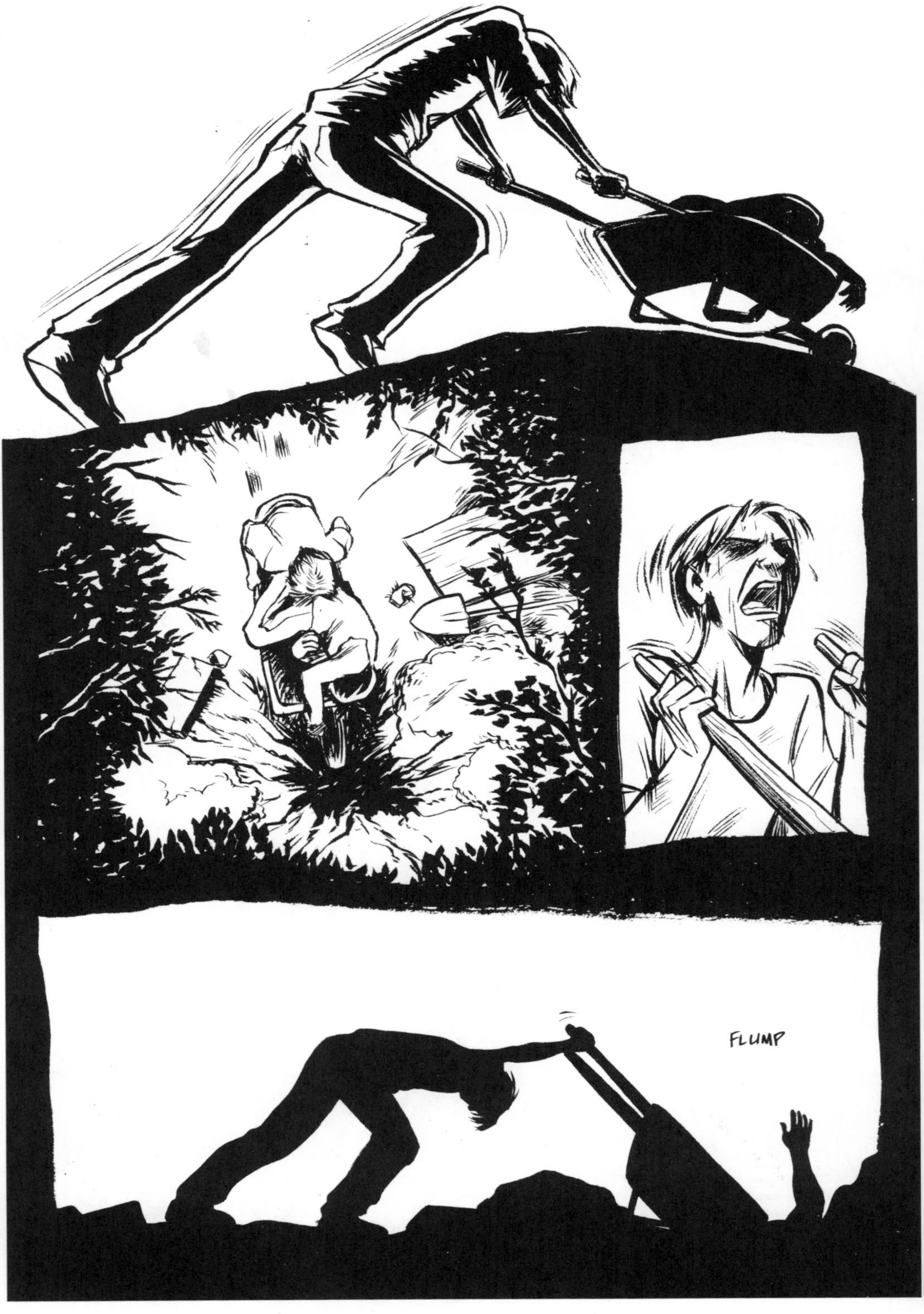
FLUMP

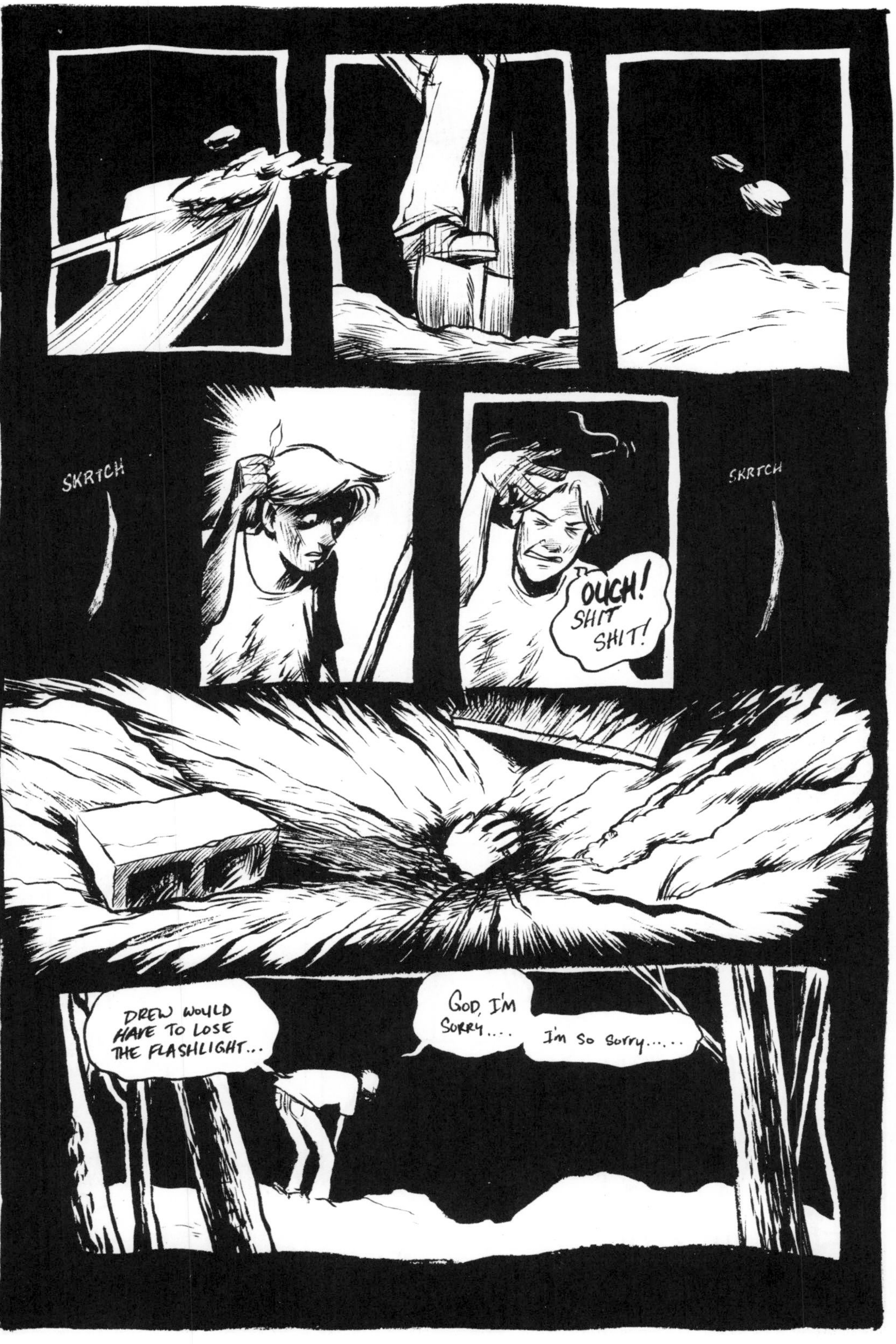
SKRTCH
OUCH! SHIT SHIT!
SKRTCH
DREW WOULD HAVE TO LOSE THE FLASHLIGHT...
GOD, I'M SORRY....
I'm so sorry......

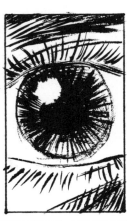

HEY, AIN'T IT COOL WHEN EVERYONE'S OFF WORKIN' AND SHIT?

IT'S MY FAVORITE TIME OF DAY.

BUGGSY DON'T LIKE ME, JOSH...

NEITHER DOES ANYBODY ELSE, YOU LI'L PUNK!

LEAVE HIM ALONE, ALBERT!!

OF COURSE HE LIKES YOU, DREW—YOU SCARED HIM IS ALL.

GOD, HE SMELLS LIKE SOME-THING...

...oh GOD.

hey, come on, man—
LET'S GO OVER TO CRUZ'S—HE'S GOT SOME GOOD REEF, FORGET ABOUT ALL THIS SHIT—

LEAVE IT FOR YOUR MOM TO TAKE CARE OF—

THAS WHAT I DO, MAN.

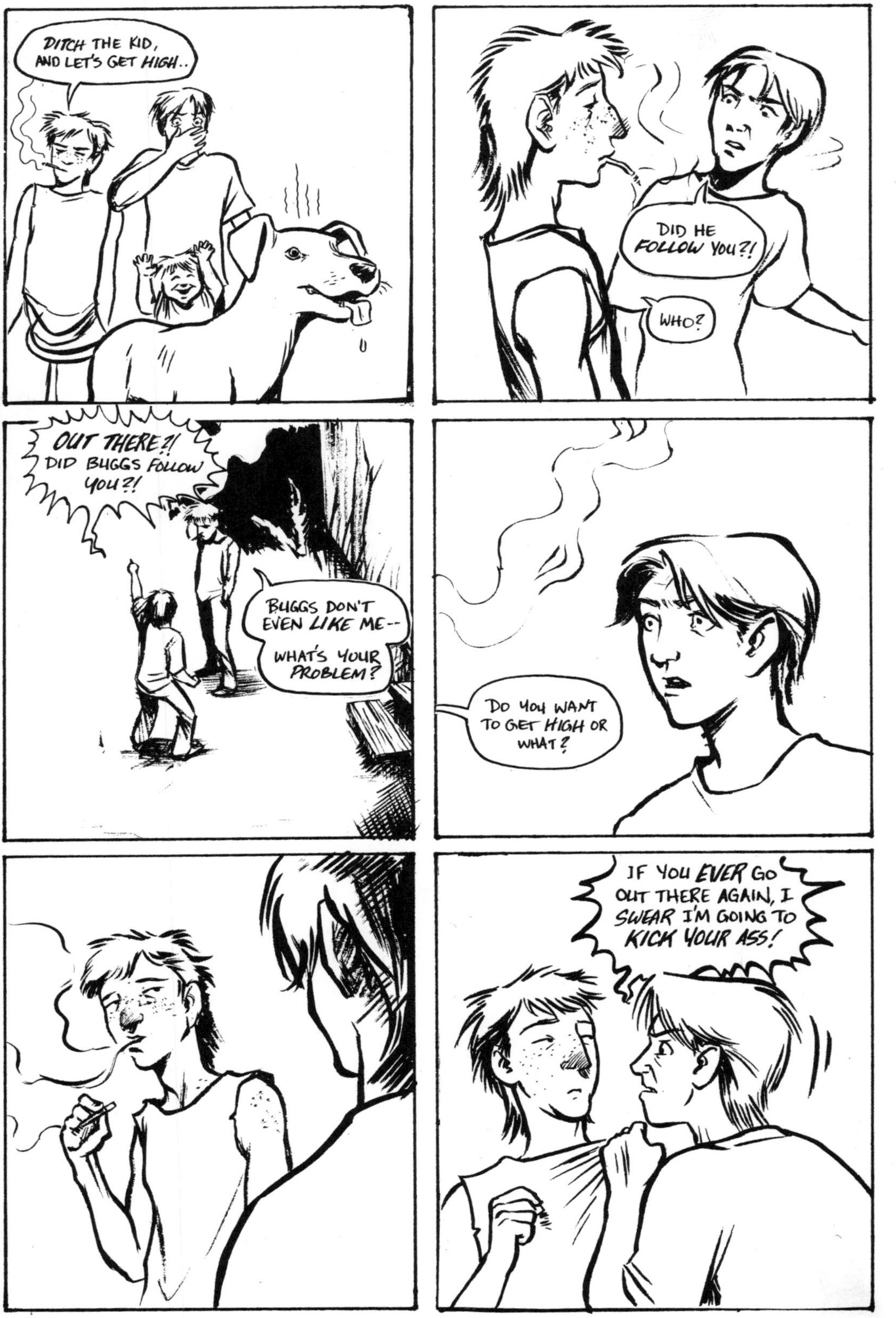
DITCH THE KID, AND LET'S GET HIGH..
DID HE FOLLOW YOU?!
WHO?
OUT THERE?! DID BUGGS FOLLOW YOU?!
BUGGS DON'T EVEN LIKE ME--
WHAT'S YOUR PROBLEM?
DO YOU WANT TO GET HIGH OR WHAT?
IF YOU EVER GO OUT THERE AGAIN, I SWEAR I'M GOING TO KICK YOUR ASS!

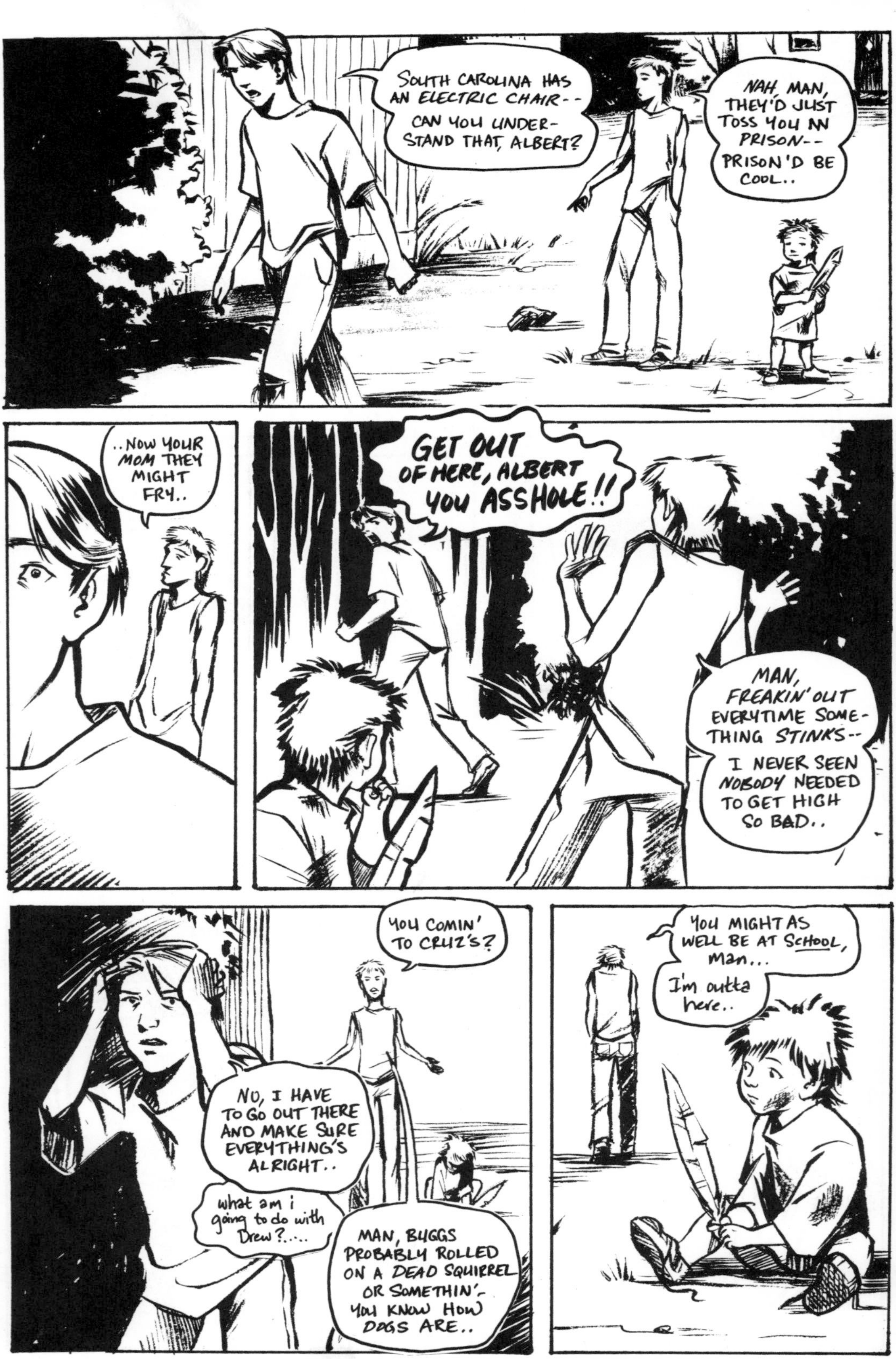
SOUTH CAROLINA HAS AN ELECTRIC CHAIR--
CAN YOU UNDERSTAND THAT, ALBERT?
NAH, MAN, THEY'D JUST TOSS YOU IN PRISON--
PRISON'D BE COOL..
..NOW YOUR MOM THEY MIGHT FRY..
GET OUT OF HERE, ALBERT YOU ASSHOLE!!
MAN, FREAKIN' OUT EVERYTIME SOMETHING STINKS--
I NEVER SEEN NOBODY NEEDED TO GET HIGH SO BAD..
YOU COMIN' TO CRUZ'S?
NO, I HAVE TO GO OUT THERE AND MAKE SURE EVERYTHING'S ALRIGHT..
what am i going to do with Drew?....
MAN, BUGGS PROBABLY ROLLED ON A DEAD SQUIRREL OR SOMETHIN'.
YOU KNOW HOW DOGS ARE..
YOU MIGHT AS WELL BE AT SCHOOL, MAN...
I'm outta here..

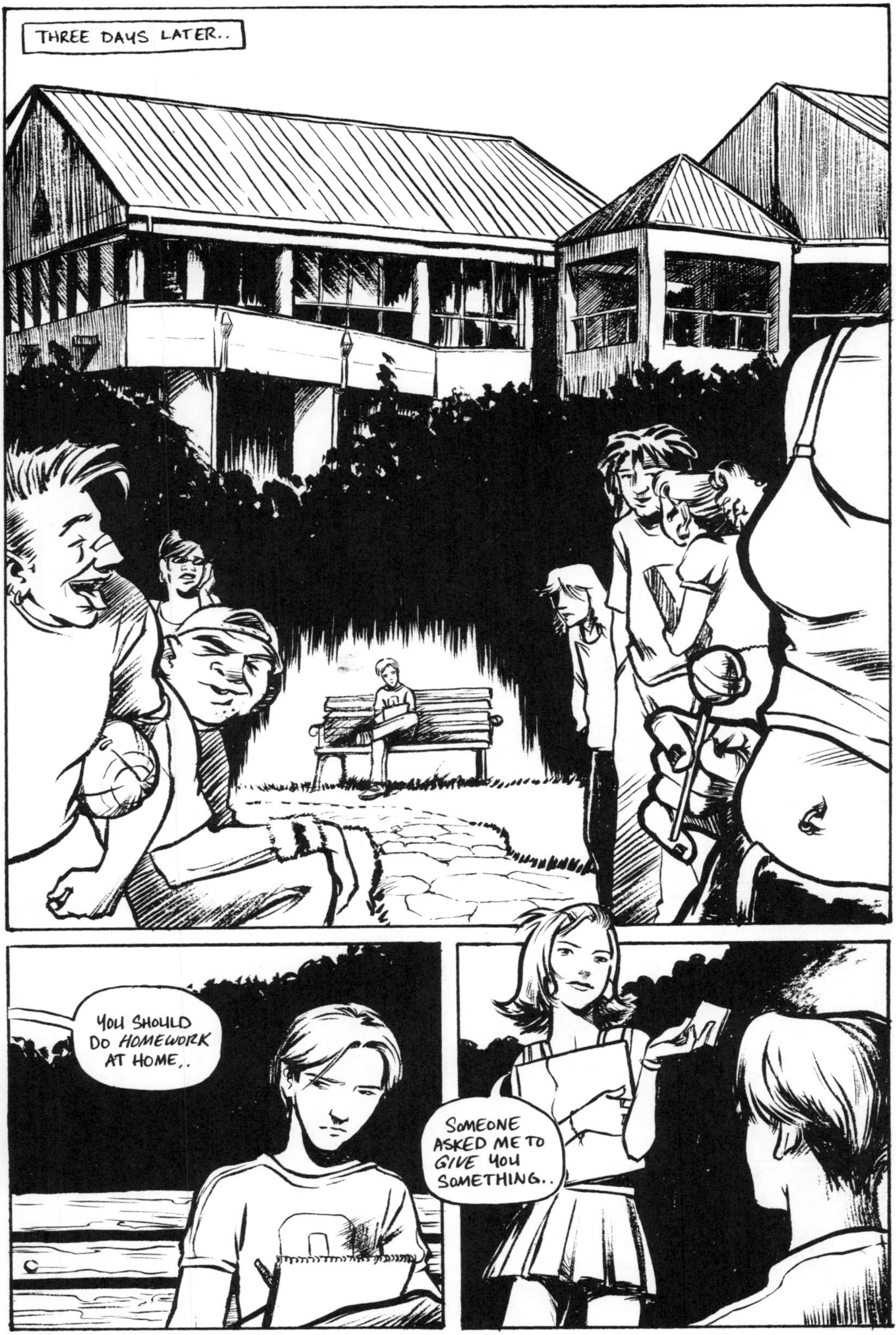
THREE DAYS LATER..
YOU SHOULD DO HOMEWORK AT HOME,.
SOMEONE ASKED ME TO GIVE YOU SOMETHING..

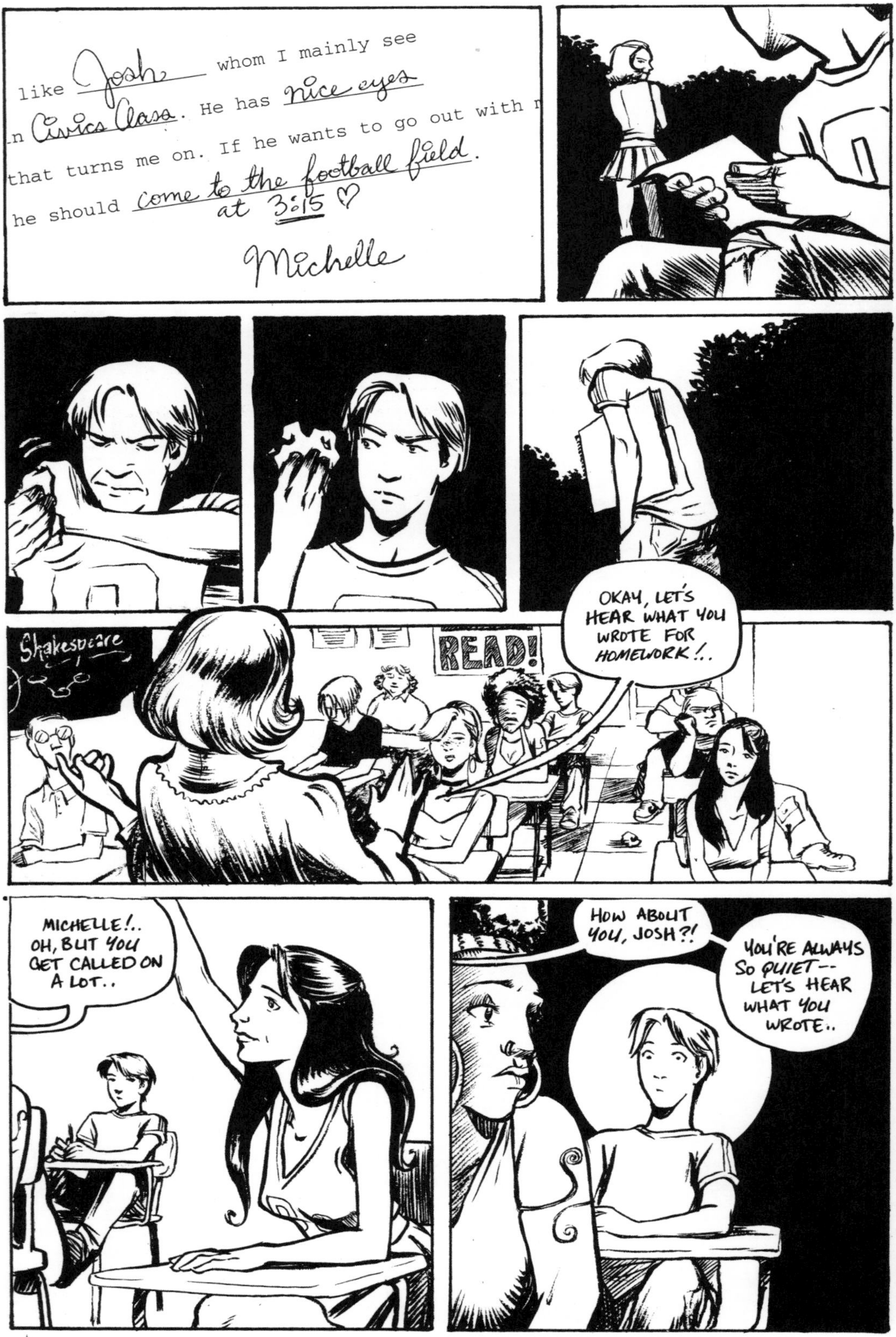

like Josh whom I mainly see
in Civics Class. He has nice eyes
that turns me on. If he wants to go out with me
he should come to the football field at 3:15 ♡
Michelle
Shakespeare
READ!
OKAY, LET'S HEAR WHAT YOU WROTE FOR HOMEWORK!..
MICHELLE!.. OH, BUT YOU GET CALLED ON A LOT..
HOW ABOUT YOU, JOSH?!
YOU'RE ALWAYS SO QUIET-- LET'S HEAR WHAT YOU WROTE..

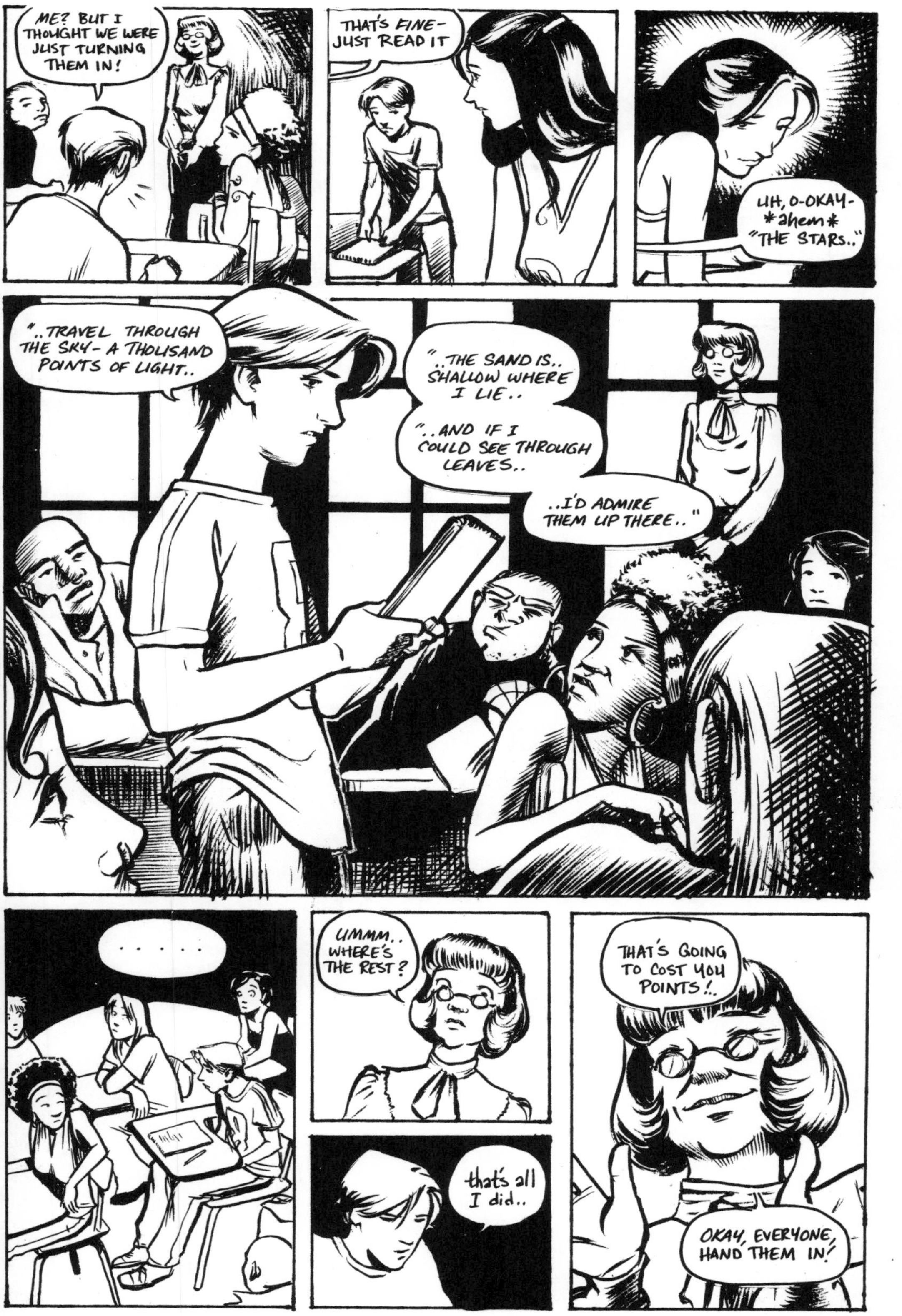
ME? BUT I THOUGHT WE WERE JUST TURNING THEM IN!
THAT'S FINE- JUST READIT
UH, O-OKAY- *ahem* "THE STARS.."
"..TRAVEL THROUGH THE SKY- A THOUSAND POINTS OF LIGHT..
"..THE SAND IS.. SHALLOW WHERE I LIE..
"..AND IF I COULD SEE THROUGH LEAVES..
..I'D ADMIRE THEM UP THERE.."
. . . . .
UMMM.. WHERE'S THE REST?
that's all I did..
THAT'S GOING TO COST YOU POINTS!..
OKAY, EVERYONE, HAND THEM IN!

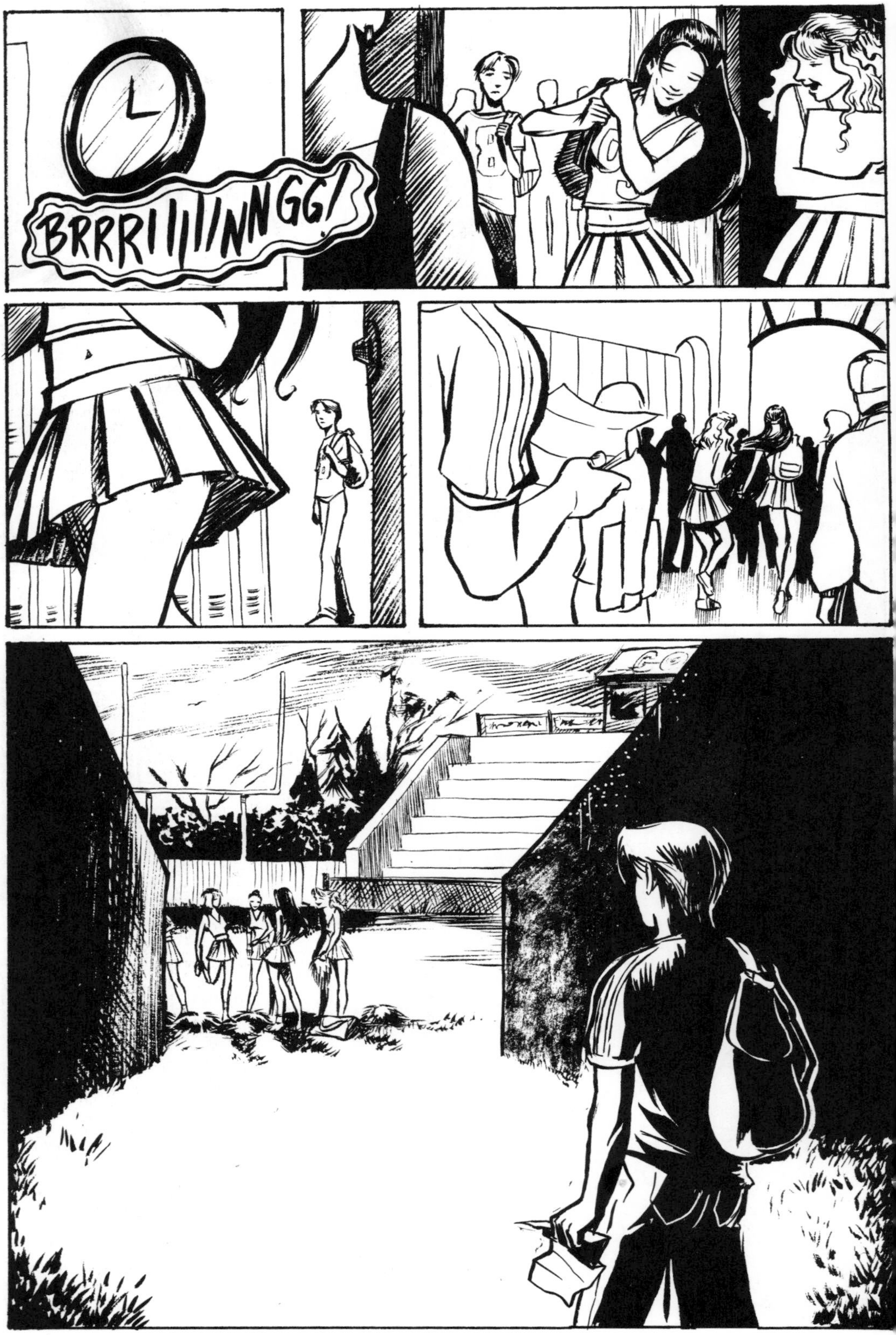
BRRRIIIIINNGG!

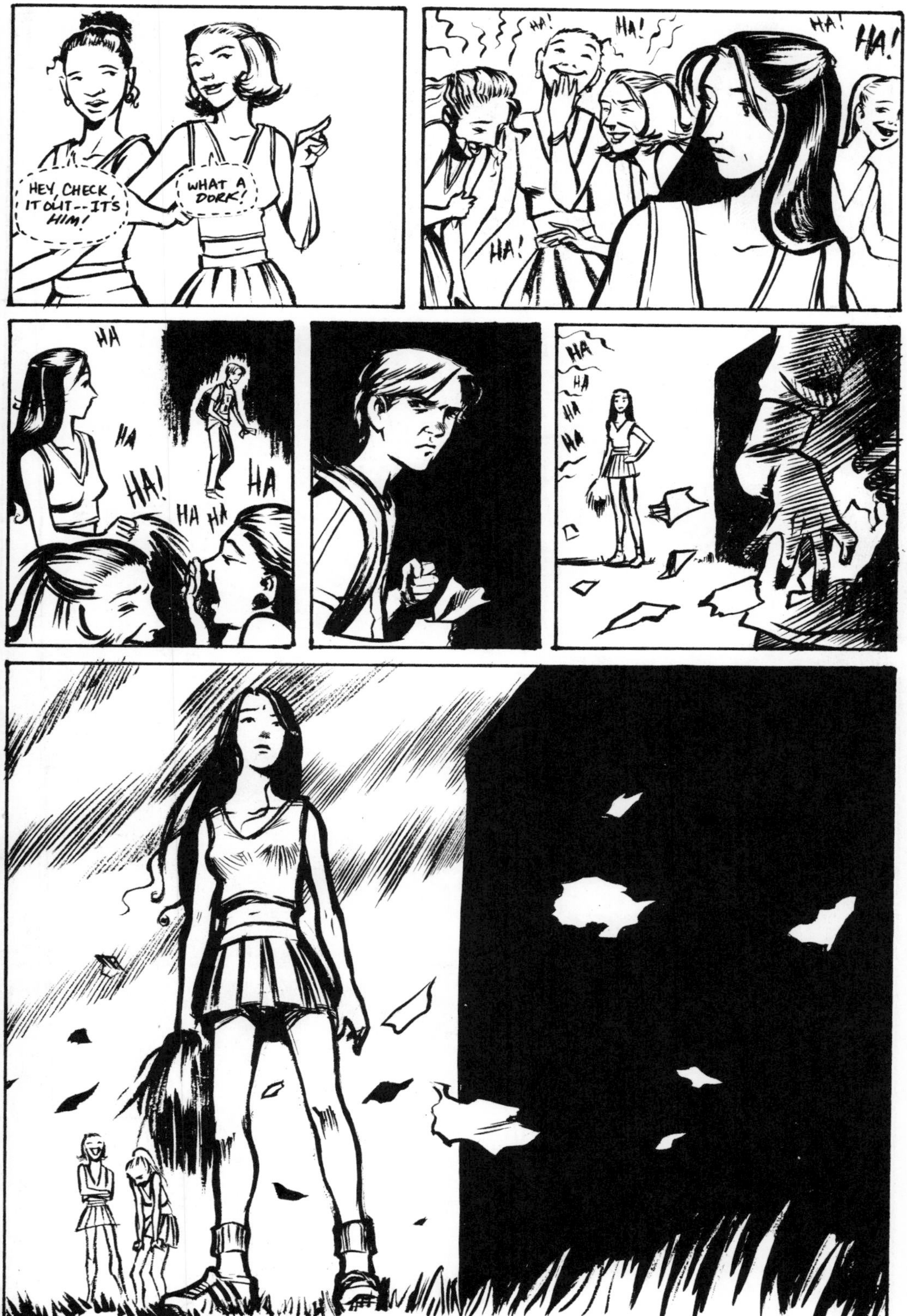
HEY, CHECK IT OUT--IT'S HIM!
WHAT A DORK!
HA!
HA!
HA!
HA!
HA!
HA
HA
HA!
HA
HA HA
HA
HA
HA
HA

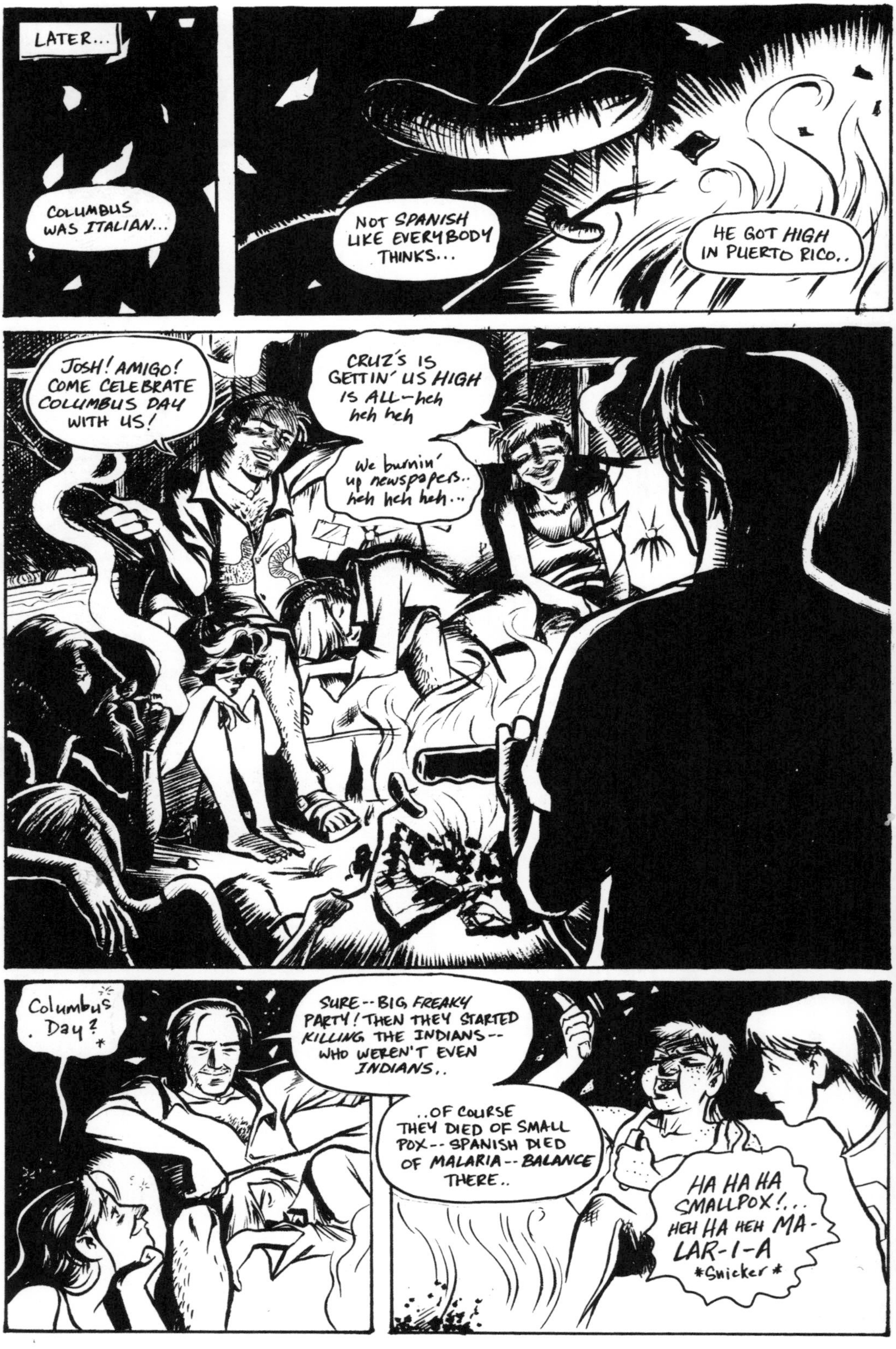
LATER...
COLUMBUS WAS ITALIAN...
NOT SPANISH LIKE EVERYBODY THINKS...
HE GOT HIGH IN PUERTO RICO..
JOSH! AMIGO! COME CELEBRATE COLUMBUS DAY WITH US!
CRUZ'S IS GETTIN' US HIGH IS ALL—heh heh heh
We burnin' up newspapers.. heh heh heh...
Columbus Day? *
SURE--BIG FREAKY PARTY! THEN THEY STARTED KILLING THE INDIANS--WHO WEREN'T EVEN INDIANS..
..OF COURSE THEY DIED OF SMALL POX--SPANISH DIED OF MALARIA--BALANCE THERE..
HA HA HA SMALLPOX!... HEH HA HEH MA-LAR-I-A
Snicker

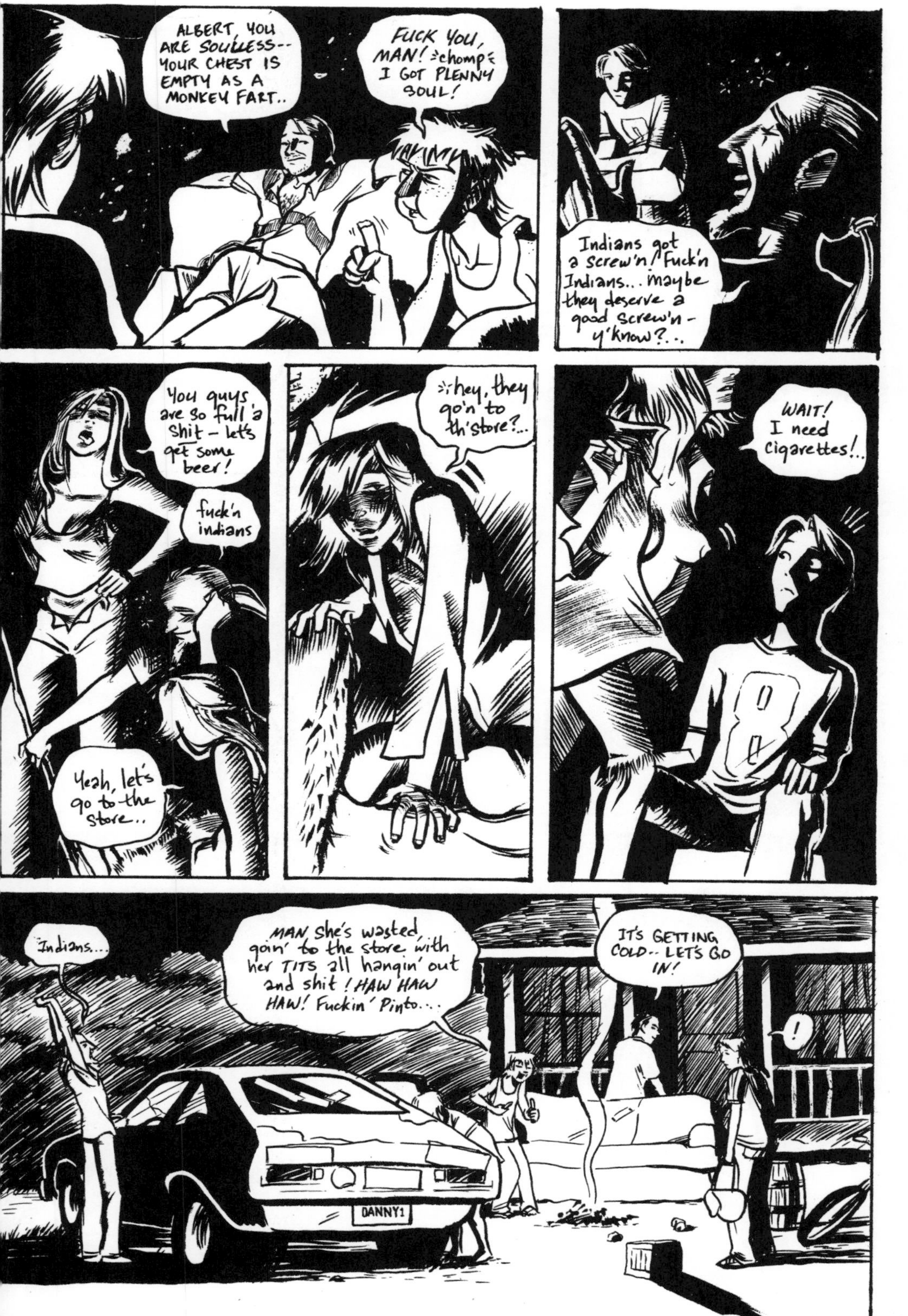
ALBERT, YOU ARE SOULLESS-- YOUR CHEST IS EMPTY AS A MONKEY FART..
FUCK YOU, MAN! *chomp* I GOT PLENNY SOUL!
Indians got a screw'n! Fuck'n Indians... maybe they deserve a good screw'n - y'know?..
You guys are so full a shit - let's get some beer!
fuck'n indians
Yeah, let's go to the store..
hey, they go'n to th'store?..
WAIT! I need Cigarettes!..
Indians....
MAN she's wasted, goin' to the store with her TITS all hangin' out and shit! HAW HAW HAW! Fuckin' Pinto...
IT'S GETTING COLD.. LET'S GO IN!
!
DANNY1

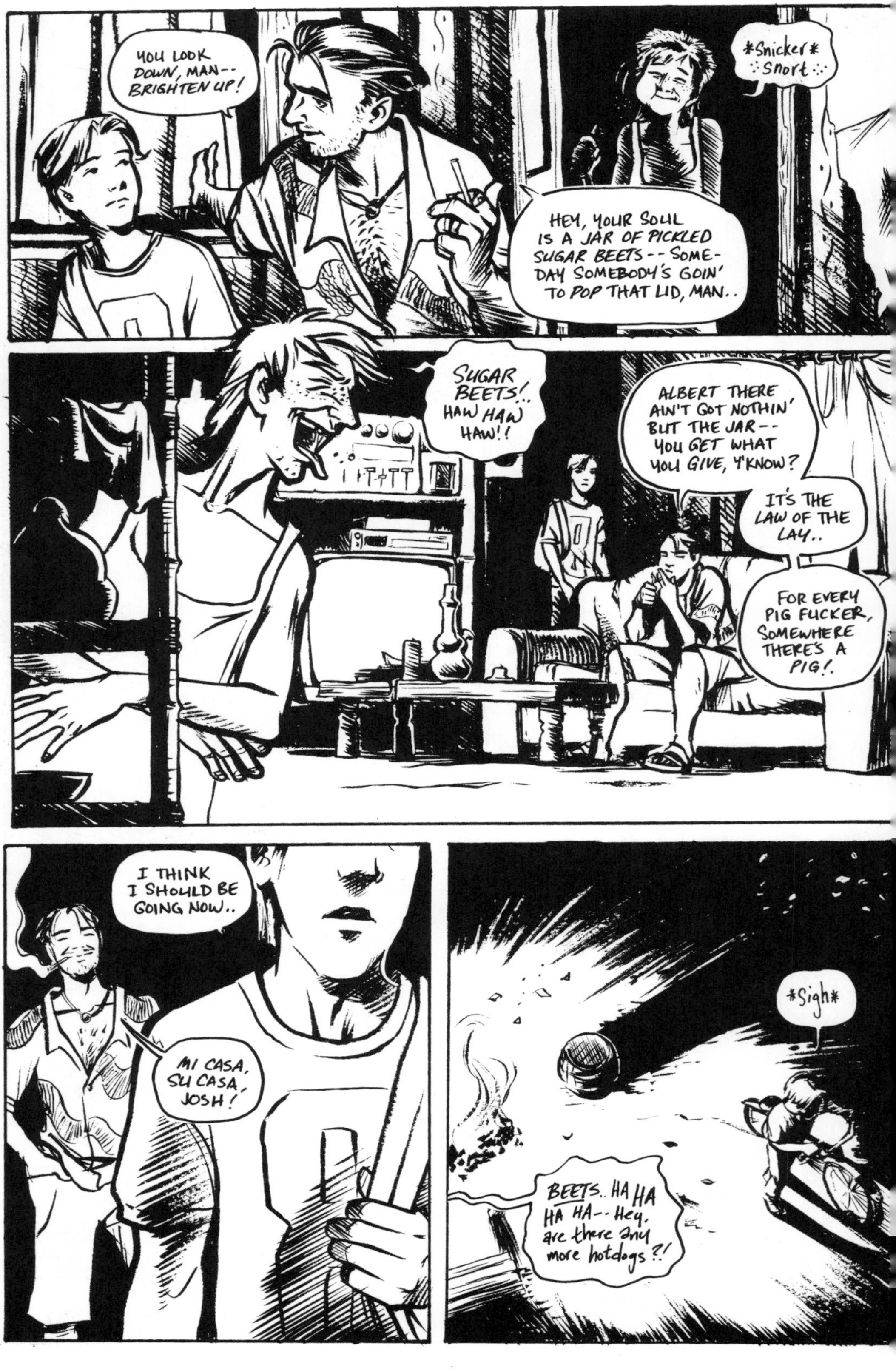
YOU LOOK DOWN, MAN-- BRIGHTEN UP!
Snicker Snort
HEY, YOUR SOUL IS A JAR OF PICKLED SUGAR BEETS -- SOMEDAY SOMEBODY'S GOIN' TO POP THAT LID, MAN..
SUGAR BEETS!.. HAW HAW HAW!!
ALBERT THERE AIN'T GOT NOTHIN' BUT THE JAR -- YOU GET WHAT YOU GIVE, Y'KNOW?
IT'S THE LAW OF THE LAY..
FOR EVERY PIG FUCKER, SOMEWHERE THERE'S A PIG!.
I THINK I SHOULD BE GOING NOW..
MI CASA, SU CASA, JOSH!
Sigh
BEETS.. HA HA HA HA-- Hey, are there any more hotdogs?!

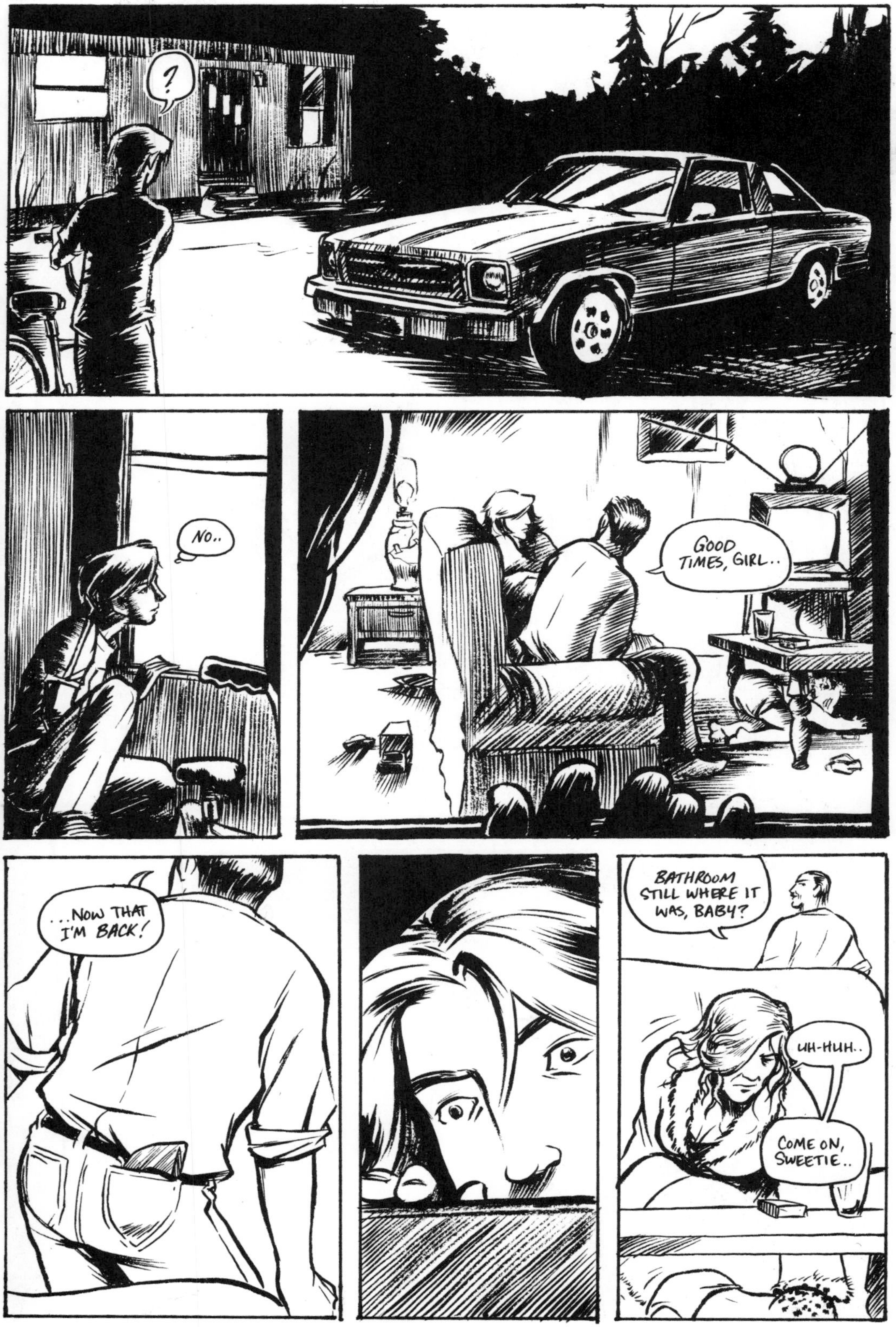
?
NO..
GOOD TIMES, GIRL..
...NOW THAT I'M BACK!
BATHROOM STILL WHERE IT WAS, BABY?
UH-HUH..
COME ON, SWEETIE..

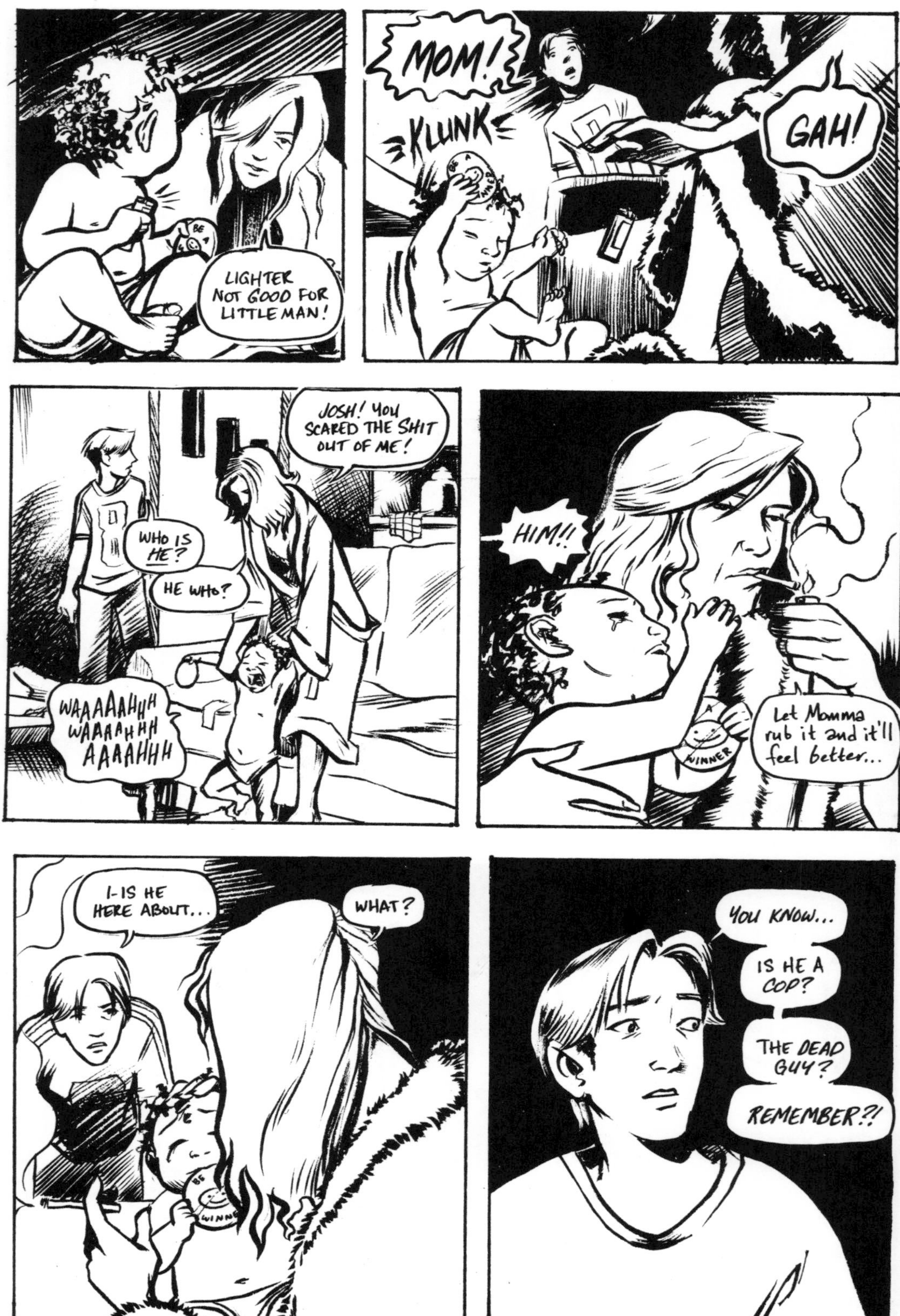
BE A
LIGHTER NOT GOOD FOR LITTLE MAN!
MOM!
KLUNK
GAH!
JOSH! YOU SCARED THE SHIT OUT OF ME!
WHO IS HE?
HE WHO?
WAAAAAHHH WAAAAHHH AAAAHHH
HIM!!
Let Momma rub it and it'll feel better...
WINNER
I-IS HE HERE ABOUT...
WHAT?
YOU KNOW...
IS HE A COP?
THE DEAD GUY?
REMEMBER?!

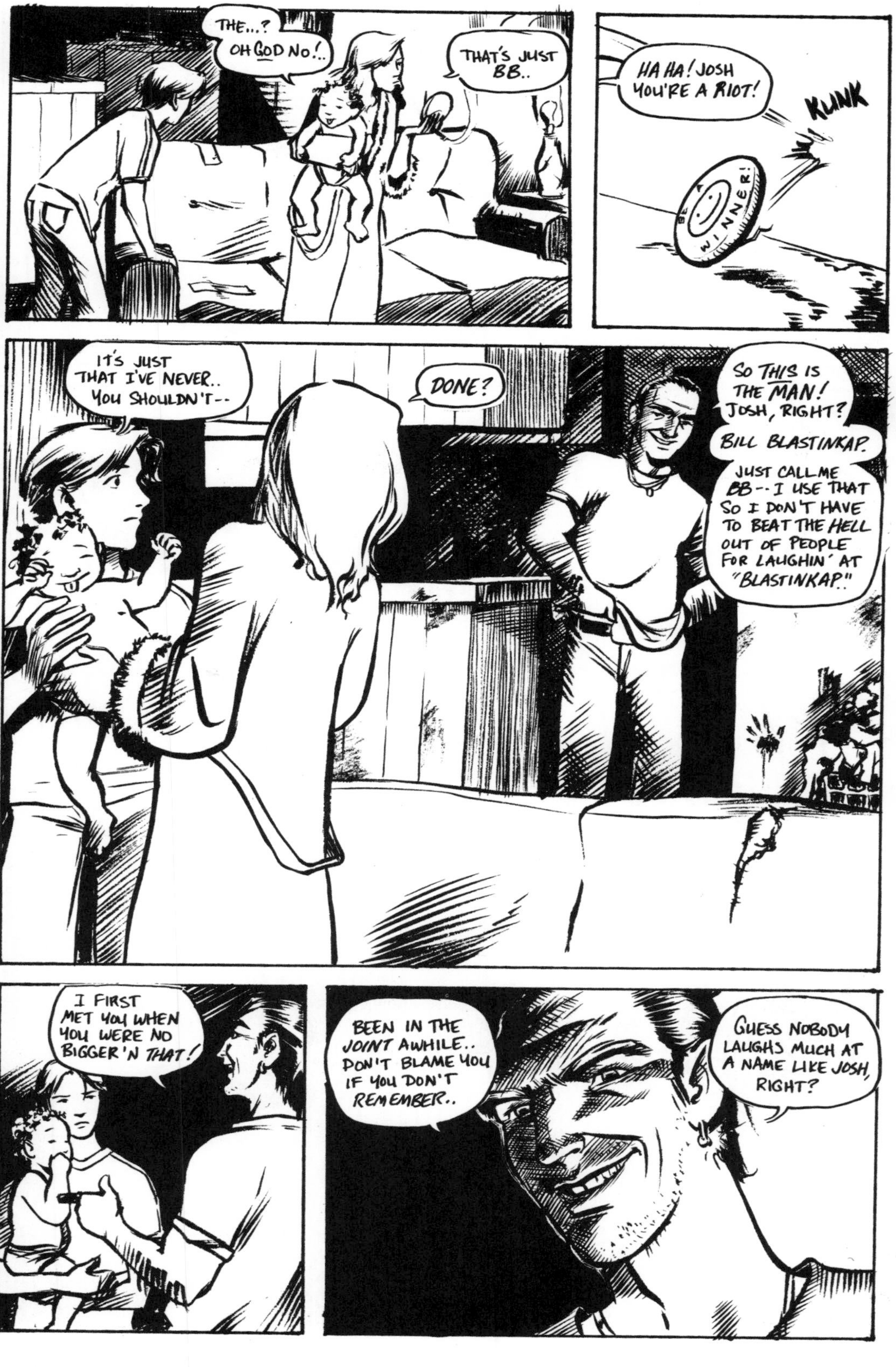
THE...? OH GOD NO!..
THAT'S JUST BB..
HA HA! JOSH YOU'RE A RIOT!
KLUNK
BE A WINNER!
IT'S JUST THAT I'VE NEVER.. YOU SHOULDN'T--
DONE?
SO THIS IS THE MAN! JOSH, RIGHT?
BILL BLASTINKAP.
JUST CALL ME BB--I USE THAT SO I DON'T HAVE TO BEAT THE HELL OUT OF PEOPLE FOR LAUGHIN' AT "BLASTINKAP."
I FIRST MET YOU WHEN YOU WERE NO BIGGER'N THAT!
BEEN IN THE JOINT AWHILE.. DON'T BLAME YOU IF YOU DON'T REMEMBER..
GUESS NOBODY LAUGHS MUCH AT A NAME LIKE JOSH, RIGHT?

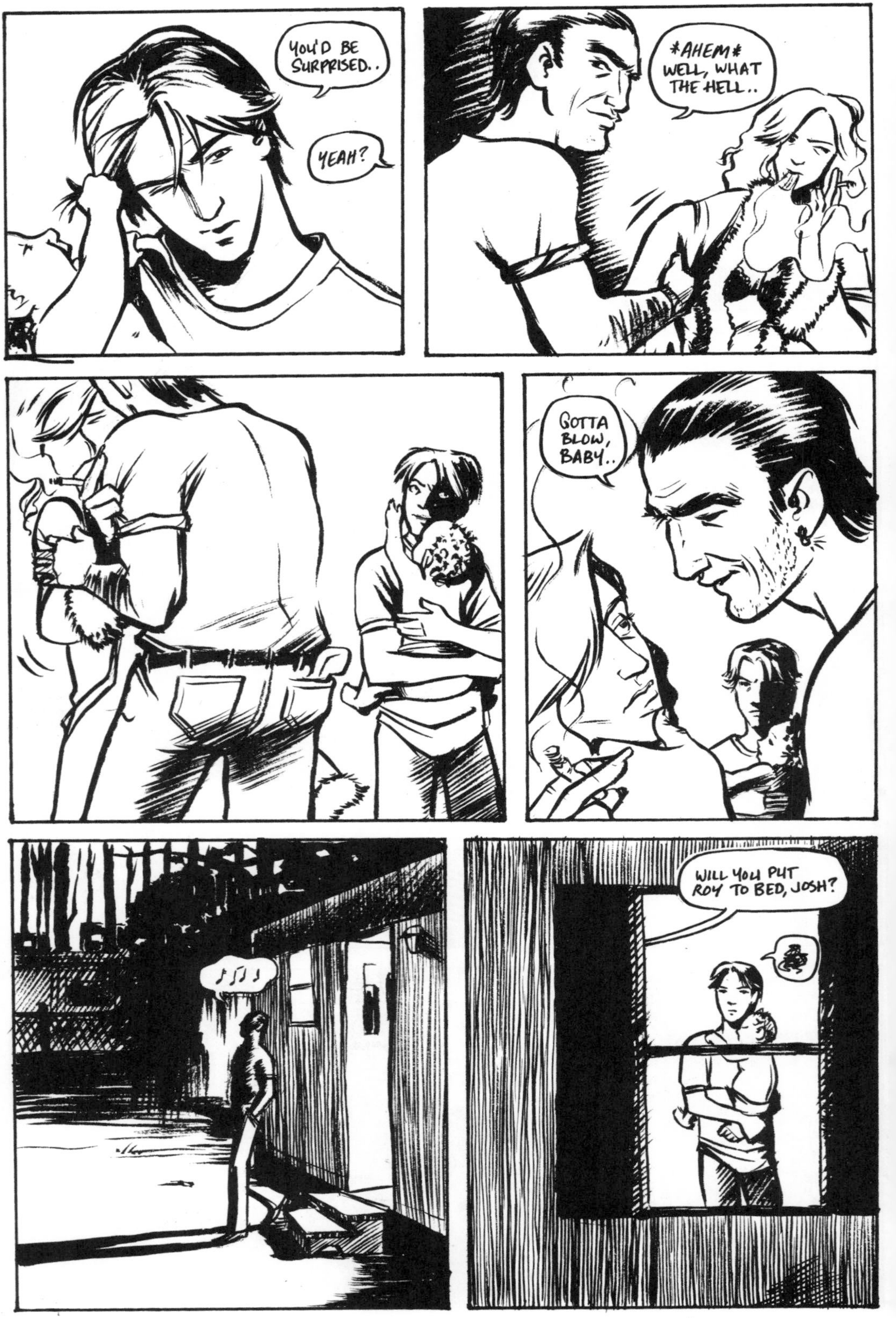
YOU'D BE SURPRISED..
YEAH?
AHEM WELL, WHAT THE HELL..
GOTTA BLOW, BABY..
♪♫♪
WILL YOU PUT ROY TO BED, JOSH?

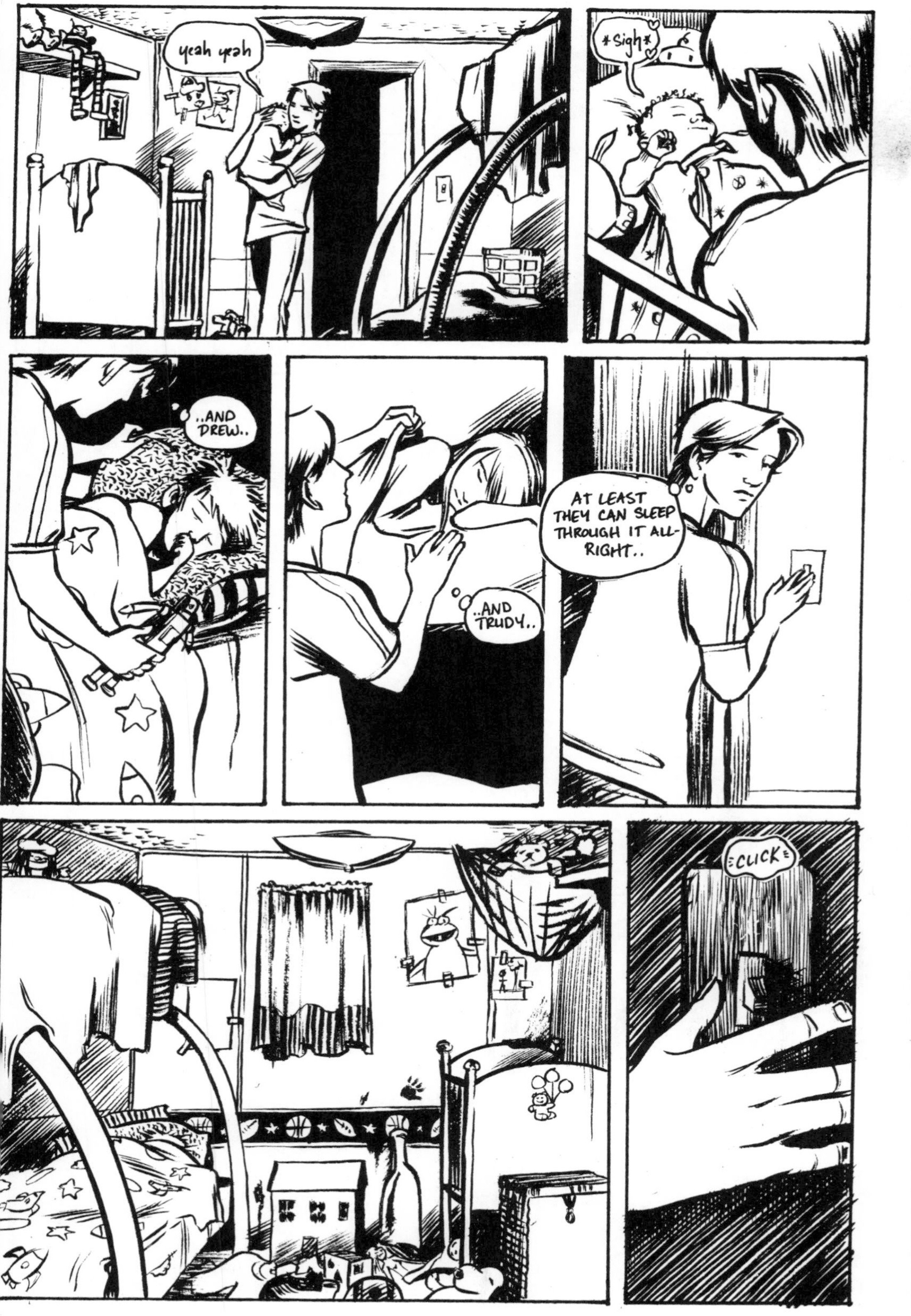
yeah yeah
sigh
..AND DREW..
..AND TRUDY..
AT LEAST THEY CAN SLEEP THROUGH IT ALL-RIGHT..
CLICK

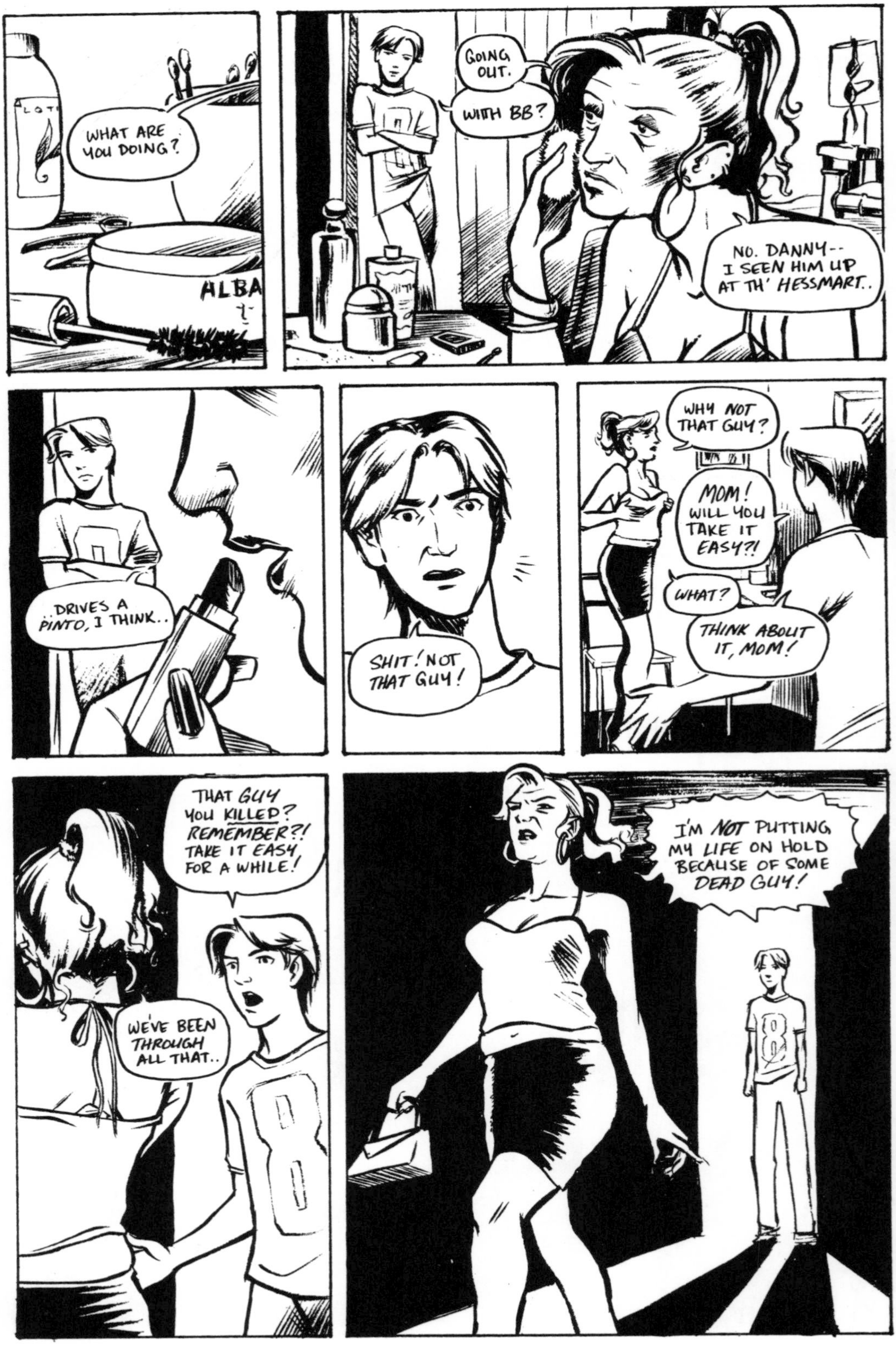
WHAT ARE YOU DOING?
ALBA
GOING OUT.
WITH BB?
NO. DANNY-- I SEEN HIM UP AT TH' HESSMART..
DRIVES A PINTO, I THINK..
SHIT! NOT THAT GUY!
WHY NOT THAT GUY?
MOM! WILL YOU TAKE IT EASY?!
WHAT?
THINK ABOUT IT, MOM!
THAT GUY YOU KILLED? REMEMBER?! TAKE IT EASY FOR A WHILE!
WE'VE BEEN THROUGH ALL THAT..
I'M NOT PUTTING MY LIFE ON HOLD BECAUSE OF SOME DEAD GUY!

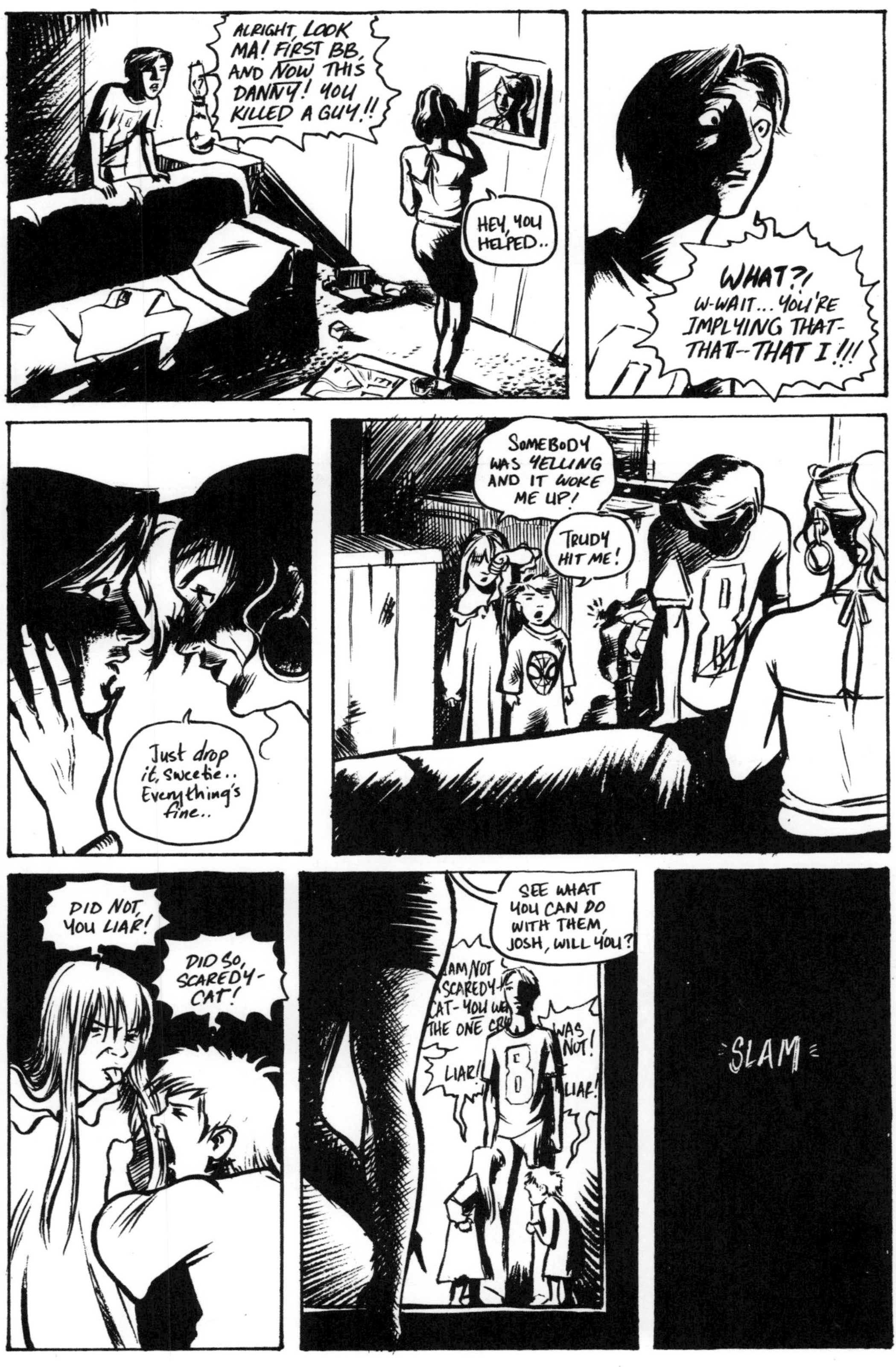
ALRIGHT, LOOK MA! FIRST BB, AND NOW THIS DANNY! YOU KILLED A GUY!!
HEY, YOU HELPED..
WHAT?! W-WAIT... YOU'RE IMPLYING THAT-THAT--THAT I!!!
Just drop it, sweetie.. Everything's fine..
SOMEBODY WAS YELLING AND IT WOKE ME UP!
TRUDY HIT ME!
DID NOT, YOU LIAR!
DID SO, SCAREDY-CAT!
SEE WHAT YOU CAN DO WITH THEM, JOSH, WILL YOU?
I AM NOT SCAREDY-CAT-
THE ONE
WAS NOT!
LIAR!
LIAR!
SLAM

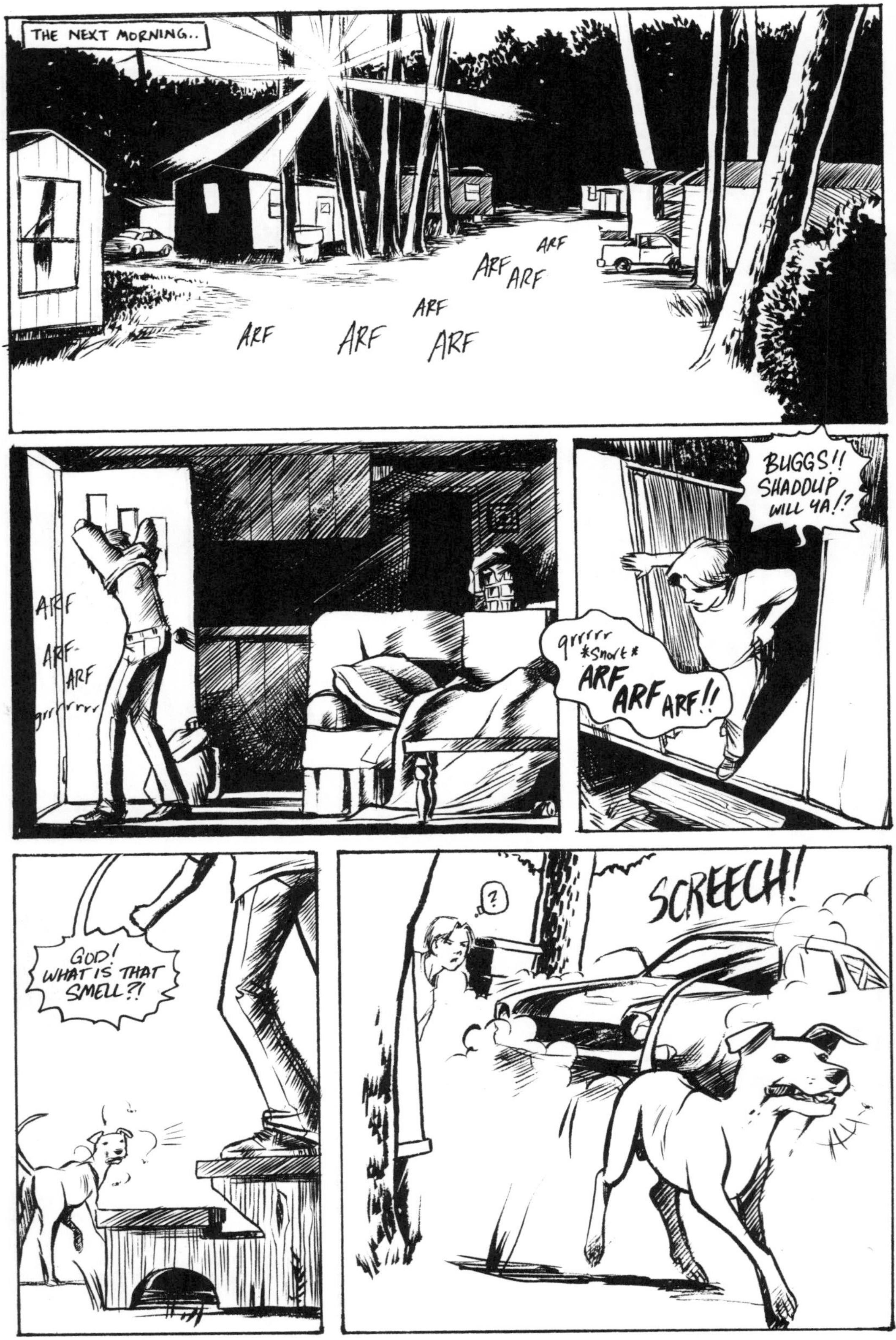
THE NEXT MORNING..
ARF
ARF
ARF
ARF
ARF
ARF
ARF
ARF
ARF
ARF
ARF
grrrrrrr
BUGGS!! SHADDUP WILL YA!?
grrrrr *snort* ARF ARF ARF!!
GOD! WHAT IS THAT SMELL?!
?
SCREECH!

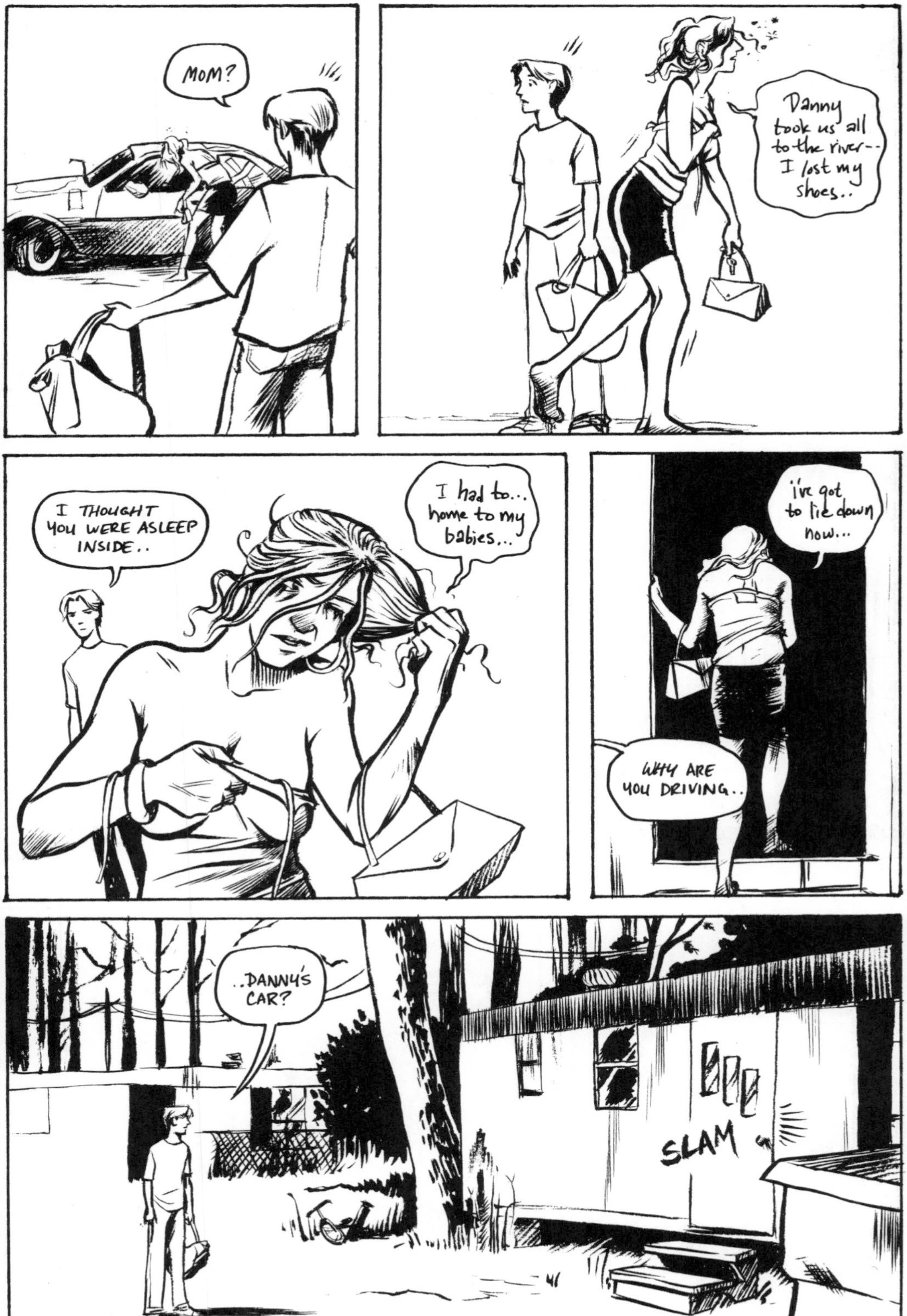
MOM?
Danny took us all to the river-- I lost my shoes..
I THOUGHT YOU WERE ASLEEP INSIDE..
I had to... home to my babies...
i've got to lie down now...
WHY ARE YOU DRIVING..
..DANNY'S CAR?
SLAM

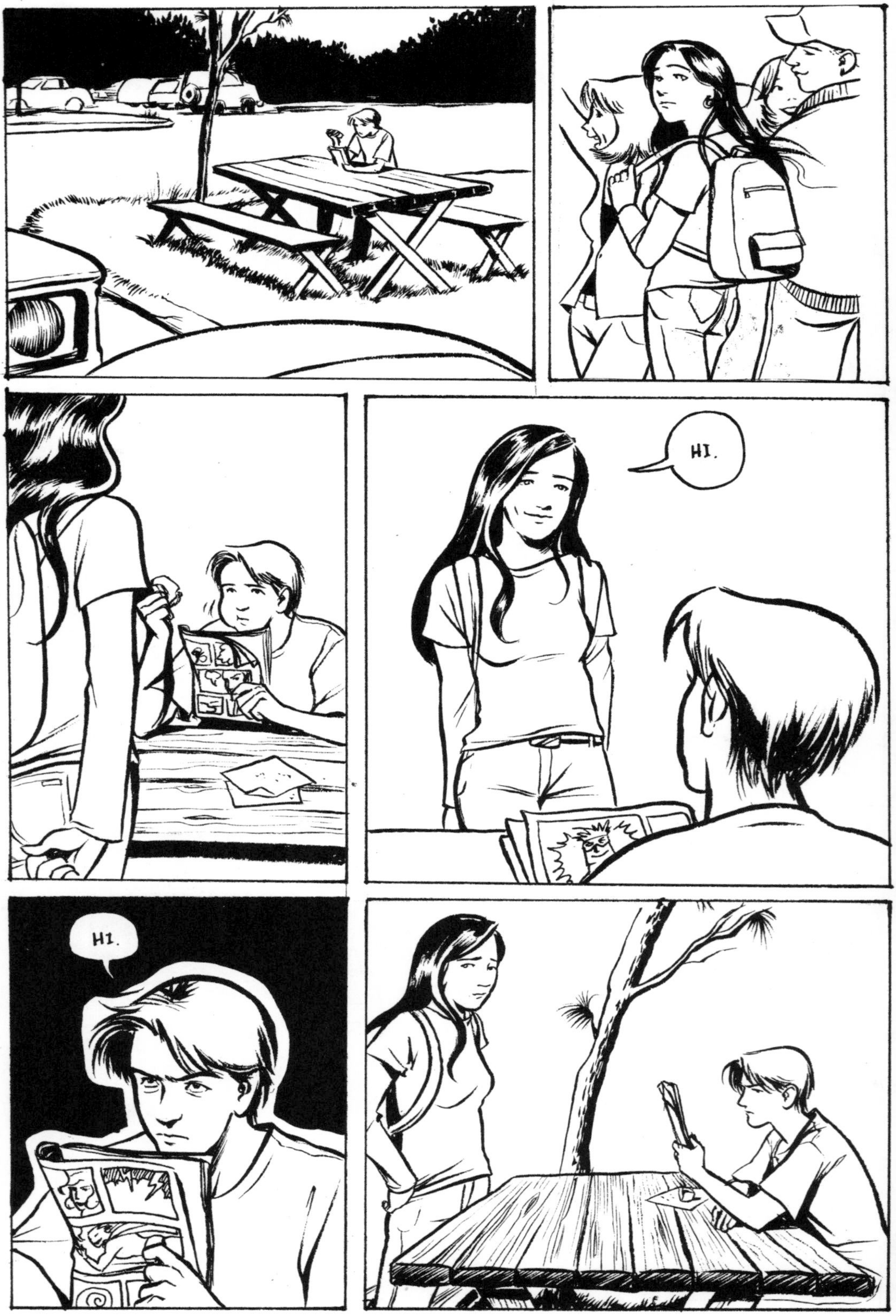
HI.
HI.

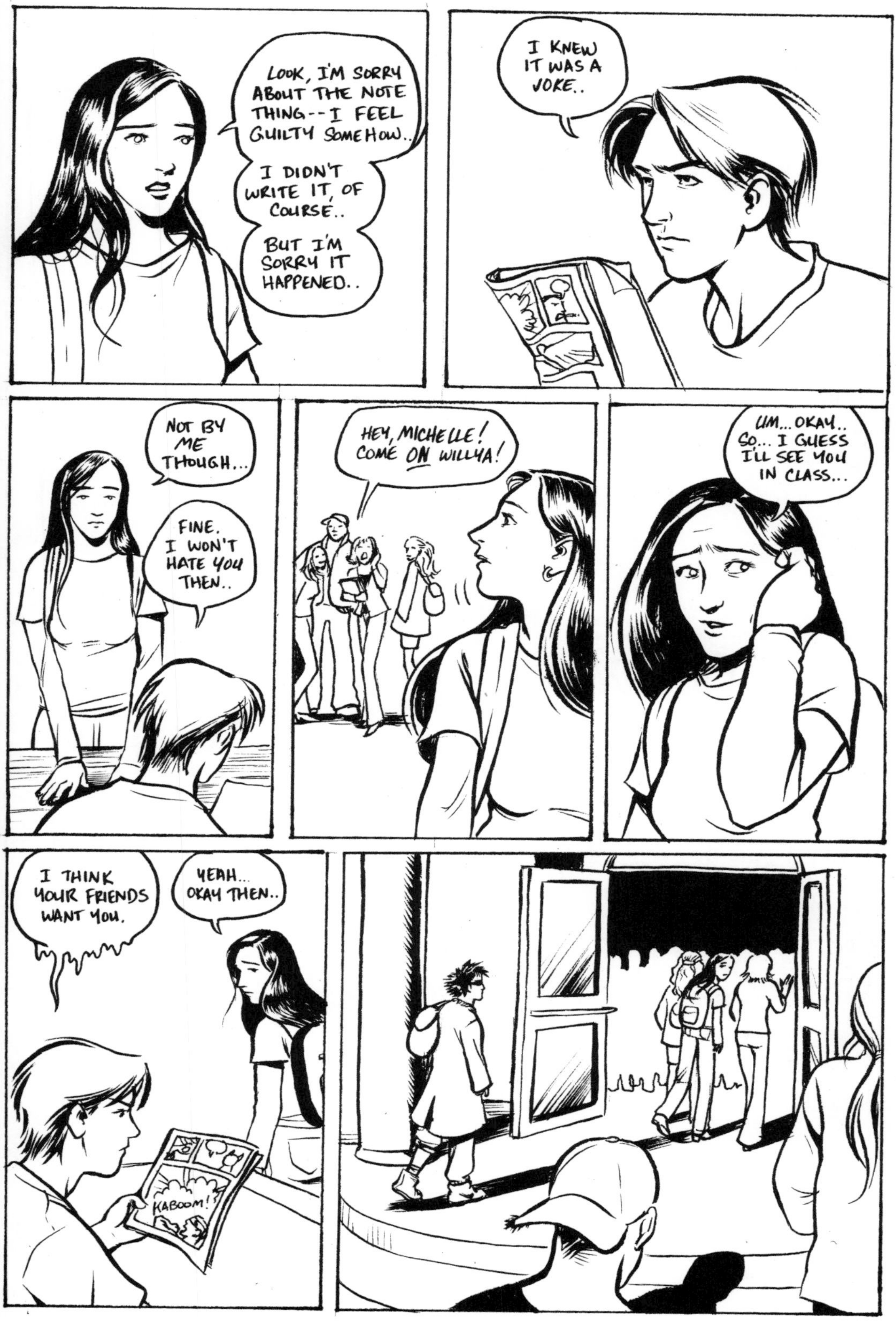
LOOK, I'M SORRY ABOUT THE NOTE THING--I FEEL GUILTY SOMEHOW..
I DIDN'T WRITE IT, OF COURSE..
BUT I'M SORRY IT HAPPENED..
I KNEW IT WAS A JOKE..
NOT BY ME THOUGH...
FINE. I WON'T HATE YOU THEN..
HEY, MICHELLE! COME ON WILLYA!
UM... OKAY.. SO... I GUESS I'LL SEE YOU IN CLASS...
I THINK YOUR FRIENDS WANT YOU.
YEAH... OKAY THEN..
KABOOM!

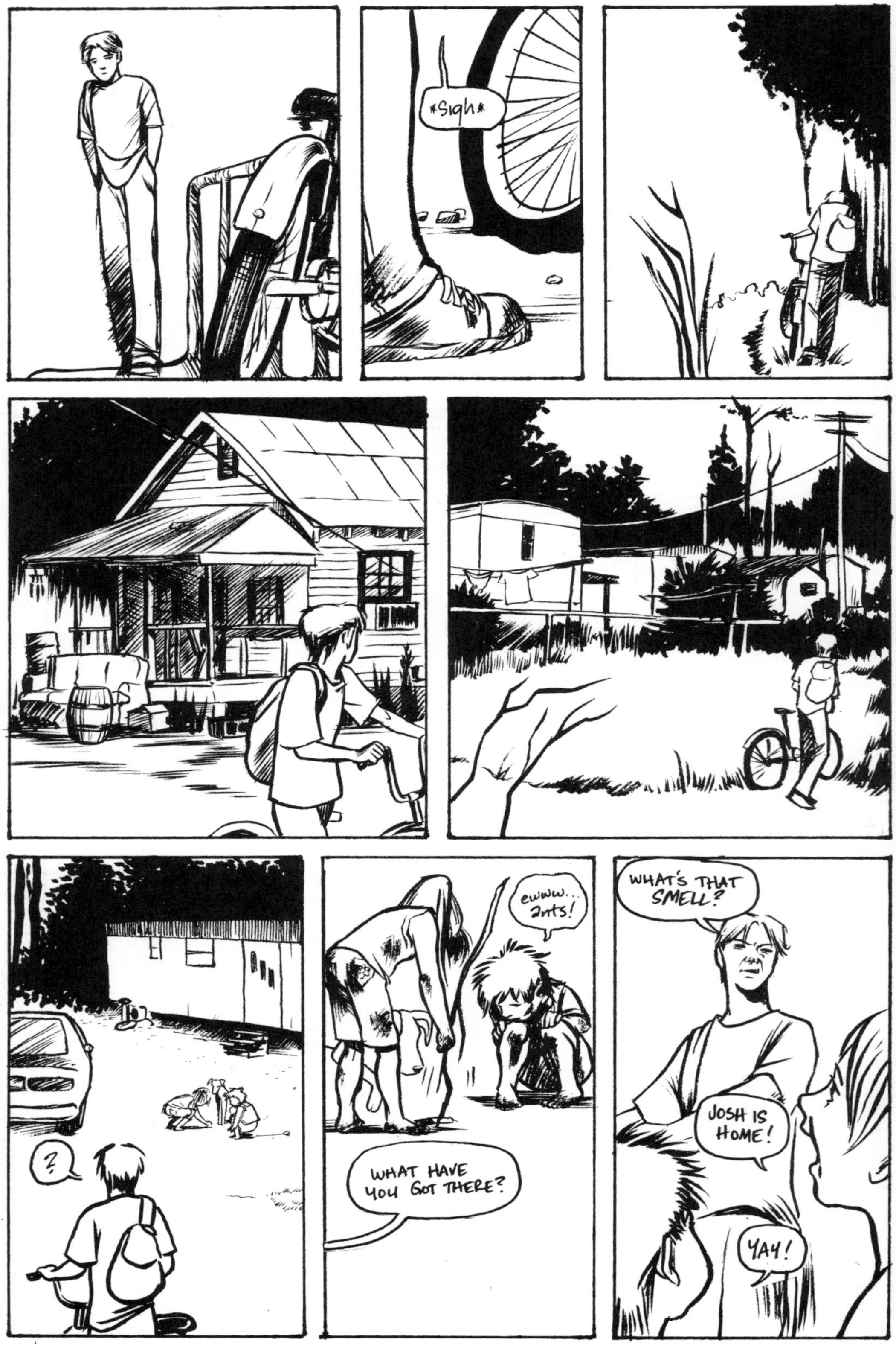
sigh
?
ewww... ants!
WHAT HAVE YOU GOT THERE?
WHAT'S THAT SMELL?
JOSH IS HOME!
YAY!

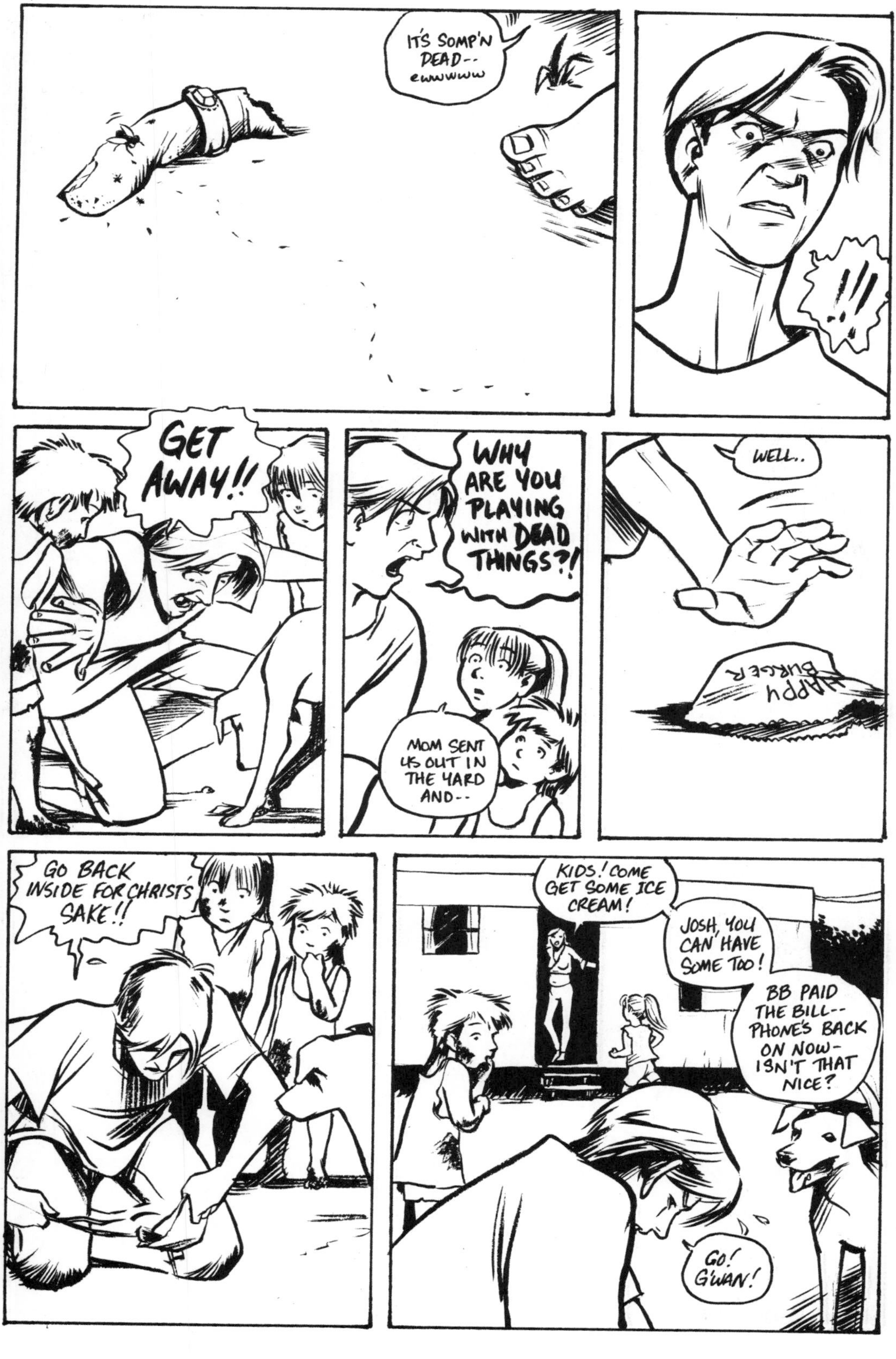
IT'S SOMP'N DEAD-- ewwwwww
!!!
GET AWAY!!
WHY ARE YOU PLAYING WITH DEAD THINGS?!
MOM SENT US OUT IN THE YARD AND--
WELL..
HAPPY BURGER
GO BACK INSIDE FOR CHRIST'S SAKE!!
KIDS! COME GET SOME ICE CREAM!
JOSH, YOU CAN HAVE SOME TOO!
BB PAID THE BILL-- PHONE'S BACK ON NOW- ISN'T THAT NICE?
GO! G'WAN!

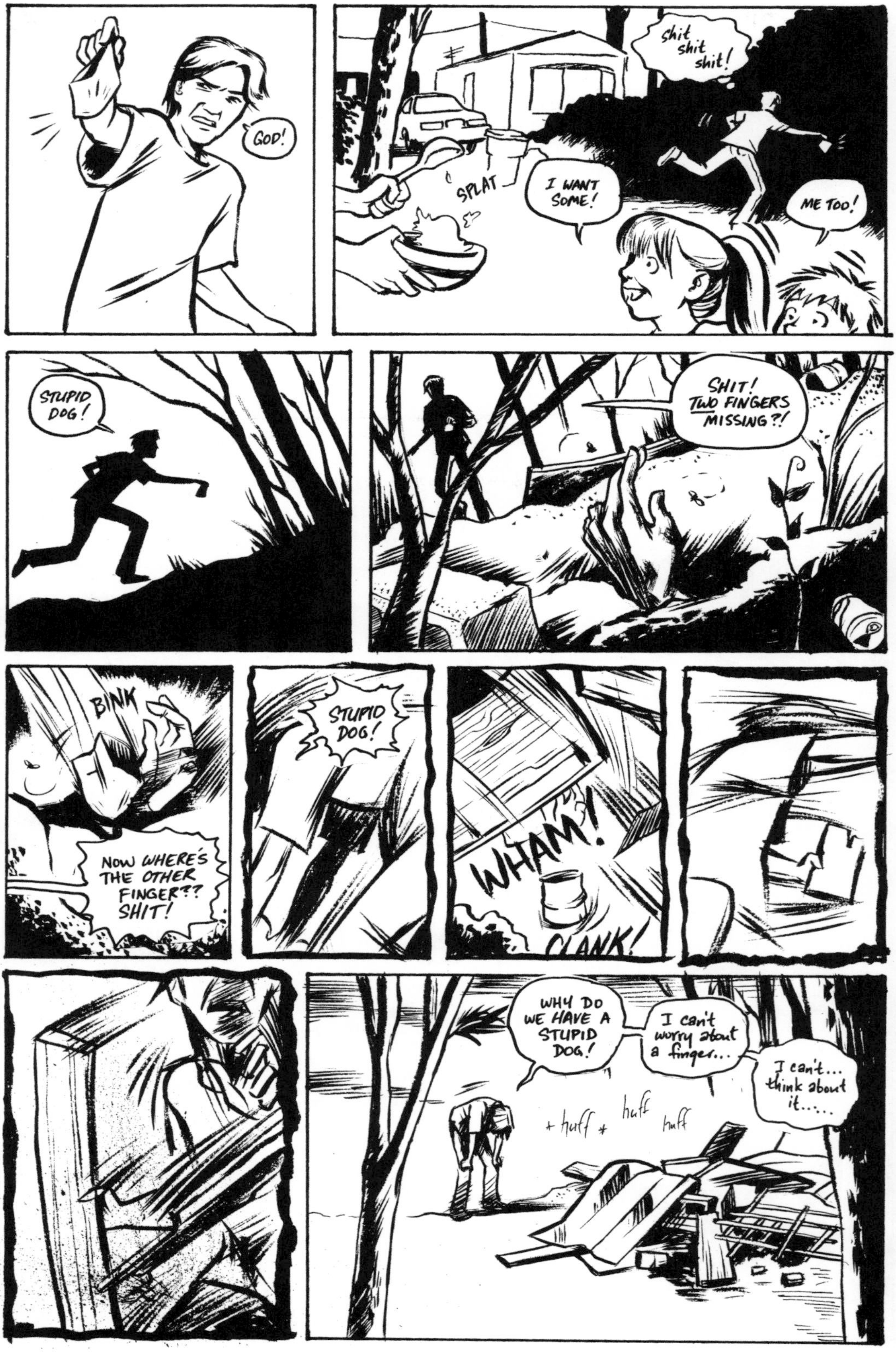
GOD!
shit shit shit!
SPLAT
I WANT SOME!
ME TOO!
STUPID DOG!
SHIT! TWO FINGERS MISSING?!
BINK
NOW WHERE'S THE OTHER FINGER?? SHIT!
STUPID DOG!
WHAM!
CLANK!
WHY DO WE HAVE A STUPID DOG!
I can't worry about a finger...
I can't... think about it.....
huff
huff
huff

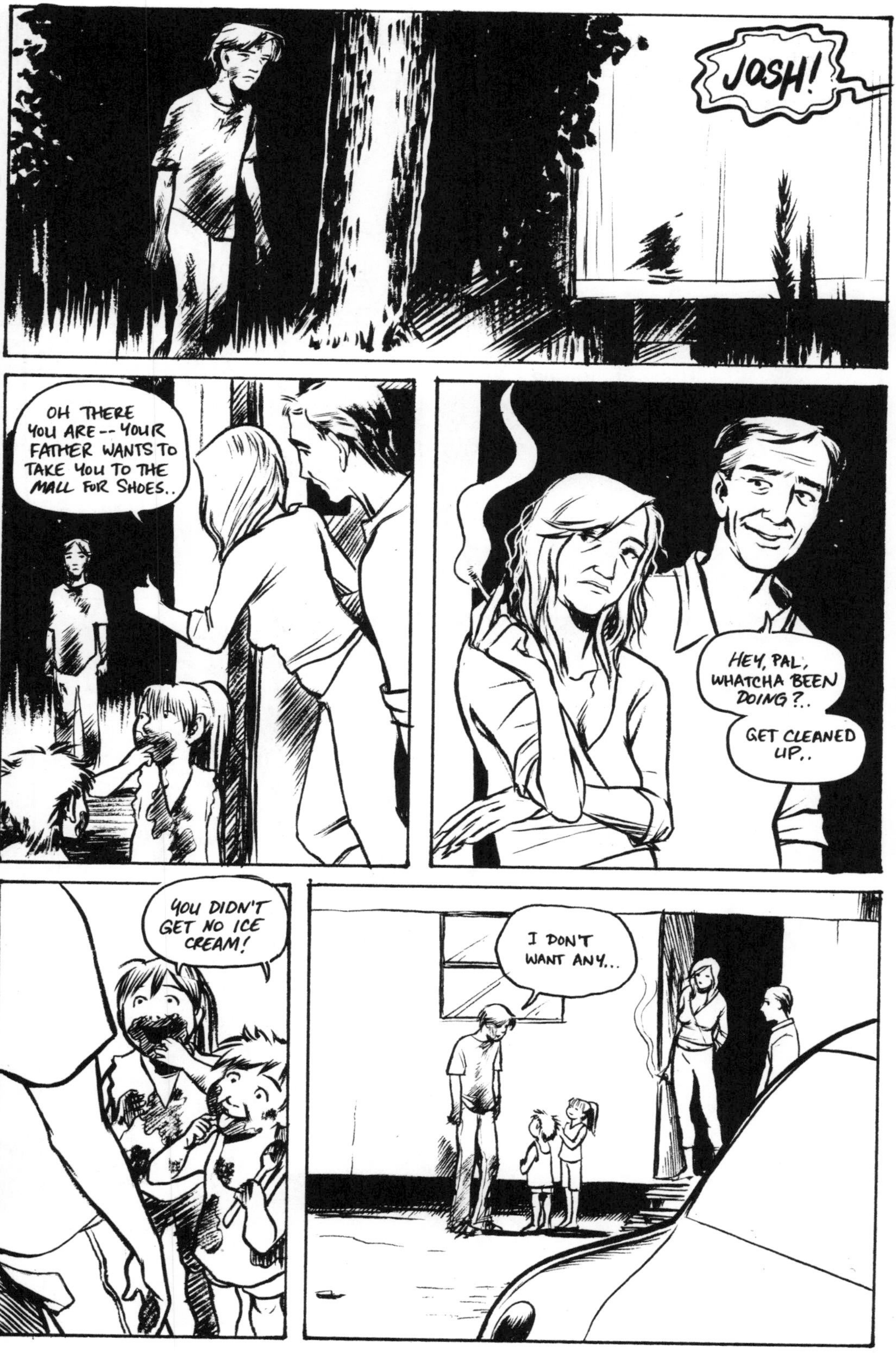
JOSH!
OH THERE YOU ARE-- YOUR FATHER WANTS TO TAKE YOU TO THE MALL FOR SHOES..
HEY, PAL, WHATCHA BEEN DOING?..
GET CLEANED UP..
YOU DIDN'T GET NO ICE CREAM!
I DON'T WANT ANY...

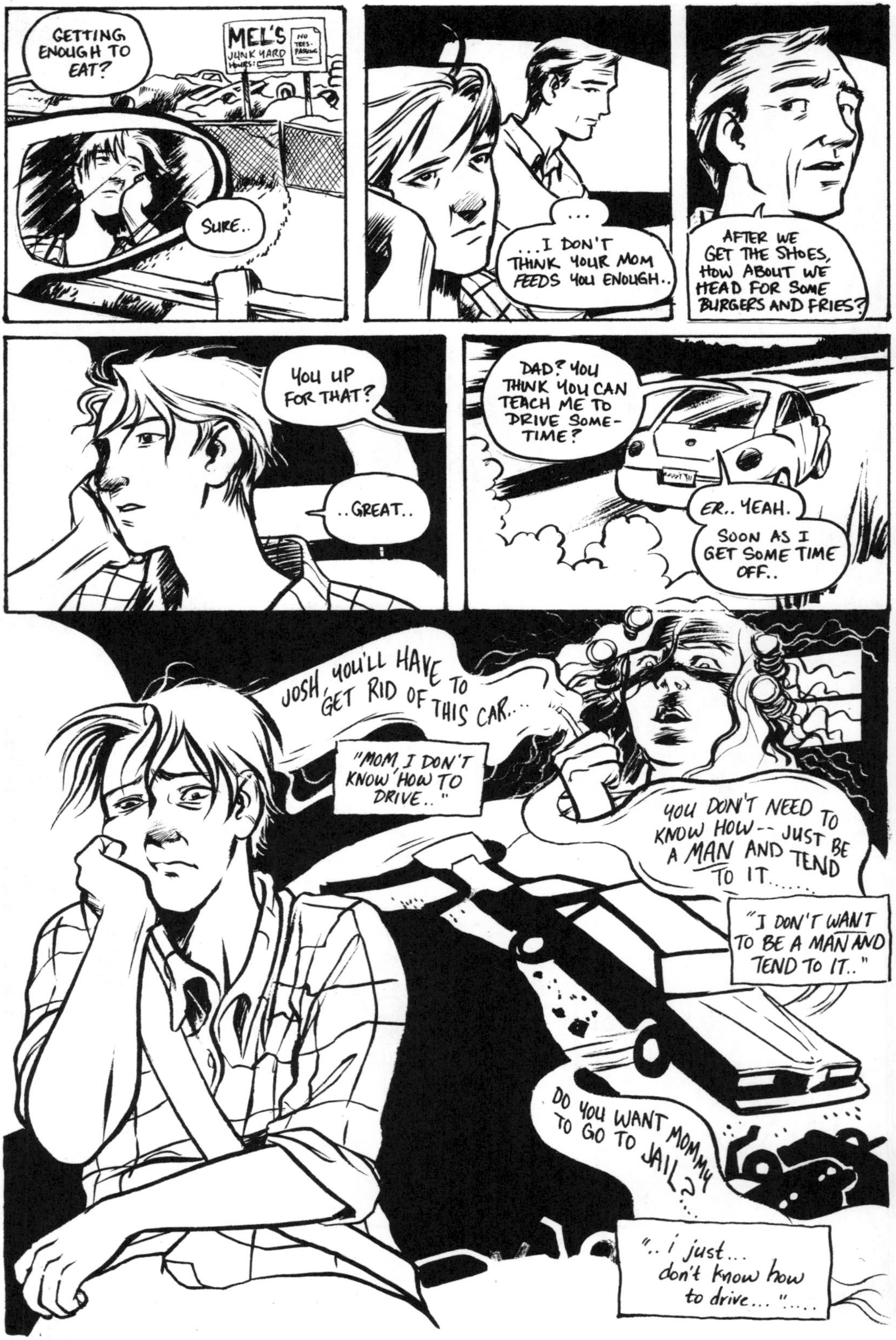
GETTING ENOUGH TO EAT?
MEL'S JUNK YARD HOURS:
NO TRES-PASSING
SURE..
...
...I DON'T THINK YOUR MOM FEEDS YOU ENOUGH..
AFTER WE GET THE SHOES, HOW ABOUT WE HEAD FOR SOME BURGERS AND FRIES?
YOU UP FOR THAT?
..GREAT..
DAD? YOU THINK YOU CAN TEACH ME TO DRIVE SOME-TIME?
ER.. YEAH.
SOON AS I GET SOME TIME OFF..
JOSH, YOU'LL HAVE TO GET RID OF THIS CAR...
"MOM, I DON'T KNOW HOW TO DRIVE.."
YOU DON'T NEED TO KNOW HOW-- JUST BE A MAN AND TEND TO IT......
"I DON'T WANT TO BE A MAN AND TEND TO IT.."
DO YOU WANT MOMMY TO GO TO JAIL?
"..i just... don't know how to drive..."....

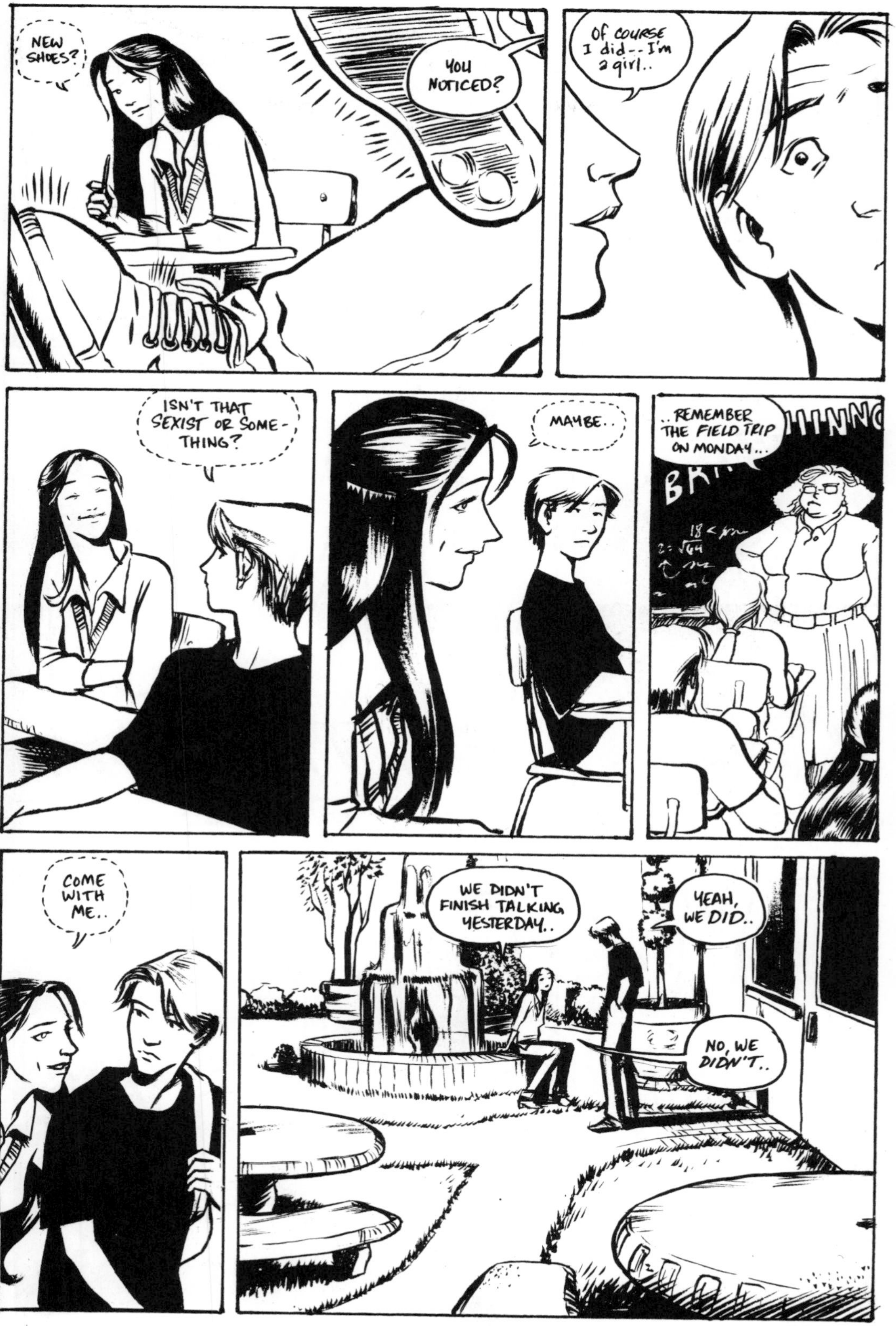
NEW SHOES?
YOU NOTICED?
OF COURSE I did-- I'm a girl..
ISN'T THAT SEXIST OR SOME-THING?
MAYBE..
..REMEMBER THE FIELD TRIP ON MONDAY...
COME WITH ME..
WE DIDN'T FINISH TALKING YESTERDAY..
YEAH, WE DID..
NO, WE DIDN'T..

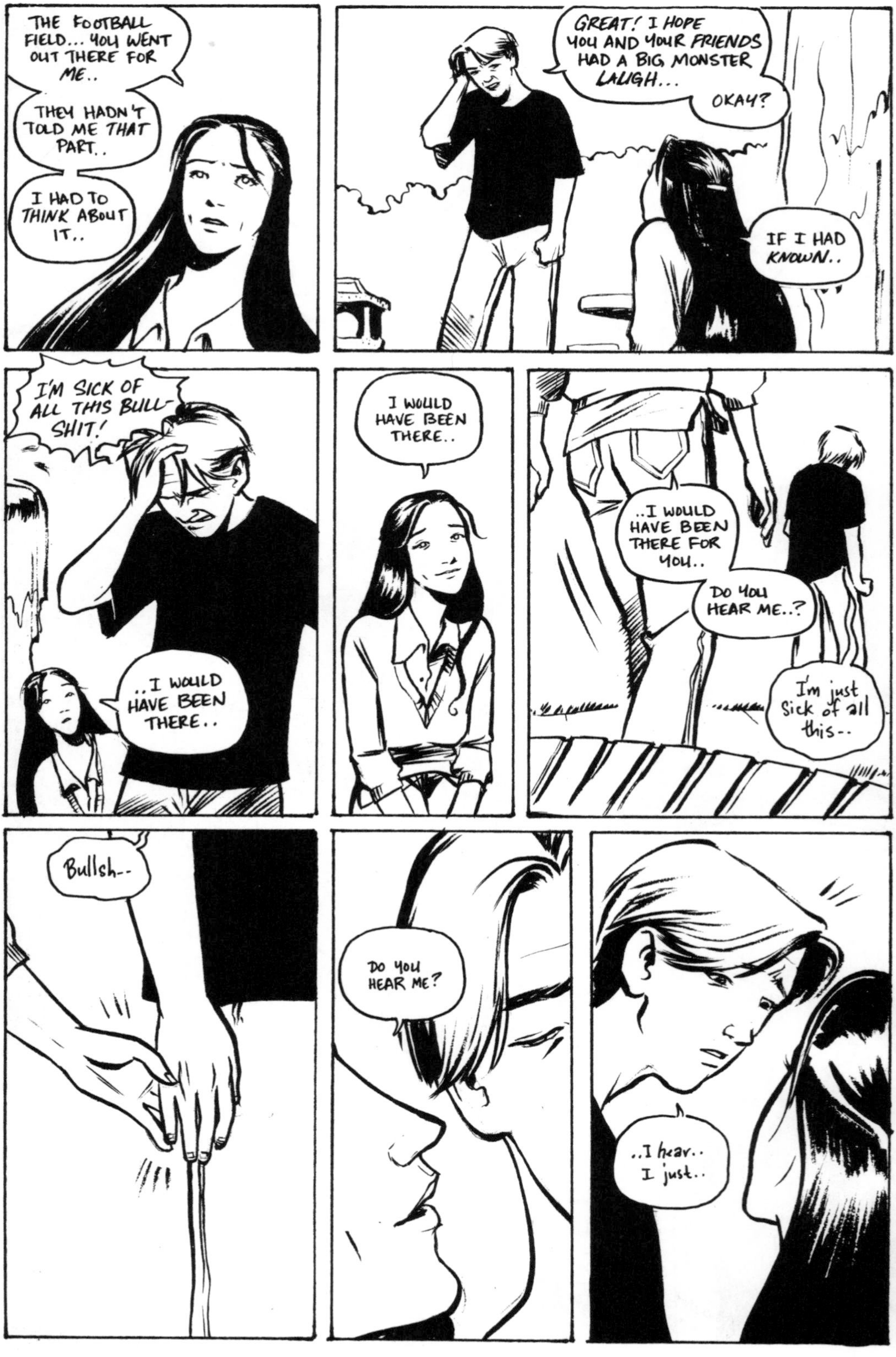
THE FOOTBALL FIELD... YOU WENT OUT THERE FOR ME..
THEY HADN'T TOLD ME THAT PART..
I HAD TO THINK ABOUT IT..
GREAT! I HOPE YOU AND YOUR FRIENDS HAD A BIG MONSTER LAUGH...
OKAY?
IF I HAD KNOWN..
I'M SICK OF ALL THIS BULL-SHIT!
..I WOULD HAVE BEEN THERE..
I WOULD HAVE BEEN THERE..
..I WOULD HAVE BEEN THERE FOR YOU..
DO YOU HEAR ME..?
I'm just sick of all this--
Bullsh--
DO YOU HEAR ME?
..I hear.. I just..

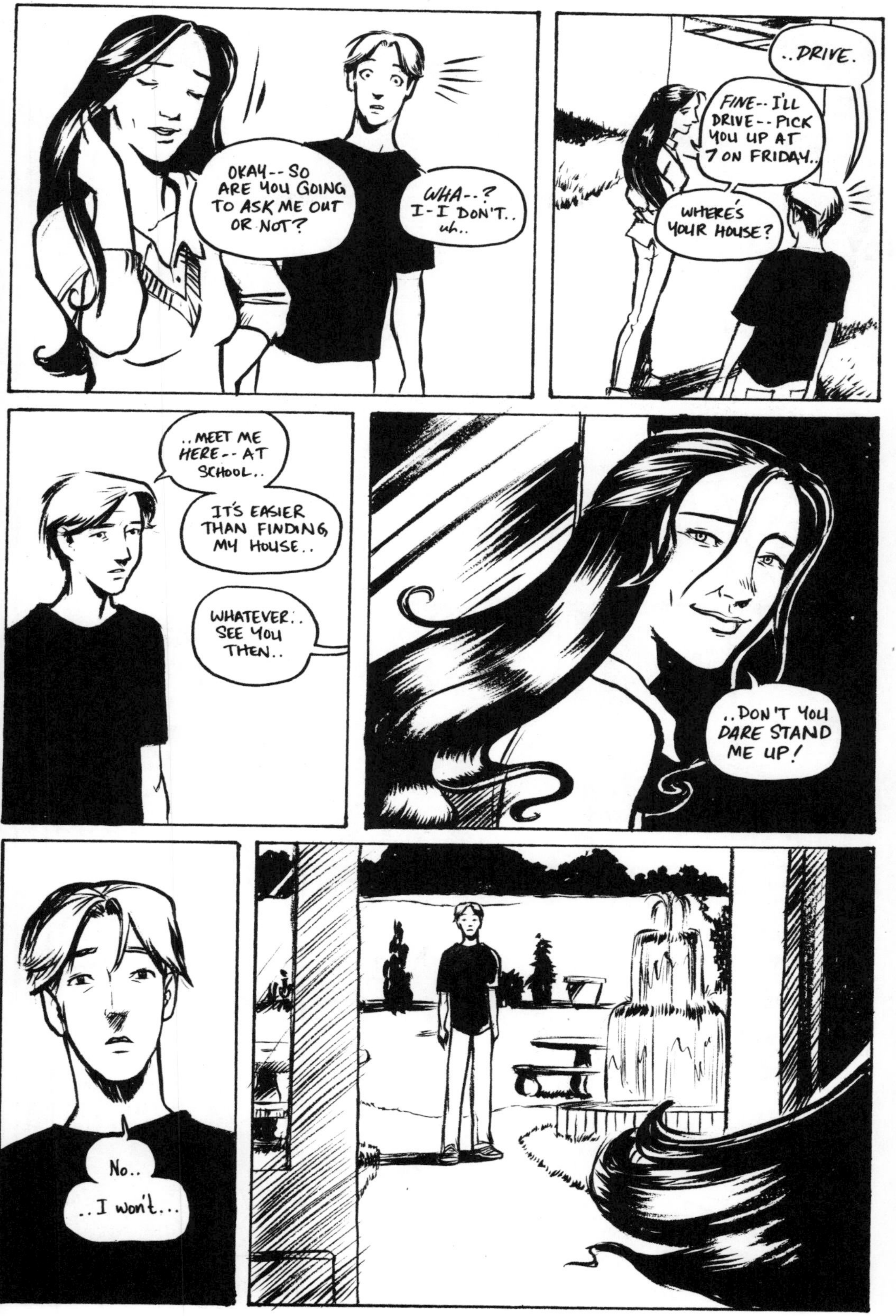
OKAY-- SO ARE YOU GOING TO ASK ME OUT OR NOT?
WHA--? I-I DON'T.. uh..
FINE-- I'LL DRIVE-- PICK YOU UP AT 7 ON FRIDAY..
..DRIVE.
WHERE'S YOUR HOUSE?
..MEET ME HERE-- AT SCHOOL..
IT'S EASIER THAN FINDING MY HOUSE..
WHATEVER.. SEE YOU THEN..
..DON'T YOU DARE STAND ME UP!
No..
..I won't...

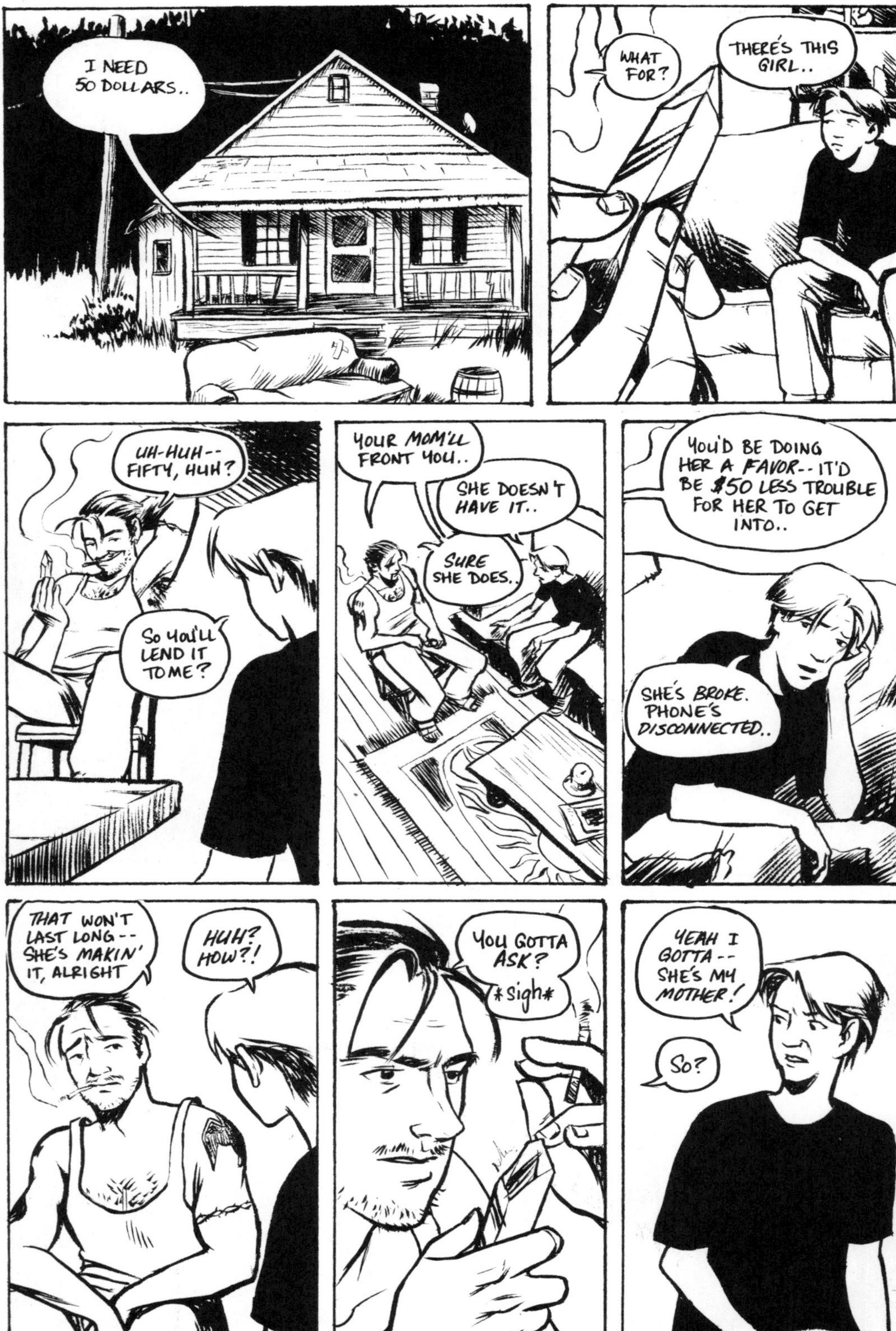
I NEED 50 DOLLARS..
WHAT FOR?
THERE'S THIS GIRL..
UH-HUH-- FIFTY, HUH?
SO YOU'LL LEND IT TO ME?
YOUR MOM'LL FRONT YOU..
SHE DOESN'T HAVE IT..
SURE SHE DOES..
YOU'D BE DOING HER A FAVOR-- IT'D BE $50 LESS TROUBLE FOR HER TO GET INTO..
SHE'S BROKE. PHONE'S DISCONNECTED..
THAT WON'T LAST LONG-- SHE'S MAKIN' IT, ALRIGHT
HUH? HOW?!
YOU GOTTA ASK?
sigh
YEAH I GOTTA-- SHE'S MY MOTHER!
SO?

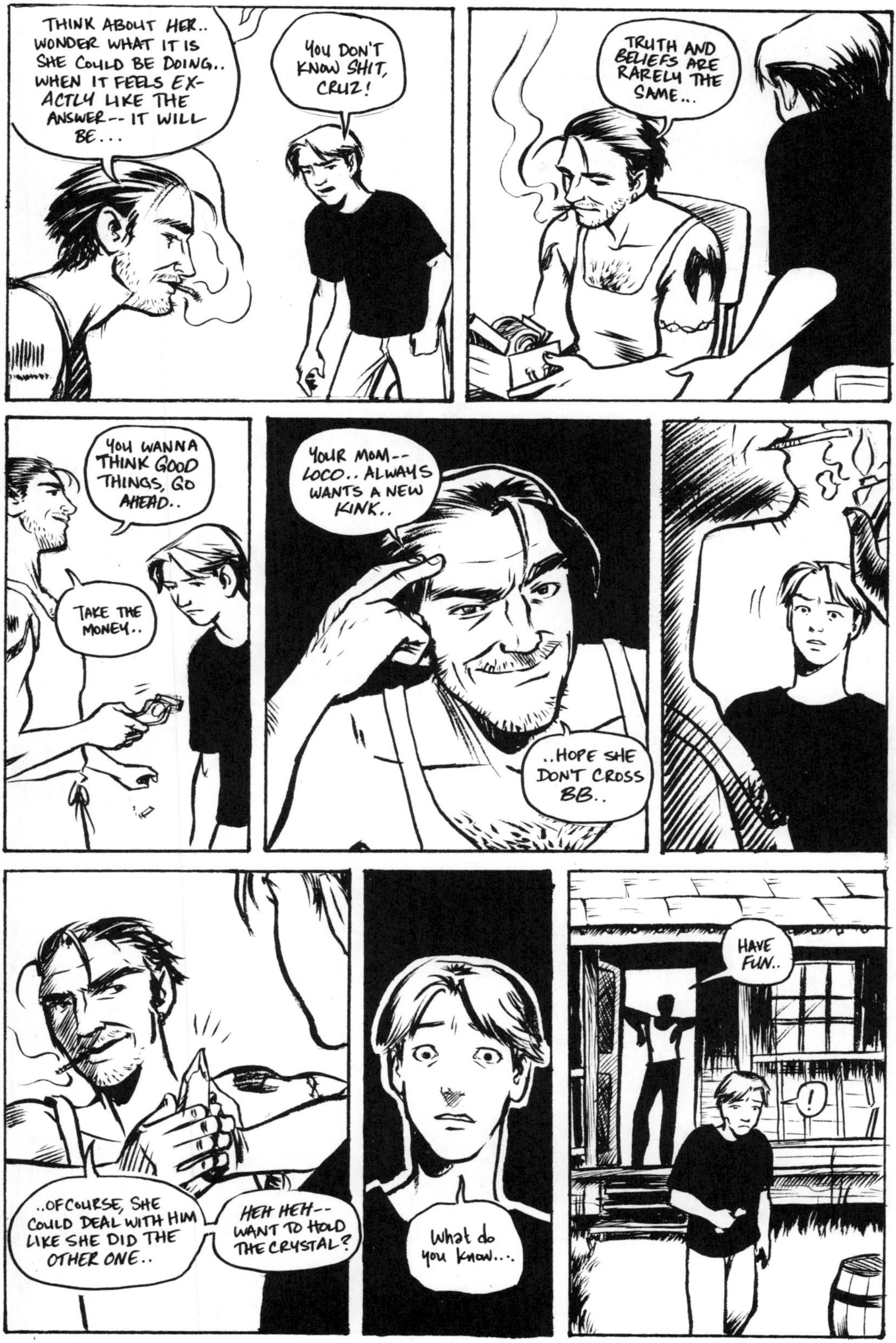
THINK ABOUT HER.. WONDER WHAT IT IS SHE COULD BE DOING.. WHEN IT FEELS EXACTLY LIKE THE ANSWER-- IT WILL BE...
YOU DON'T KNOW SHIT, CRUZ!
TRUTH AND BELIEFS ARE RARELY THE SAME...
YOU WANNA THINK GOOD THINGS, GO AHEAD..
TAKE THE MONEY..
YOUR MOM-- LOCO.. ALWAYS WANTS A NEW KINK..
..HOPE SHE DON'T CROSS BB..
..OF COURSE, SHE COULD DEAL WITH HIM LIKE SHE DID THE OTHER ONE..
HEH HEH-- WANT TO HOLD THE CRYSTAL?
What do you know...
HAVE FUN..
!

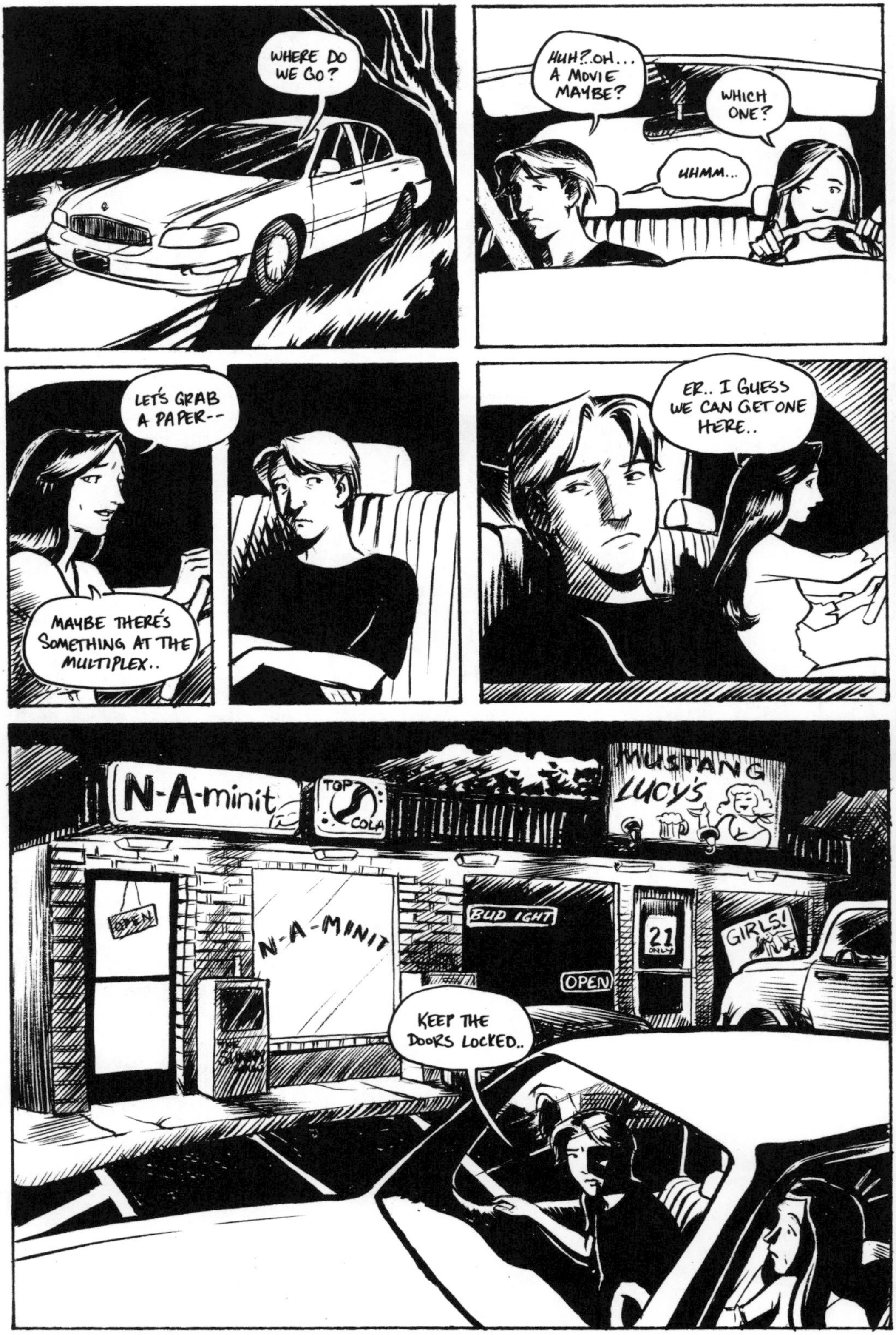
WHERE DO WE GO?
HUH?..OH... A MOVIE MAYBE?
WHICH ONE?
UHMM...
LET'S GRAB A PAPER--
MAYBE THERE'S SOMETHING AT THE MULTIPLEX..
ER.. I GUESS WE CAN GET ONE HERE..
N-A-minit
TOP COLA
MUSTANG LUCY'S
OPEN
N-A-MINIT
BUD IGHT
21 ONLY
GIRLS!
OPEN
KEEP THE DOORS LOCKED..

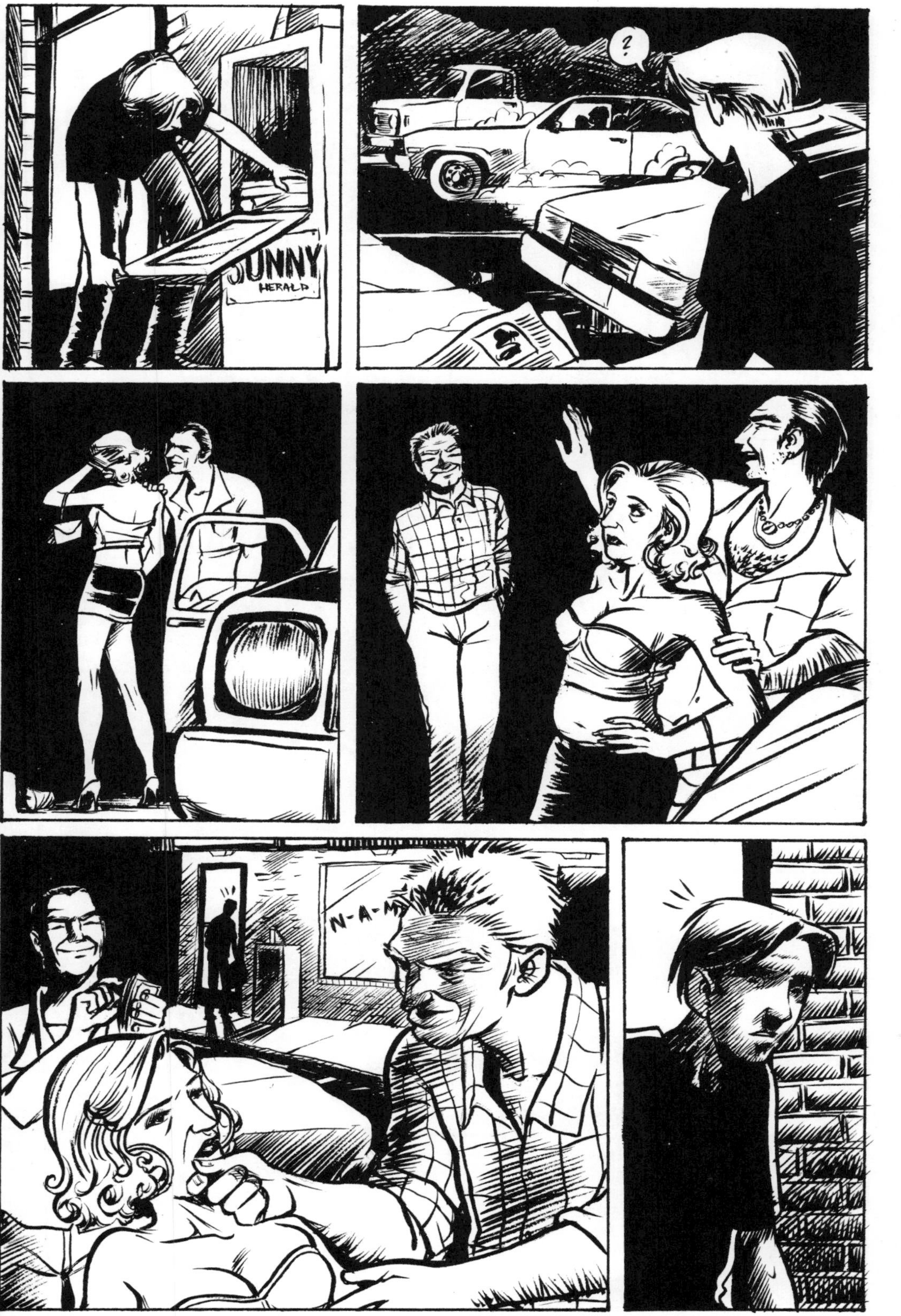
SUNNY
HERALD
?
N-A-M

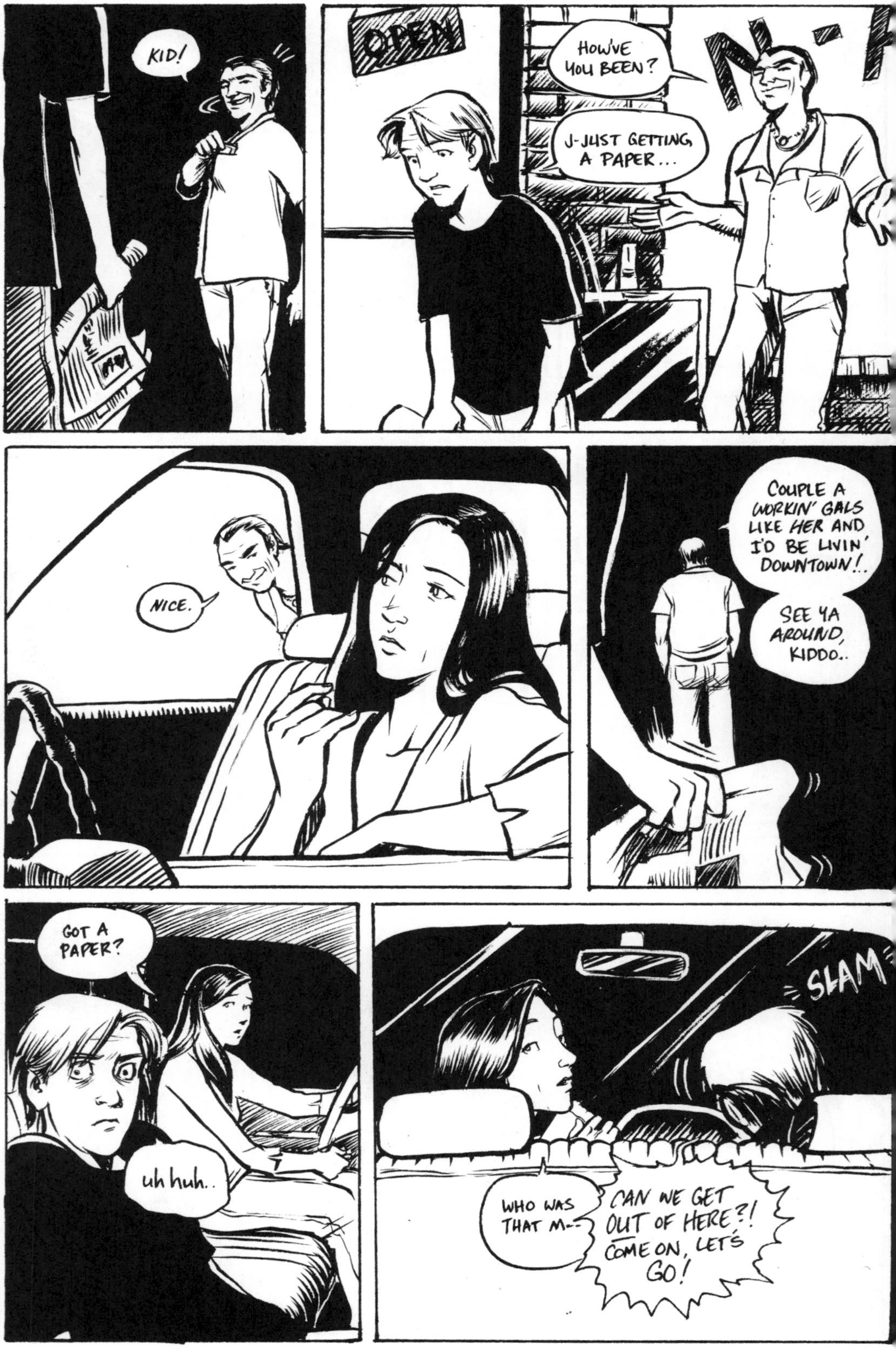
KID!
OPEN
HOW'VE YOU BEEN?
J-JUST GETTING A PAPER...
NICE.
COUPLE A WORKIN' GALS LIKE HER AND I'D BE LIVIN' DOWNTOWN!..
SEE YA AROUND, KIDDO..
GOT A PAPER?
uh huh..
SLAM
WHO WAS THAT M--
CAN WE GET OUT OF HERE?! COME ON, LET'S GO!

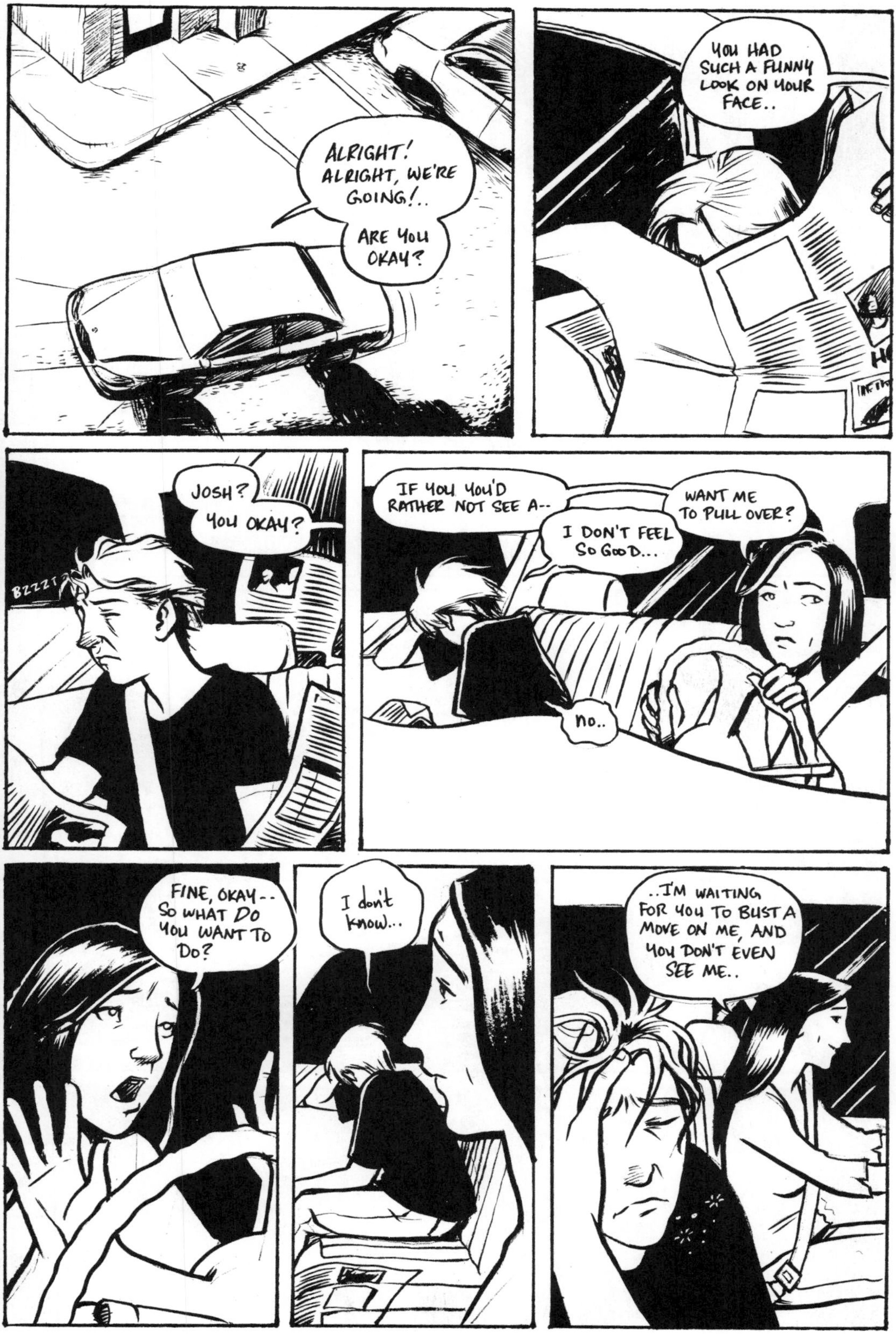
ALRIGHT! ALRIGHT, WE'RE GOING!..
ARE YOU OKAY?
YOU HAD SUCH A FUNNY LOOK ON YOUR FACE..
JOSH?
YOU OKAY?
BZZZT
IF YOU YOU'D RATHER NOT SEE A--
I DON'T FEEL SO GOOD...
WANT ME TO PULL OVER?
no..
FINE, OKAY-- SO WHAT DO YOU WANT TO DO?
I don't know...
..I'M WAITING FOR YOU TO BUST A MOVE ON ME, AND YOU DON'T EVEN SEE ME..

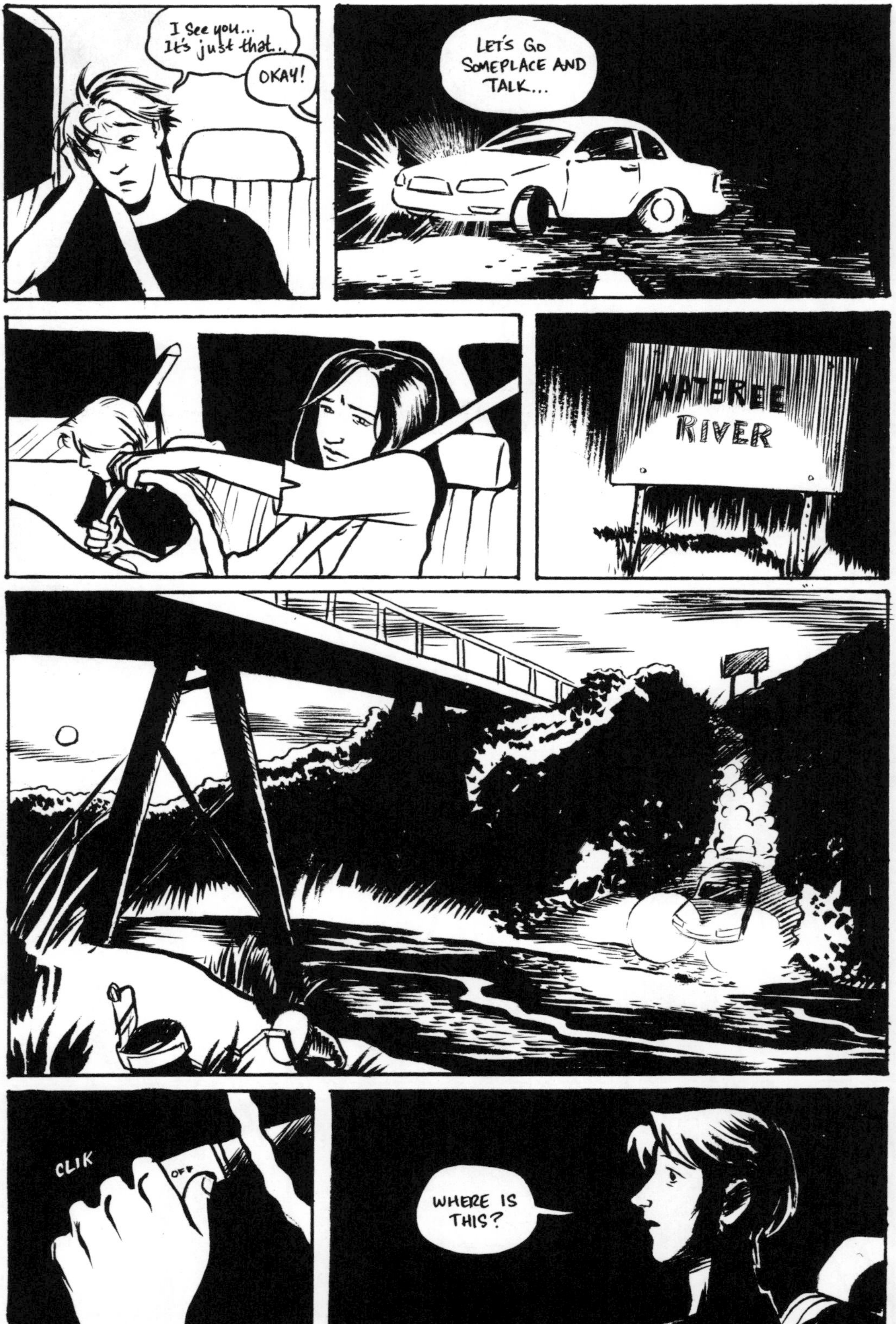
I see you... It's just that..
OKAY!
LET'S GO SOMEPLACE AND TALK...
WATEREE
RIVER
CLIK
OFF
WHERE IS THIS?

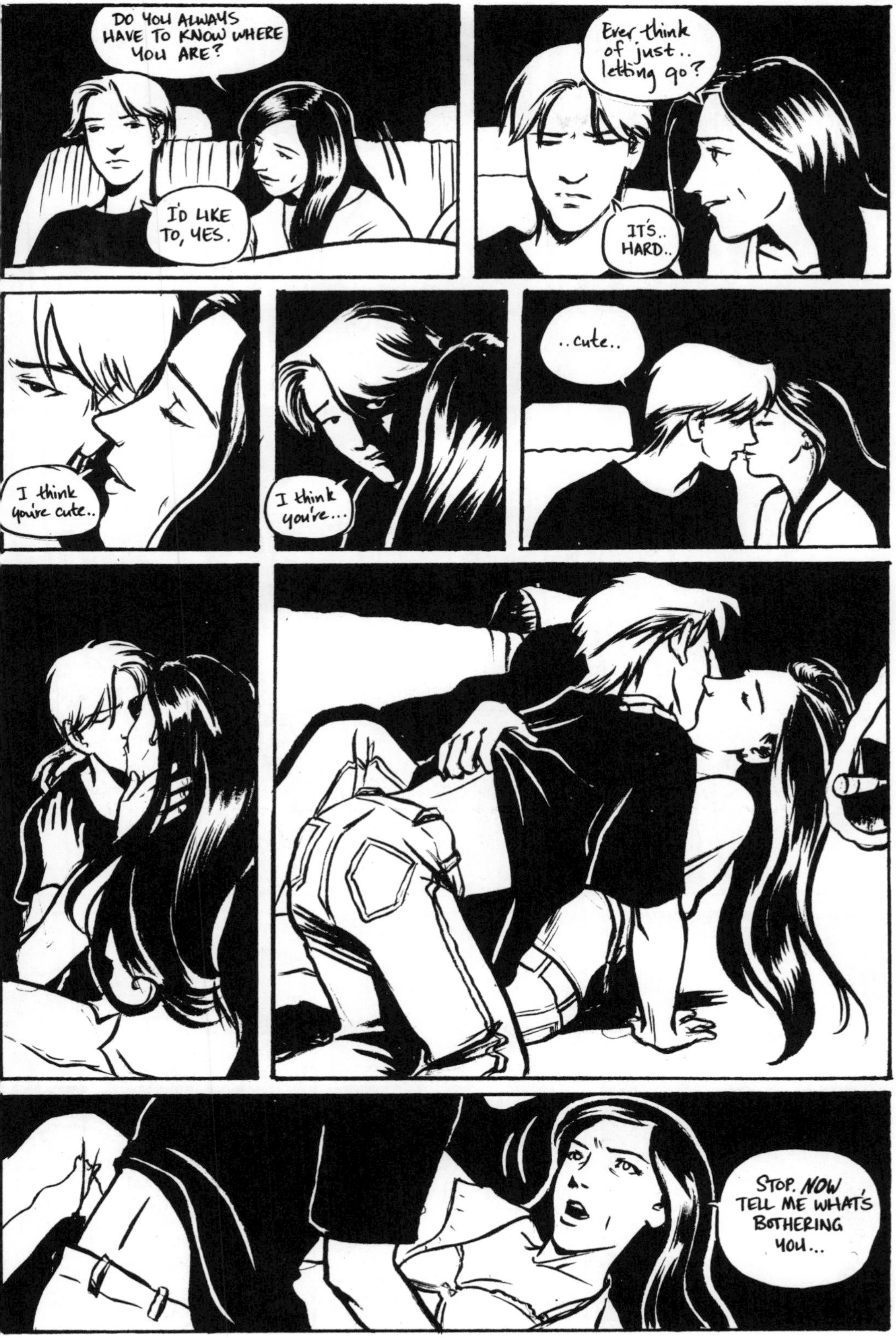
DO YOU ALWAYS HAVE TO KNOW WHERE YOU ARE?
I'D LIKE TO, YES.
Ever think of just.. letting go?
IT'S.. HARD..
I think you're cute..
I think you're...
..cute..
STOP. NOW TELL ME WHAT'S BOTHERING YOU...

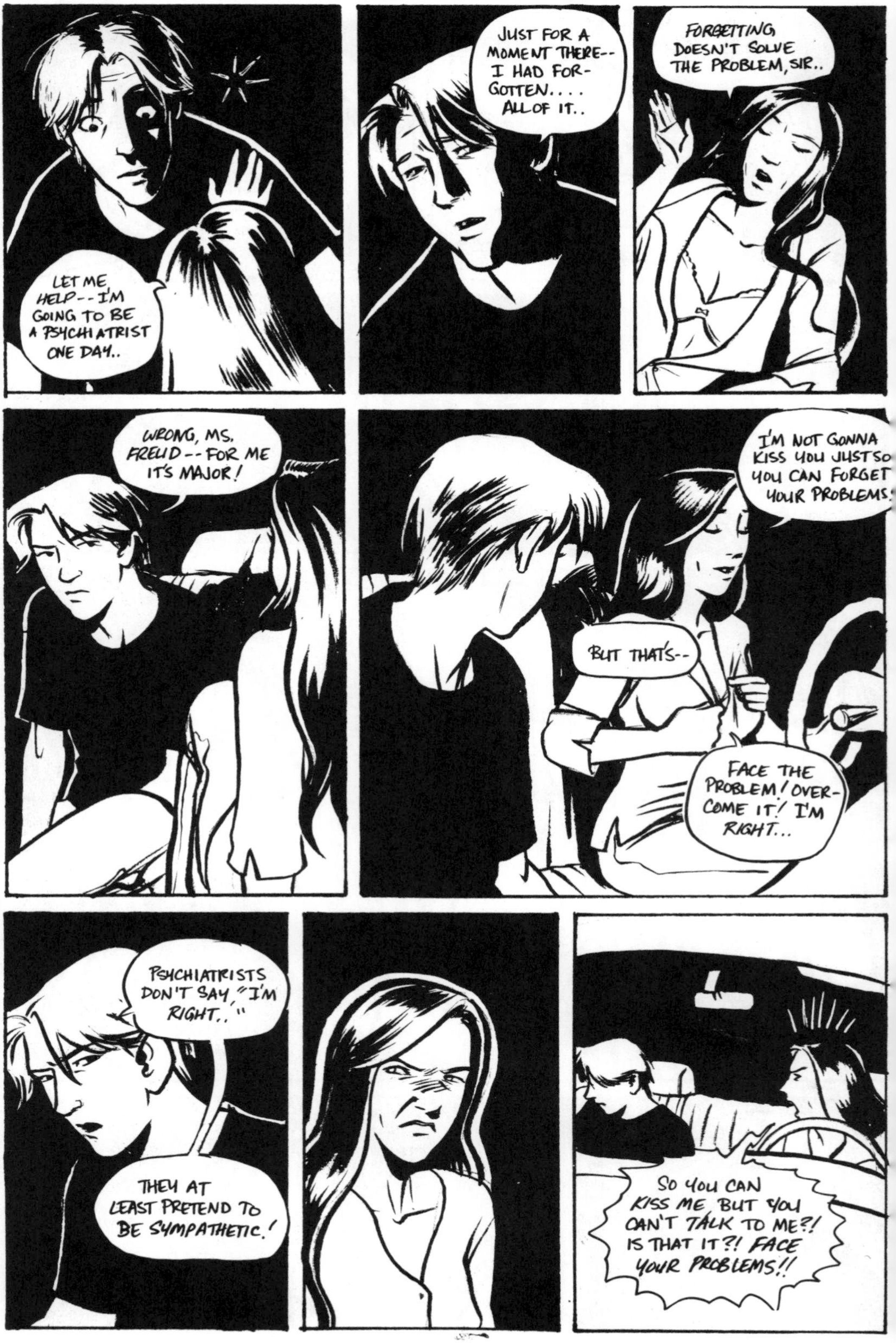
LET ME HELP--I'M GOING TO BE A PSYCHIATRIST ONE DAY..
JUST FOR A MOMENT THERE--I HAD FORGOTTEN.... ALL OF IT..
FORGETTING DOESN'T SOLVE THE PROBLEM, SIR..
WRONG, MS. FREUD--FOR ME IT'S MAJOR!
I'M NOT GONNA KISS YOU JUST SO YOU CAN FORGET YOUR PROBLEMS.
BUT THAT'S--
FACE THE PROBLEM! OVERCOME IT! I'M RIGHT...
PSYCHIATRISTS DON'T SAY "I'M RIGHT.."
THEY AT LEAST PRETEND TO BE SYMPATHETIC!
SO YOU CAN KISS ME BUT YOU CAN'T TALK TO ME?! IS THAT IT?! FACE YOUR PROBLEMS!!

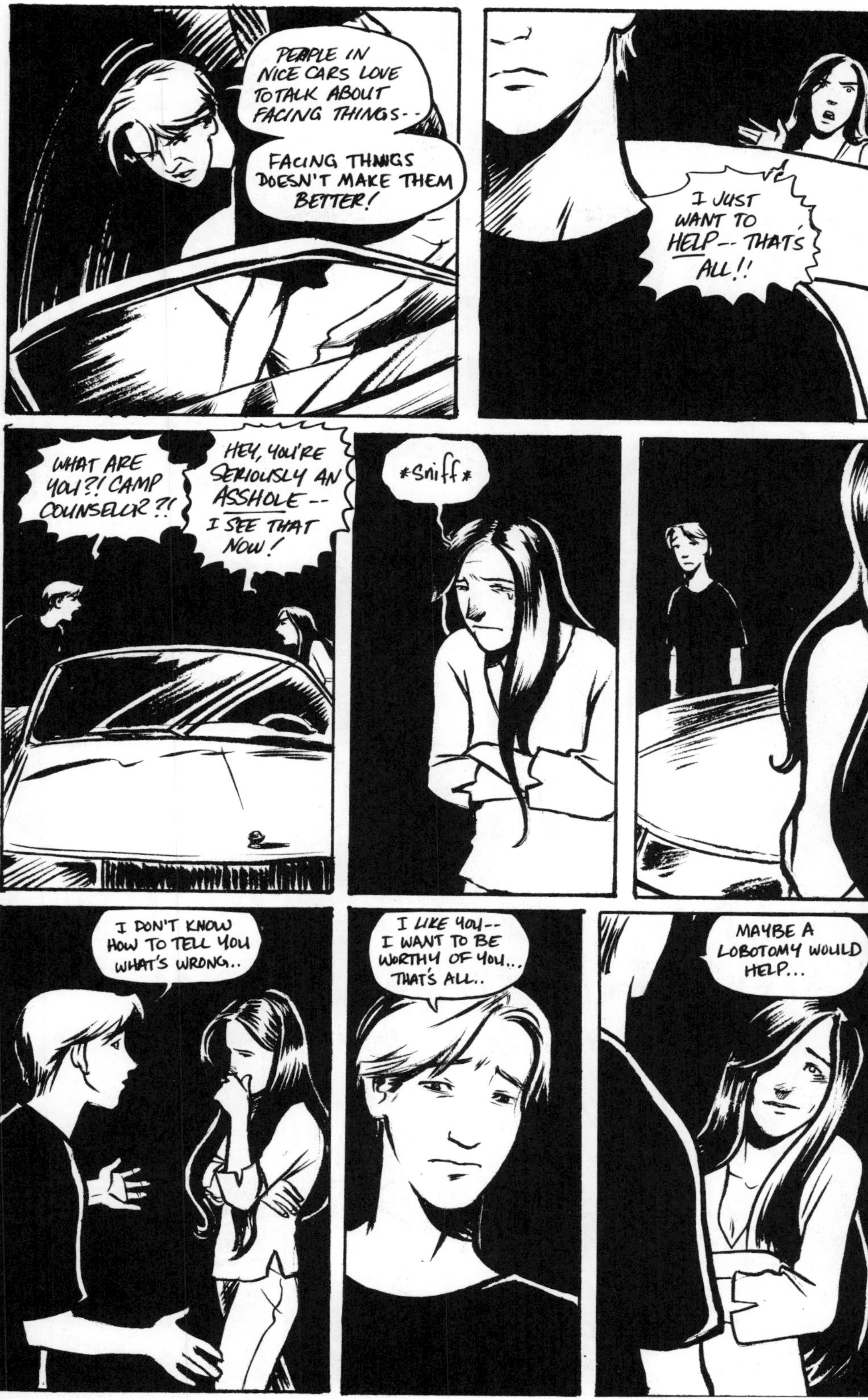
PEOPLE IN NICE CARS LOVE TO TALK ABOUT FACING THINGS--
FACING THINGS DOESN'T MAKE THEM BETTER!
I JUST WANT TO HELP-- THAT'S ALL!!
WHAT ARE YOU?! CAMP COUNSELOR?!
HEY, YOU'RE SERIOUSLY AN ASSHOLE-- I SEE THAT NOW!
sniff
I DON'T KNOW HOW TO TELL YOU WHAT'S WRONG..
I LIKE YOU-- I WANT TO BE WORTHY OF YOU... THAT'S ALL..
MAYBE A LOBOTOMY WOULD HELP...

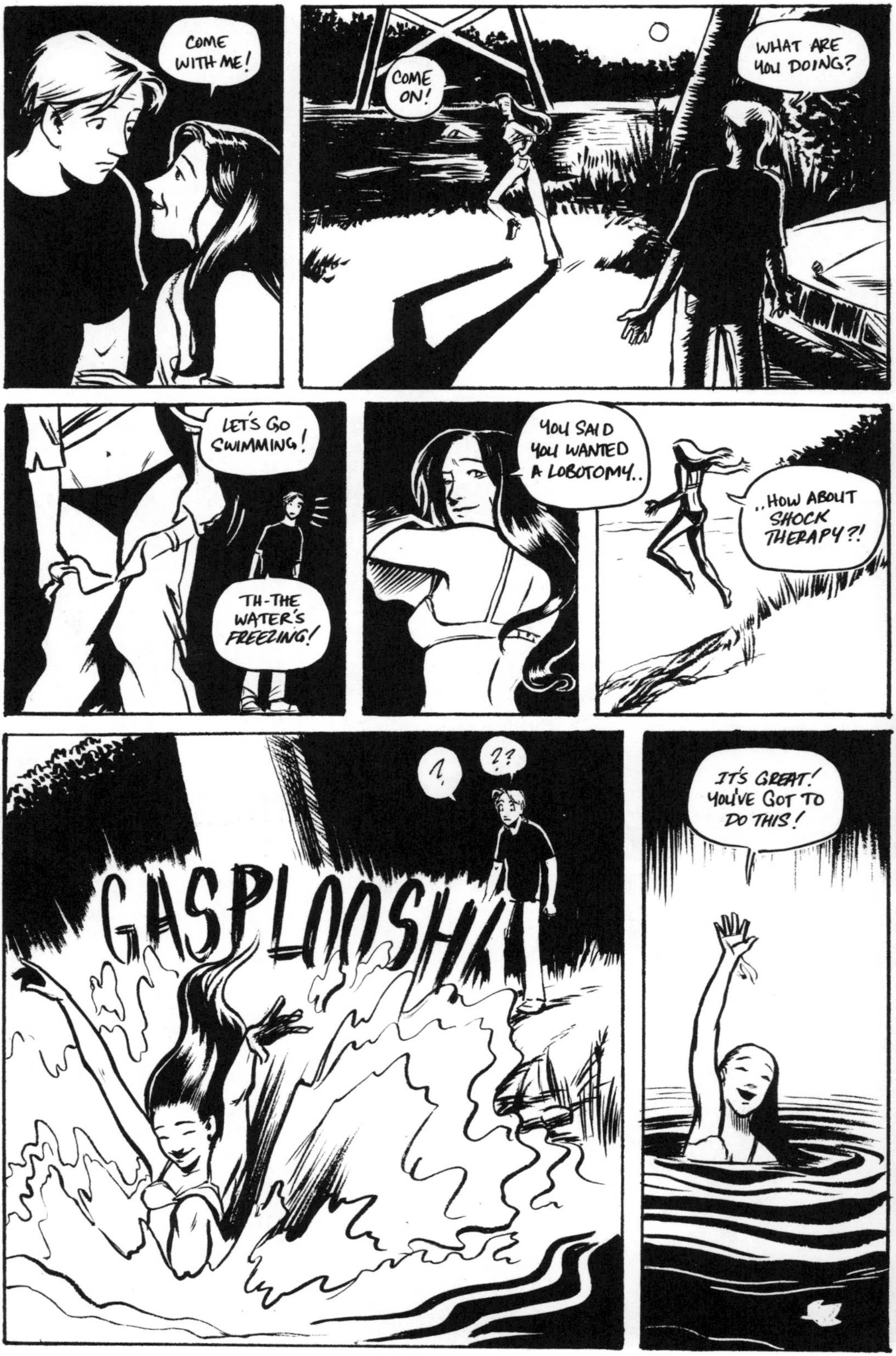
COME WITH ME!
COME ON!
WHAT ARE YOU DOING?
LET'S GO SWIMMING!
TH-THE WATER'S FREEZING!
YOU SAID YOU WANTED A LOBOTOMY..
..HOW ABOUT SHOCK THERAPY?!
GASPLOOSH!
?
??
IT'S GREAT! YOU'VE GOT TO DO THIS!

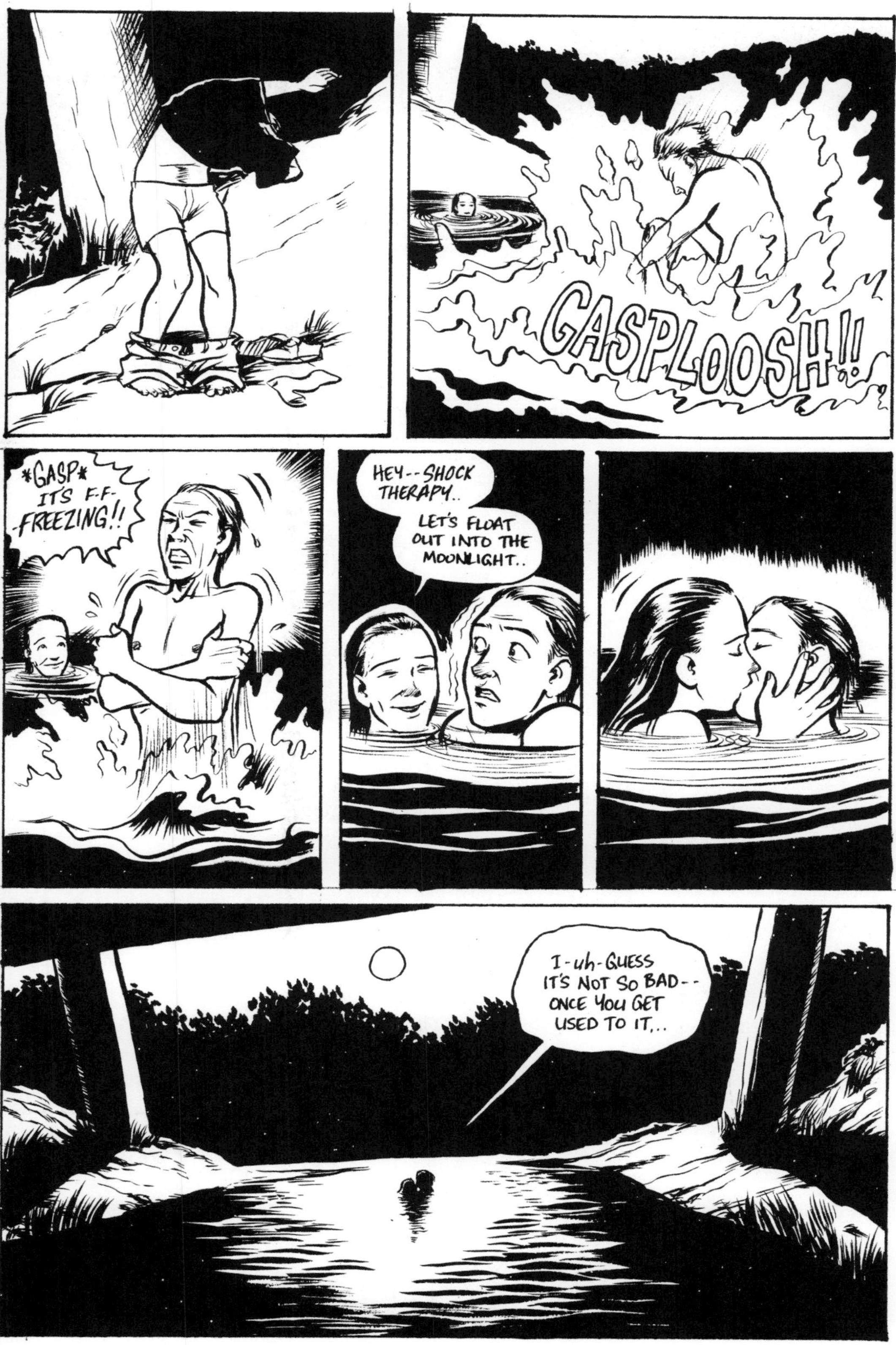
GASPLOOSH!!
GASP IT'S F-F--FREEZING!!
HEY--SHOCK THERAPY..
LET'S FLOAT OUT INTO THE MOONLIGHT..
I-uh-GUESS IT'S NOT SO BAD--ONCE YOU GET USED TO IT,..

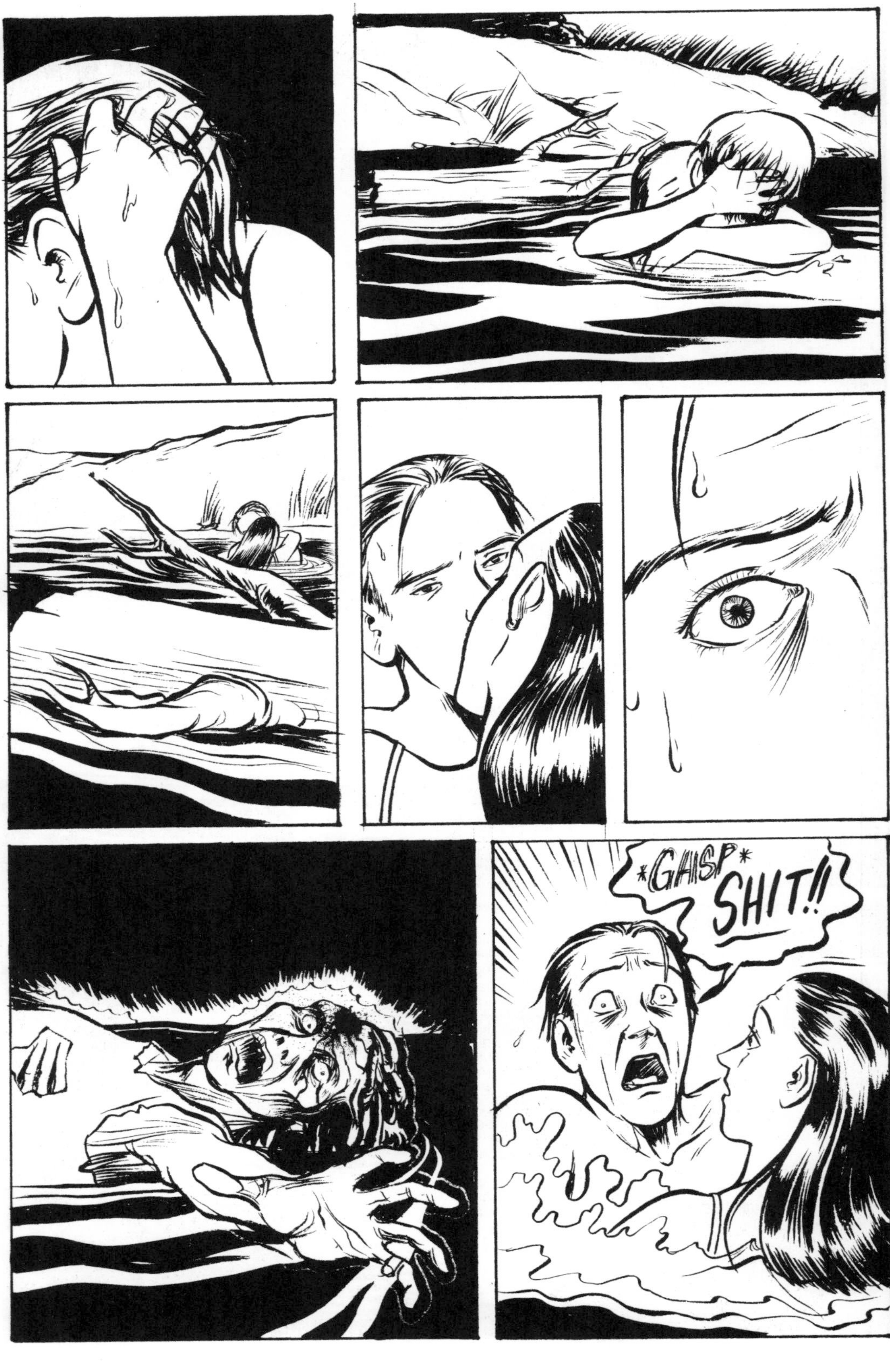
GASP
SHIT!!

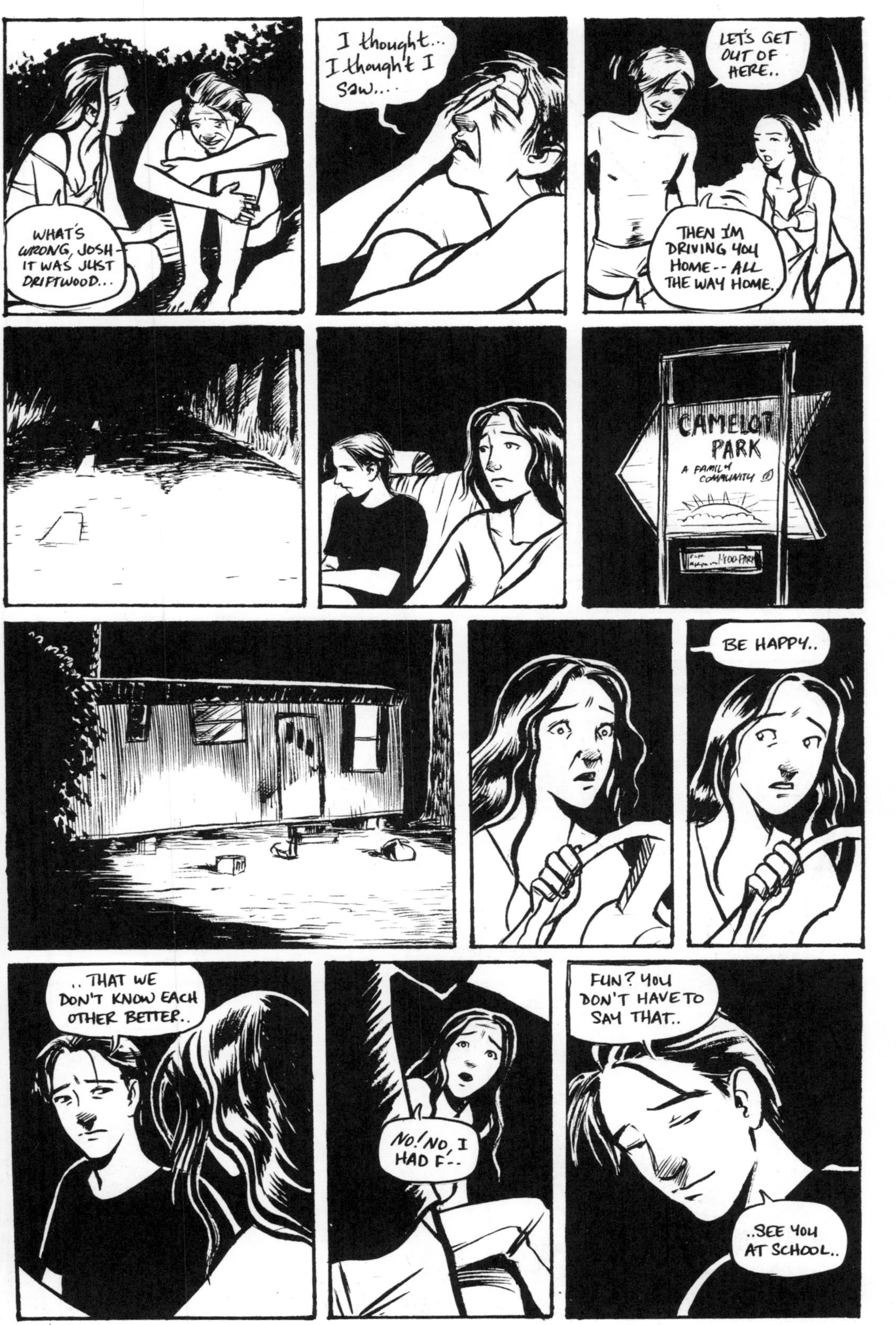
WHAT'S WRONG, JOSH - IT WAS JUST DRIFTWOOD...
I thought... I thought I saw....
LET'S GET OUT OF HERE..
THEN I'M DRIVING YOU HOME -- ALL THE WAY HOME.
CAMELOT PARK
A FAMILY COMMUNITY
BE HAPPY..
.. THAT WE DON'T KNOW EACH OTHER BETTER..
NO! NO, I HAD F- -
FUN? YOU DON'T HAVE TO SAY THAT..
..SEE YOU AT SCHOOL..

MOM?

POPS

CABLE?..

CHIPS

OH, YOU LITTLE SHITS..

KAT JAMMIES

prrrrr prrrrrr prrrrr...

prrrrrrrrrr

GOD, ROY!!

sigh

prrrrrr prrrrr

TTLE HAMP

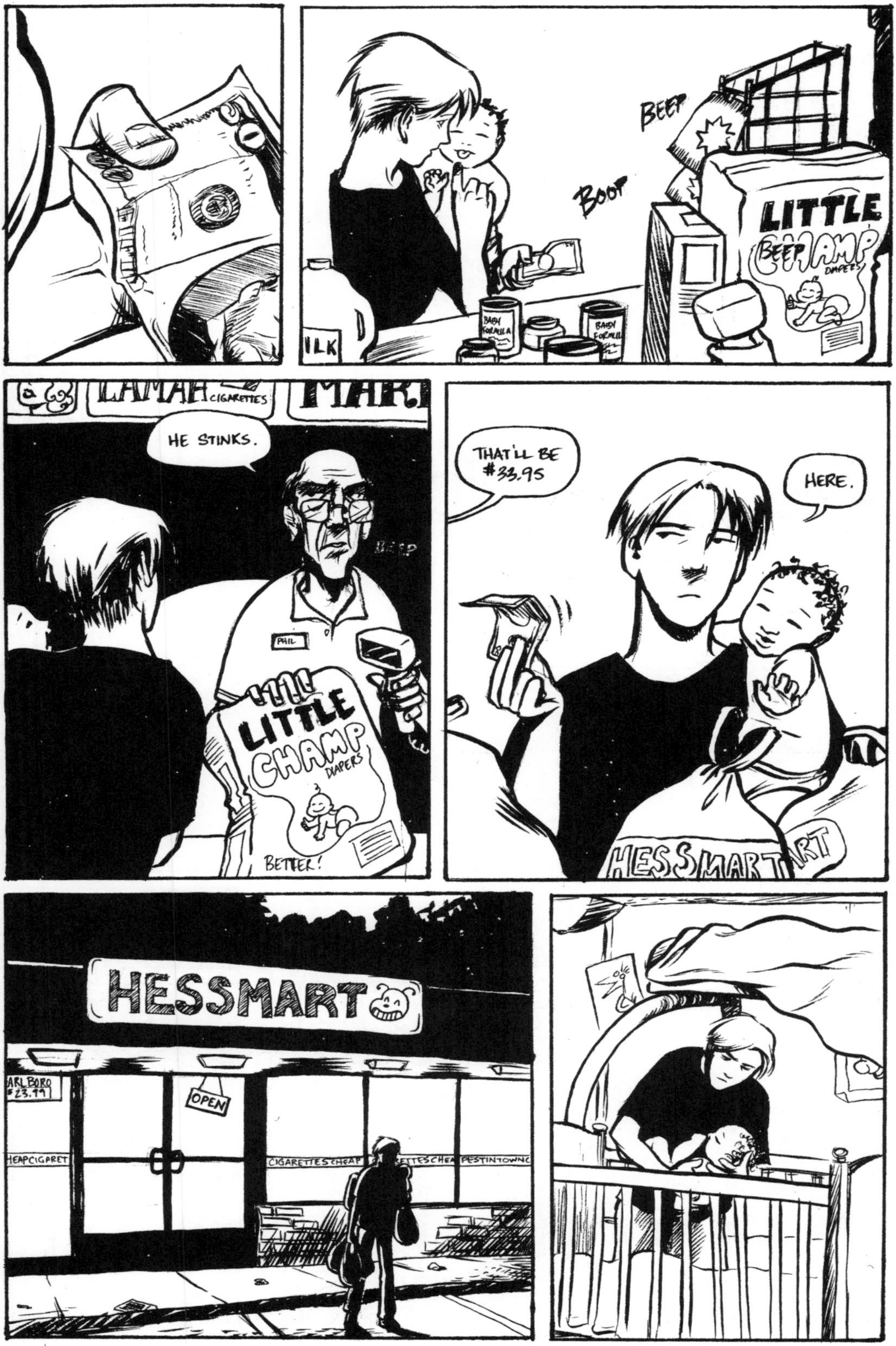

BEEP
BOOP
LITTLE
BEEP
CHAMP
DIAPERS
BABY FORMULA
BABY FORMULA
ILK
CIGARETTES
HE STINKS.
BEEP
PHIL
LITTLE CHAMP
DIAPERS
BETTER!
THAT'LL BE $33.95
HERE.
HESSMART
HESSMART
ARLBORO $23.99
OPEN
HEAPCIGARET
CIGARETTESCHEAP
ETTESCHEAPESTINTOWNC

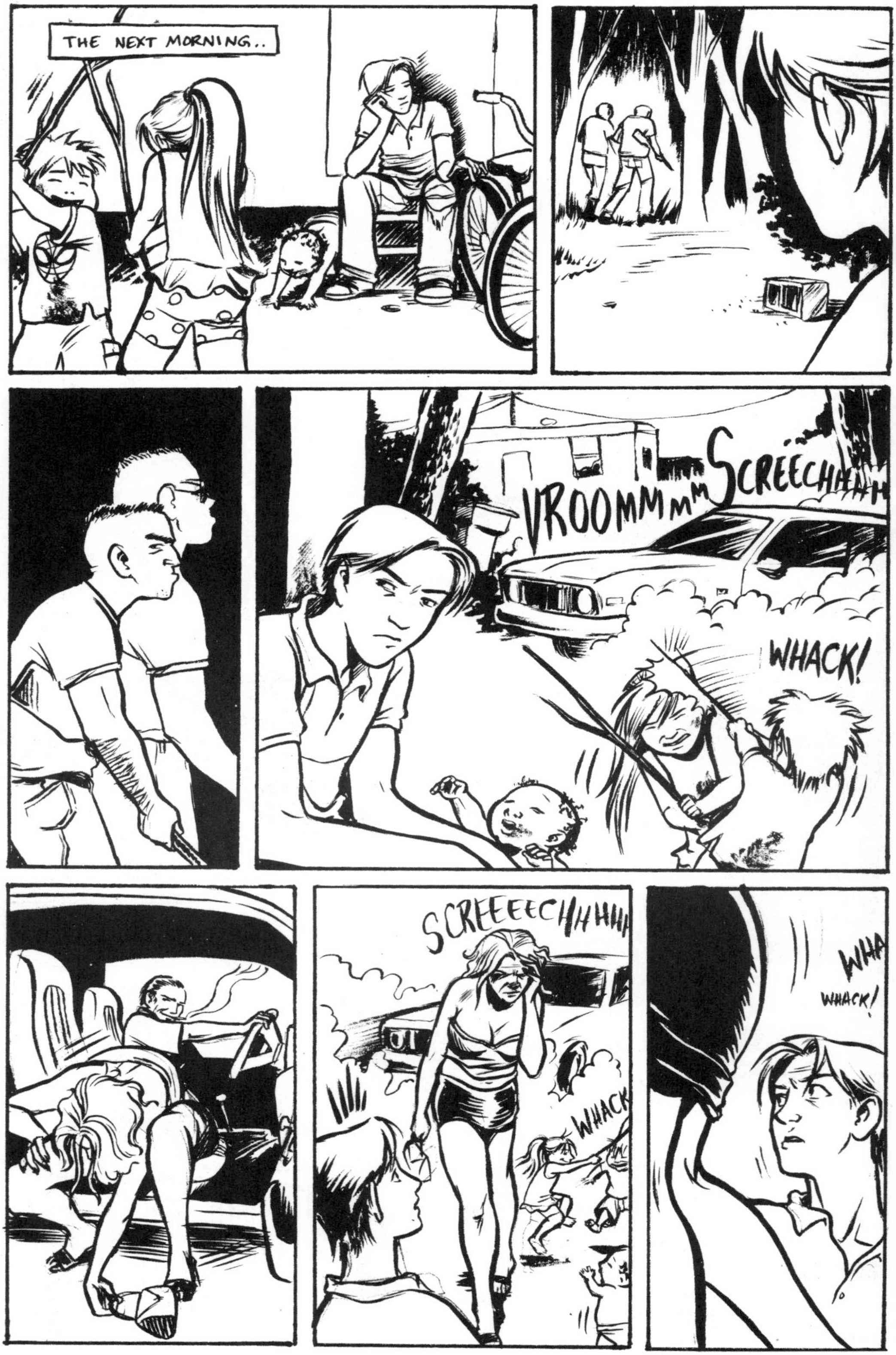
THE NEXT MORNING..
VROOMMMMM
SCREECHHHH
WHACK!
SCREEEECHHHH
WHACK
WHA
WHACK!

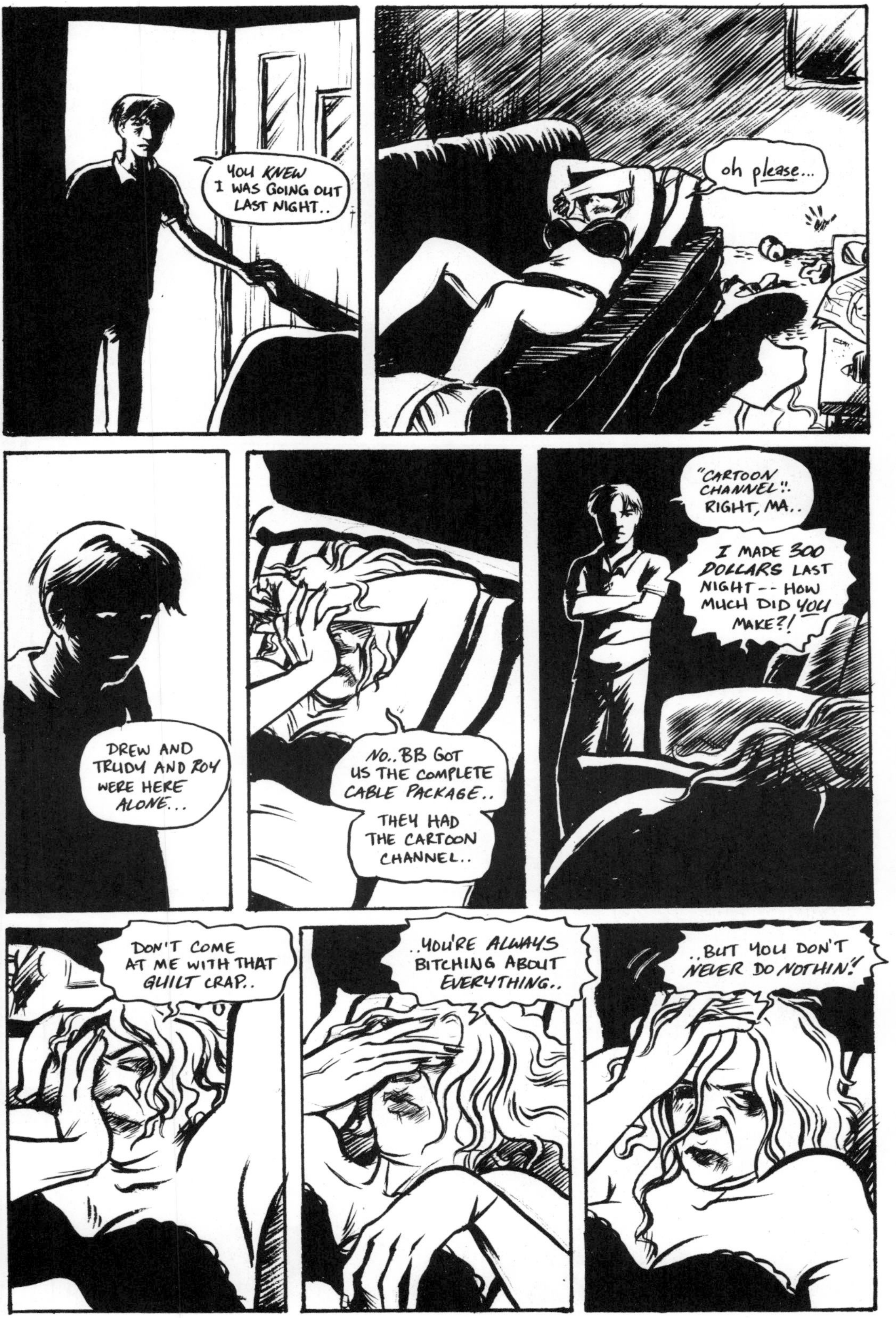
YOU KNEW I WAS GOING OUT LAST NIGHT..
oh please...
DREW AND TRUDY AND ROY WERE HERE ALONE...
NO.. BB GOT US THE COMPLETE CABLE PACKAGE..
THEY HAD THE CARTOON CHANNEL..
"CARTOON CHANNEL"!. RIGHT, MA..
I MADE 300 DOLLARS LAST NIGHT-- HOW MUCH DID YOU MAKE?!
DON'T COME AT ME WITH THAT GUILT CRAP..
..YOU'RE ALWAYS BITCHING ABOUT EVERYTHING..
..BUT YOU DON'T NEVER DO NOTHIN'!

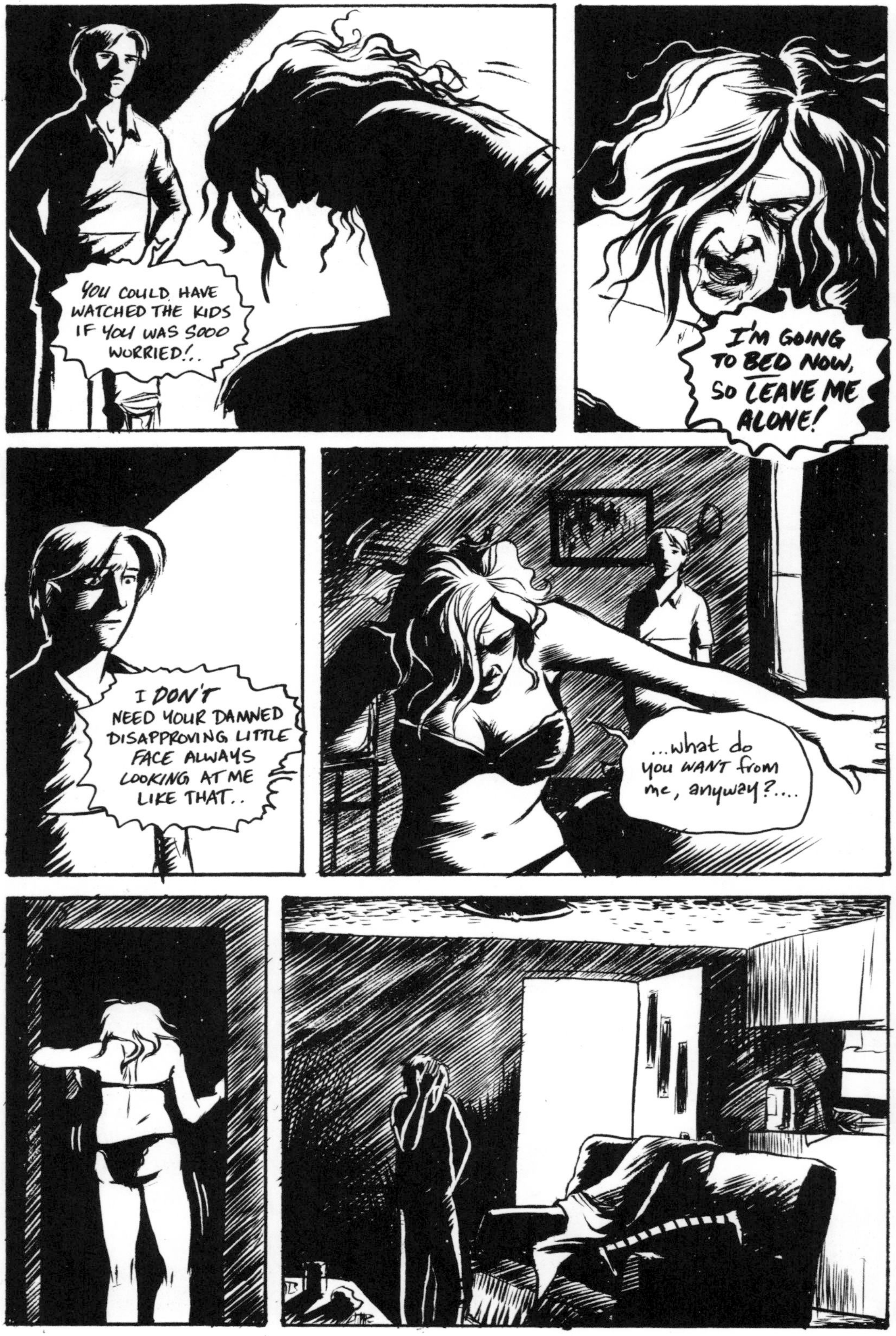
YOU COULD HAVE WATCHED THE KIDS IF YOU WAS SOOO WORRIED!..
I'M GOING TO BED NOW, SO LEAVE ME ALONE!
I DON'T NEED YOUR DAMNED DISAPPROVING LITTLE FACE ALWAYS LOOKING AT ME LIKE THAT..
...what do you WANT from me, anyway?....

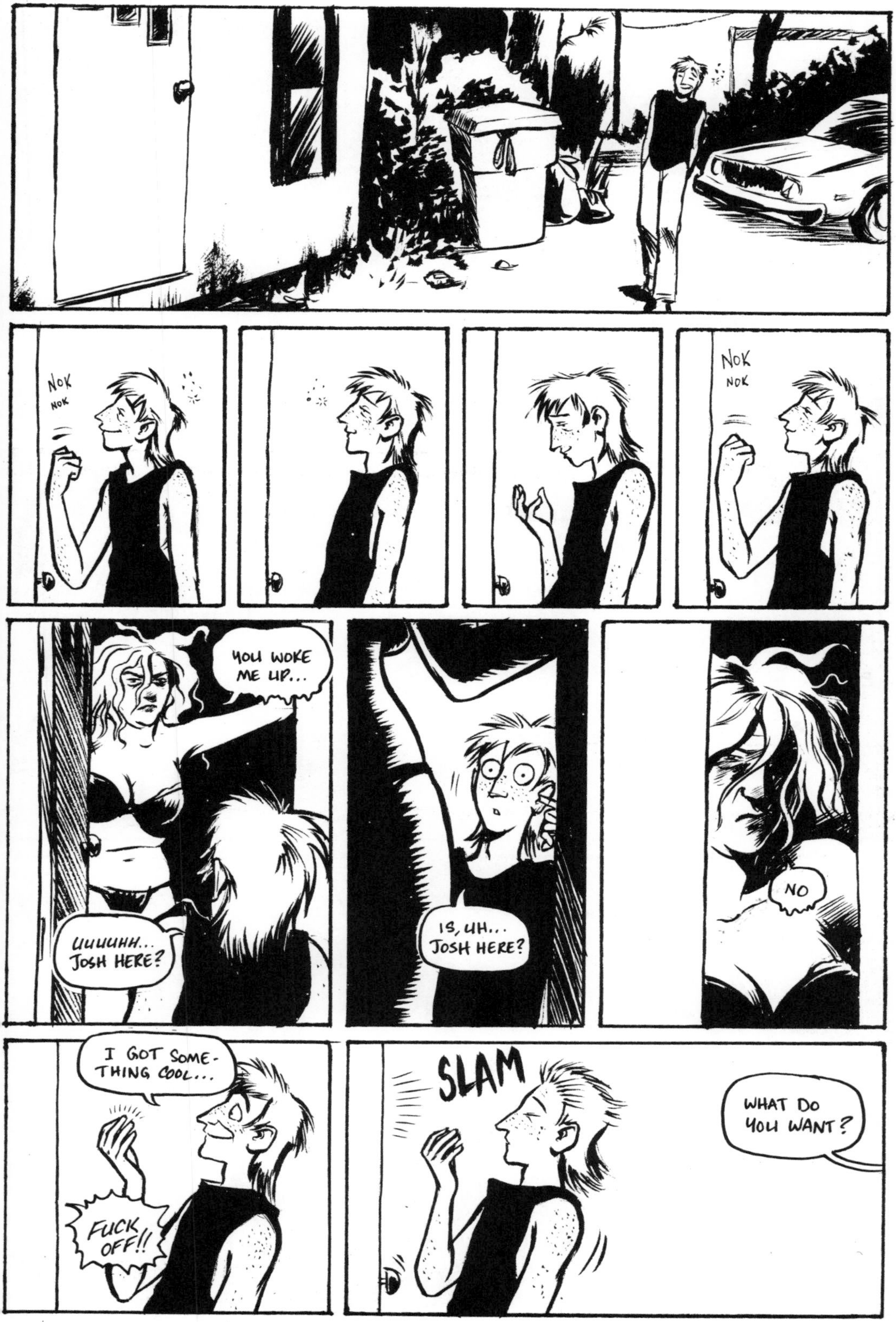

NOK
NOK
NOK
NOK
YOU WOKE ME UP...
UUUUHH... JOSH HERE?
IS, UH... JOSH HERE?
NO
I GOT SOME-THING COOL...
FUCK OFF!!
SLAM
WHAT DO YOU WANT?

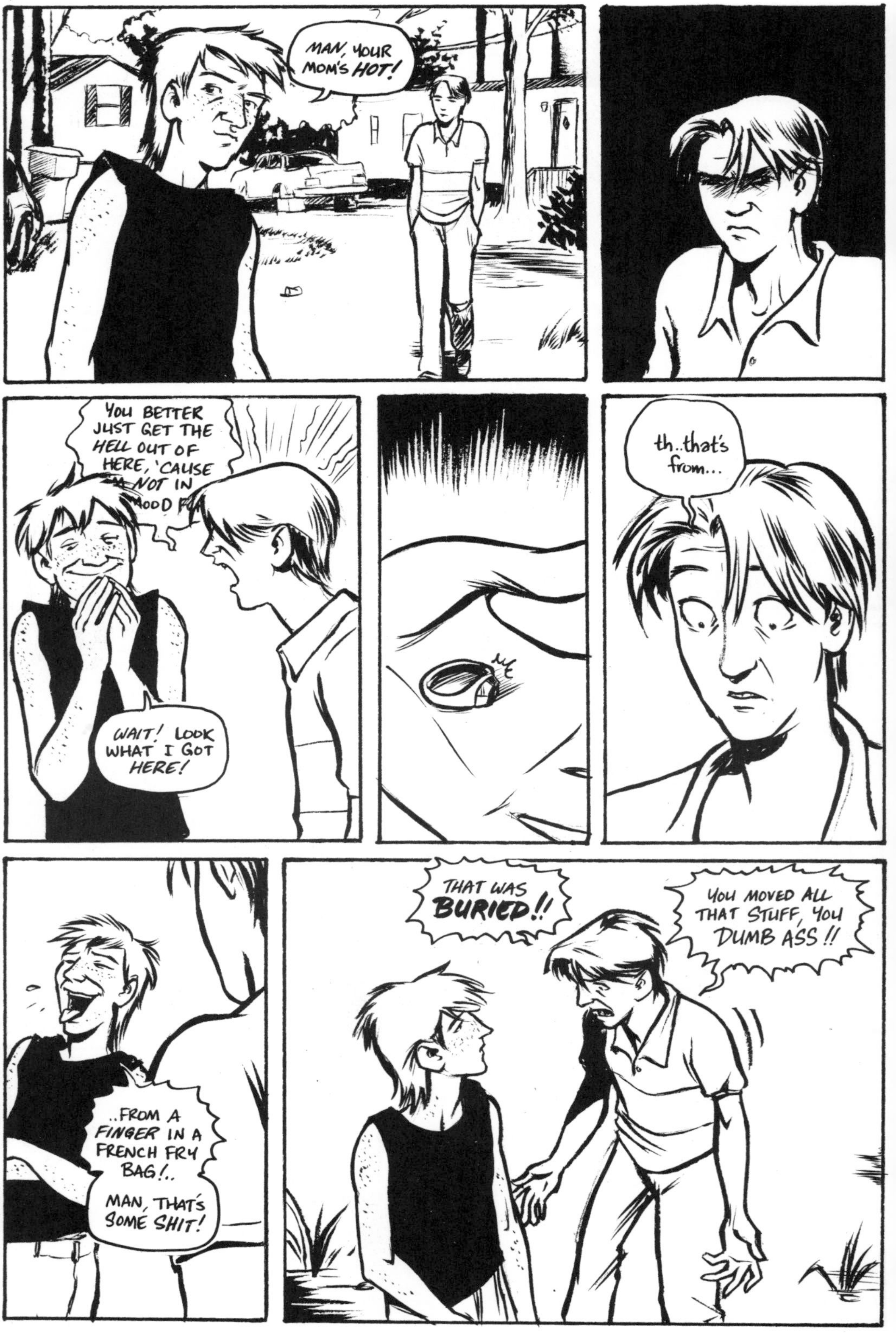

MAN, YOUR MOM'S HOT!
YOU BETTER JUST GET THE HELL OUT OF HERE, 'CAUSE NOT IN MOOD F
WAIT! LOOK WHAT I GOT HERE!
th..that's from...
..FROM A FINGER IN A FRENCH FRY BAG!..
MAN, THAT'S SOME SHIT!
THAT WAS BURIED!!
YOU MOVED ALL THAT STUFF, YOU DUMB ASS!!

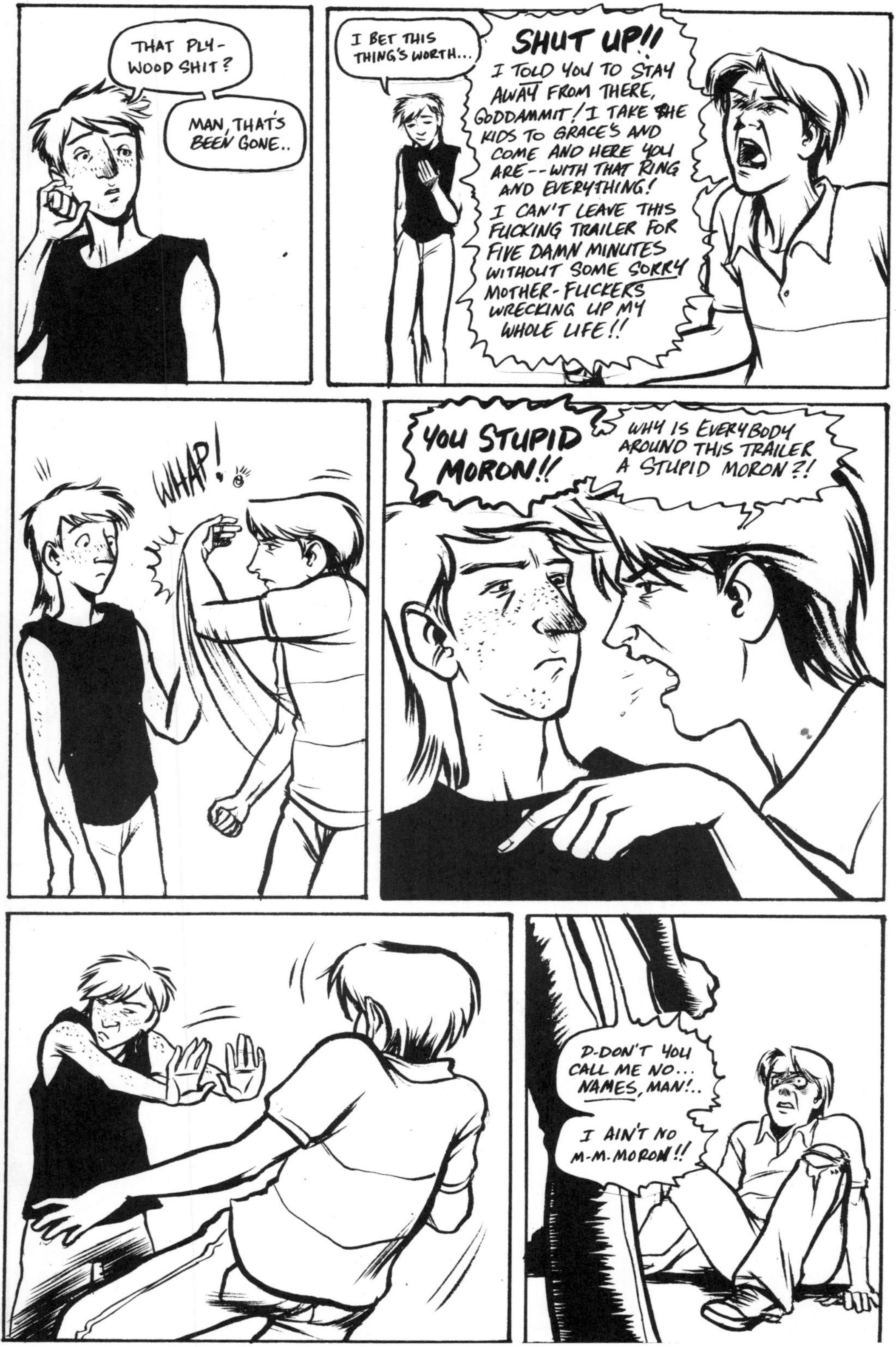
THAT PLY-WOOD SHIT?
MAN, THAT'S BEEN GONE..
I BET THIS THING'S WORTH...
SHUT UP!! I TOLD YOU TO STAY AWAY FROM THERE, GODDAMMIT! I TAKE THE KIDS TO GRACE'S AND COME AND HERE YOU ARE--WITH THAT RING AND EVERYTHING! I CAN'T LEAVE THIS FUCKING TRAILER FOR FIVE DAMN MINUTES WITHOUT SOME SORRY MOTHER-FUCKERS WRECKING UP MY WHOLE LIFE!!
WHAP!
YOU STUPID MORON!!
WHY IS EVERYBODY AROUND THIS TRAILER A STUPID MORON?!
D-DON'T YOU CALL ME NO... NAMES, MAN!...
I AIN'T NO M-M-MORON!!

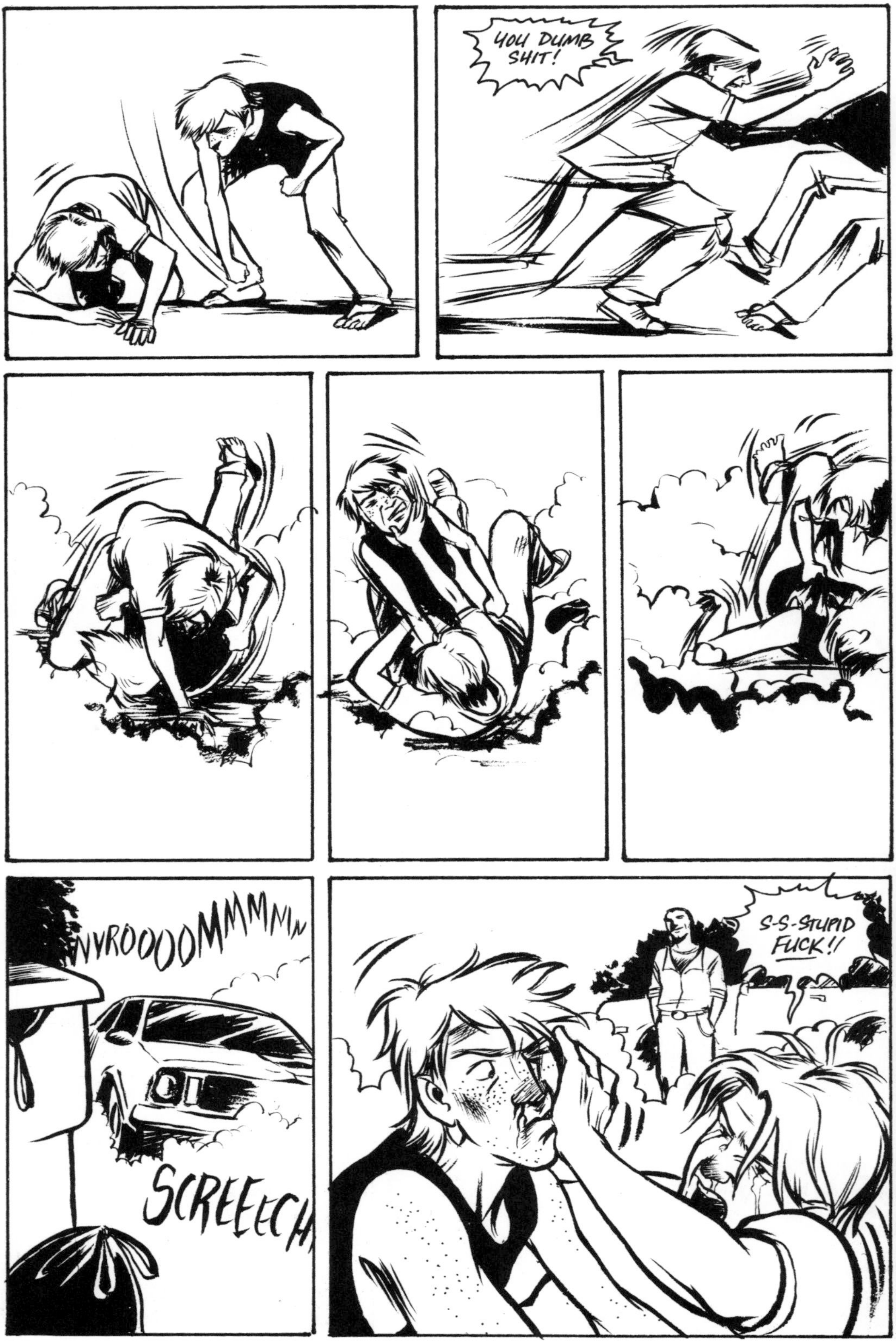
YOU DUMB SHIT!
NVROOOOOMMMNN
SCREEECH
S-S-STUPID FUCK!!

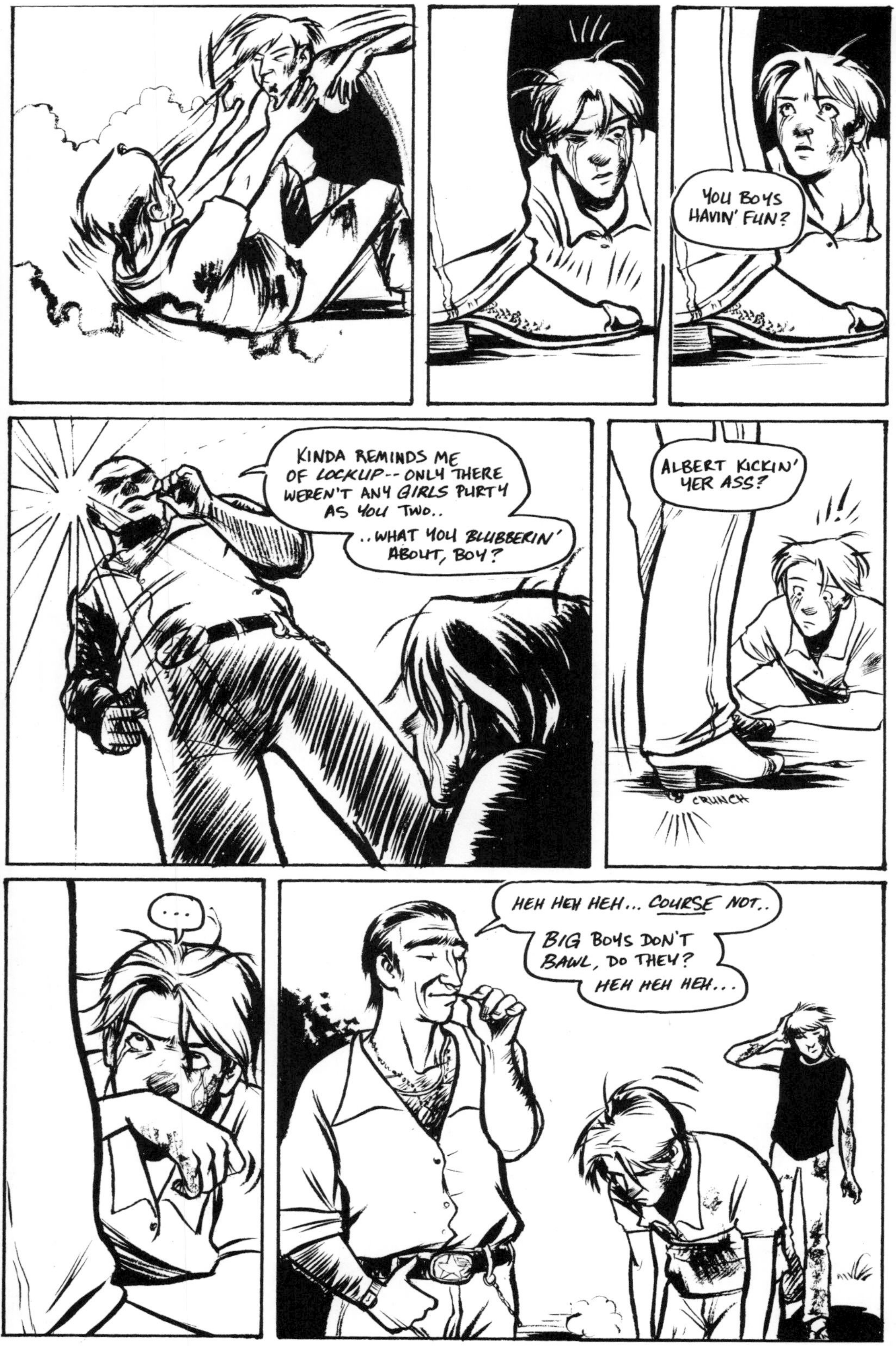
YOU BOYS HAVIN' FUN?
KINDA REMINDS ME OF LOCKUP-- ONLY THERE WEREN'T ANY GIRLS PURTY AS YOU TWO..
..WHAT YOU BLUBBERIN' ABOUT, BOY?
ALBERT KICKIN' YER ASS?
CRUNCH
...
HEH HEH HEH... COURSE NOT..
BIG BOYS DON'T BAWL, DO THEY? HEH HEH HEH...

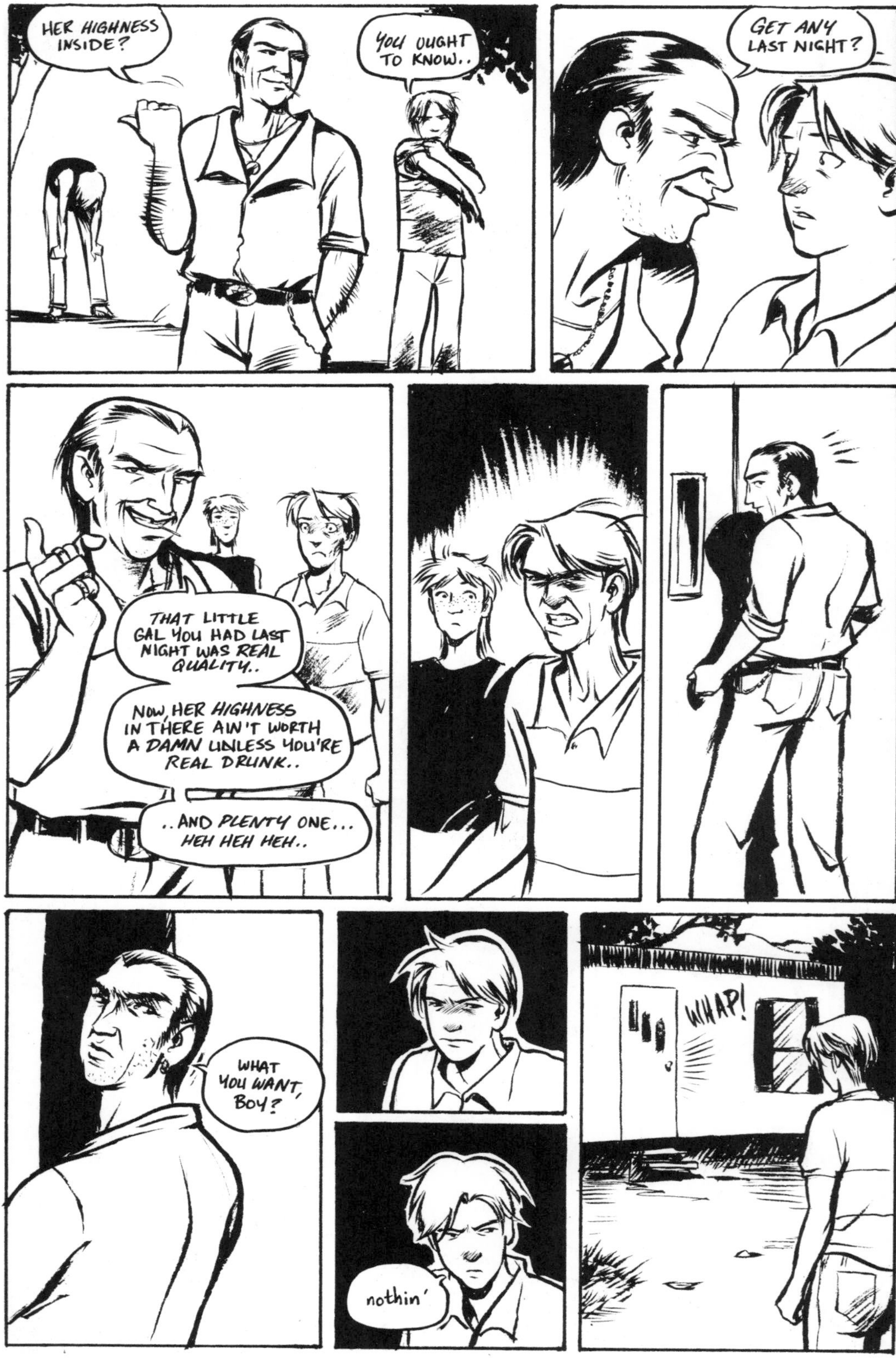
HER HIGHNESS INSIDE?
YOU OUGHT TO KNOW..
GET ANY LAST NIGHT?
THAT LITTLE GAL YOU HAD LAST NIGHT WAS REAL QUALITY..
NOW, HER HIGHNESS IN THERE AIN'T WORTH A DAMN UNLESS YOU'RE REAL DRUNK..
..AND PLENTY ONE... HEH HEH HEH..
WHAT YOU WANT, BOY?
nothin'
WHAP!

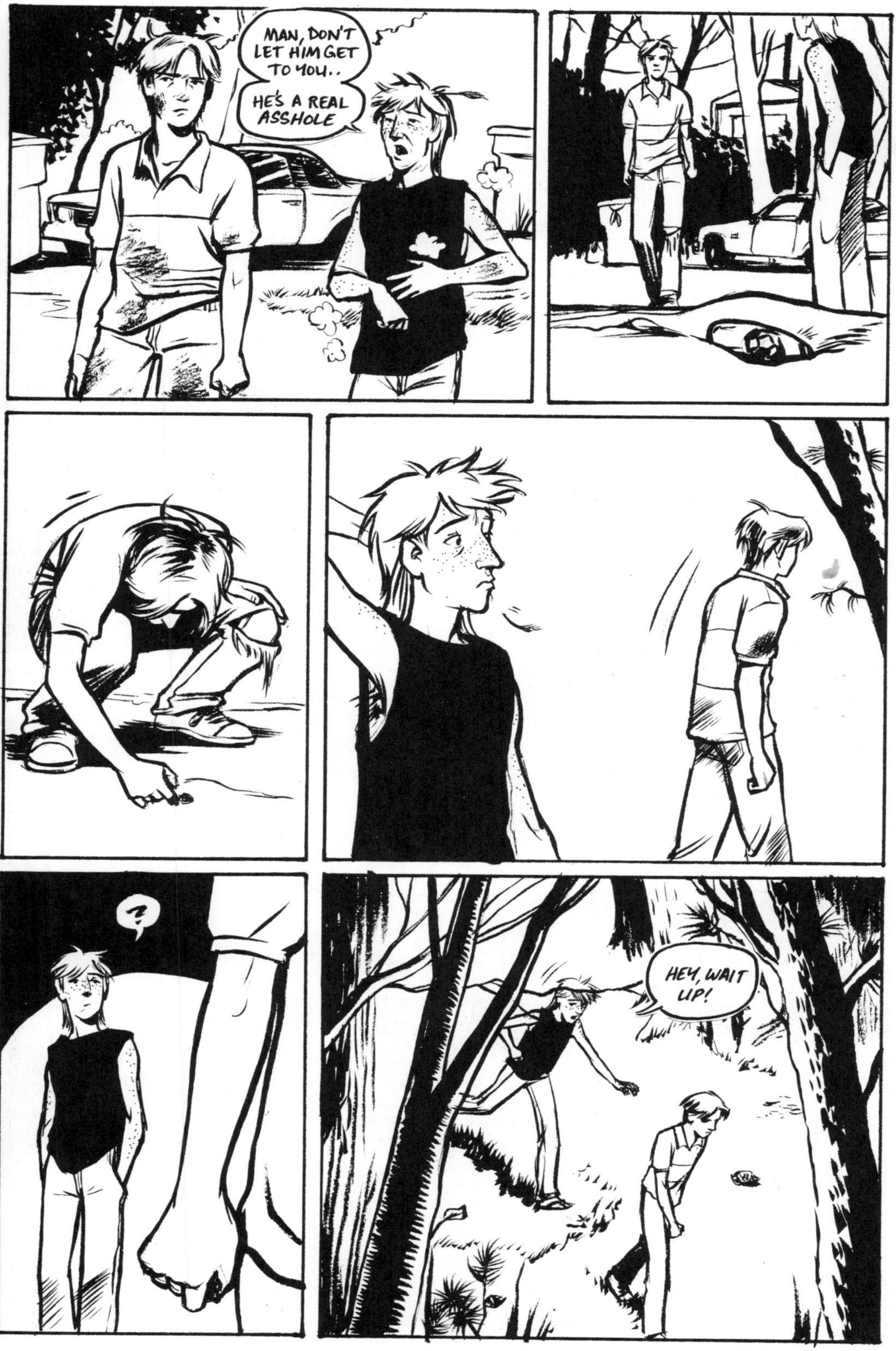
MAN, DON'T LET HIM GET TO YOU..
HE'S A REAL ASSHOLE
?
HEY, WAIT UP!

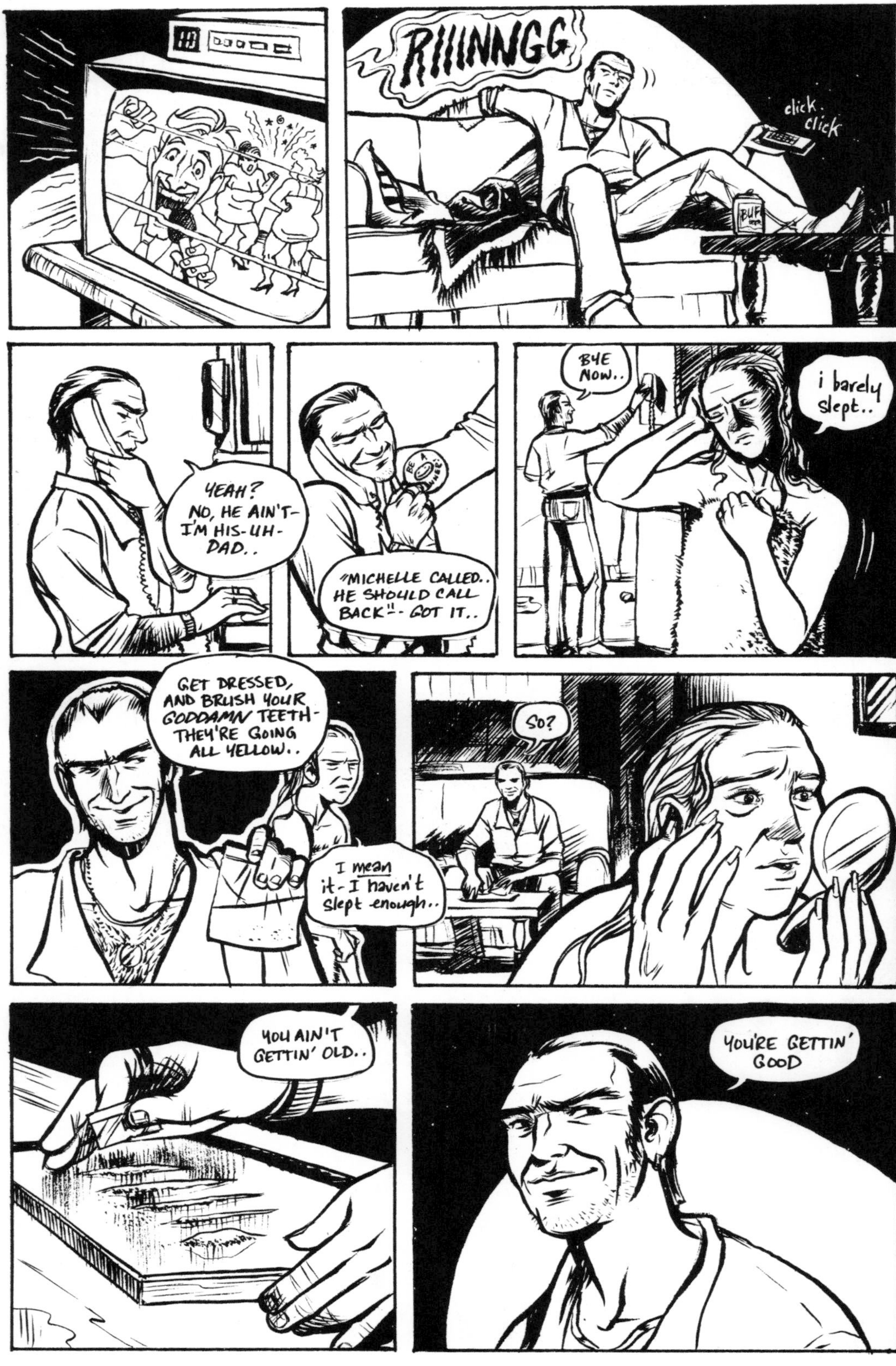
RIIINNGG
click. click
YEAH? NO, HE AIN'T- I'M HIS-UH- DAD..
BE A WINNER!
"MICHELLE CALLED.. HE SHOULD CALL BACK"- GOT IT..
BYE NOW..
i barely slept..
GET DRESSED, AND BRUSH YOUR GODDAMN TEETH- THEY'RE GOING ALL YELLOW..
I mean it- I haven't slept enough..
So?
YOU AIN'T GETTIN' OLD..
YOU'RE GETTIN' GOOD

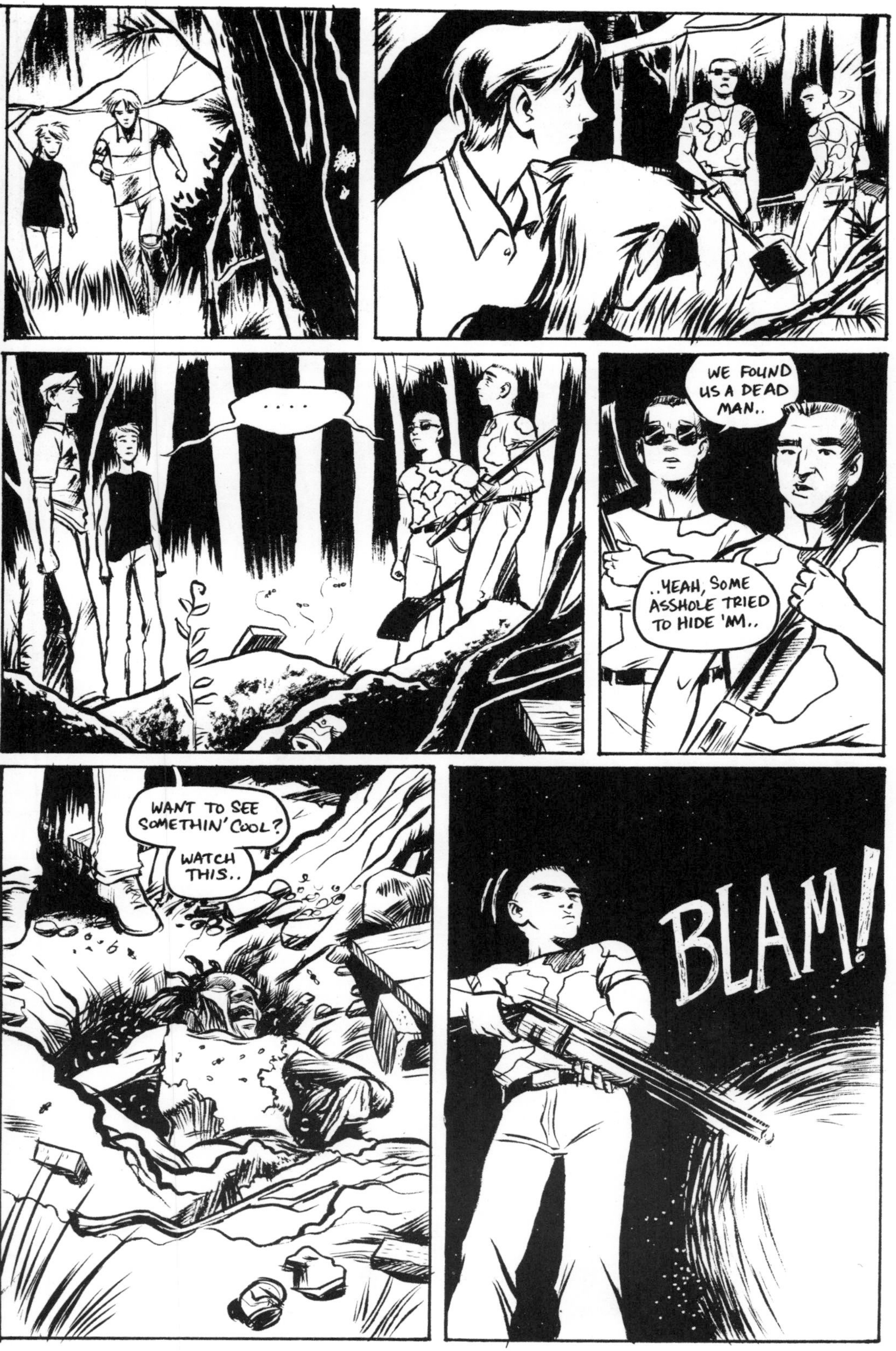
....
WE FOUND US A DEAD MAN..
..YEAH, SOME ASSHOLE TRIED TO HIDE 'IM..
WANT TO SEE SOMETHIN' COOL?
WATCH THIS..
BLAM!

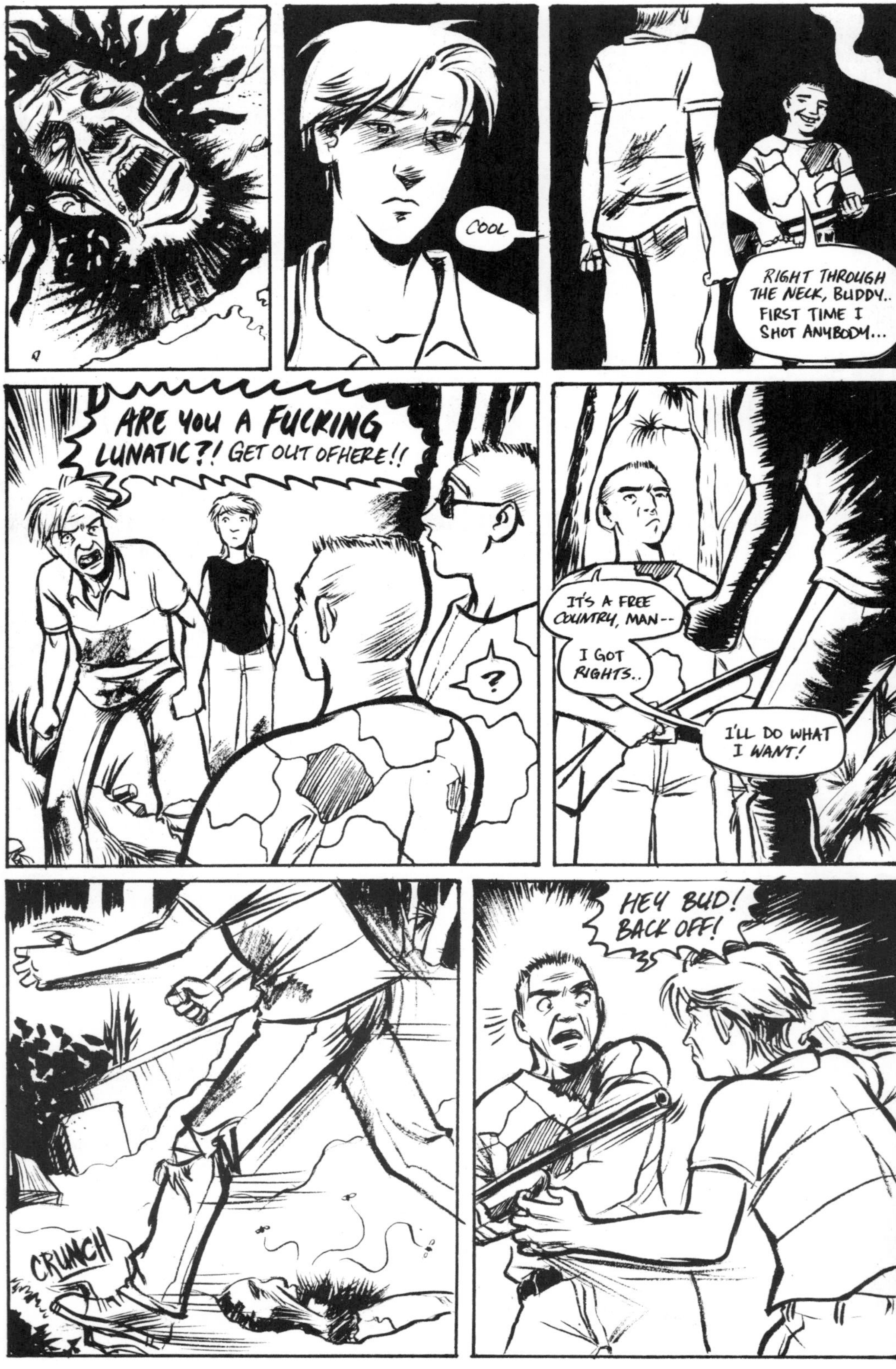
COOL
RIGHT THROUGH THE NECK, BUDDY.. FIRST TIME I SHOT ANYBODY...
ARE YOU A FUCKING LUNATIC?! GET OUT OFHERE!!
?
IT'S A FREE COUNTRY, MAN--
I GOT RIGHTS..
I'LL DO WHAT I WANT!
CRUNCH
HEY BUD! BACK OFF!

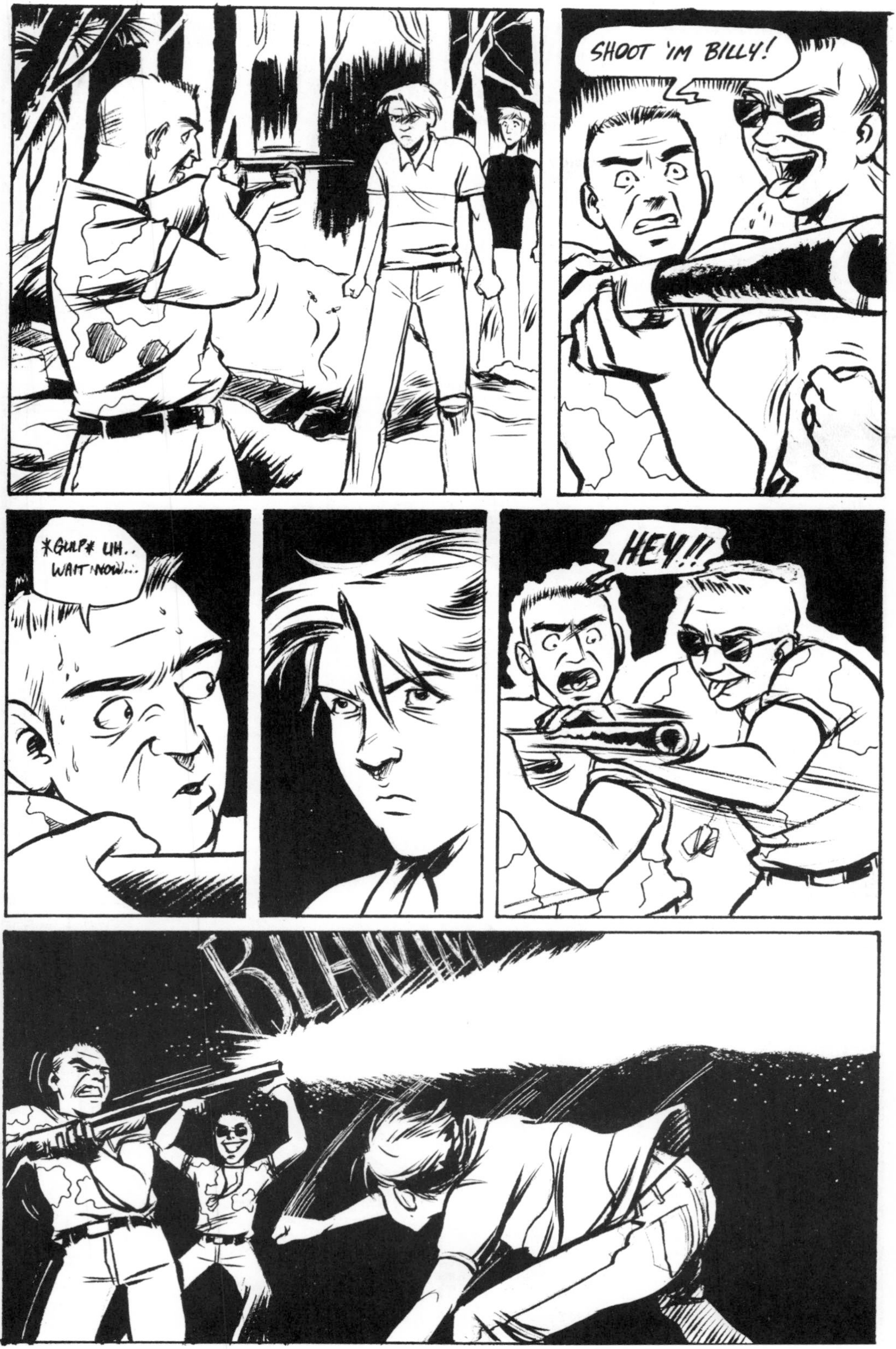
SHOOT 'IM BILLY!
GULP UH.. WAIT NOW...
HEY!!

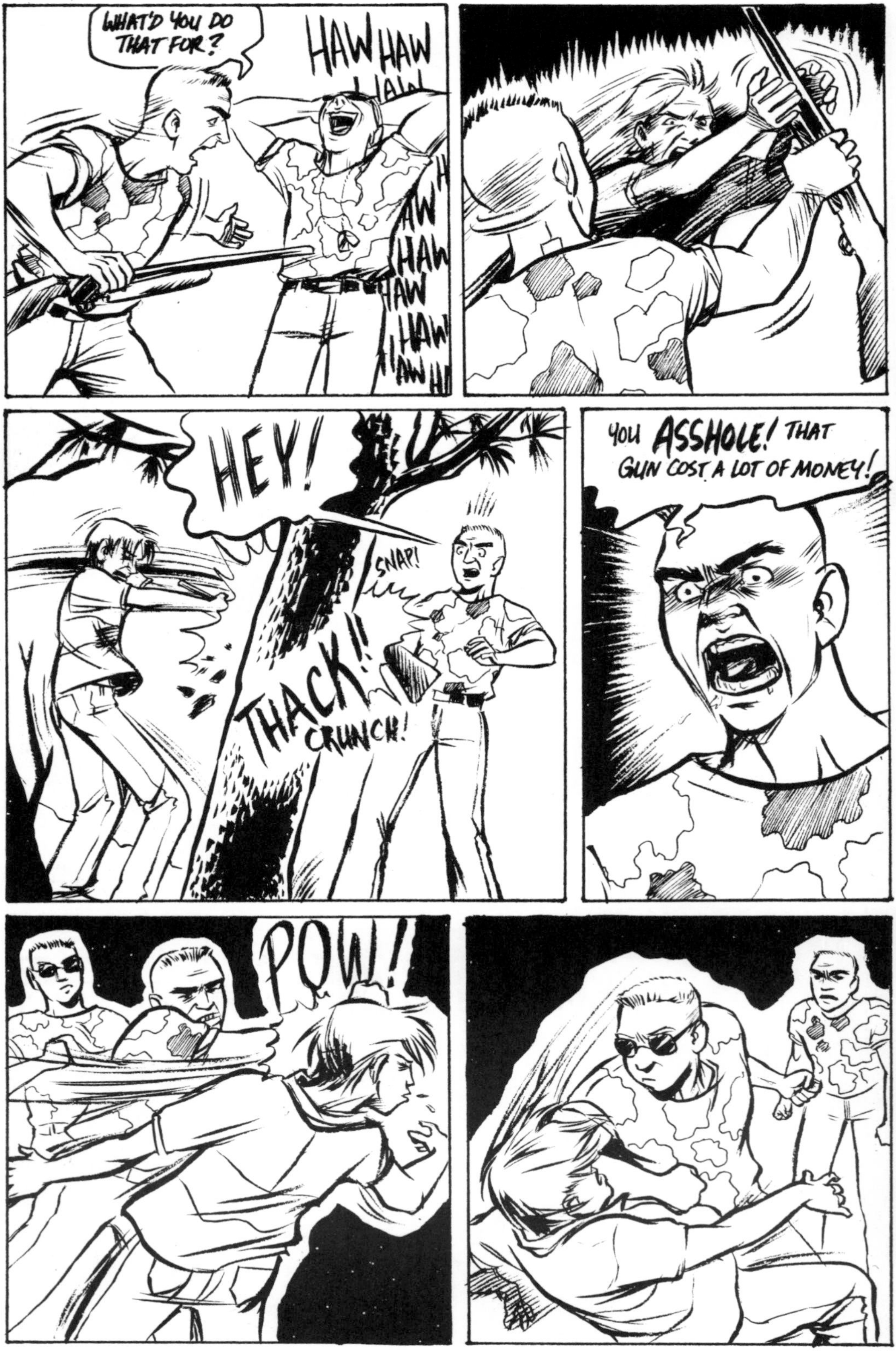

WHAT'D YOU DO THAT FOR?
HAW HAW HAW
HAW HAW HAW HAW HAW HAW
HEY!
SNAP!
THACK!!
CRUNCH!
YOU ASSHOLE! THAT GUN COST A LOT OF MONEY!
POW!

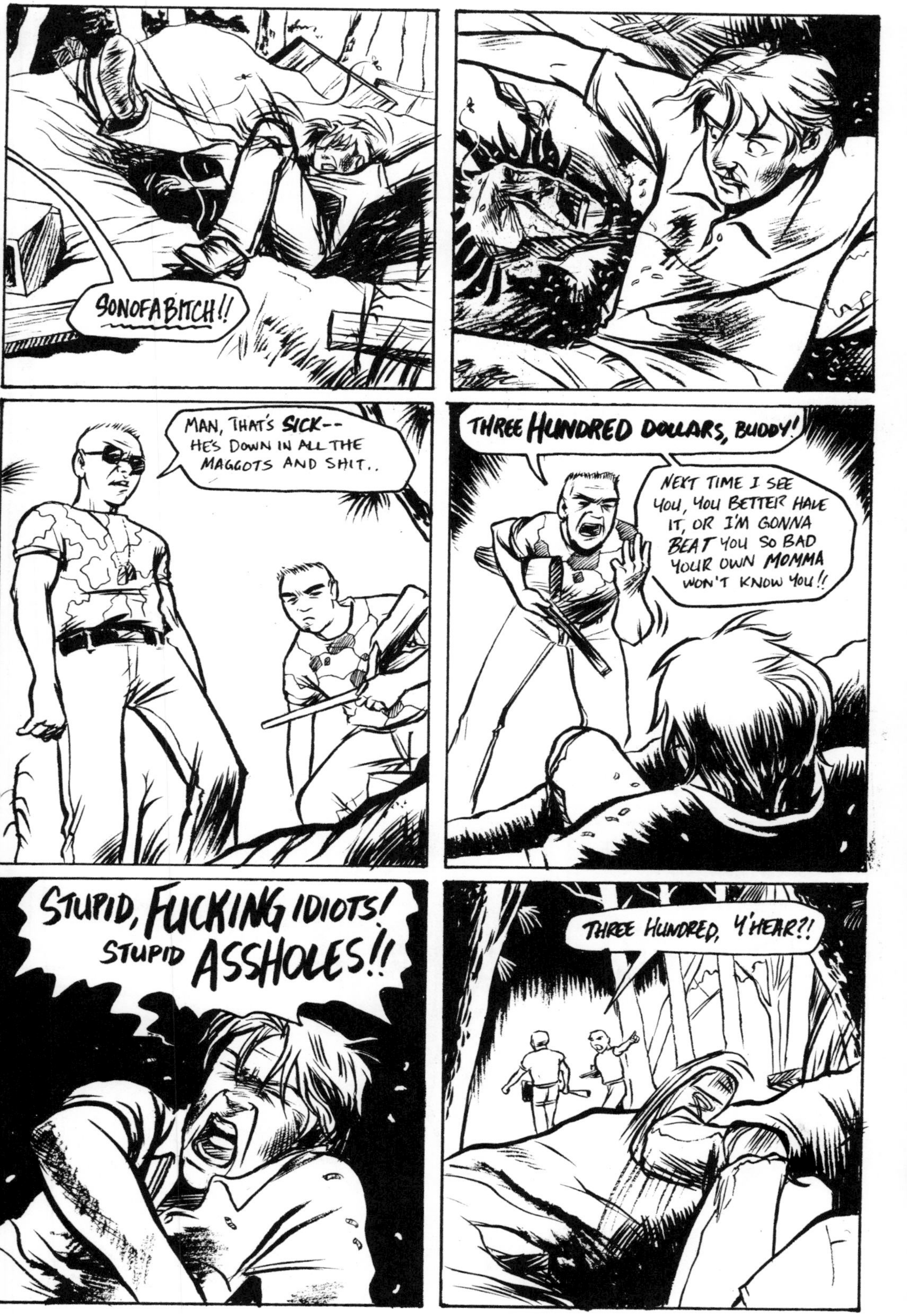
SONOFABITCH!!
MAN, THAT'S SICK-- HE'S DOWN IN ALL THE MAGGOTS AND SHIT..
THREE HUNDRED DOLLARS, BUDDY!
NEXT TIME I SEE YOU, YOU BETTER HAVE IT, OR I'M GONNA BEAT YOU SO BAD YOUR OWN MOMMA WON'T KNOW YOU!!
STUPID, FUCKING IDIOTS! STUPID ASSHOLES!!
THREE HUNDRED, Y'HEAR?!

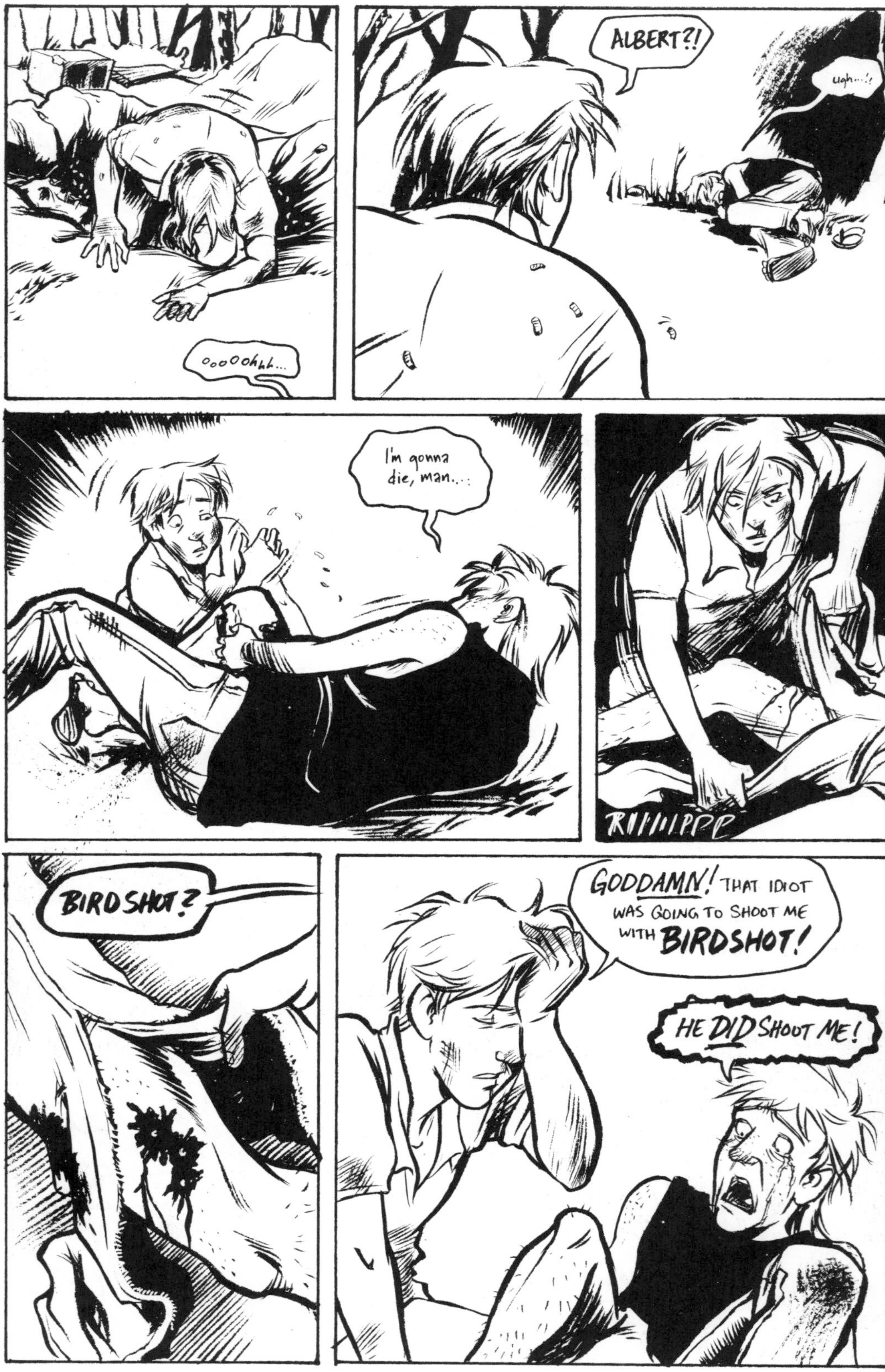
oooOOhhh...
ALBERT?!
ugh...!
I'm gonna die, man...
RIIIIPPP
BIRDSHOT?
GODDAMN! THAT IDIOT WAS GOING TO SHOOT ME WITH BIRDSHOT!
HE DID SHOOT ME!

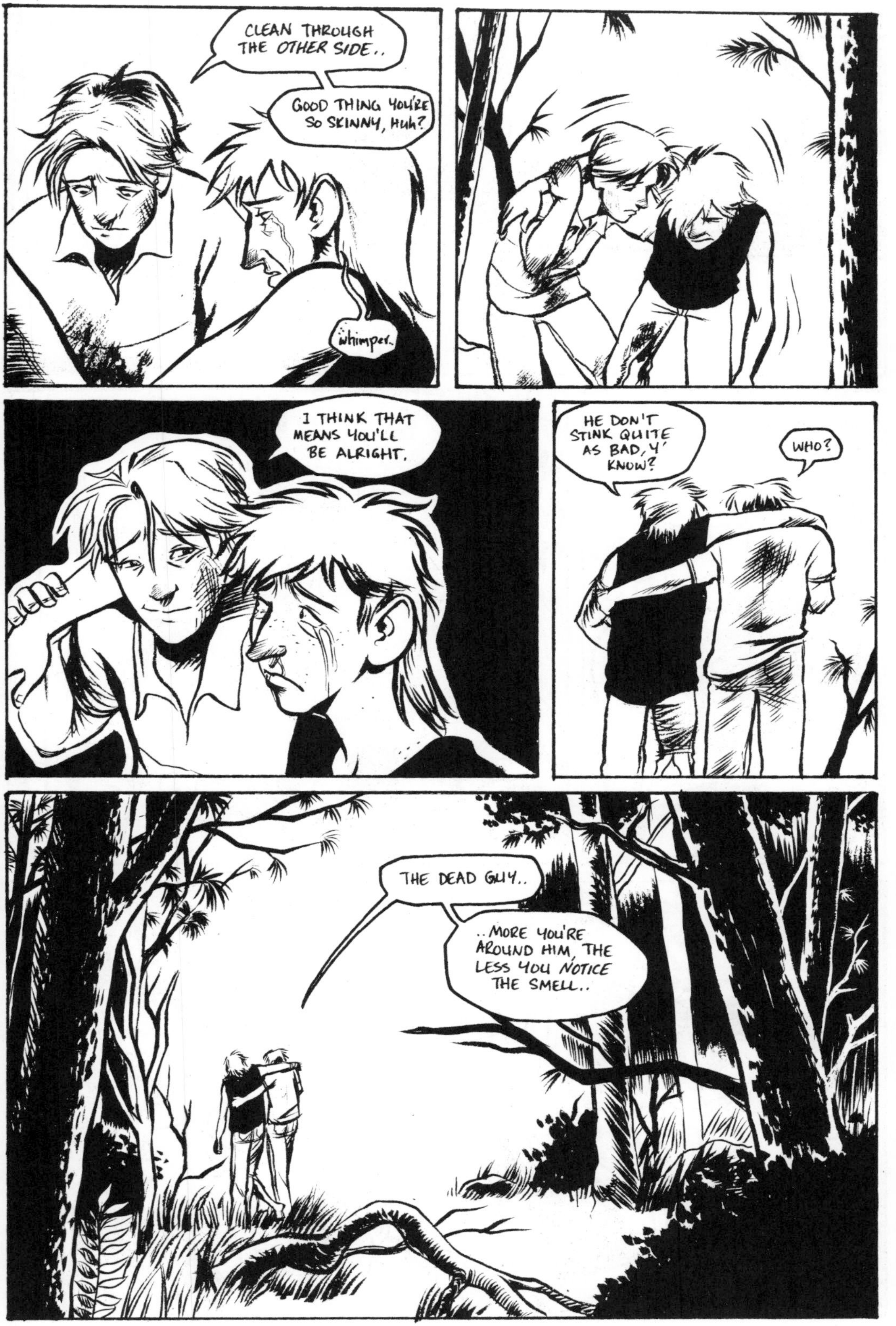
CLEAN THROUGH THE OTHER SIDE..
GOOD THING YOU'RE SO SKINNY, Huh?
whimper..
I THINK THAT MEANS YOU'LL BE ALRIGHT.
HE DON'T STINK QUITE AS BAD, Y' KNOW?
WHO?
THE DEAD GUY..
..MORE YOU'RE AROUND HIM, THE LESS YOU NOTICE THE SMELL..

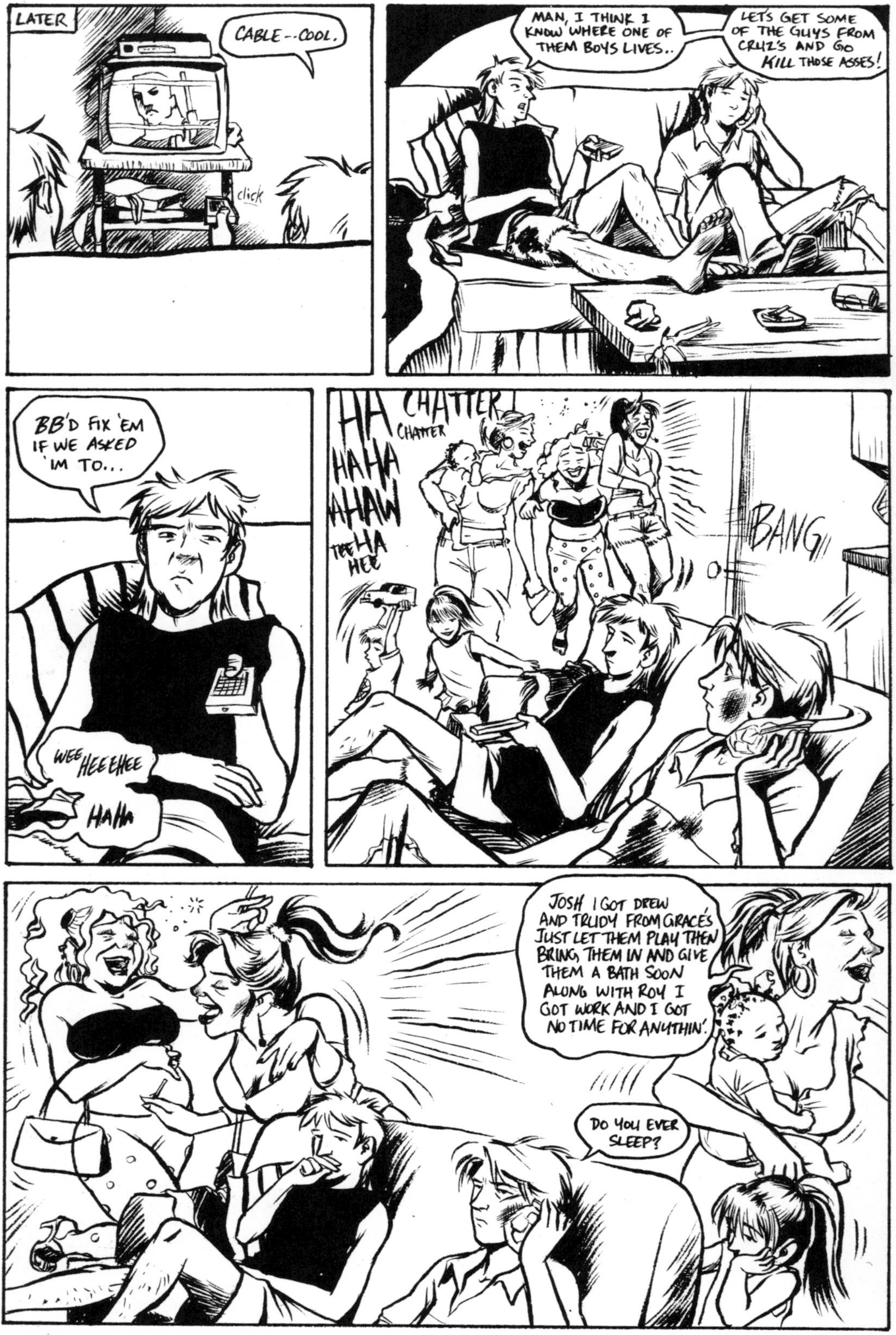
LATER
CABLE--COOL.
click
MAN, I THINK I KNOW WHERE ONE OF THEM BOYS LIVES..
LET'S GET SOME OF THE GUYS FROM CRUZ'S AND GO KILL THOSE ASSES!
BB'D FIX 'EM IF WE ASKED 'IM TO...
WEE HEE EHEE
HAHA
HA
CHATTER!
CHATTER
HAHA
AHAW
TEE HA HEE
BANG
JOSH I GOT DREW AND TRUDY FROM GRACE'S JUST LET THEM PLAY THEN BRING THEM IN AND GIVE THEM A BATH SOON ALONG WITH ROY I GOT WORK AND I GOT NO TIME FOR ANYTHIN'.
DO YOU EVER SLEEP?

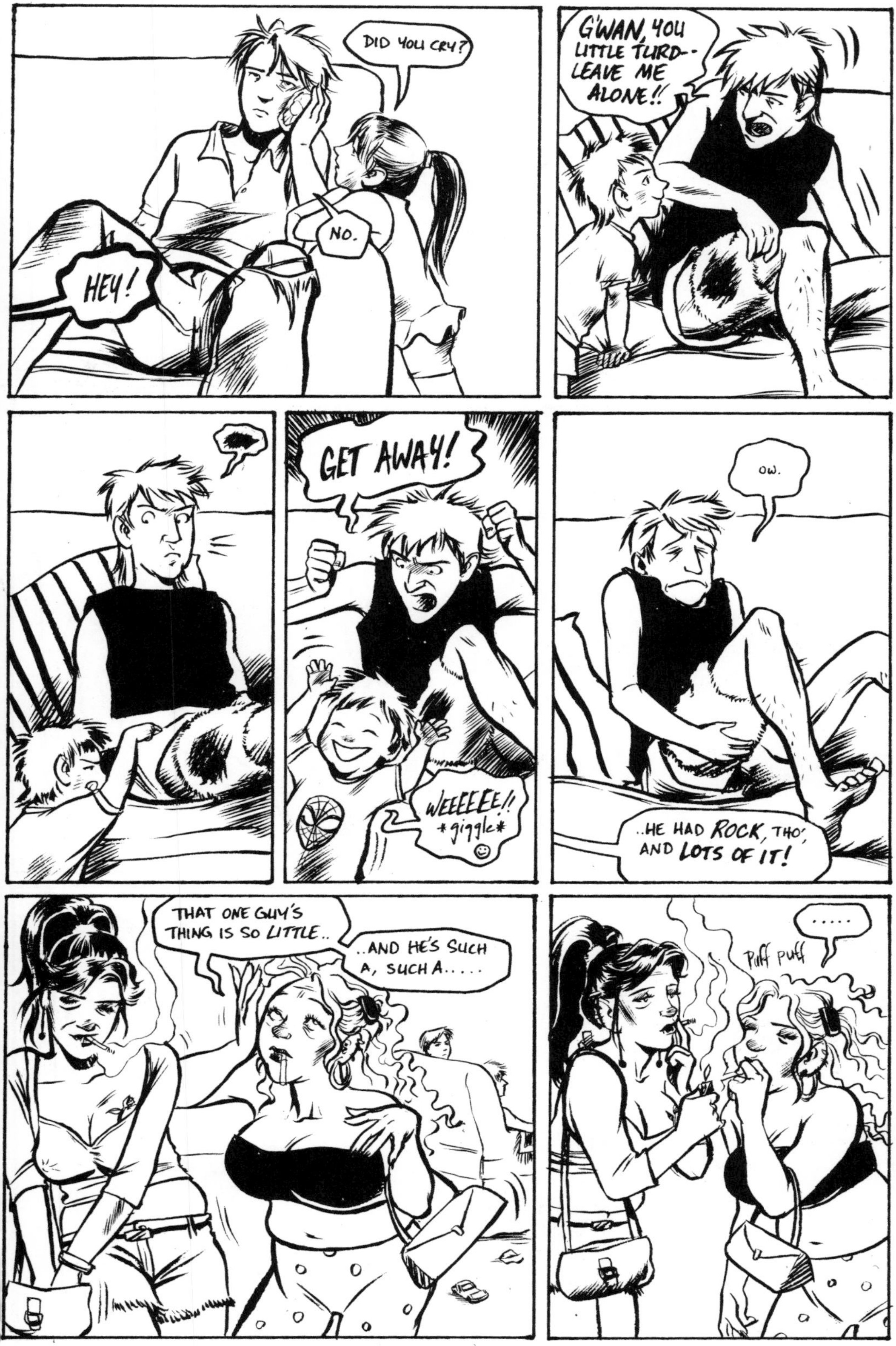
DID YOU CRY?
NO.
HEY!
G'WAN, YOU LITTLE TURD-- LEAVE ME ALONE!!
GET AWAY!
WEEEEEE!! *giggle*
OW.
..HE HAD ROCK, THO', AND LOTS OF IT!
THAT ONE GUY'S THING IS SO LITTLE..
..AND HE'S SUCH A, SUCH A.....
puff puff
.....

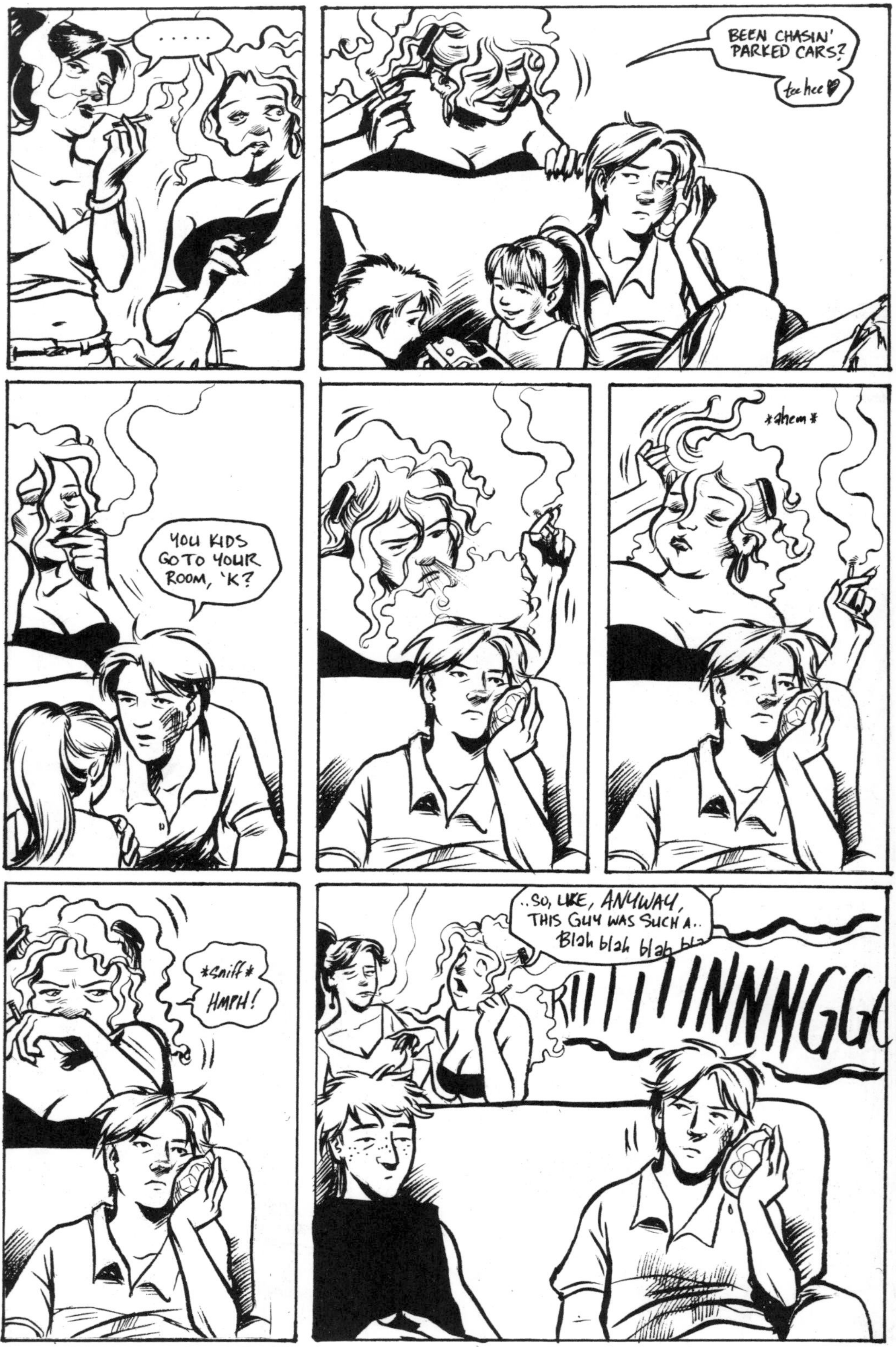

......
BEEN CHASIN' PARKED CARS?
tee hee ♥
YOU KIDS GO TO YOUR ROOM, 'K?
ahem
sniff HMPH!
..SO, LIKE, ANYWAY, THIS GUY WAS SUCH A.. Blah blah blah bla
RIIIINNNNGG

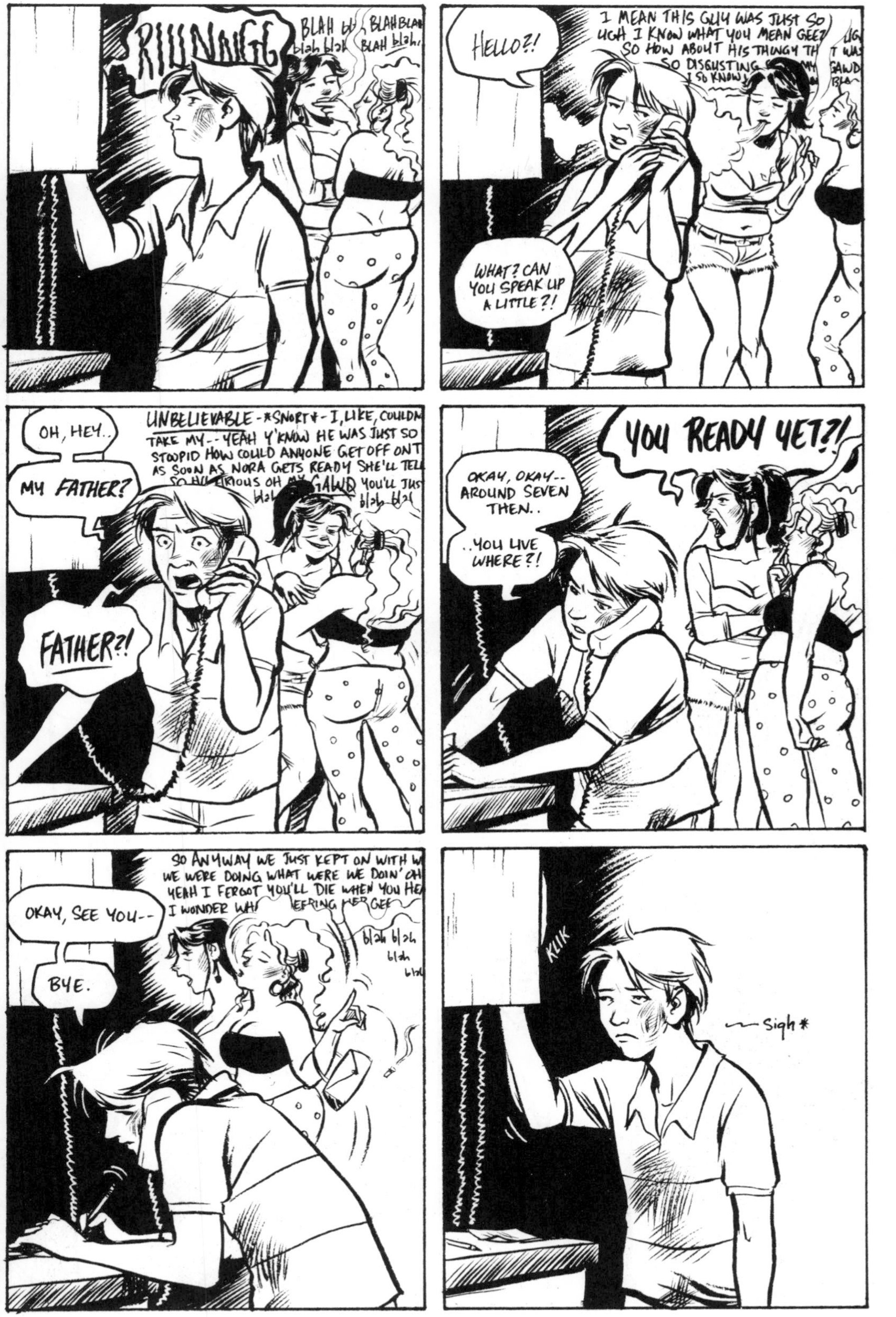
RIIUNNGG
BLAH BLAH BLAH BLAH
BLAH blah
HELLO?!
I MEAN THIS GUY WAS JUST SO
UGH I KNOW WHAT YOU MEAN GEEZ
SO HOW ABOUT HIS THINGY TH
SO DISGUSTING
I SO KNOW
MY GAWD
WHAT? CAN YOU SPEAK UP A LITTLE?!
OH, HEY..
MY FATHER?
FATHER?!
UNBELIEVABLE - *SNORT* - I, LIKE, COULDN
TAKE MY-- YEAH Y'KNOW HE WAS JUST SO
STOOPID HOW COULD ANYONE GET OFF ONT
AS SOON AS NORA GETS READY SHE'LL TELL
RIOUS OH GAWD YOU'LL JUST
YOU READY YET?!
OKAY, OKAY-- AROUND SEVEN THEN..
..YOU LIVE WHERE?!
OKAY, SEE YOU--
BYE.
SO ANYWAY WE JUST KEPT ON WITH W
WE WERE DOING WHAT WERE WE DOIN' OH
YEAH I FERGOT YOU'LL DIE WHEN YOU HE
I WONDER WH EFRING HER GEE
blah blah
blah
KLIK
~sigh*

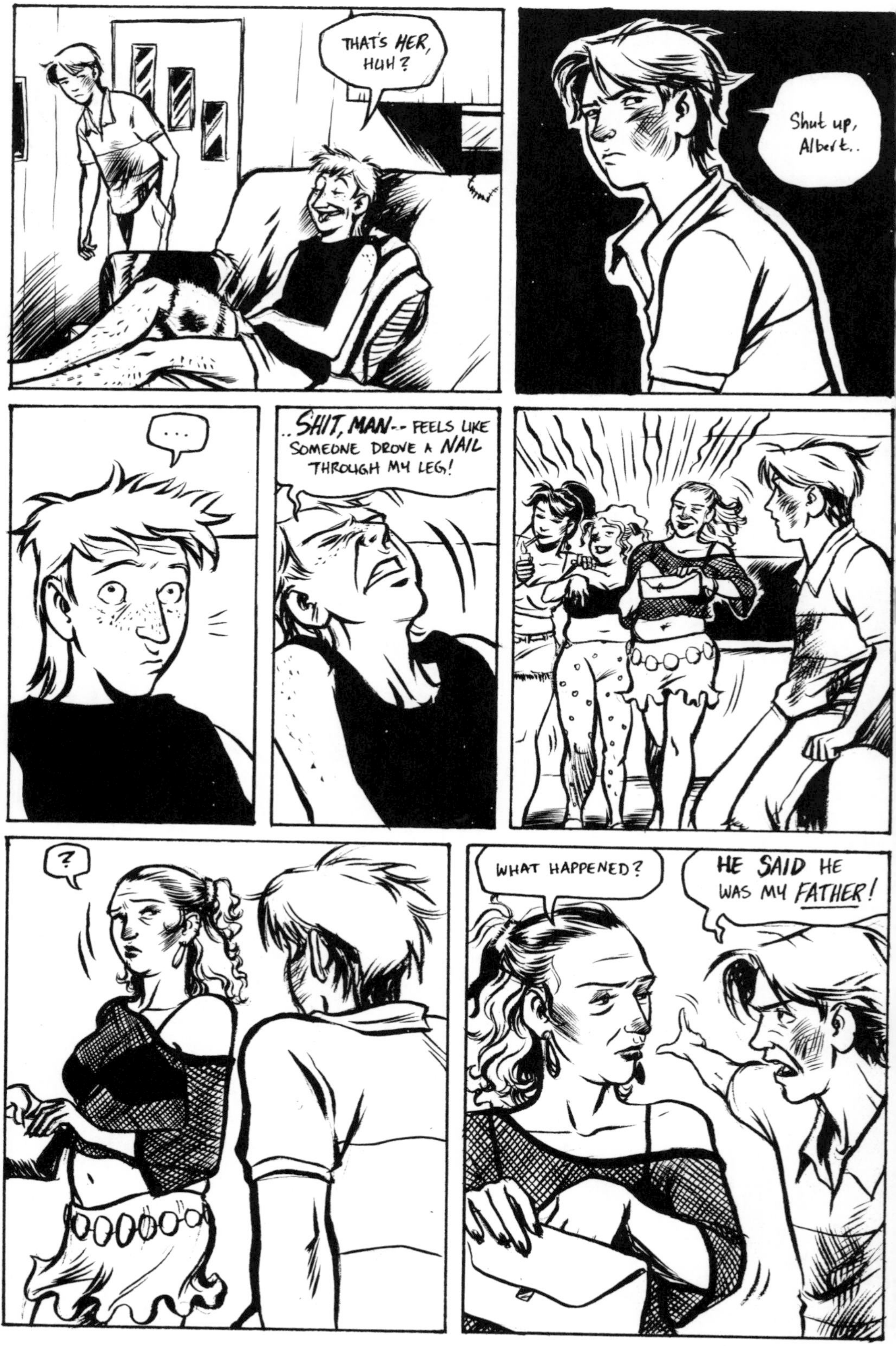
THAT'S HER, HUH?
Shut up, Albert..
...
..SHIT, MAN-- FEELS LIKE SOMEONE DROVE A NAIL THROUGH MY LEG!
?
WHAT HAPPENED?
HE SAID HE WAS MY FATHER!

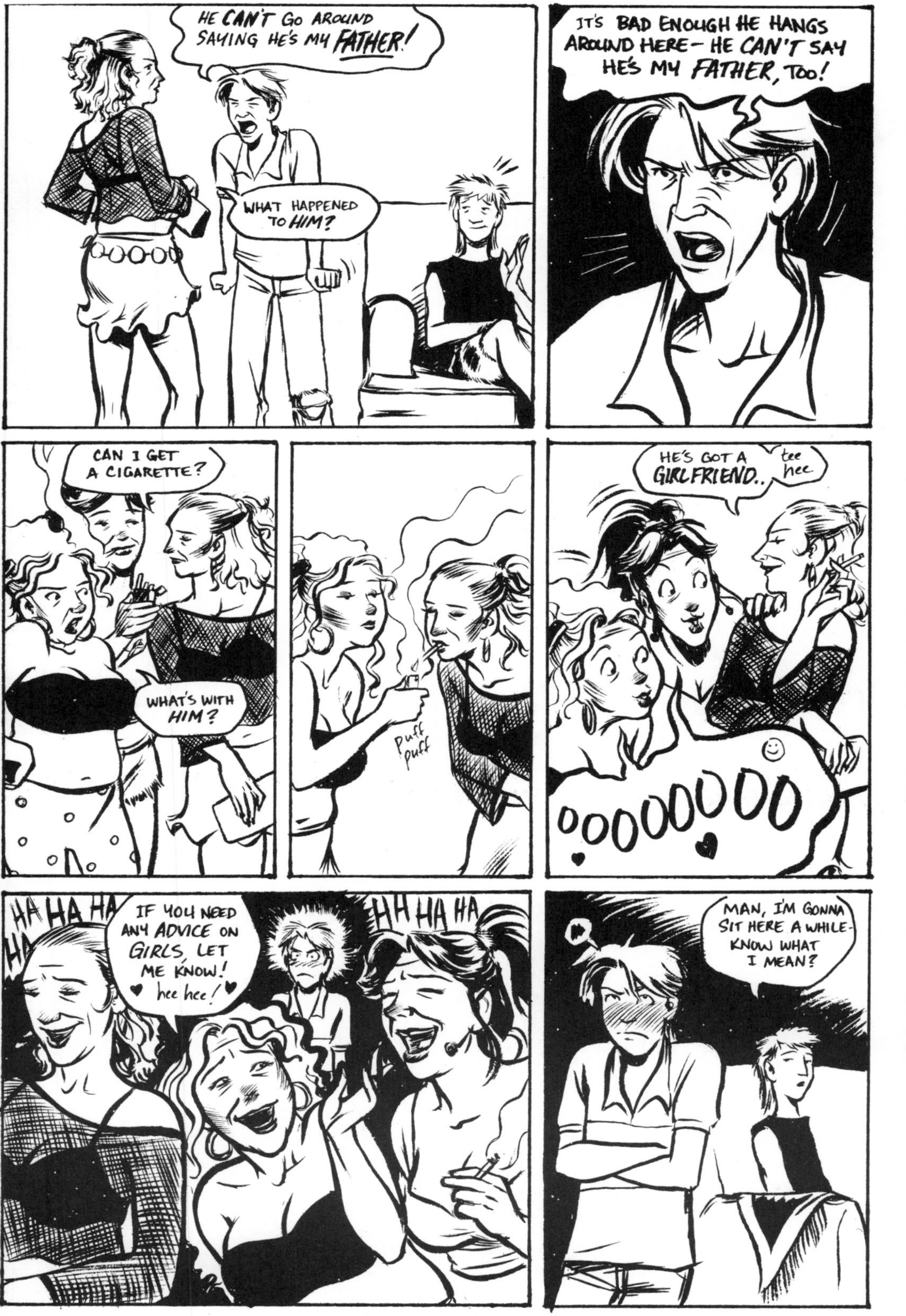
HE CAN'T GO AROUND SAYING HE'S MY FATHER!
WHAT HAPPENED TO HIM?
IT'S BAD ENOUGH HE HANGS AROUND HERE— HE CAN'T SAY HE'S MY FATHER, TOO!
CAN I GET A CIGARETTE?
WHAT'S WITH HIM?
puff puff
HE'S GOT A GIRLFRIEND..
tee hee
OOOOOOOO
HA HA HA HA
IF YOU NEED ANY ADVICE ON GIRLS, LET ME KNOW! hee hee!
HH HA HA
MAN, I'M GONNA SIT HERE A WHILE- KNOW WHAT I MEAN?

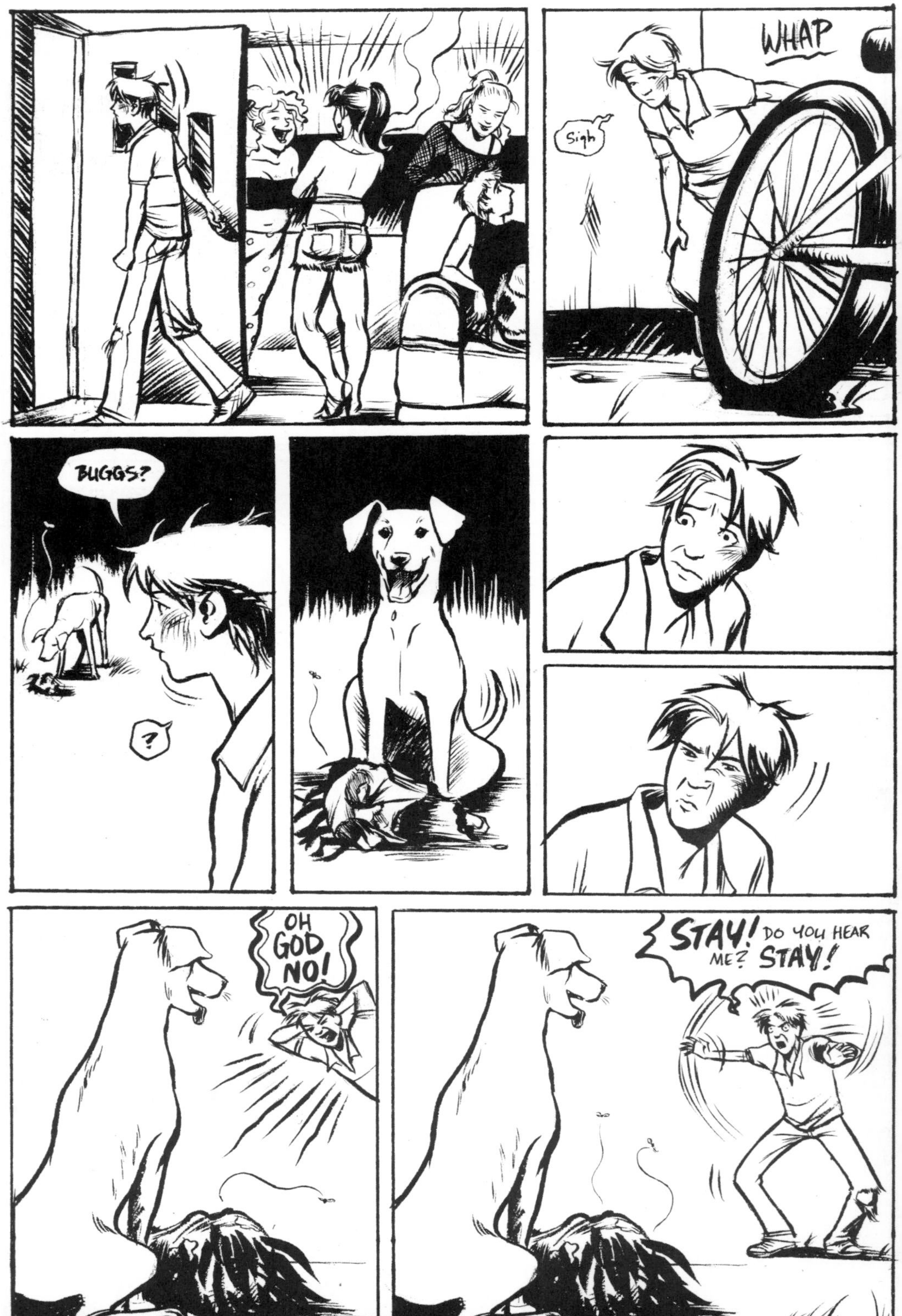
WHAP
Sigh
BUGGS?
?
OH GOD NO!
STAY! DO YOU HEAR ME? STAY!

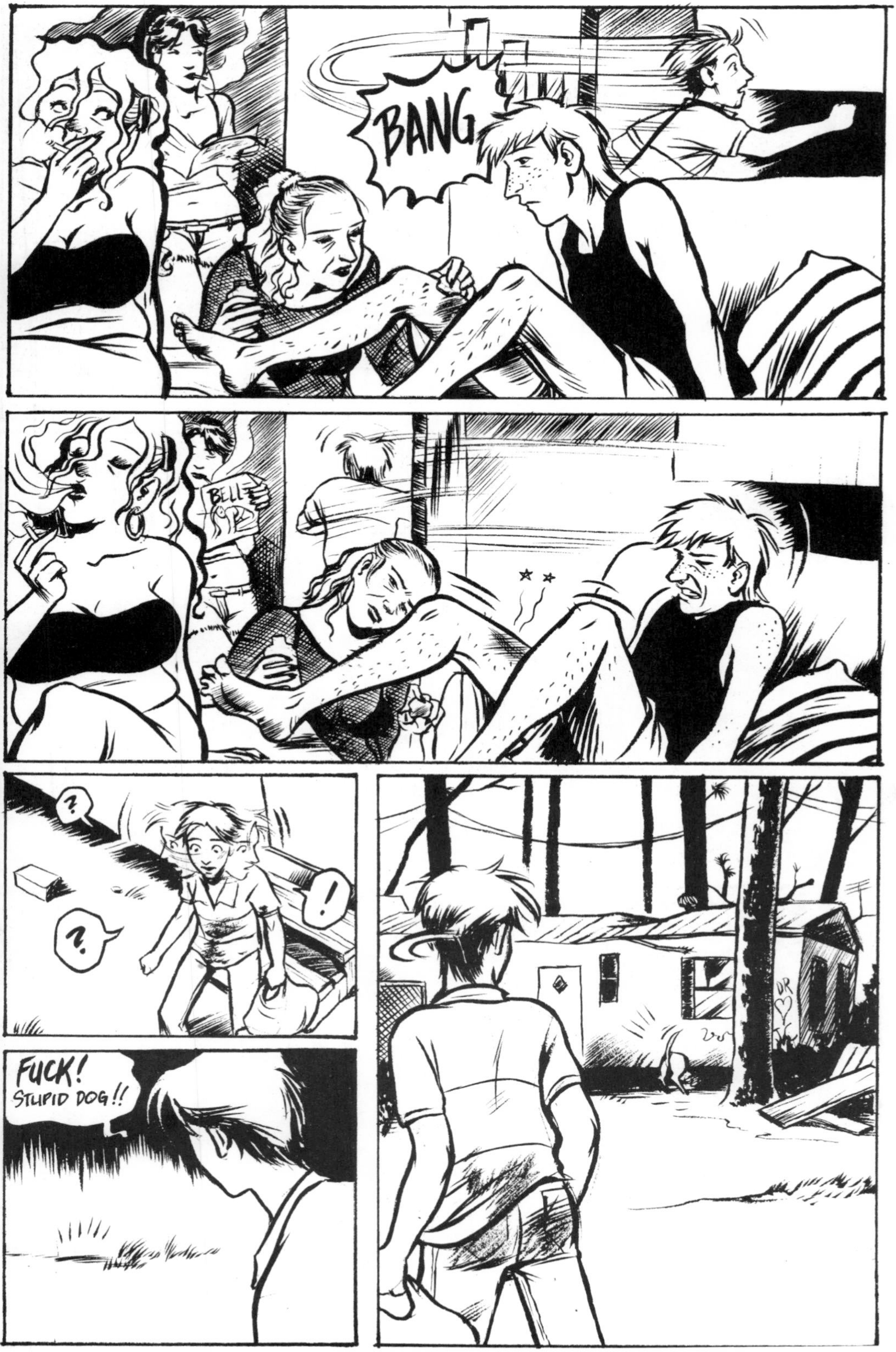
BANG
?
!
?
FUCK!
STUPID DOG!!
BELL

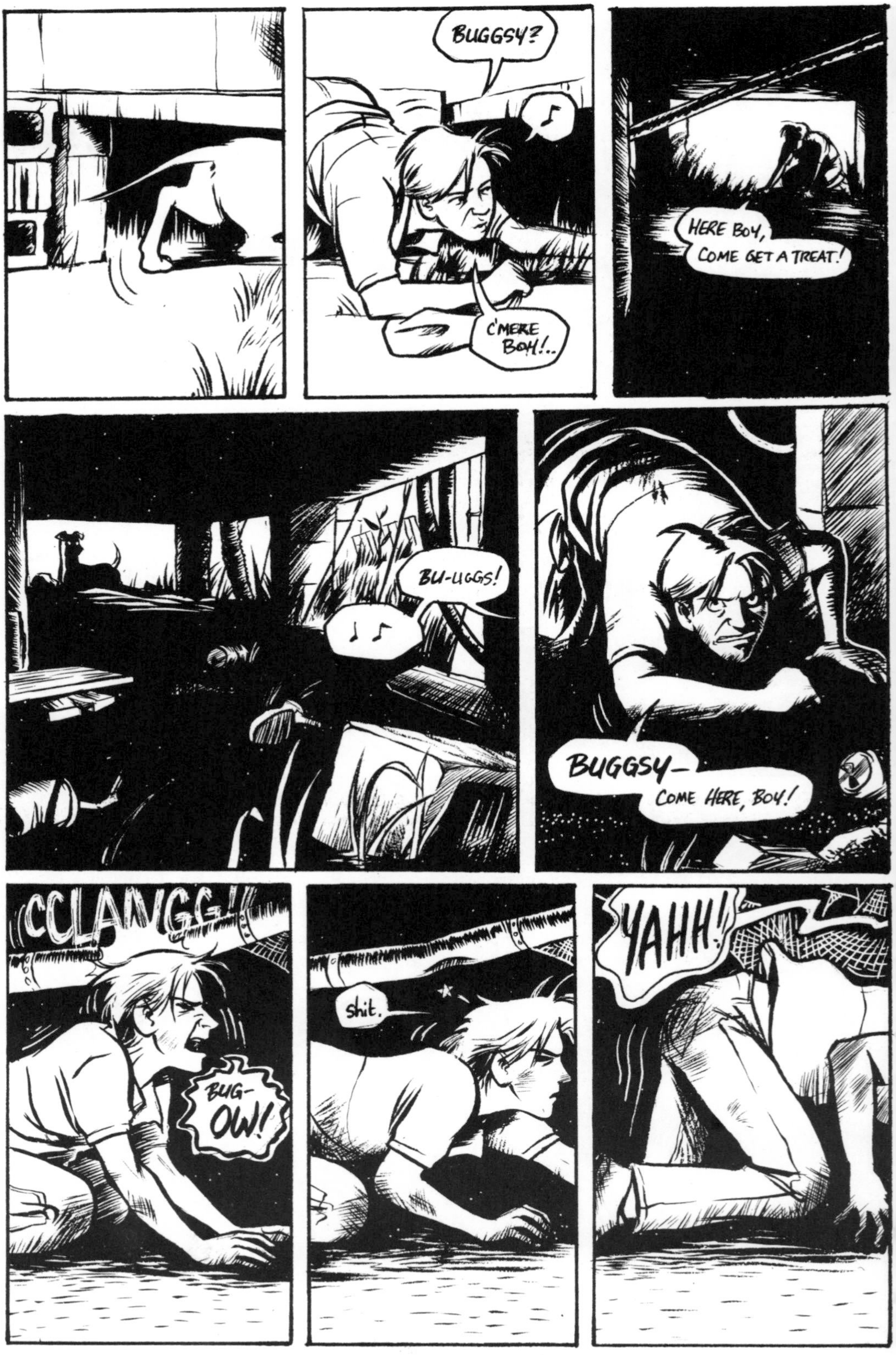
BUGGSY?
C'MERE BOY!..
HERE BOY, COME GET A TREAT!
BU-UGGS!
BUGGSY- COME HERE, BOY!
CCLANGG!!
BUG-OW!
shit.
YAHH!

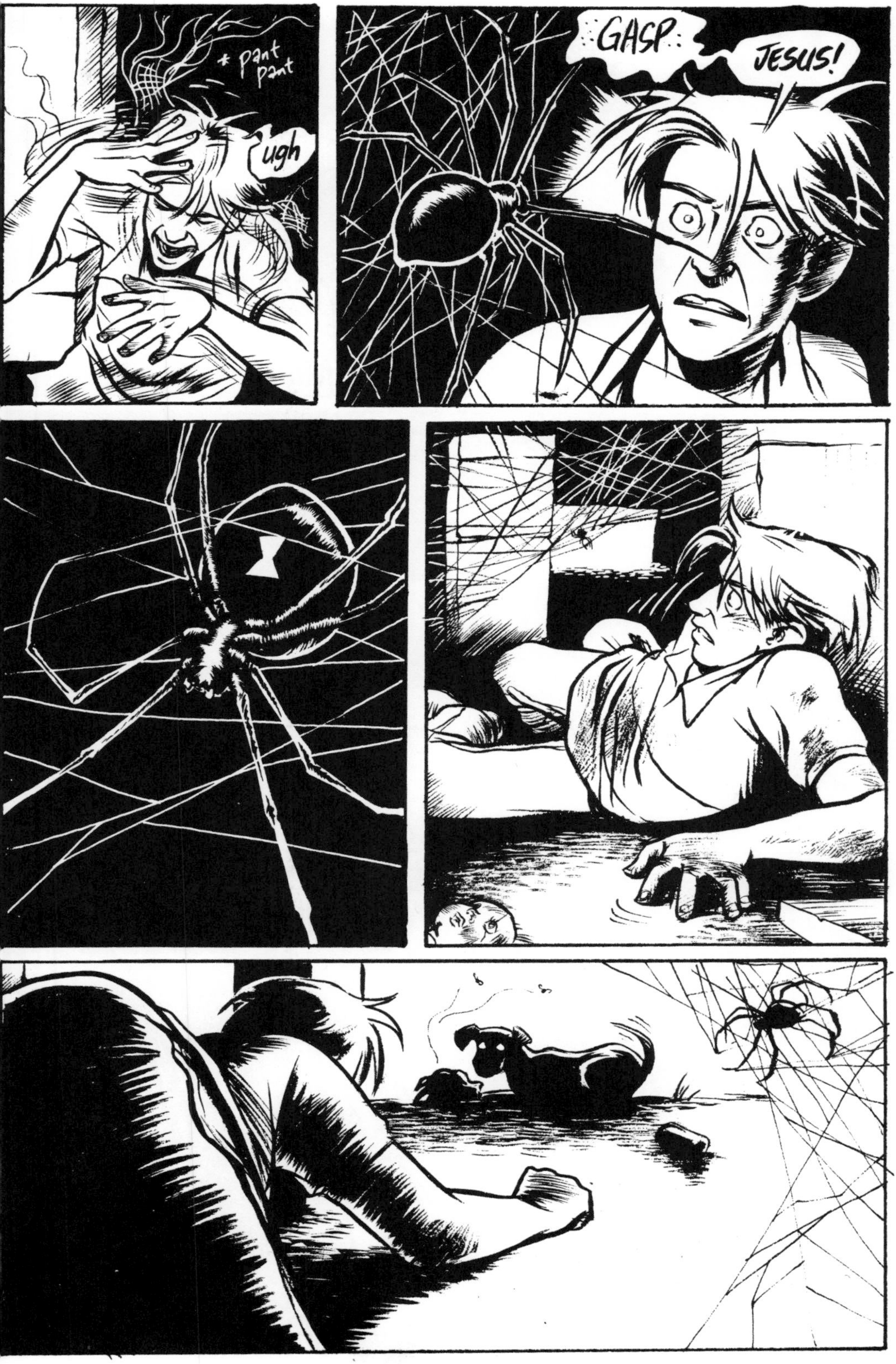
* pant pant
ugh
GASP
JESUS!

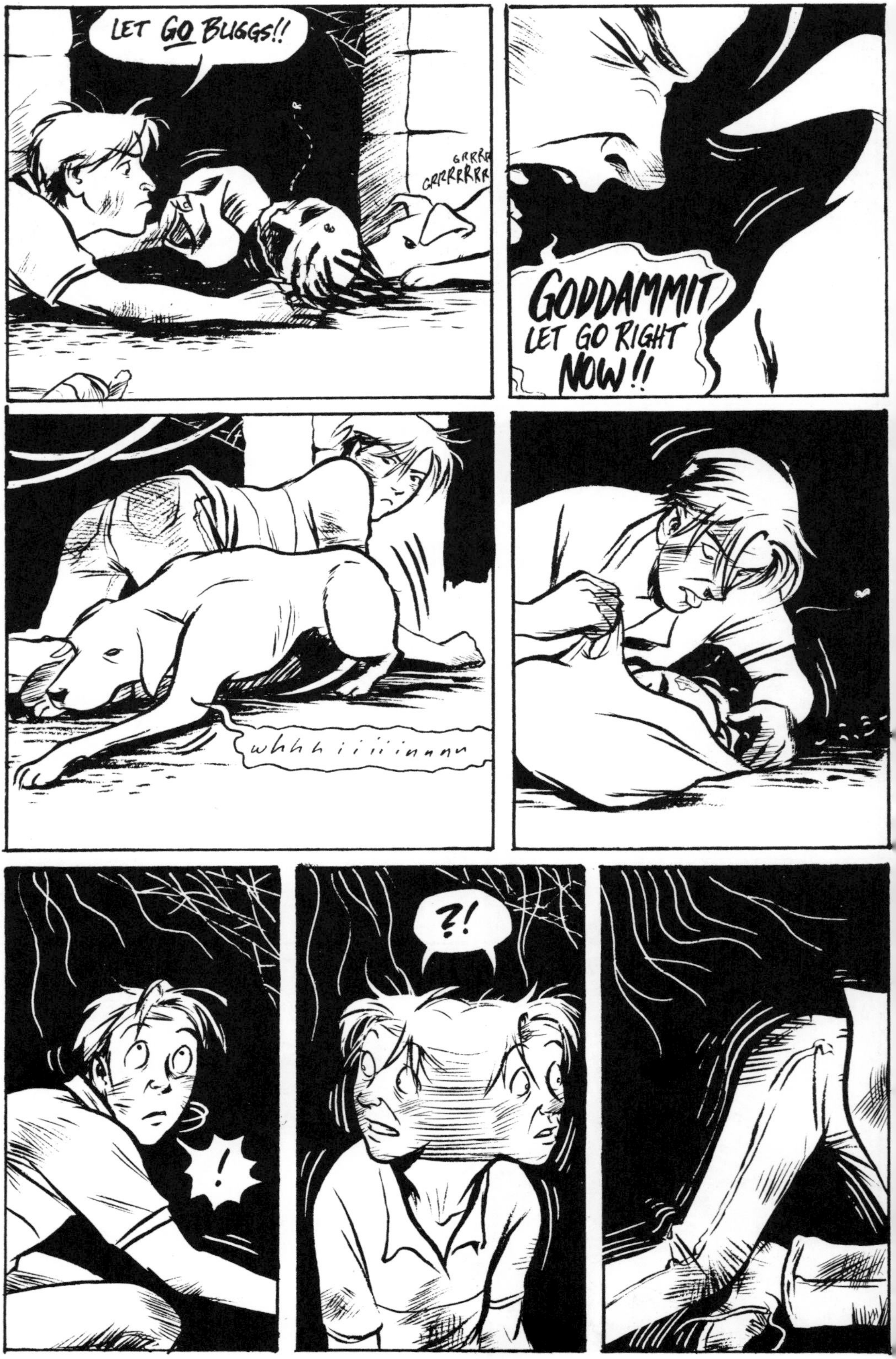
LET GO BUGGS!!
GRRRR
GRRRRRRRR
GODDAMMIT LET GO RIGHT NOW!!
whhhiiiinnnn
?!
!

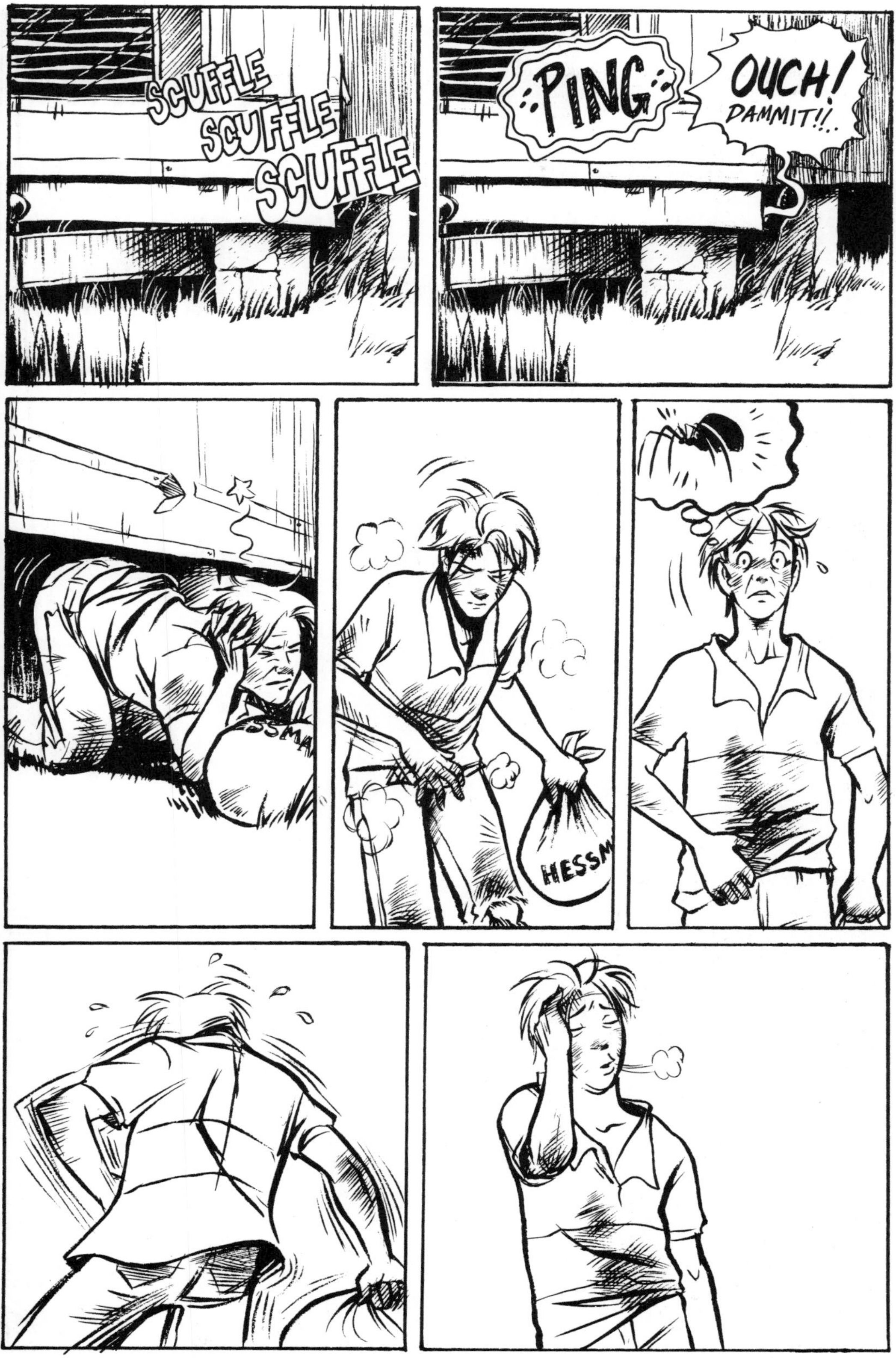
SCUFFLE
SCUFFLE
SCUFFLE
PING
OUCH! DAMMIT!!
HESSM

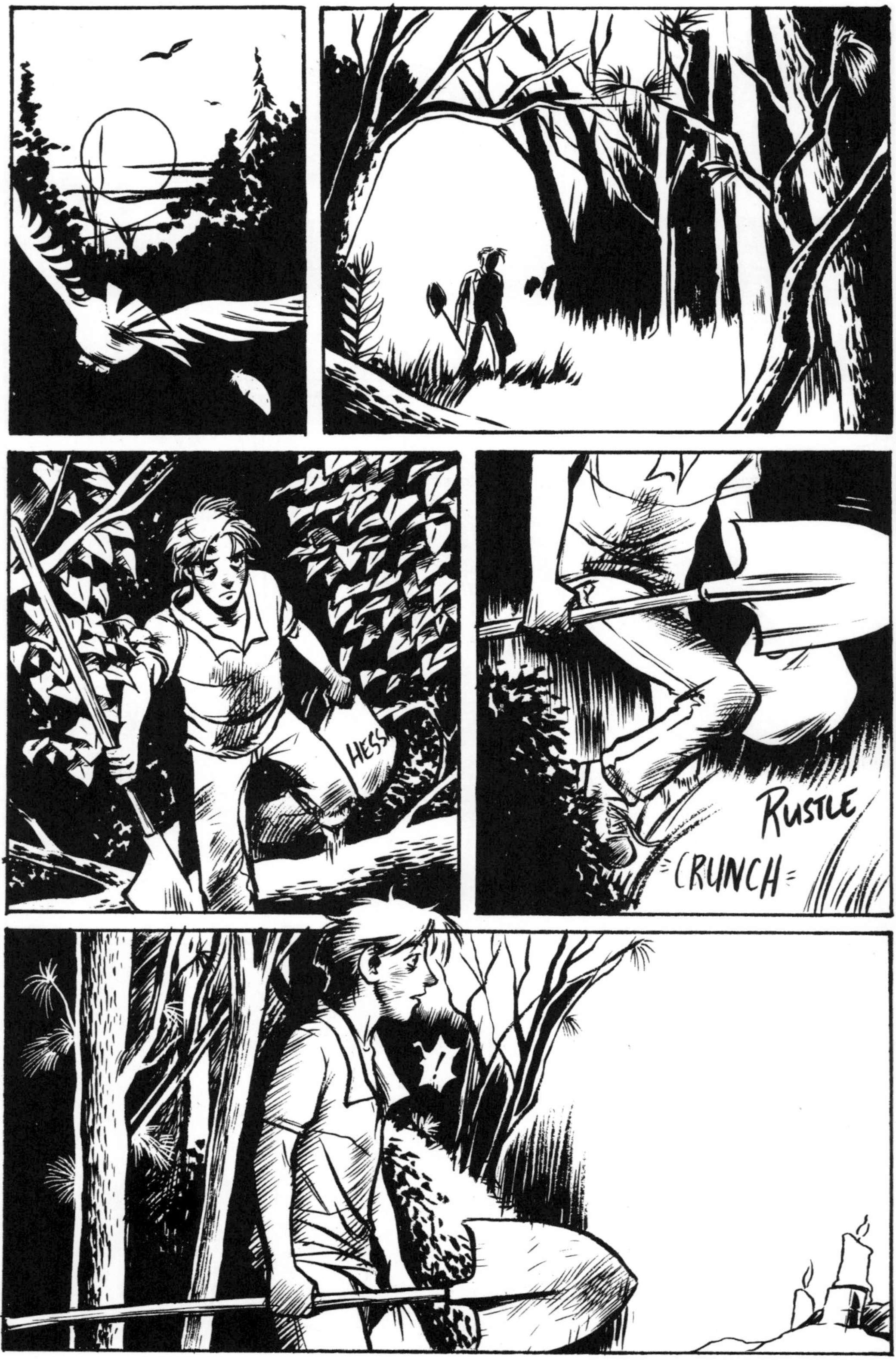
HESS
RUSTLE
CRUNCH
!

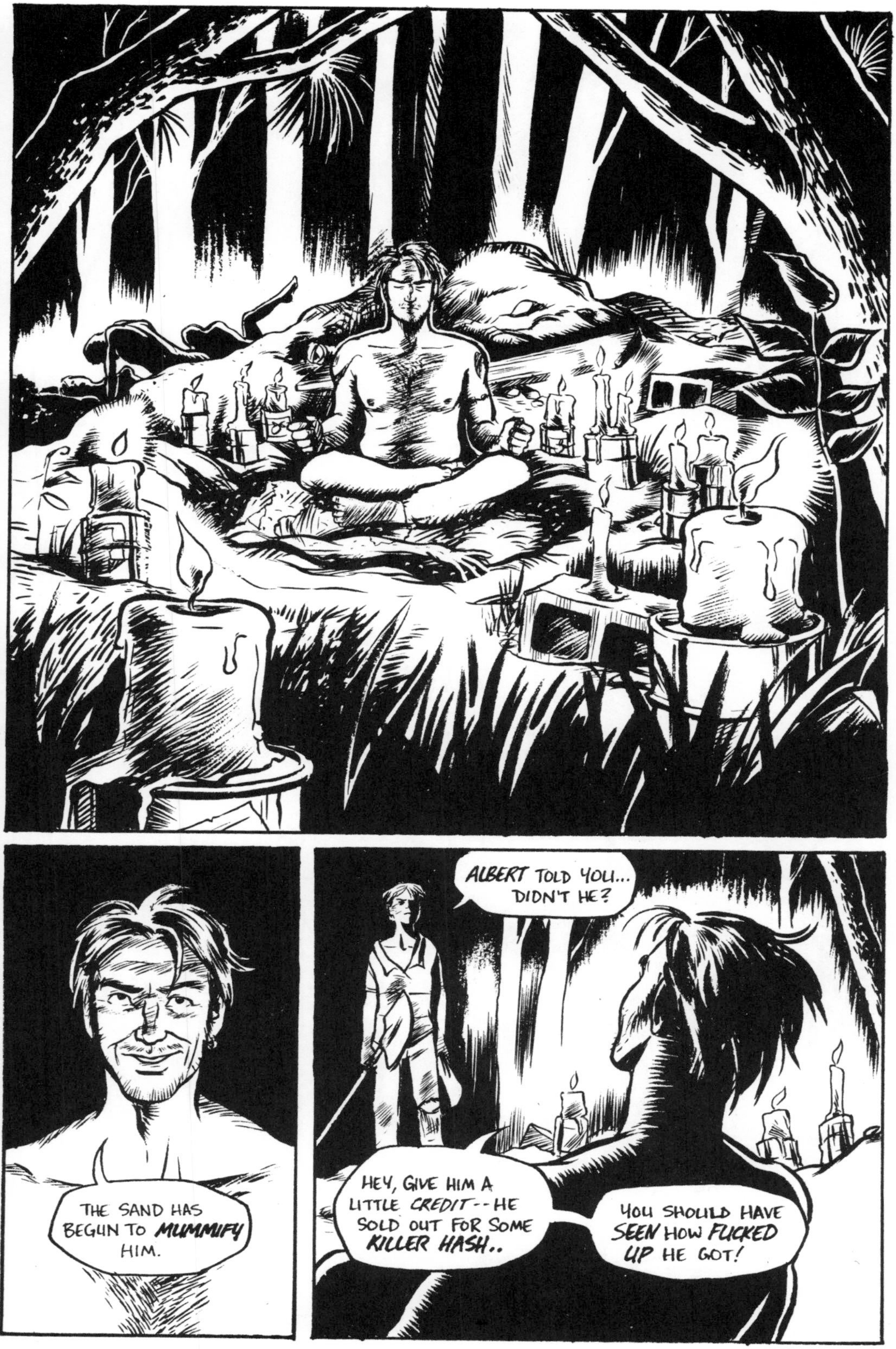
THE SAND HAS BEGUN TO MUMMIFY HIM.
ALBERT TOLD YOU... DIDN'T HE?
HEY, GIVE HIM A LITTLE CREDIT--HE SOLD OUT FOR SOME KILLER HASH..
YOU SHOULD HAVE SEEN HOW FUCKED UP HE GOT!

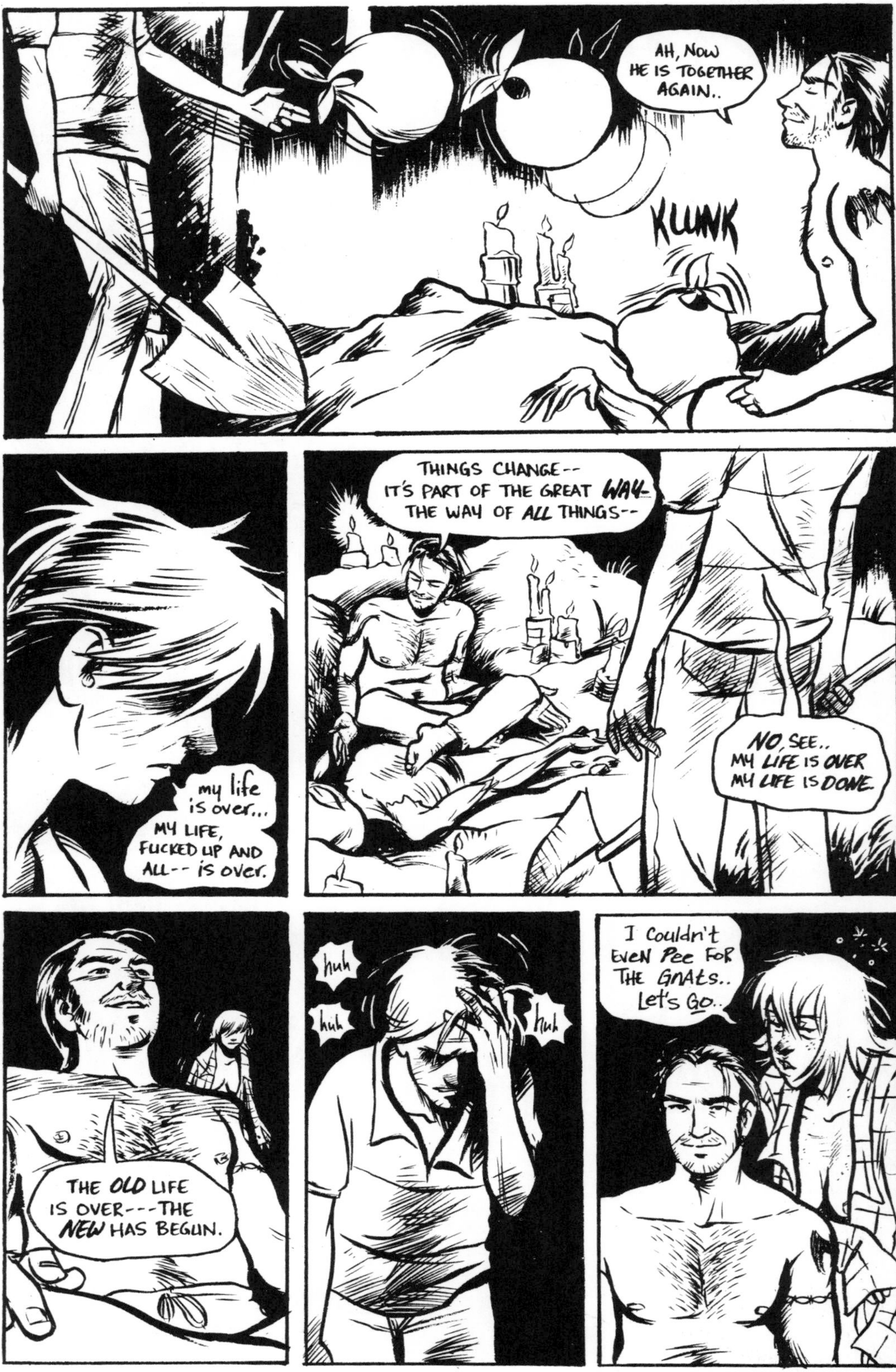
AH, NOW HE IS TOGETHER AGAIN..
KLUNK
THINGS CHANGE-- IT'S PART OF THE GREAT WAY- THE WAY OF ALL THINGS--
my life is over... MY LIFE, FUCKED UP AND ALL-- is over.
NO, SEE.. MY LIFE IS OVER MY LIFE IS DONE.
THE OLD LIFE IS OVER---THE NEW HAS BEGUN.
huh
huh
huh
I Couldn't Even Pee For The Gnats.. Let's Go..

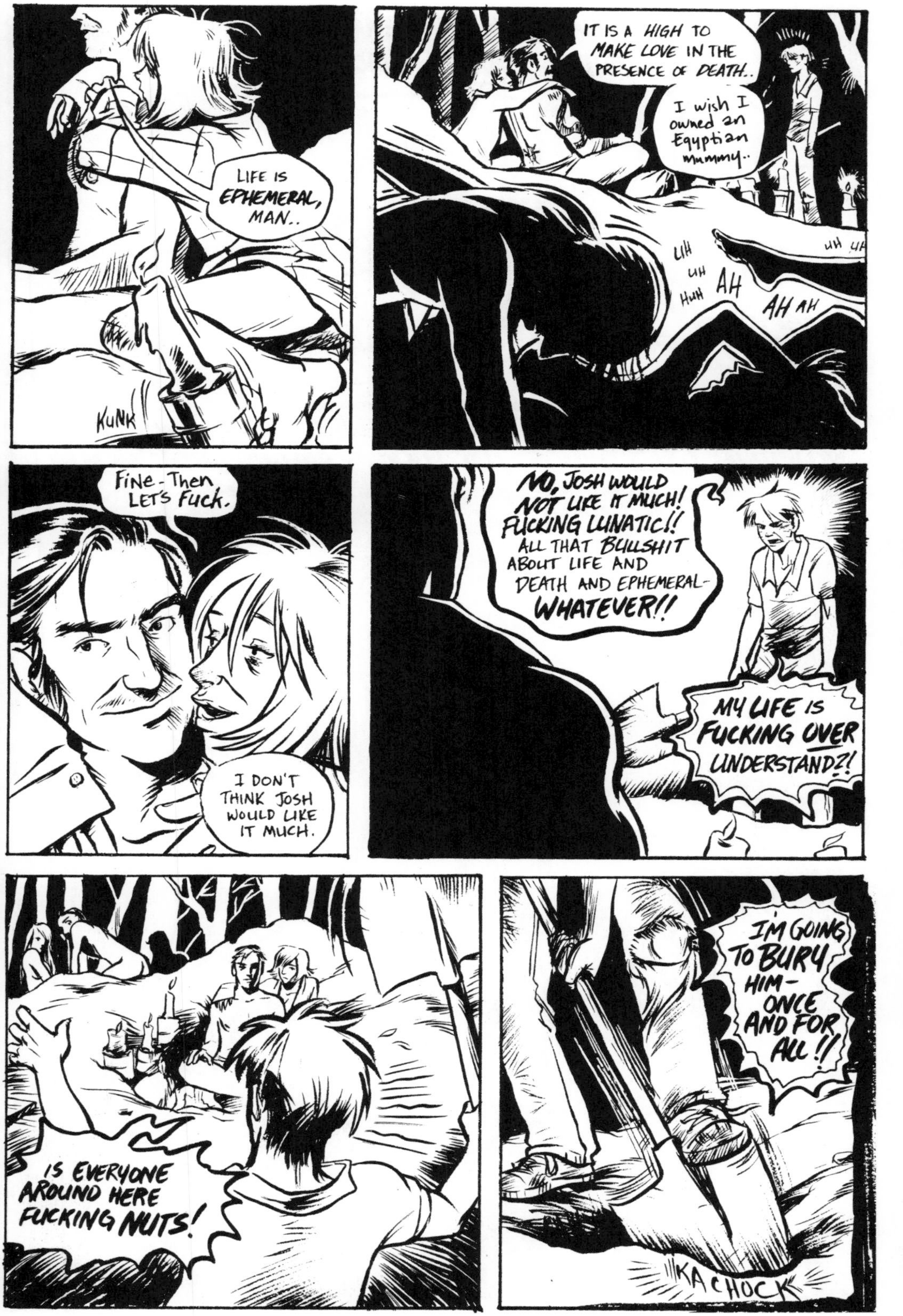
LIFE IS EPHEMERAL, MAN..
KUNK
IT IS A HIGH TO MAKE LOVE IN THE PRESENCE OF DEATH..
I wish I owned an Egyptian mummy..
UH UH HUH AH AH AH UH UH
Fine-Then LET'S Fuck.
I DON'T THINK JOSH WOULD LIKE IT MUCH.
NO, JOSH WOULD NOT LIKE IT MUCH! FUCKING LUNATIC!! ALL THAT BULLSHIT ABOUT LIFE AND DEATH AND EPHEMERAL-WHATEVER!!
MY LIFE IS FUCKING OVER UNDERSTAND?!
IS EVERYONE AROUND HERE FUCKING NUTS!
I'M GOING TO BURY HIM-ONCE AND FOR ALL!!
KACHOCK

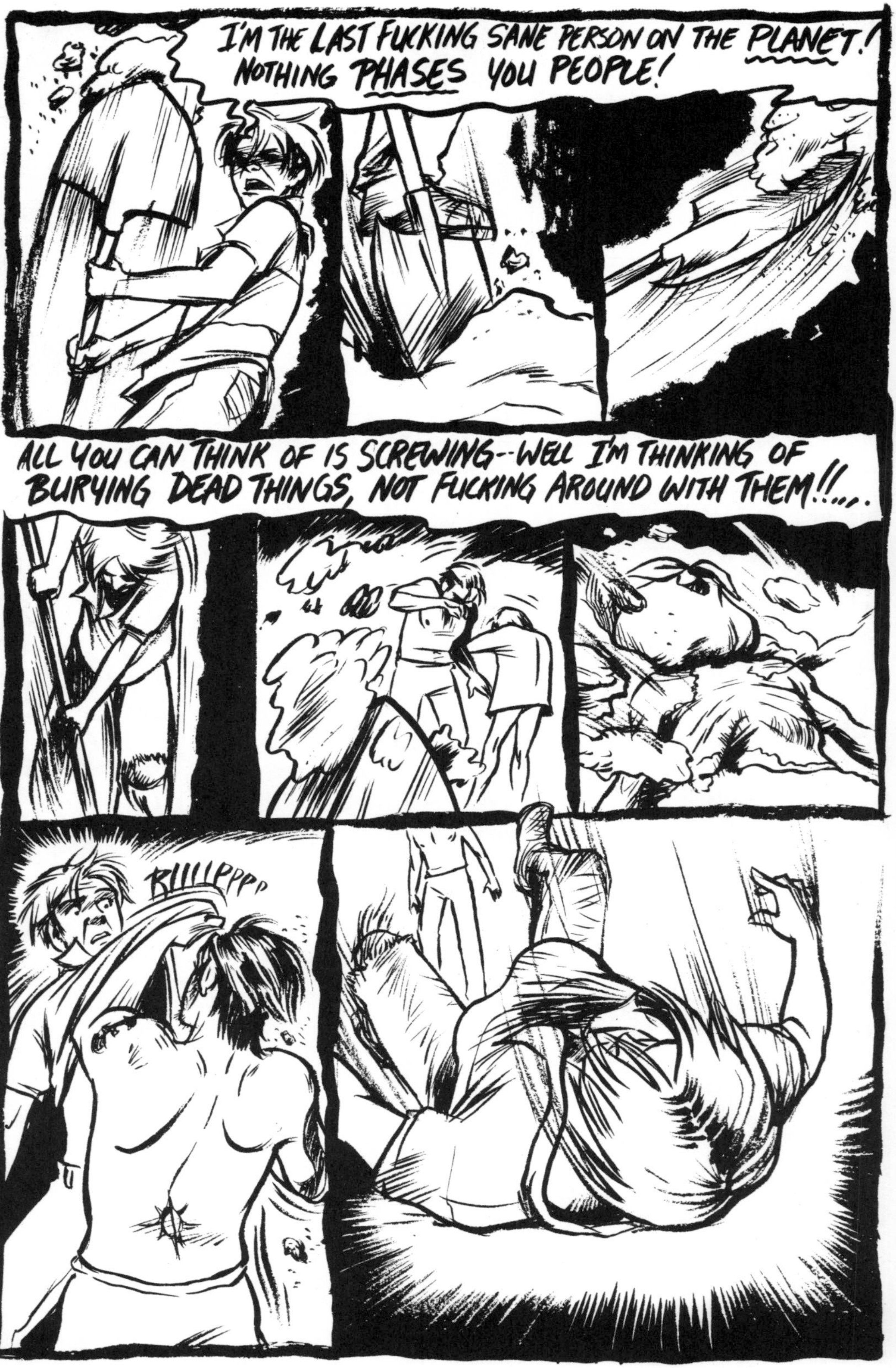
I'M THE LAST FUCKING SANE PERSON ON THE PLANET! NOTHING PHASES YOU PEOPLE!
ALL YOU CAN THINK OF IS SCREWING--WELL I'M THINKING OF BURYING DEAD THINGS, NOT FUCKING AROUND WITH THEM!!...
RIIIIPPPP

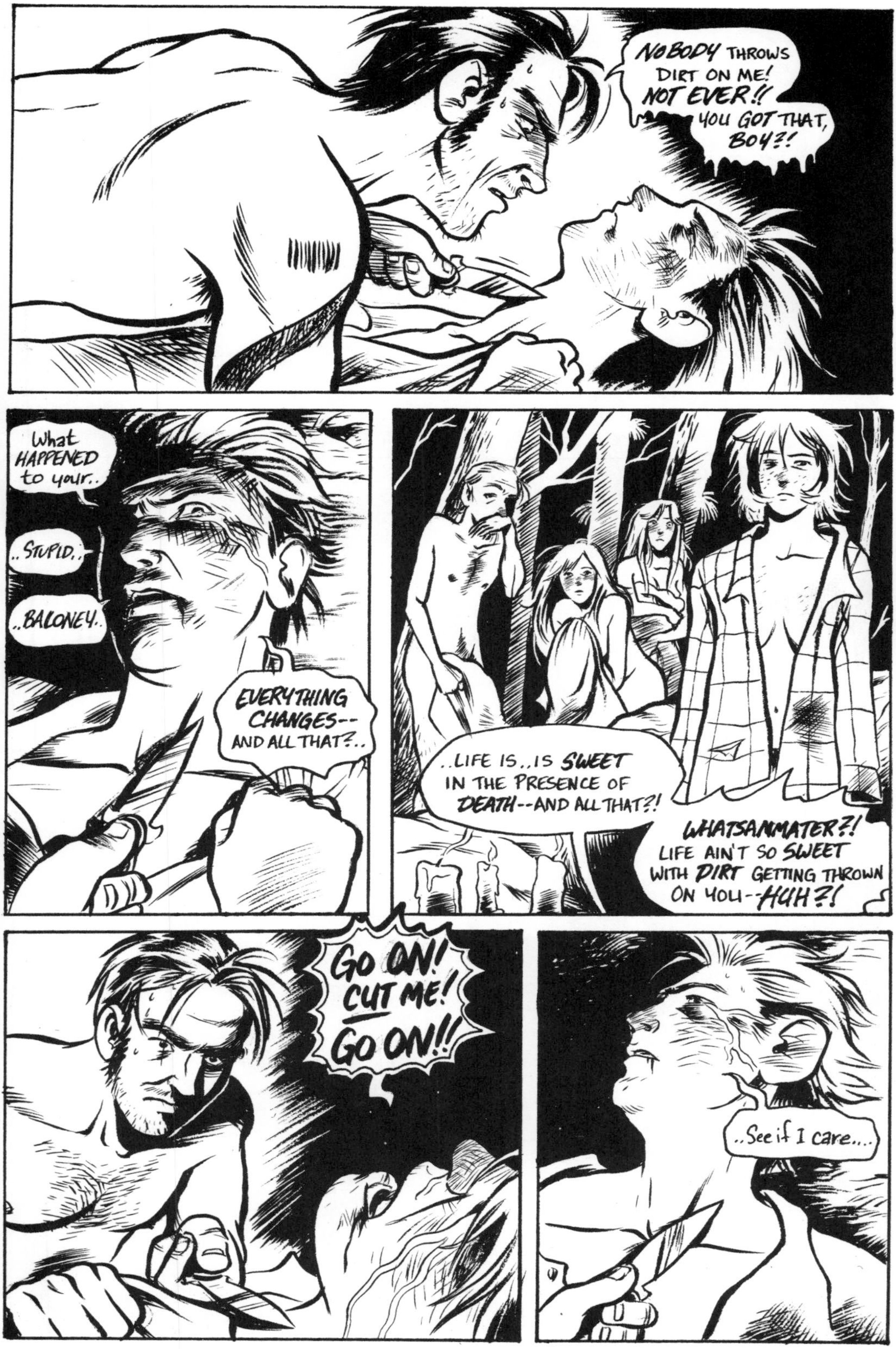
NOBODY THROWS DIRT ON ME! NOT EVER!! YOU GOT THAT, BOY?!
What HAPPENED to your..
..STUPID..
..BALONEY..
EVERYTHING CHANGES--AND ALL THAT?..
..LIFE IS..IS SWEET IN THE PRESENCE OF DEATH--AND ALL THAT?!
WHATSAMMATER?! LIFE AIN'T SO SWEET WITH DIRT GETTING THROWN ON YOU--HUH?!
GO ON! CUT ME! GO ON!!
..See if I care....

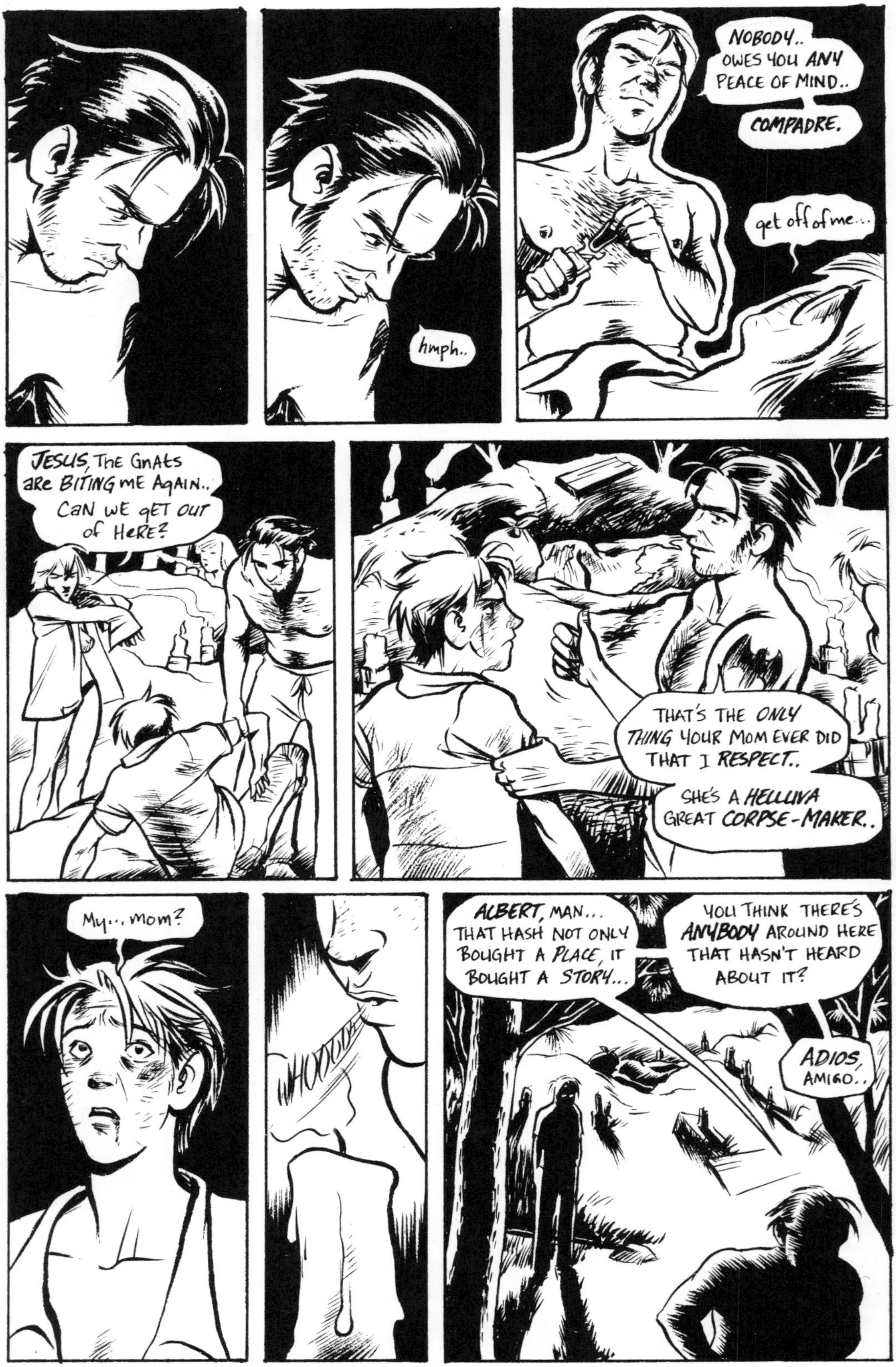
hmph..
NOBODY.. OWES YOU ANY PEACE OF MIND..
COMPADRE.
get off of me...
JESUS, THE GNATS ARE BITING ME AGAIN.. CAN WE GET OUT OF HERE?
THAT'S THE ONLY THING YOUR MOM EVER DID THAT I RESPECT..
SHE'S A HELLUVA GREAT CORPSE-MAKER..
My... mom?
WHOOOOO
ALBERT, MAN... THAT HASH NOT ONLY BOUGHT A PLACE, IT BOUGHT A STORY...
YOU THINK THERE'S ANYBODY AROUND HERE THAT HASN'T HEARD ABOUT IT?
ADIOS, AMIGO..

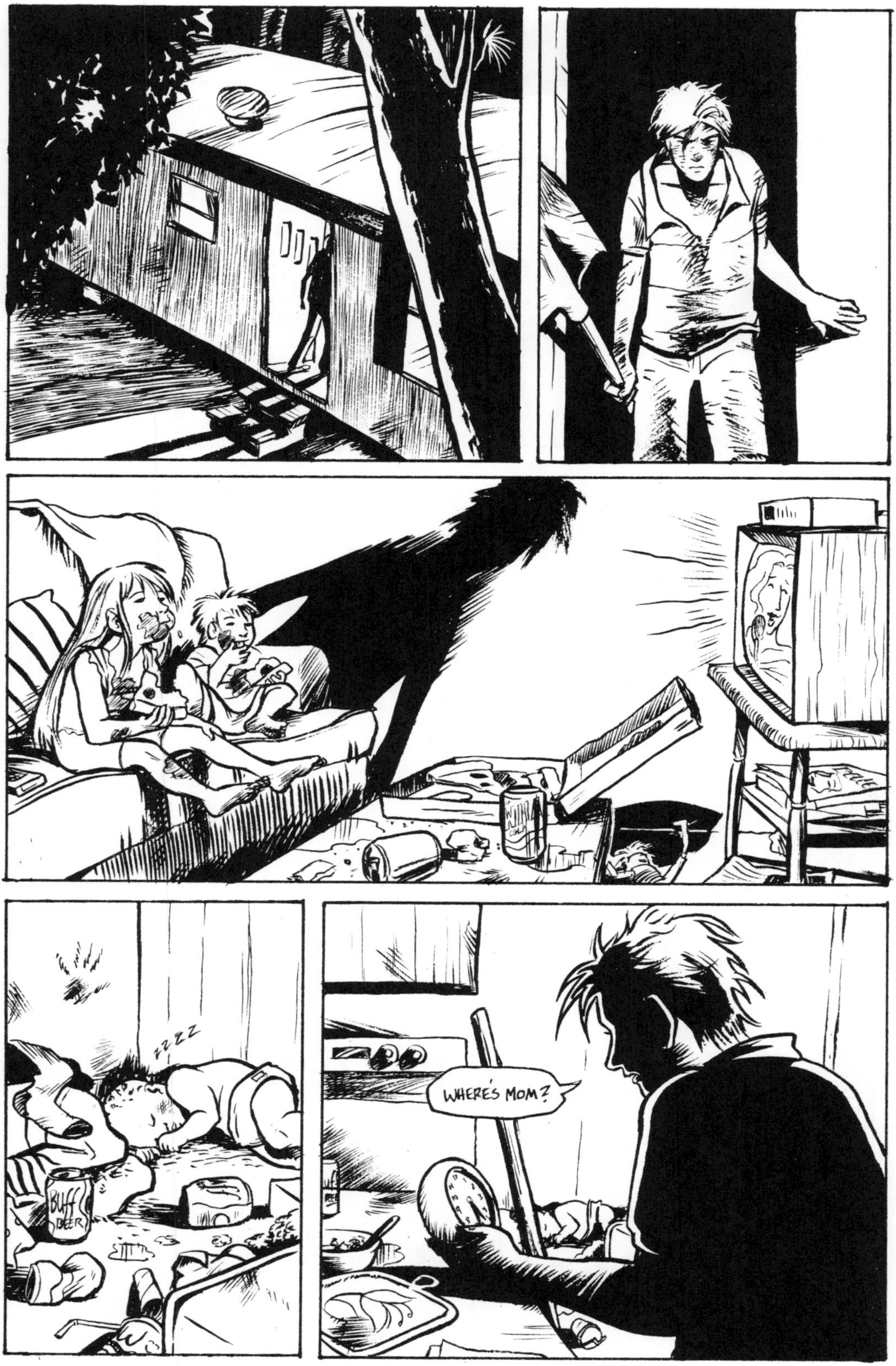
BUFF BEER
WHERE'S MOM?

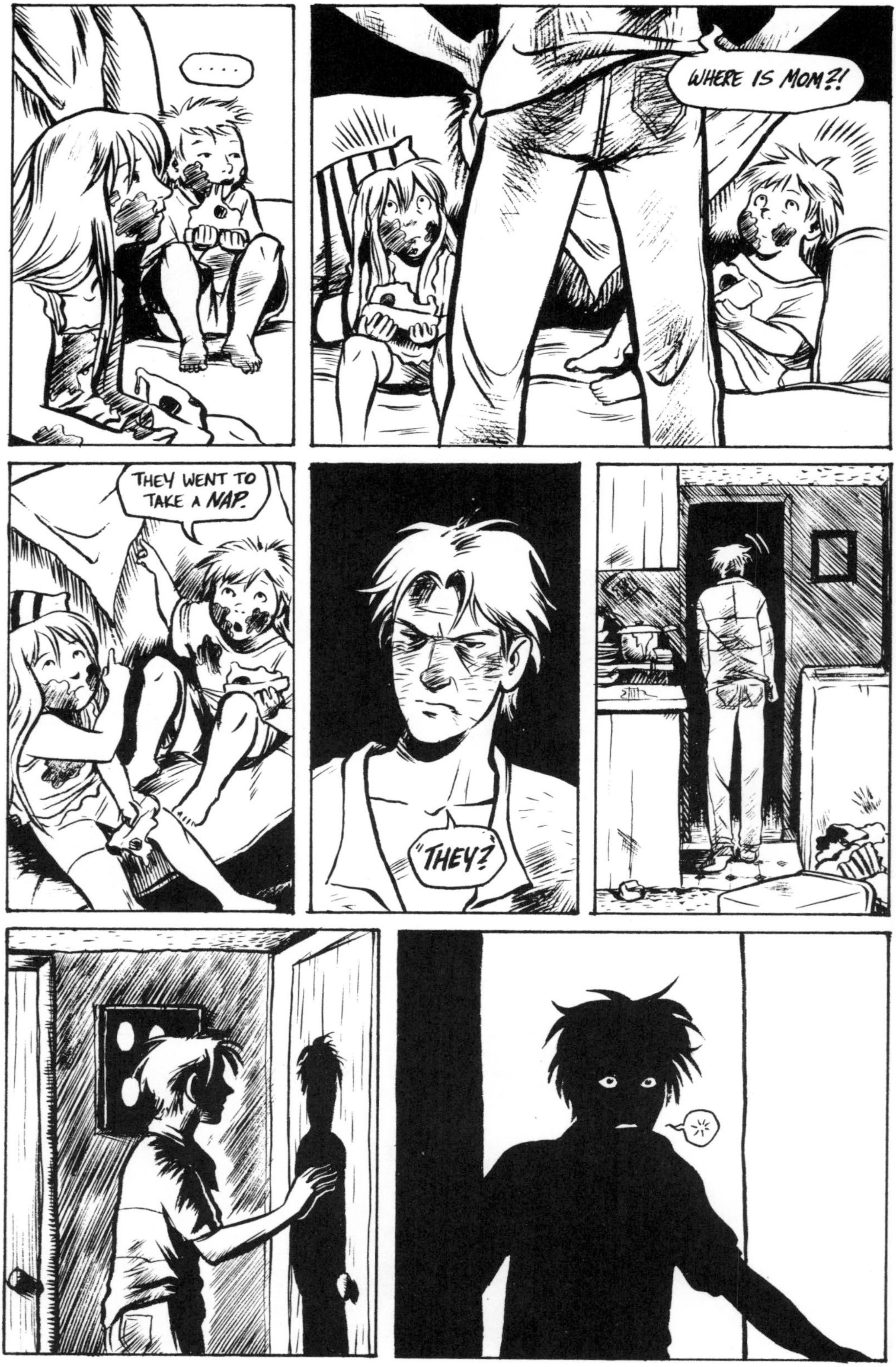
. . . .
WHERE IS MOM?!
THEY WENT TO TAKE A NAP.
"THEY?"

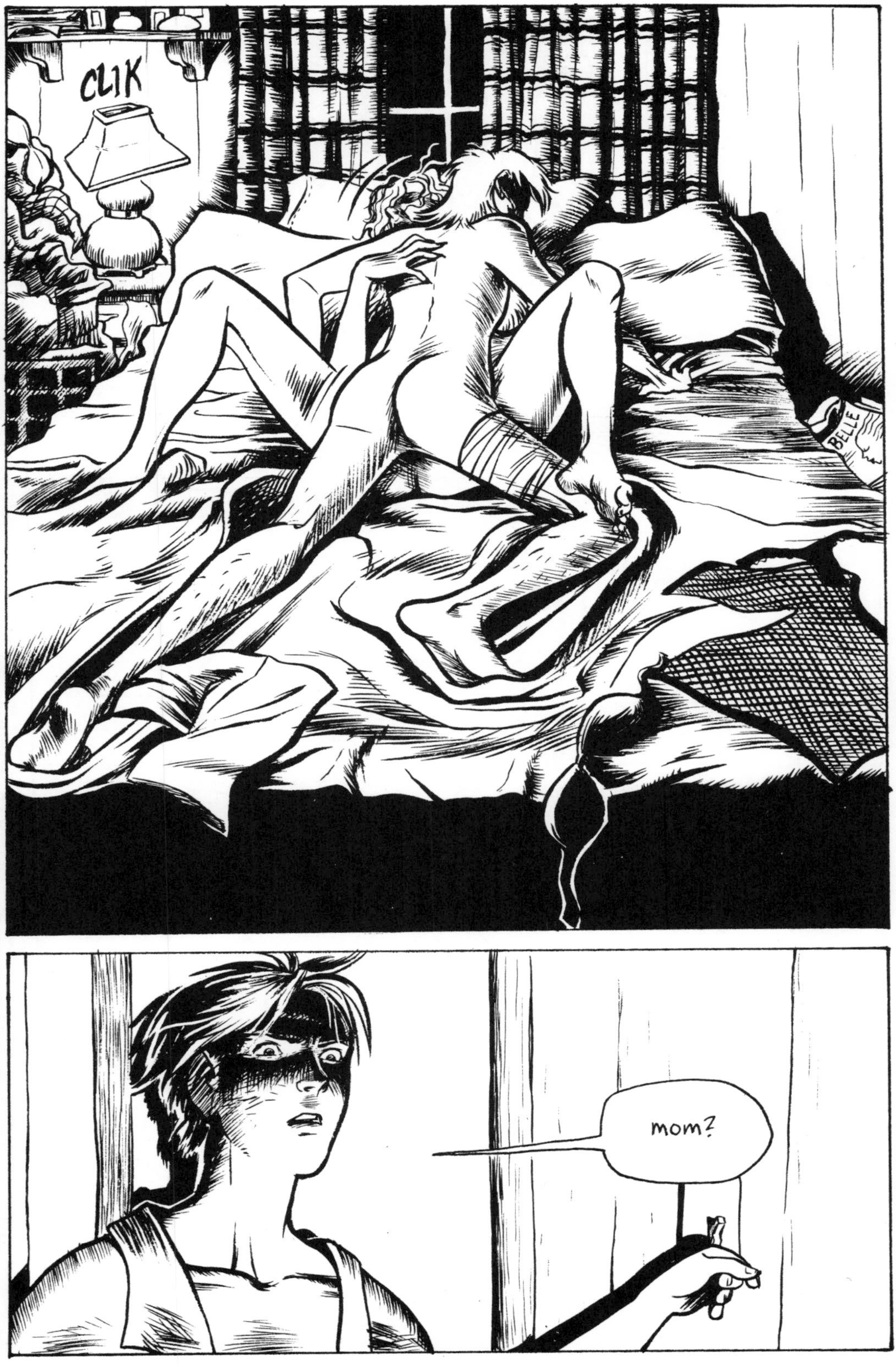
CLIK
BELLE
mom?

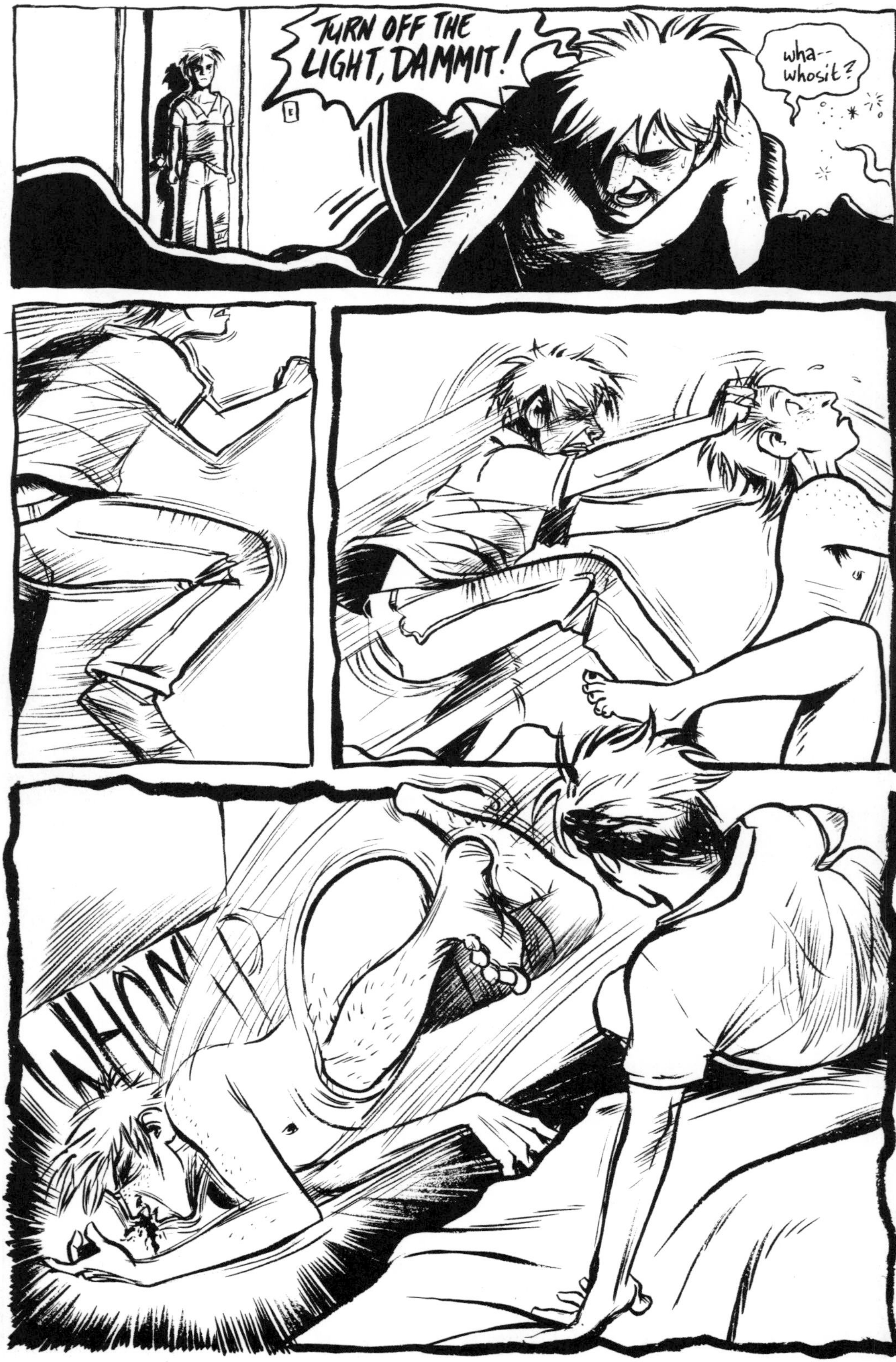
TURN OFF THE LIGHT, DAMMIT!
wha-- whosit?
WHOMP

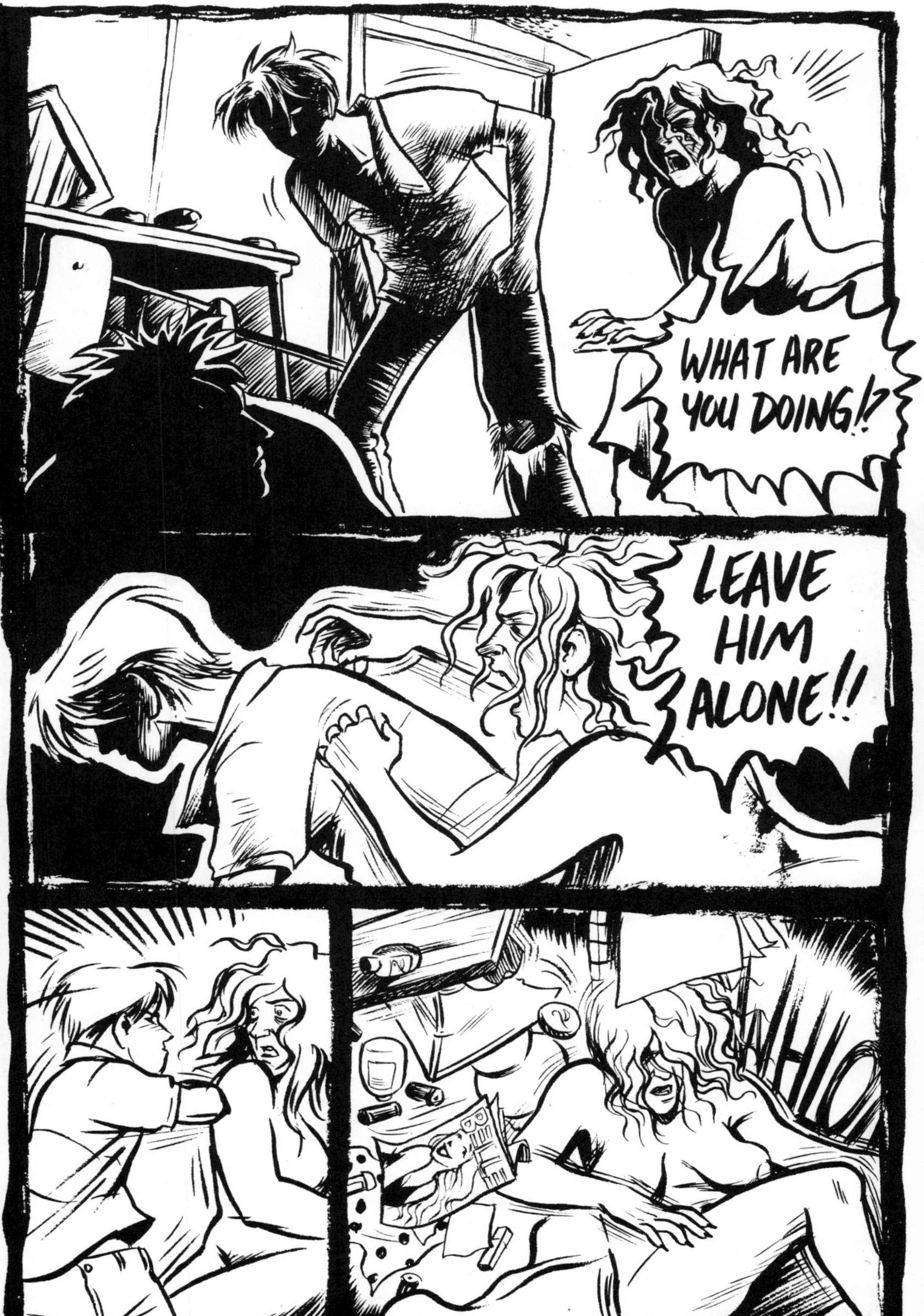
WHAT ARE YOU DOING!?
LEAVE HIM ALONE!!

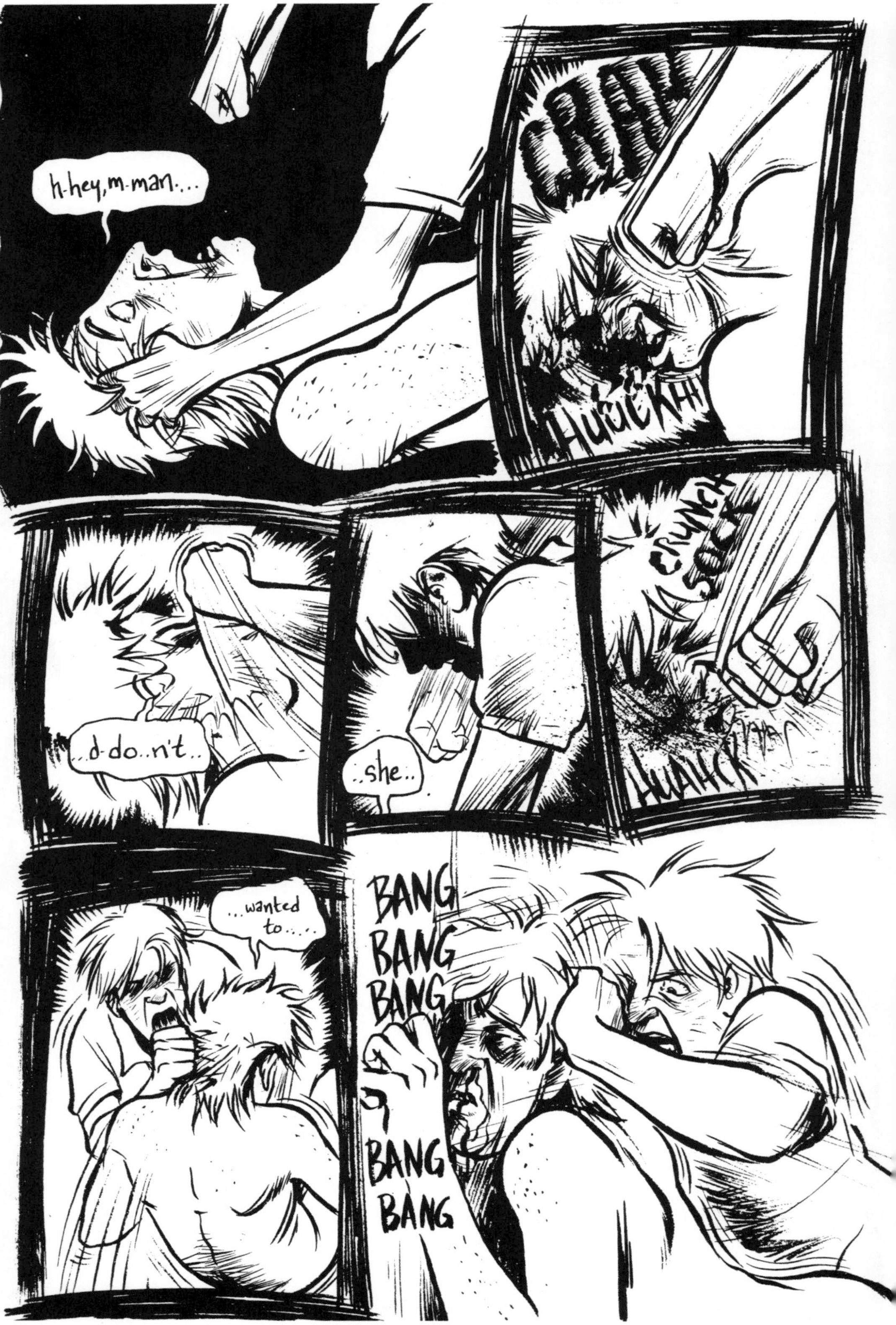
h-hey, m-man....
CRUNCH
SOCK
...d-do...n't...
...she...
...wanted to.....
BANG
BANG
BANG
BANG
BANG

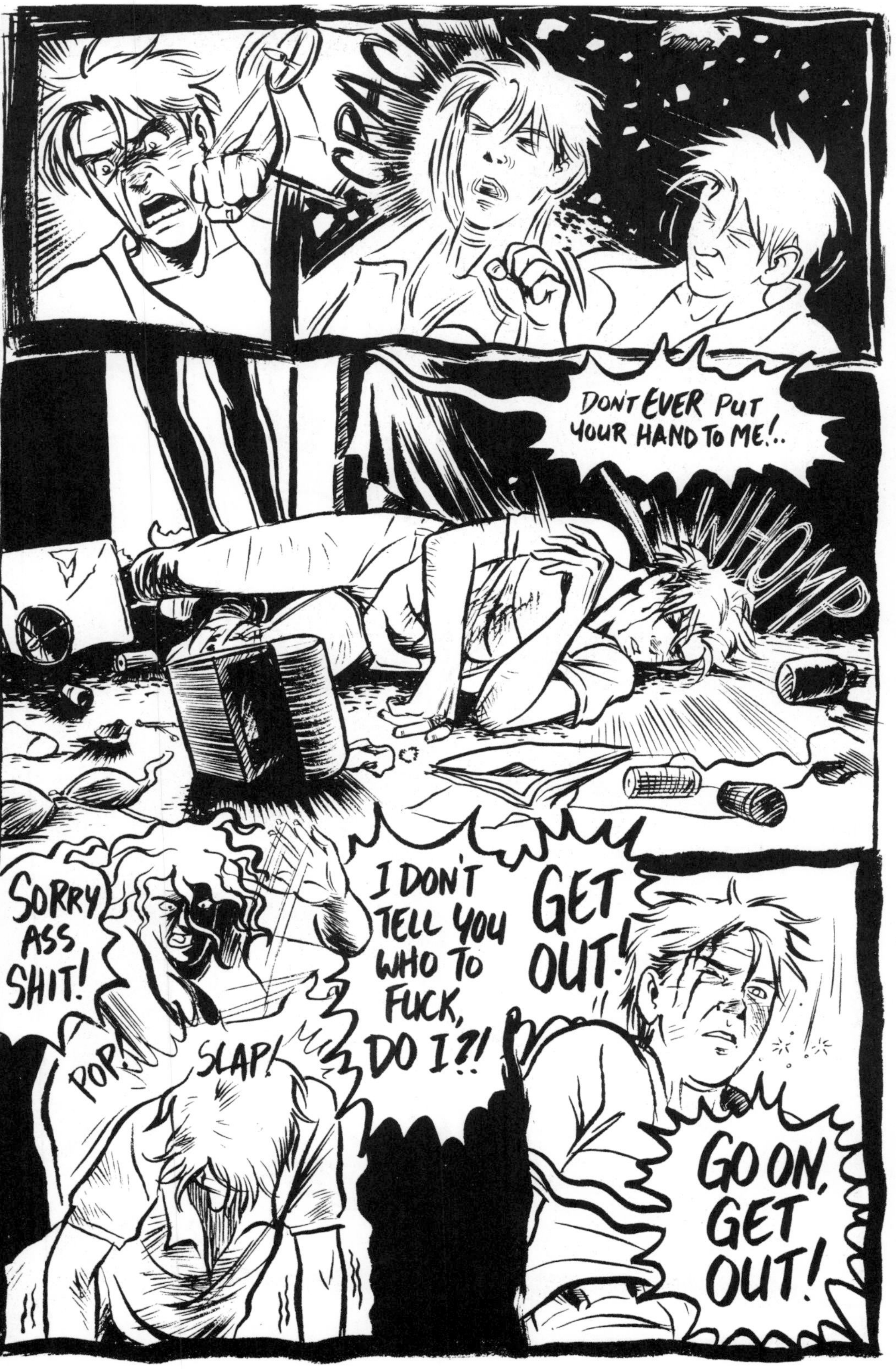

DON'T EVER PUT YOUR HAND TO ME!..
WHOMP
SORRY ASS SHIT!
I DON'T TELL YOU WHO TO FUCK, DO I?!
GET OUT!
POP!
SLAP!
GO ON, GET OUT!

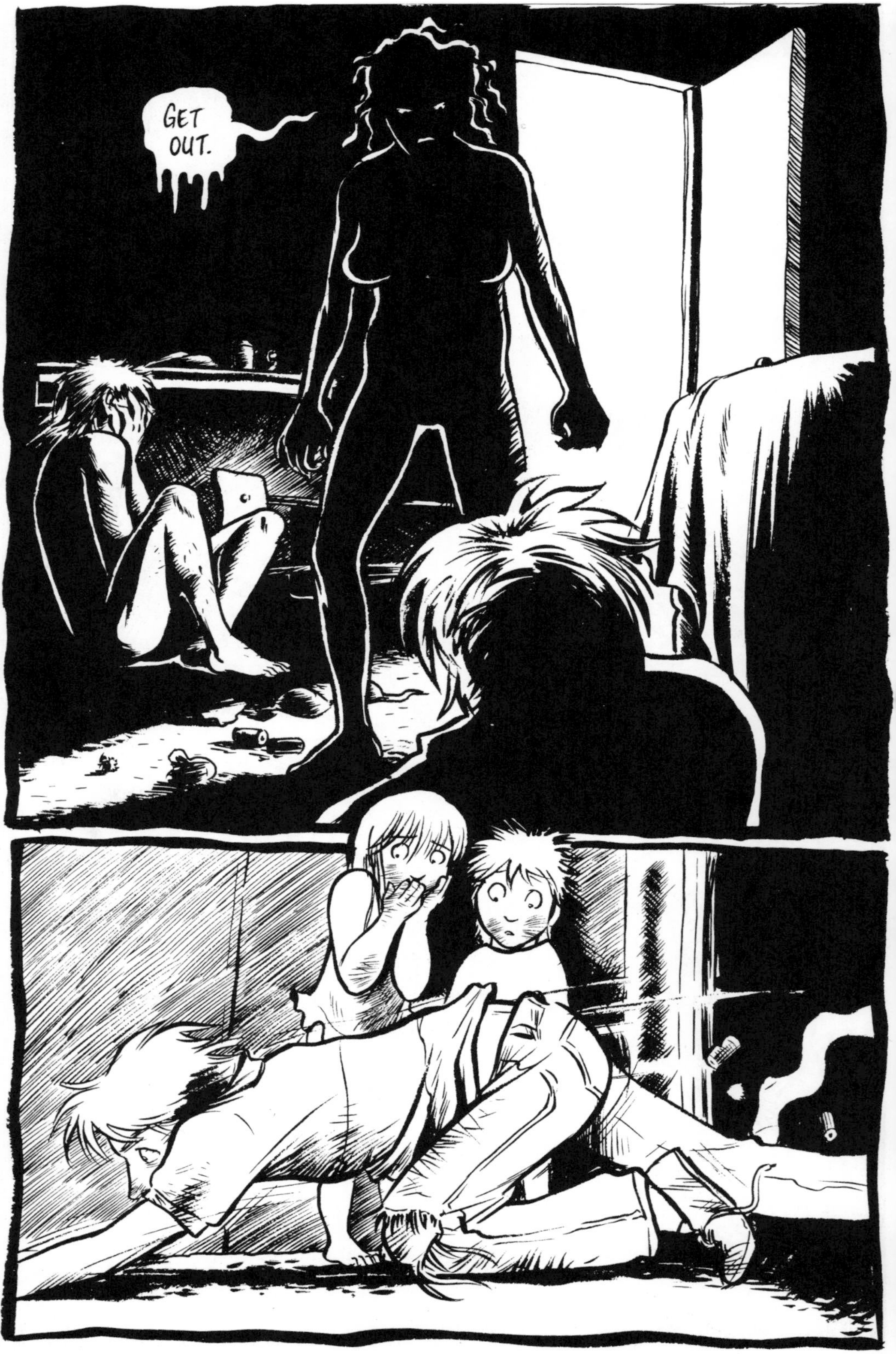
GET OUT.

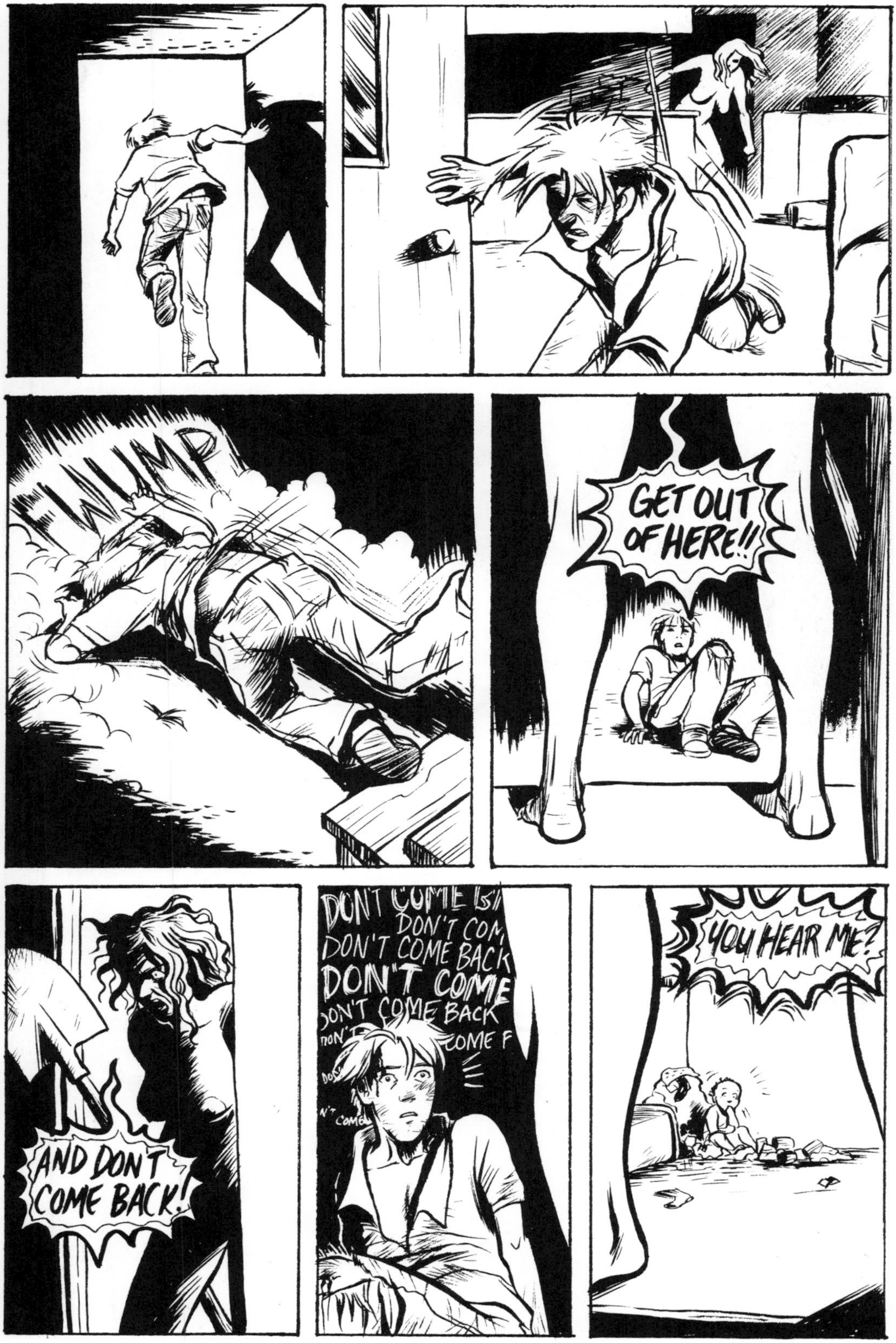
FWUMP
GET OUT OF HERE!!
AND DON'T COME BACK!
DON'T COM
DON'T COME BACK
DON'T COME
YOU HEAR ME?

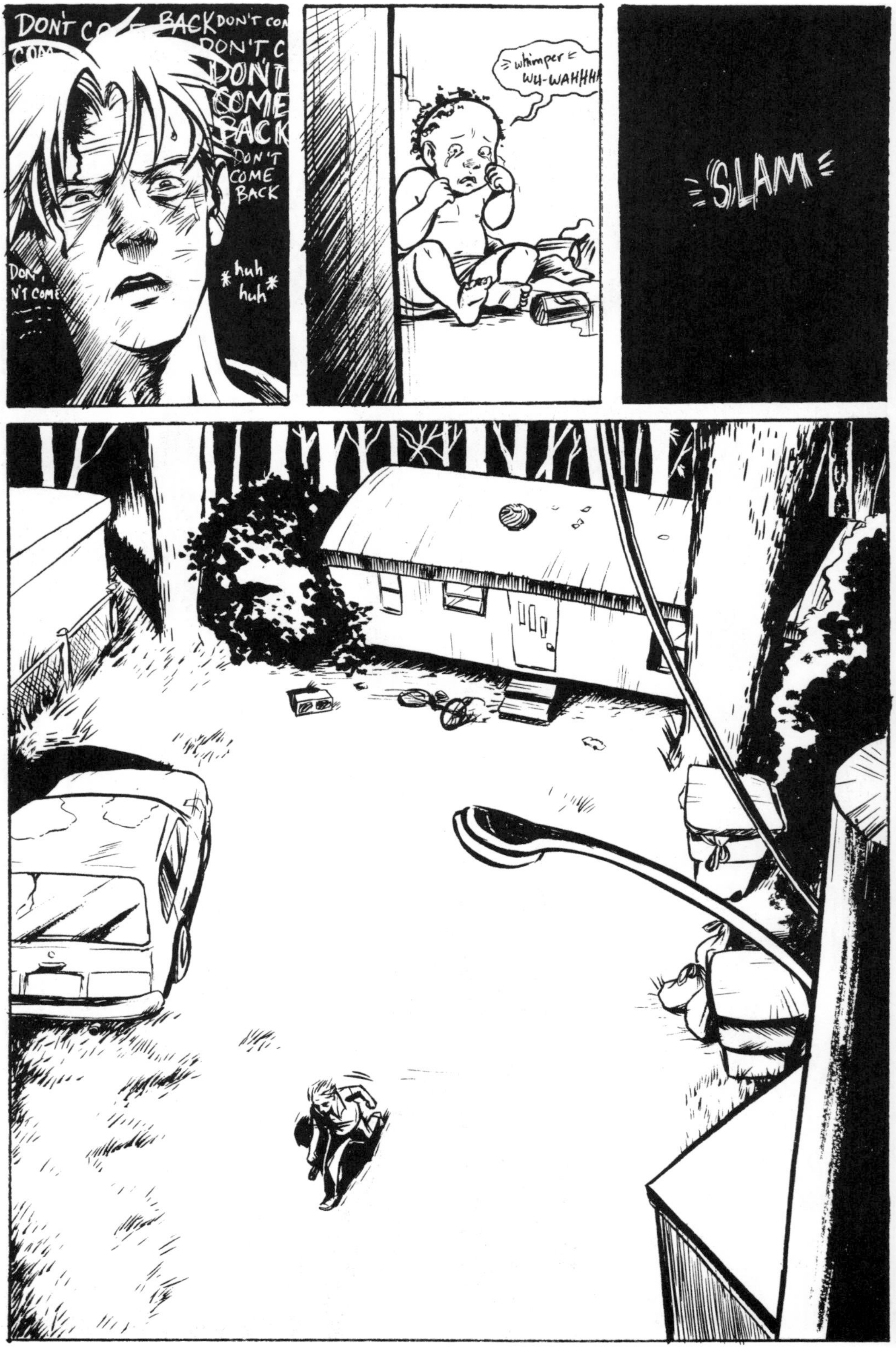
DON'T CO BACK DON'T CO
DON'T C
DON'T COME BACK
DON'T COME BACK
N'T COME
huh huh
whimper
WU-WAHHH
SLAM

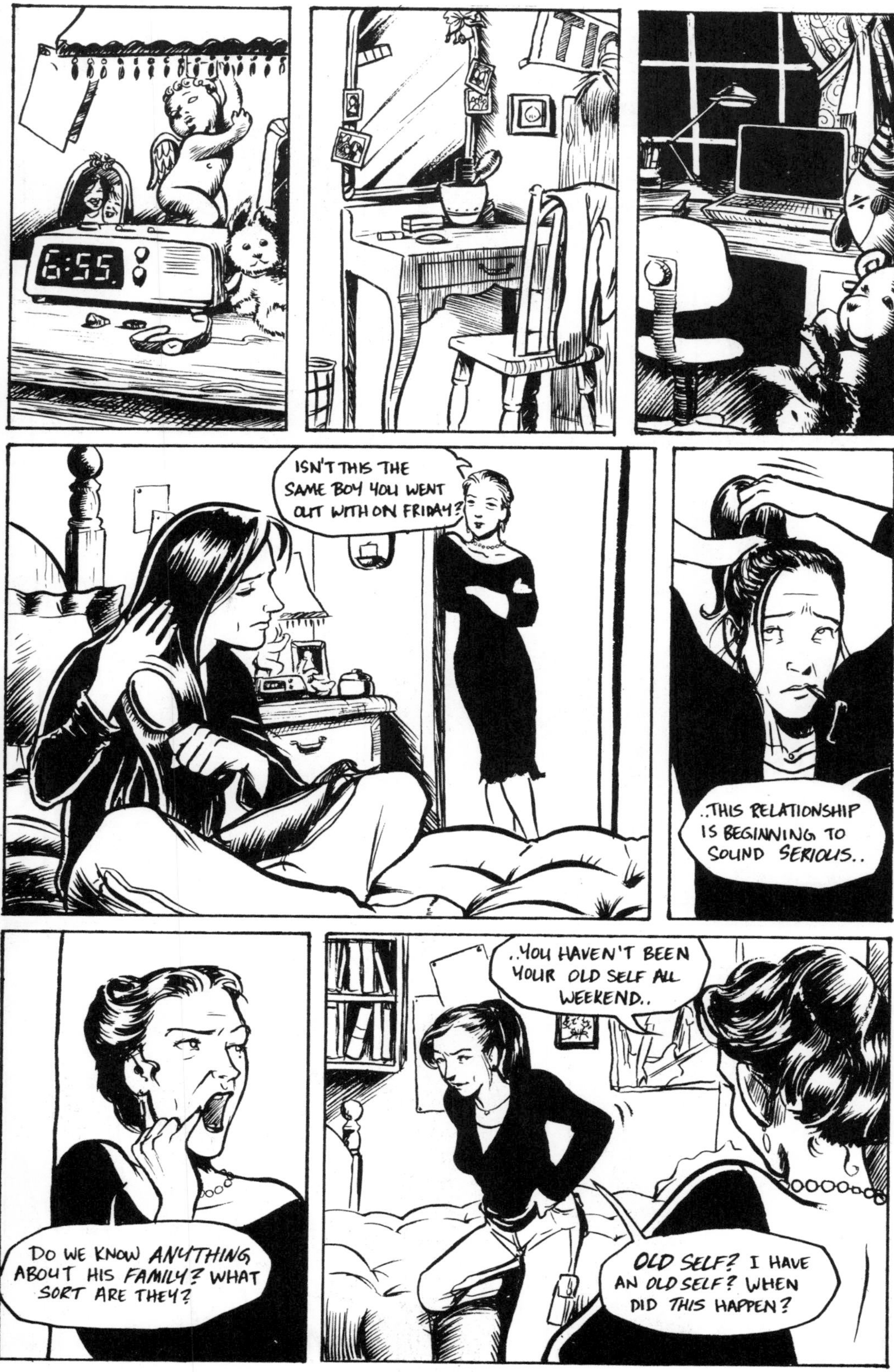

ISN'T THIS THE SAME BOY YOU WENT OUT WITH ON FRIDAY?
..THIS RELATIONSHIP IS BEGINNING TO SOUND SERIOUS..
DO WE KNOW *ANYTHING* ABOUT HIS *FAMILY*? WHAT SORT ARE THEY?
..YOU HAVEN'T BEEN YOUR OLD SELF ALL WEEKEND..
OLD SELF? I HAVE AN *OLD SELF*? WHEN DID *THIS* HAPPEN?

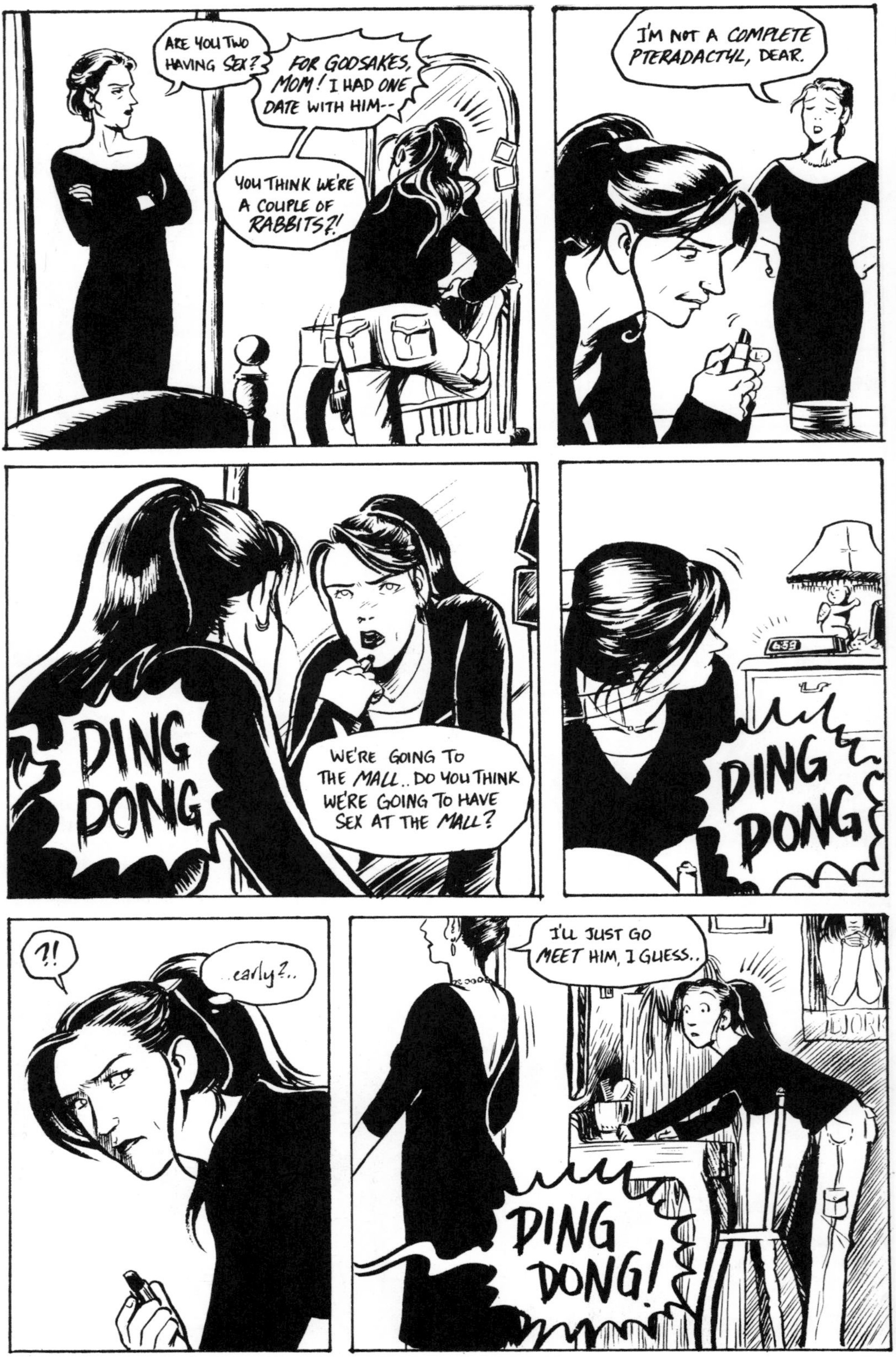
ARE YOU TWO HAVING SEX?
FOR GODSAKES, MOM! I HAD ONE DATE WITH HIM--
YOU THINK WE'RE A COUPLE OF RABBITS?!
I'M NOT A COMPLETE PTERADACTYL, DEAR.
DING DONG
WE'RE GOING TO THE MALL.. DO YOU THINK WE'RE GOING TO HAVE SEX AT THE MALL?
DING DONG
?!
..early?..
I'LL JUST GO MEET HIM, I GUESS..
BJORK
DING DONG!

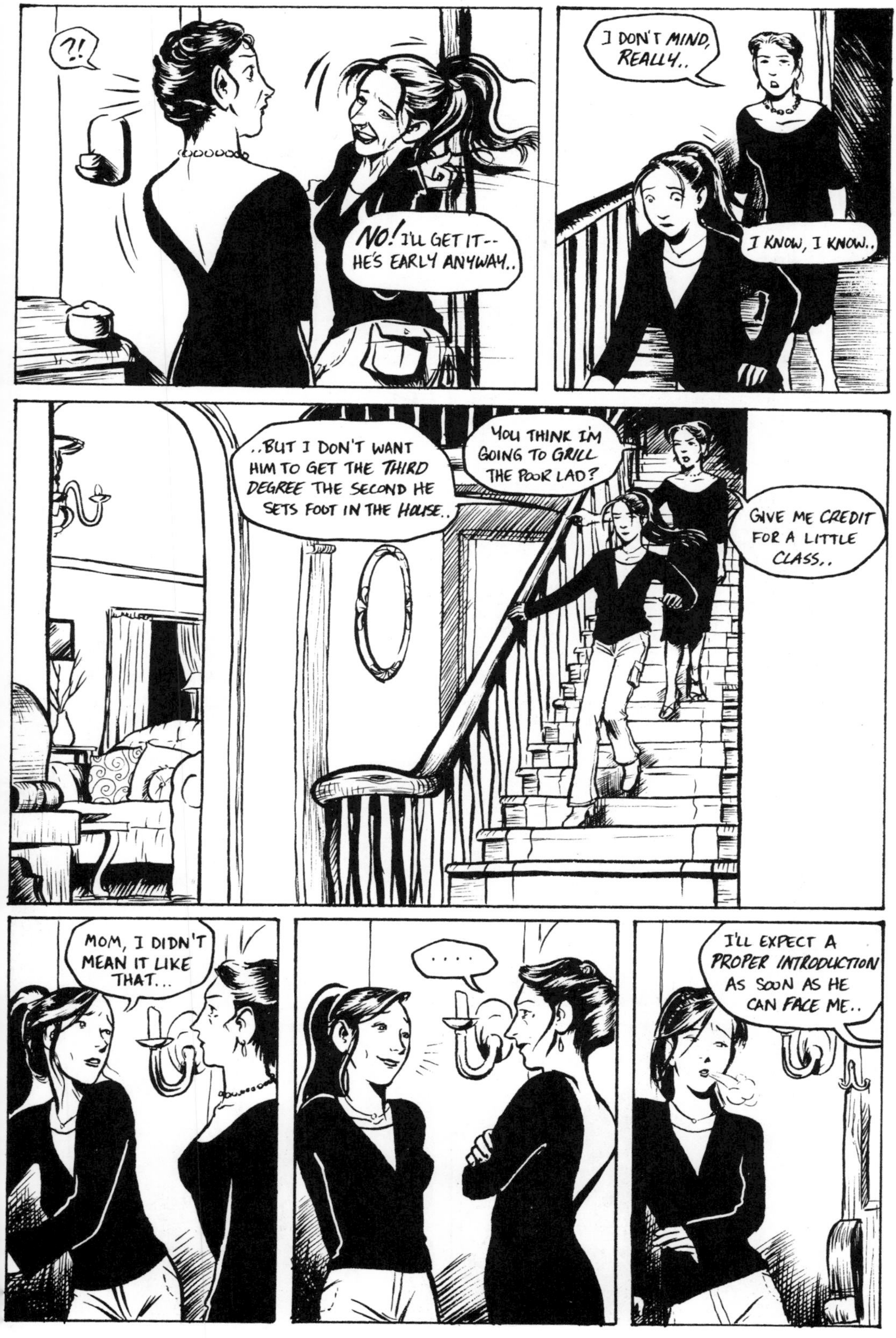
?!
NO! I'LL GET IT-- HE'S EARLY ANYWAY..
I DON'T MIND, REALLY..
I KNOW, I KNOW..
..BUT I DON'T WANT HIM TO GET THE THIRD DEGREE THE SECOND HE SETS FOOT IN THE HOUSE..
YOU THINK I'M GOING TO GRILL THE POOR LAD?
GIVE ME CREDIT FOR A LITTLE CLASS..
MOM, I DIDN'T MEAN IT LIKE THAT...
....
I'LL EXPECT A PROPER INTRODUCTION AS SOON AS HE CAN FACE ME..

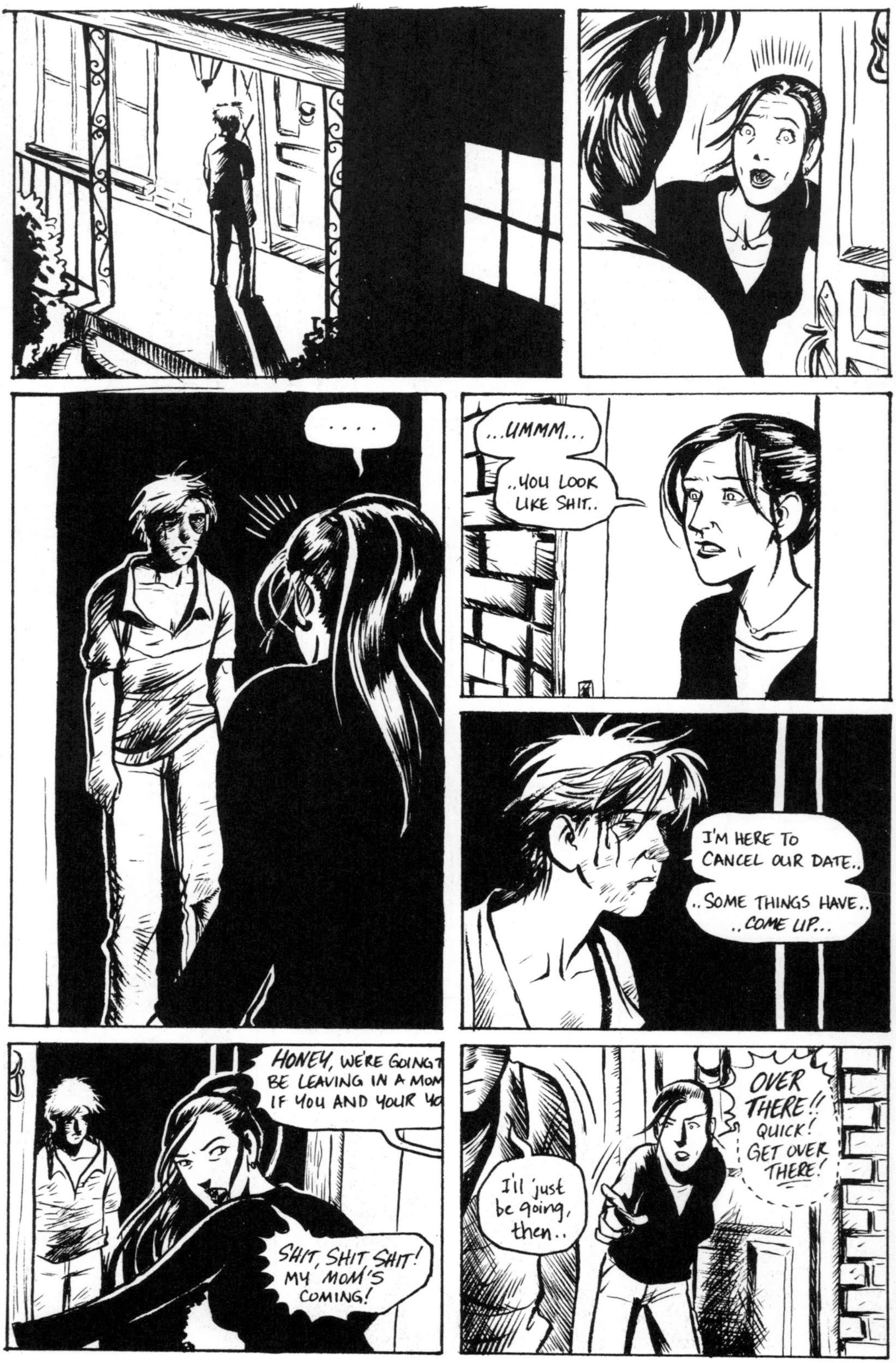
....
...UMMM...
..YOU LOOK LIKE SHIT..
I'M HERE TO CANCEL OUR DATE..
..SOME THINGS HAVE.. ..COME UP...
HONEY, WE'RE GOING T
BE LEAVING IN A MOM
IF YOU AND YOUR YO
SHIT, SHIT SHIT! MY MOM'S COMING!
I'll just be going, then..
OVER THERE!!
QUICK! GET OVER THERE!

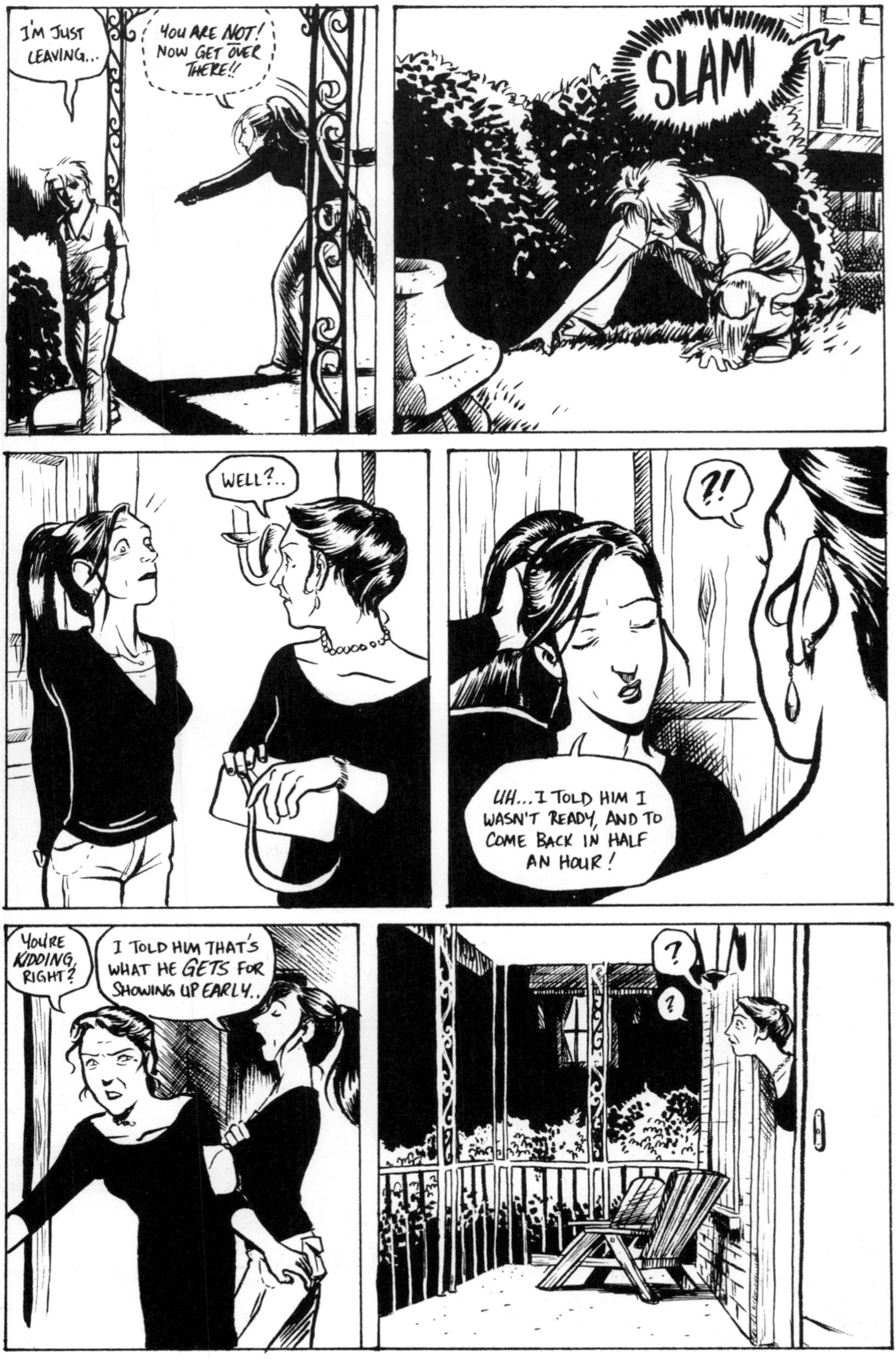
I'M JUST LEAVING...
YOU ARE NOT! NOW GET OVER THERE!!
SLAM
WELL?..
?!
UH...I TOLD HIM I WASN'T READY, AND TO COME BACK IN HALF AN HOUR!
YOU'RE KIDDING, RIGHT?
I TOLD HIM THAT'S WHAT HE GETS FOR SHOWING UP EARLY..
?
?

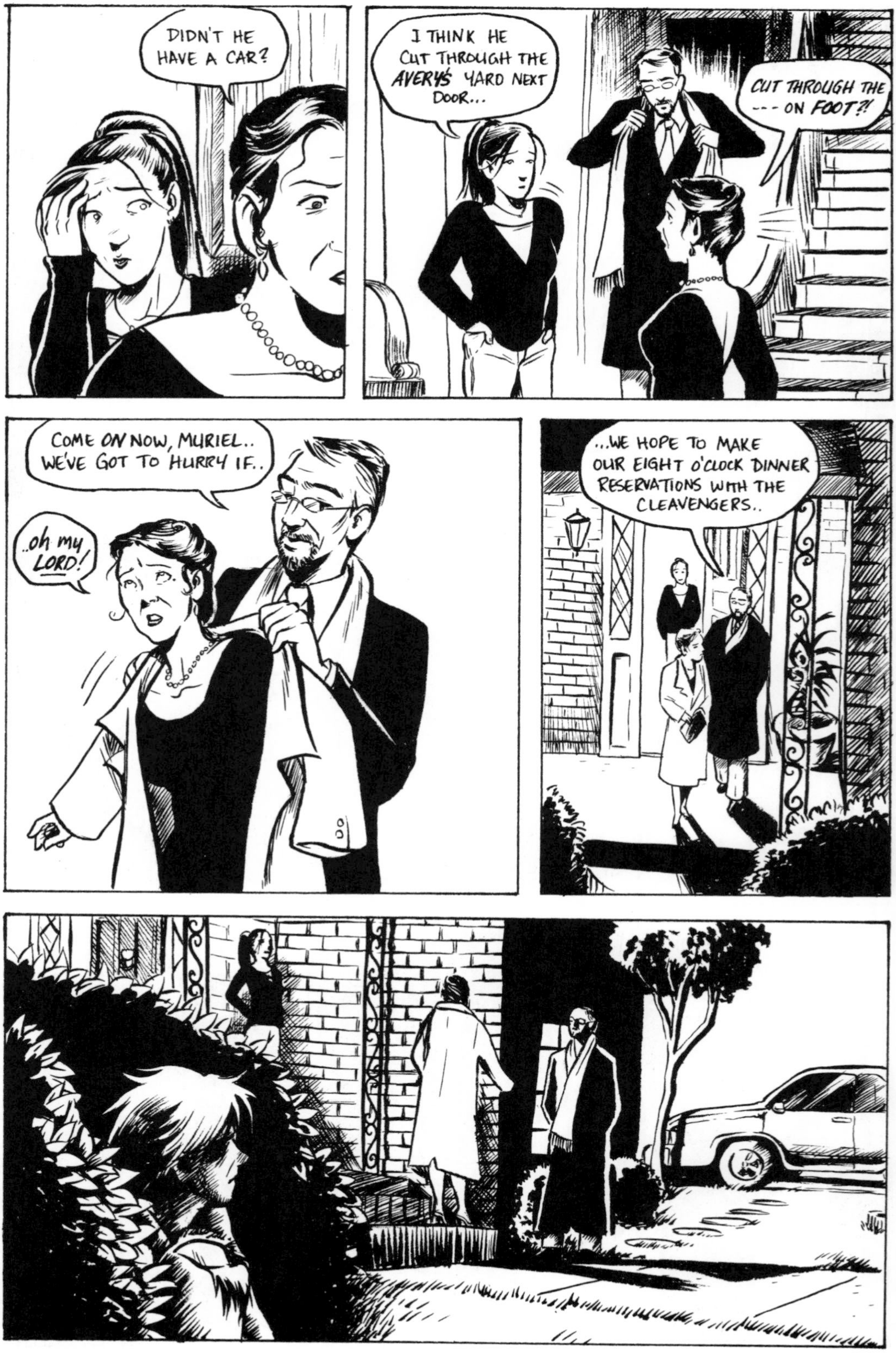
DIDN'T HE HAVE A CAR?
I THINK HE CUT THROUGH THE AVERYS' YARD NEXT DOOR...
CUT THROUGH THE --- ON FOOT?!
COME ON NOW, MURIEL.. WE'VE GOT TO HURRY IF..
..oh my LORD!
...WE HOPE TO MAKE OUR EIGHT O'CLOCK DINNER RESERVATIONS WITH THE CLEAVENGERS..

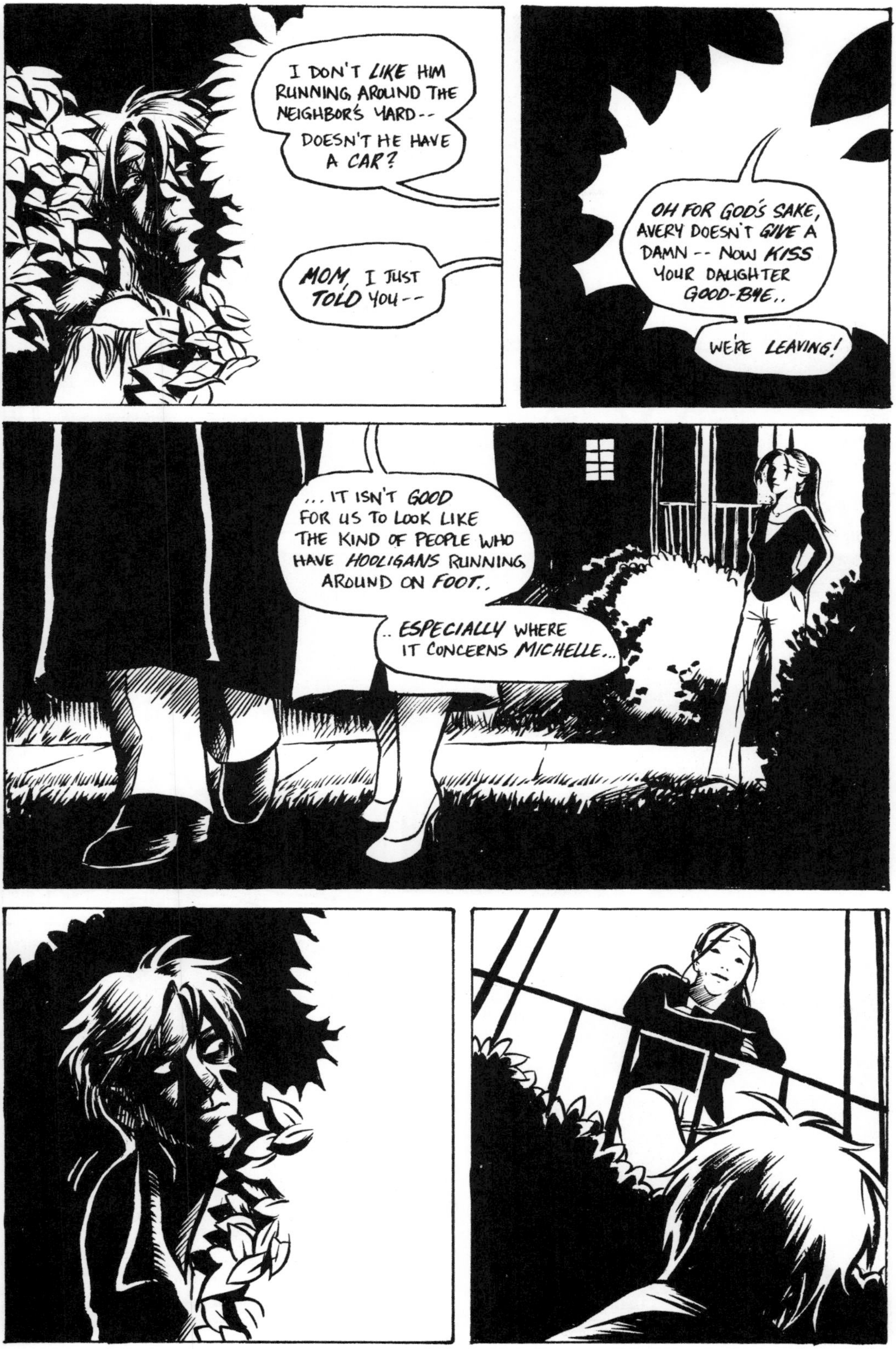
I DON'T LIKE HIM RUNNING AROUND THE NEIGHBOR'S YARD--
DOESN'T HE HAVE A CAR?
MOM, I JUST TOLD YOU--
OH FOR GOD'S SAKE, AVERY DOESN'T GIVE A DAMN -- NOW KISS YOUR DAUGHTER GOOD-BYE..
WE'RE LEAVING!
...IT ISN'T GOOD FOR US TO LOOK LIKE THE KIND OF PEOPLE WHO HAVE HOOLIGANS RUNNING AROUND ON FOOT..
..ESPECIALLY WHERE IT CONCERNS MICHELLE...

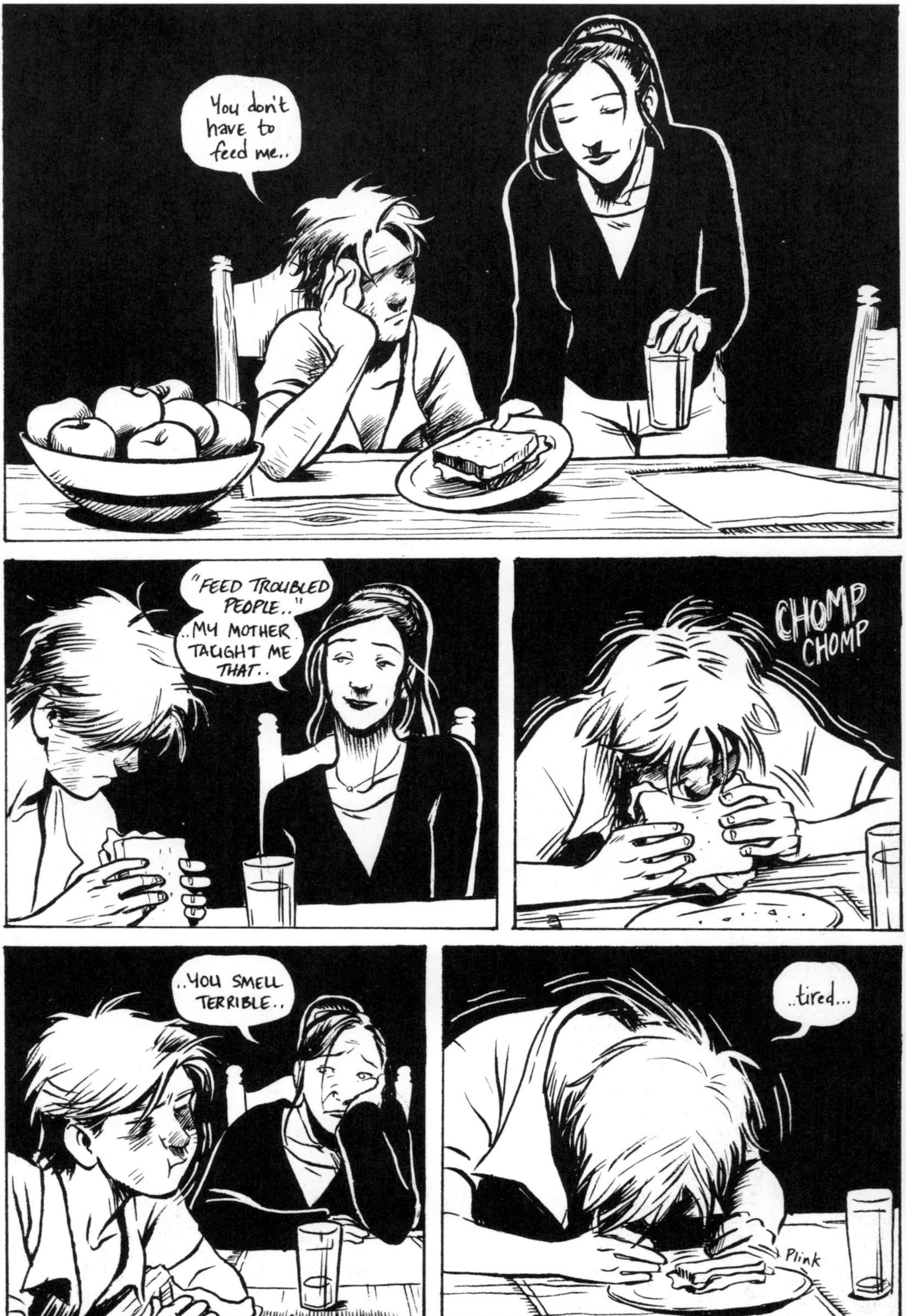
You don't have to feed me..
"FEED TROUBLED PEOPLE.." ..MY MOTHER TAUGHT ME THAT..
CHOMP CHOMP
..YOU SMELL TERRIBLE..
..tired...
Plink

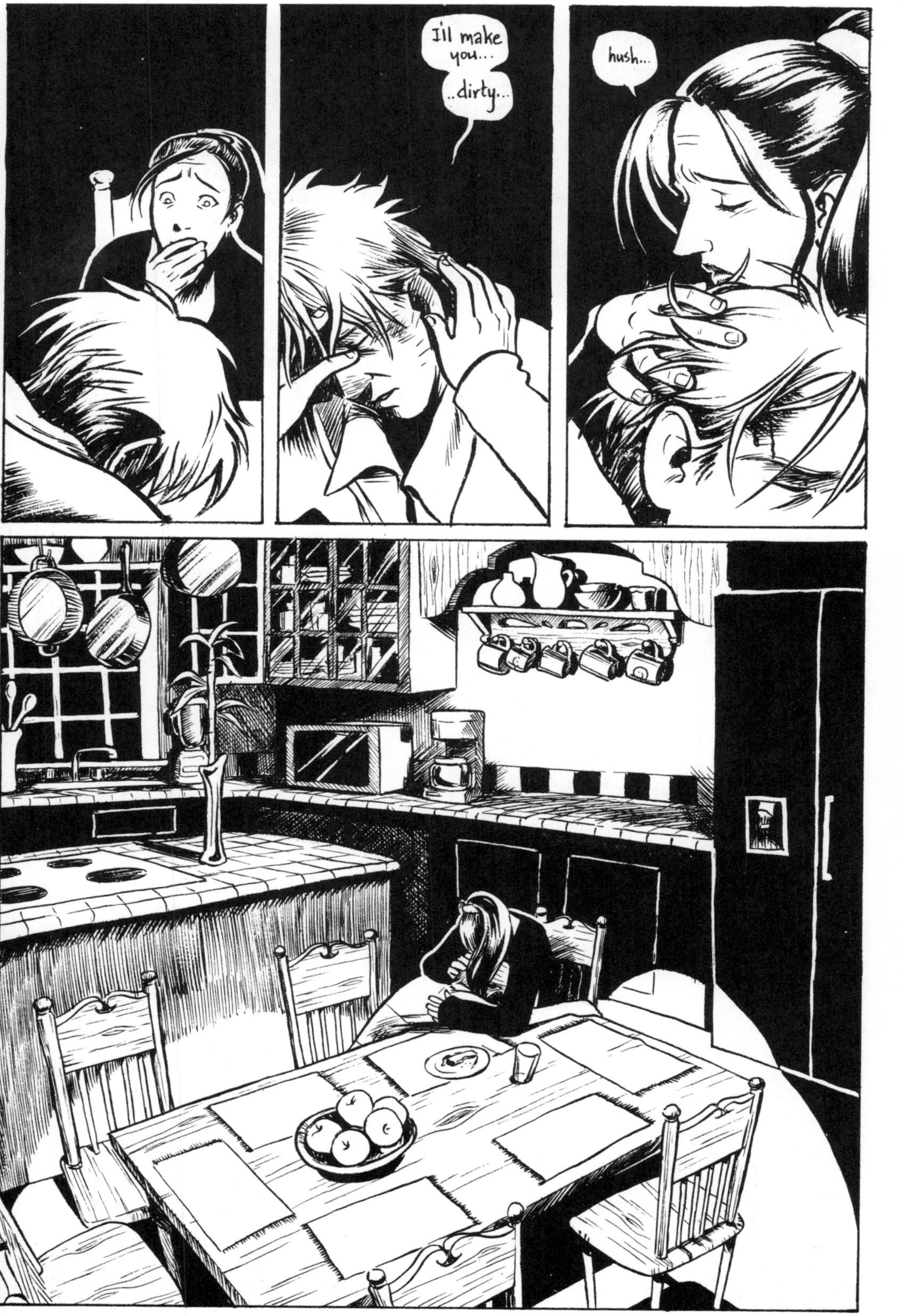
I'll make you...
..dirty...
hush...

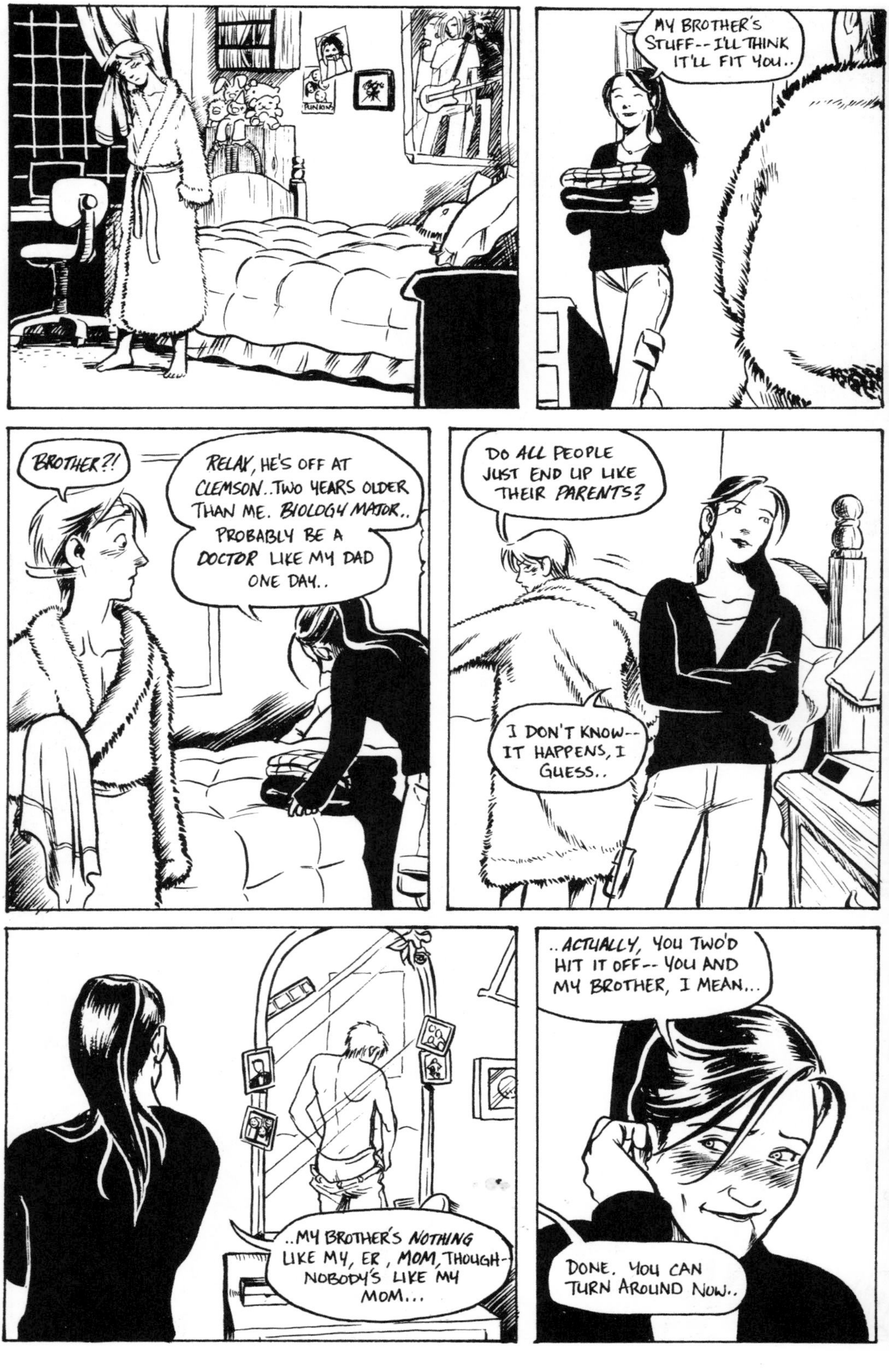
MY BROTHER'S STUFF-- I'LL THINK IT'LL FIT YOU..
BROTHER?!
RELAX, HE'S OFF AT CLEMSON..TWO YEARS OLDER THAN ME. BIOLOGY MAJOR.. PROBABLY BE A DOCTOR LIKE MY DAD ONE DAY..
DO ALL PEOPLE JUST END UP LIKE THEIR PARENTS?
I DON'T KNOW-- IT HAPPENS, I GUESS..
..MY BROTHER'S NOTHING LIKE MY, ER, MOM, THOUGH-- NOBODY'S LIKE MY MOM...
..ACTUALLY, YOU TWO'D HIT IT OFF-- YOU AND MY BROTHER, I MEAN...
DONE. YOU CAN TURN AROUND NOW..

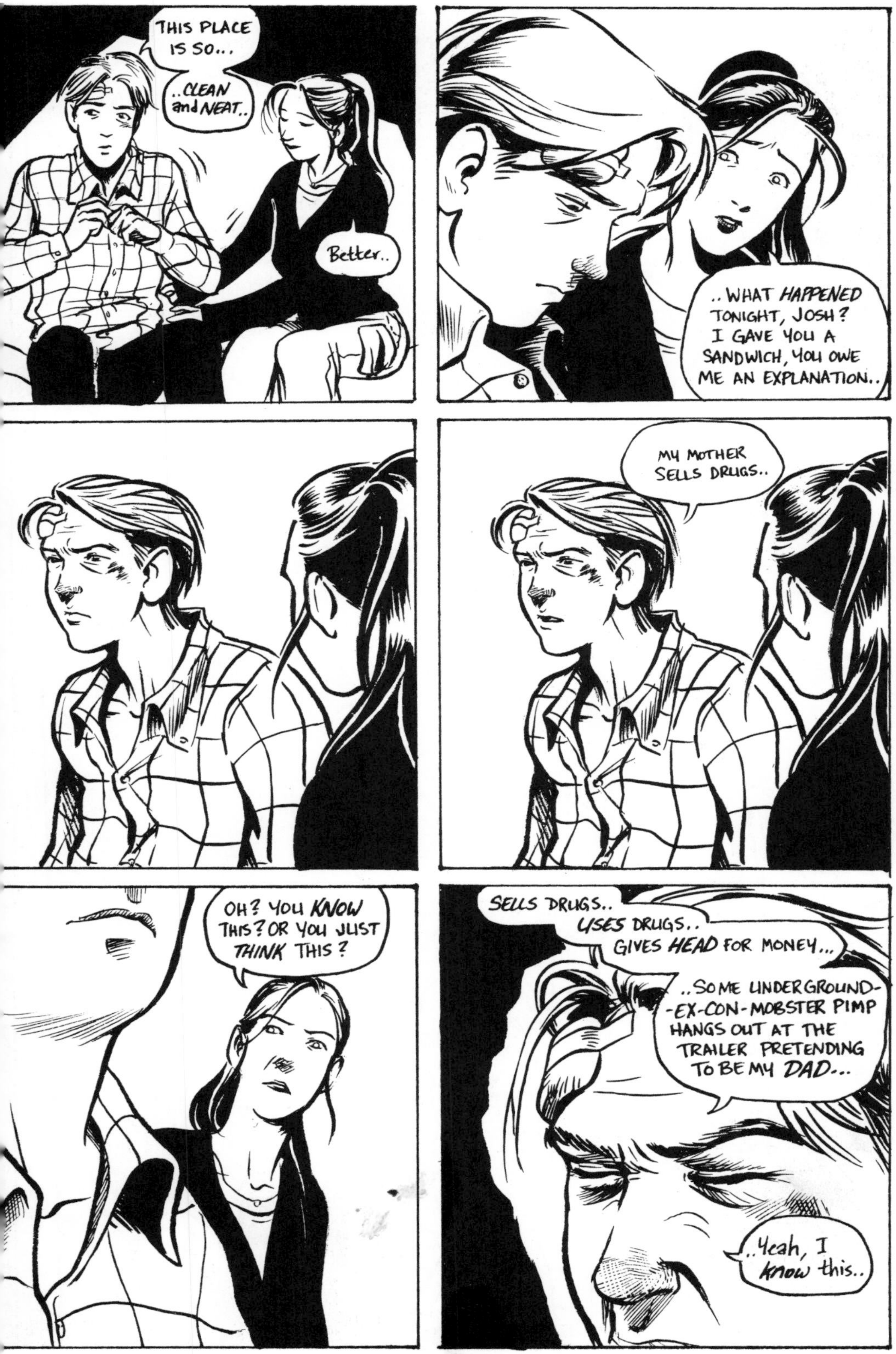
THIS PLACE IS SO...
..CLEAN and NEAT..
Better..
..WHAT HAPPENED TONIGHT, JOSH? I GAVE YOU A SANDWICH, YOU OWE ME AN EXPLANATION..
MY MOTHER SELLS DRUGS..
OH? YOU KNOW THIS? OR YOU JUST THINK THIS?
SELLS DRUGS..
USES DRUGS..
GIVES HEAD FOR MONEY...
..SOME UNDERGROUND-EX-CON-MOBSTER PIMP HANGS OUT AT THE TRAILER PRETENDING TO BE MY DAD...
..Yeah, I know this..

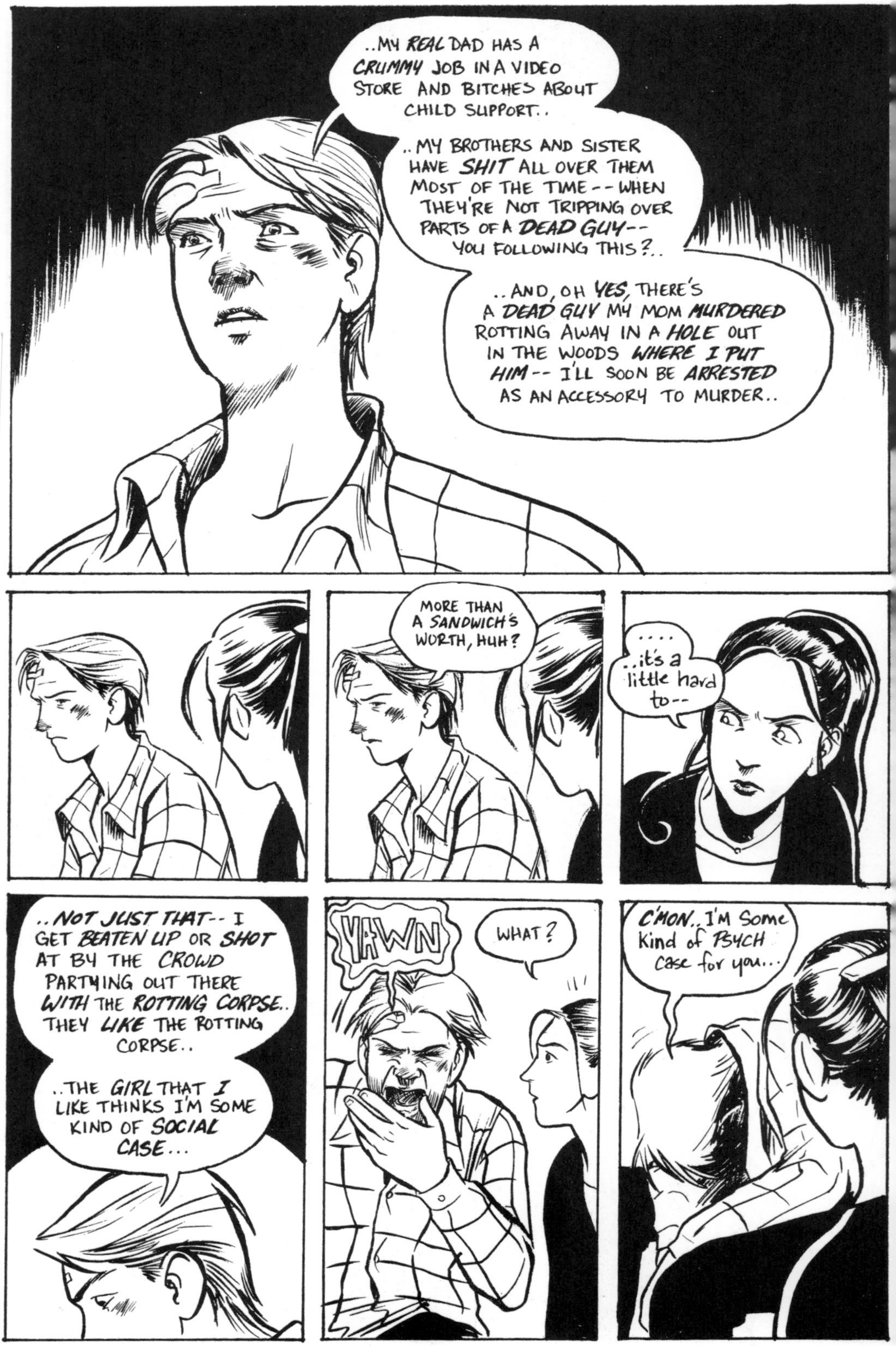
..MY REAL DAD HAS A CRUMMY JOB IN A VIDEO STORE AND BITCHES ABOUT CHILD SUPPORT..
..MY BROTHERS AND SISTER HAVE SHIT ALL OVER THEM MOST OF THE TIME -- WHEN THEY'RE NOT TRIPPING OVER PARTS OF A DEAD GUY -- YOU FOLLOWING THIS?..
..AND, OH YES, THERE'S A DEAD GUY MY MOM MURDERED ROTTING AWAY IN A HOLE OUT IN THE WOODS WHERE I PUT HIM -- I'LL SOON BE ARRESTED AS AN ACCESSORY TO MURDER..
MORE THAN A SANDWICH'S WORTH, HUH?
....
..it's a little hard to--
..NOT JUST THAT -- I GET BEATEN UP OR SHOT AT BY THE CROWD PARTYING OUT THERE WITH THE ROTTING CORPSE.. THEY LIKE THE ROTTING CORPSE..
..THE GIRL THAT I LIKE THINKS I'M SOME KIND OF SOCIAL CASE...
YAWN
WHAT?
C'MON.. I'M Some kind of PSYCH case for you...

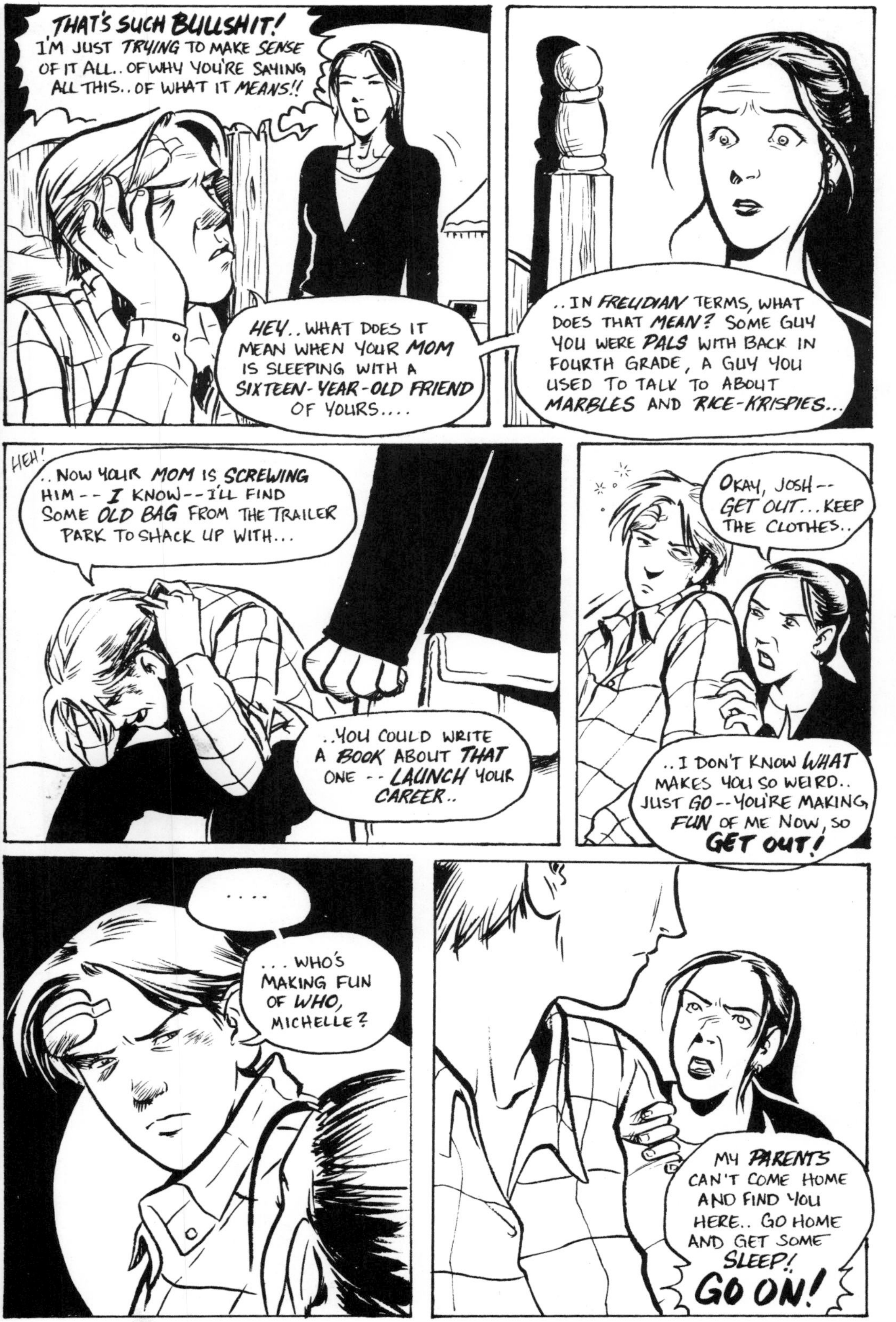
THAT'S SUCH BULLSHIT! I'M JUST TRYING TO MAKE SENSE OF IT ALL.. OF WHY YOU'RE SAYING ALL THIS.. OF WHAT IT MEANS!!
HEY.. WHAT DOES IT MEAN WHEN YOUR MOM IS SLEEPING WITH A SIXTEEN-YEAR-OLD FRIEND OF YOURS....
..IN FREUDIAN TERMS, WHAT DOES THAT MEAN? SOME GUY YOU WERE PALS WITH BACK IN FOURTH GRADE, A GUY YOU USED TO TALK TO ABOUT MARBLES AND RICE-KRISPIES...
HEH!
..NOW YOUR MOM IS SCREWING HIM -- I KNOW -- I'LL FIND SOME OLD BAG FROM THE TRAILER PARK TO SHACK UP WITH...
..YOU COULD WRITE A BOOK ABOUT THAT ONE -- LAUNCH YOUR CAREER..
OKAY, JOSH -- GET OUT... KEEP THE CLOTHES..
..I DON'T KNOW WHAT MAKES YOU SO WEIRD.. JUST GO -- YOU'RE MAKING FUN OF ME NOW, SO GET OUT!
....
...WHO'S MAKING FUN OF WHO, MICHELLE?
MY PARENTS CAN'T COME HOME AND FIND YOU HERE.. GO HOME AND GET SOME SLEEP! GO ON!

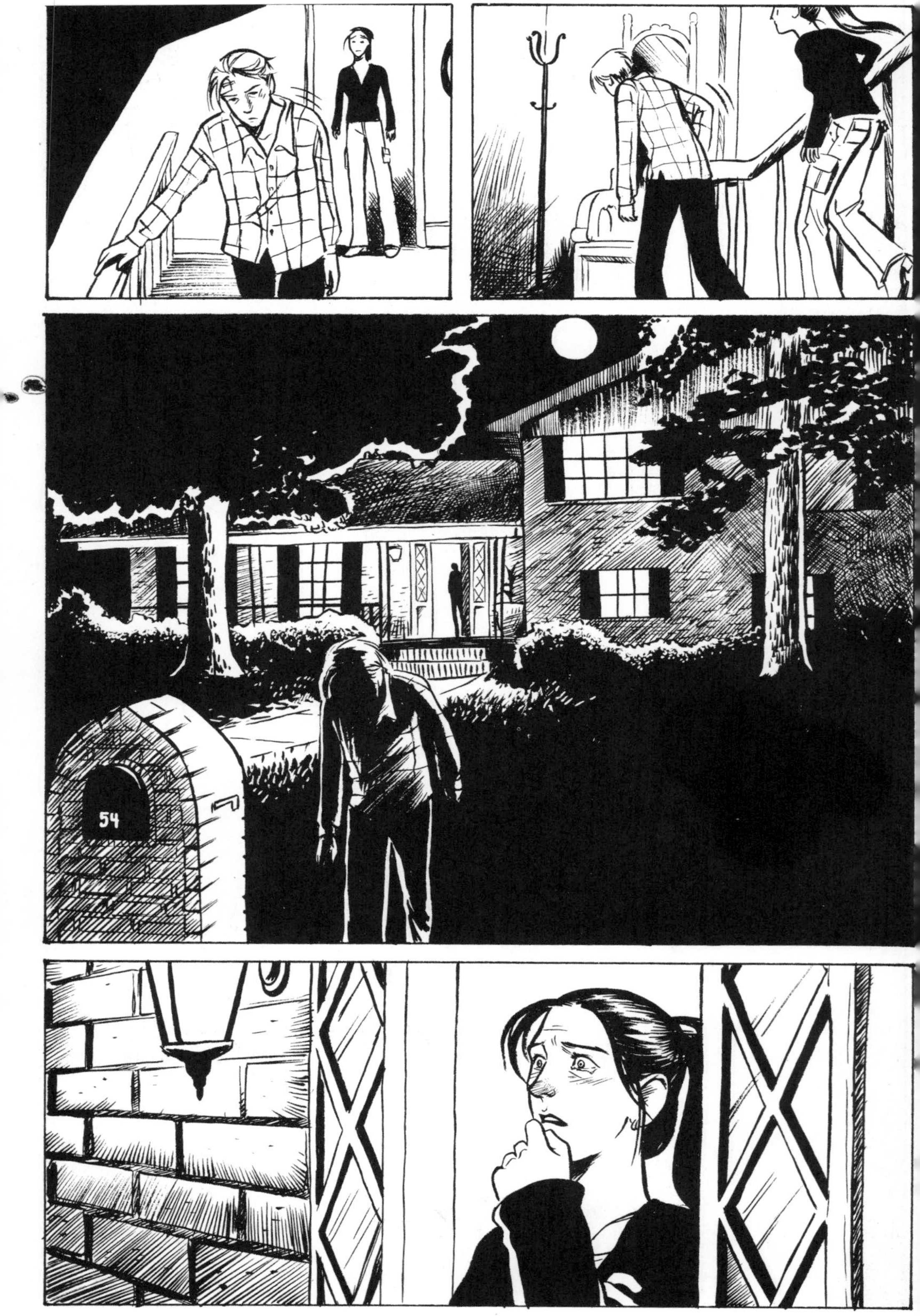
54

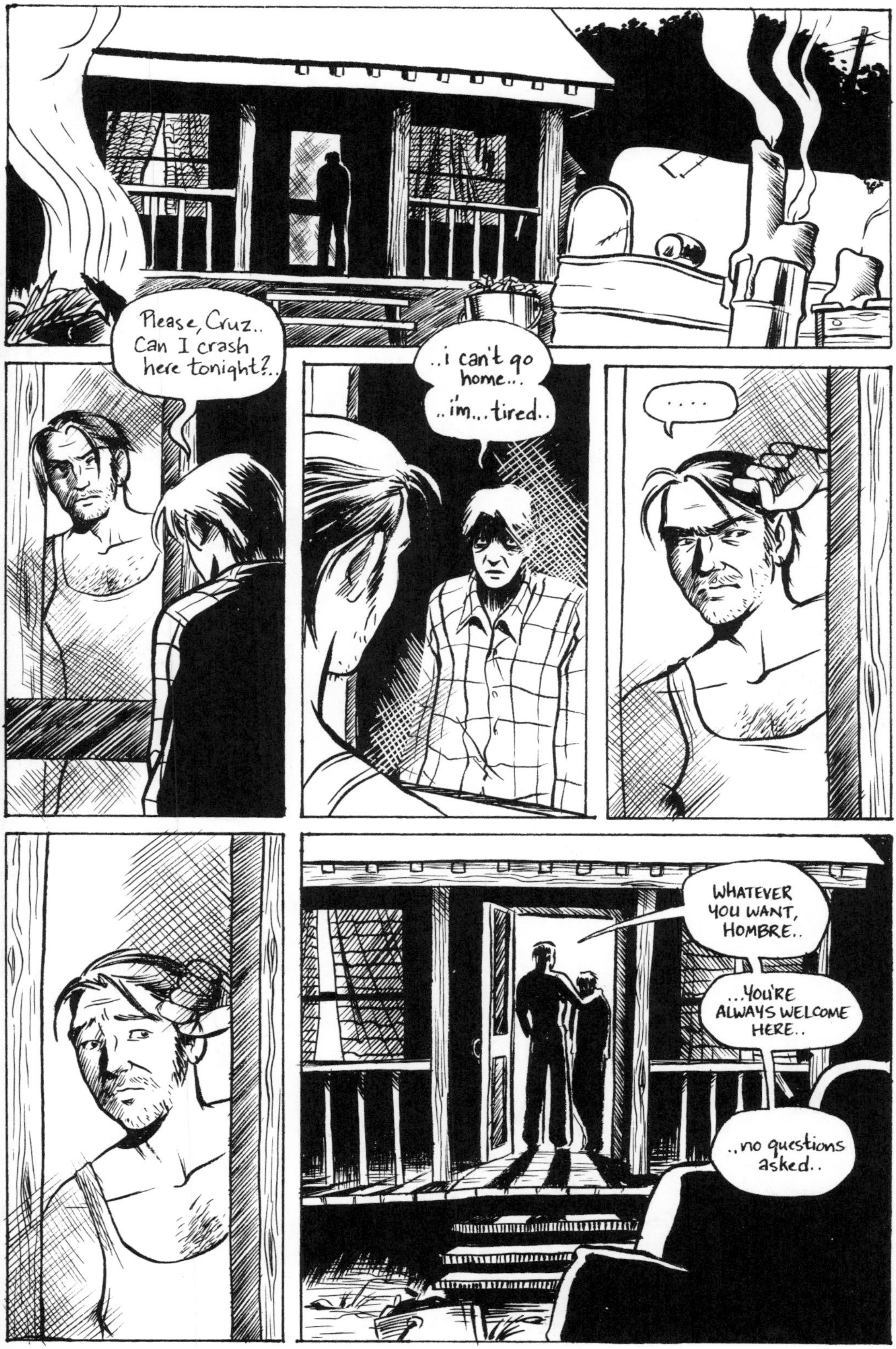
Please, Cruz.. Can I crash here tonight?..
..i can't go home..
..i'm... tired..
. . . .
WHATEVER YOU WANT, HOMBRE..
...YOU'RE ALWAYS WELCOME HERE..
..no questions asked..

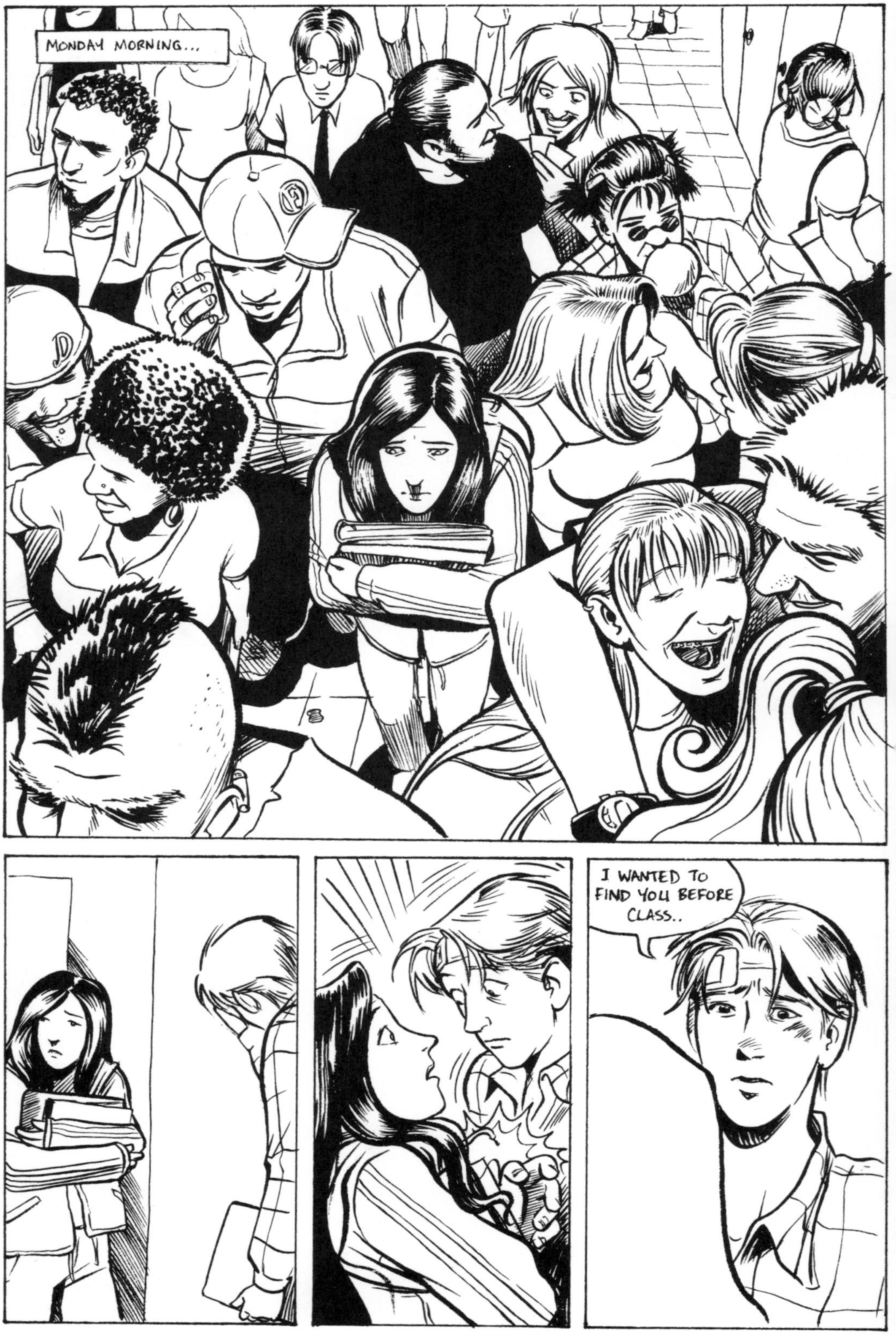
MONDAY MORNING...
I WANTED TO FIND YOU BEFORE CLASS..

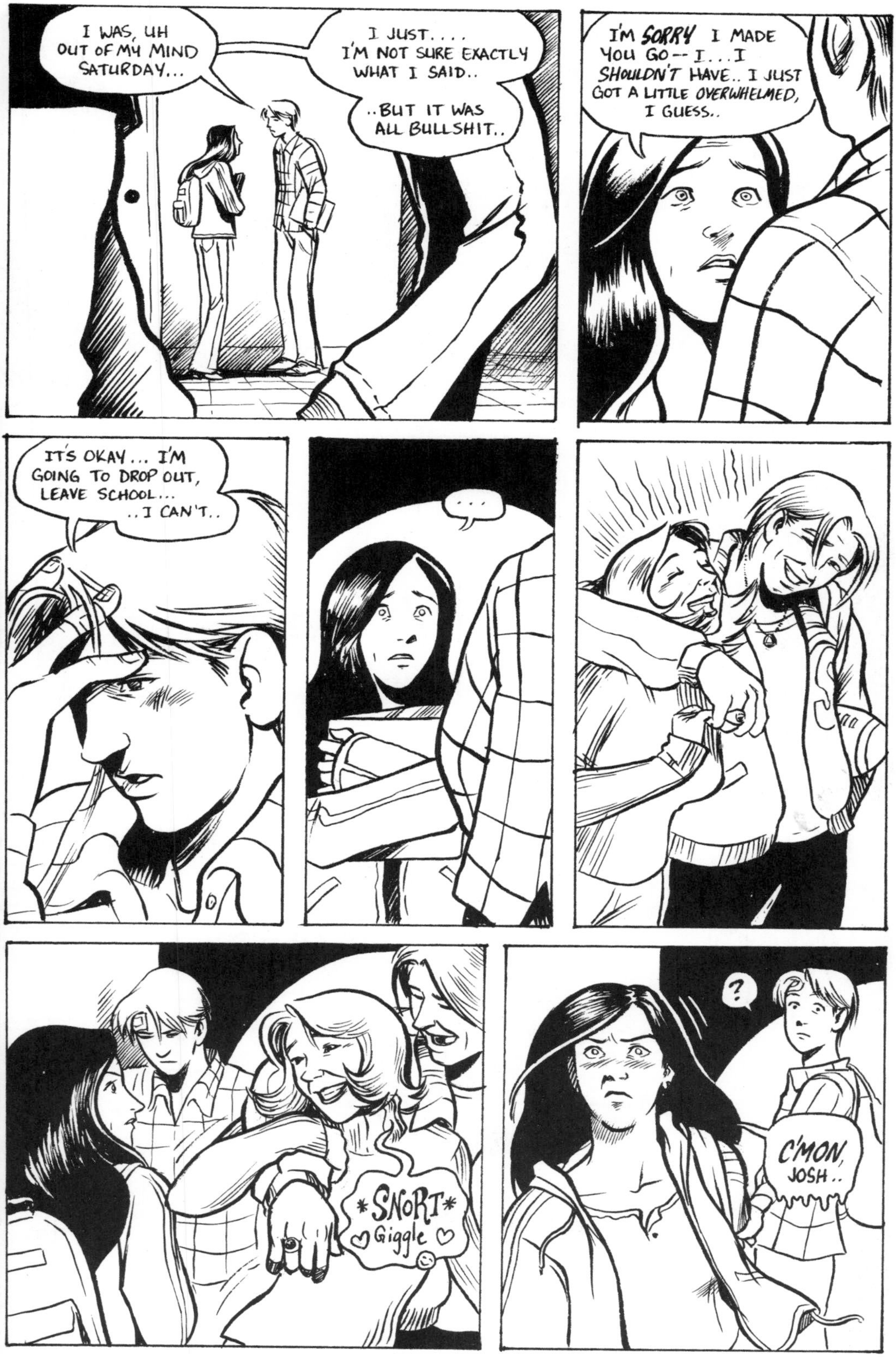
I WAS, UH OUT OF MY MIND SATURDAY...
I JUST.... I'M NOT SURE EXACTLY WHAT I SAID..
..BUT IT WAS ALL BULLSHIT..
I'M SORRY I MADE YOU GO-- I...I SHOULDN'T HAVE.. I JUST GOT A LITTLE OVERWHELMED, I GUESS..
IT'S OKAY... I'M GOING TO DROP OUT, LEAVE SCHOOL... ..I CAN'T..
...
SNORT Giggle
?
C'MON, JOSH..

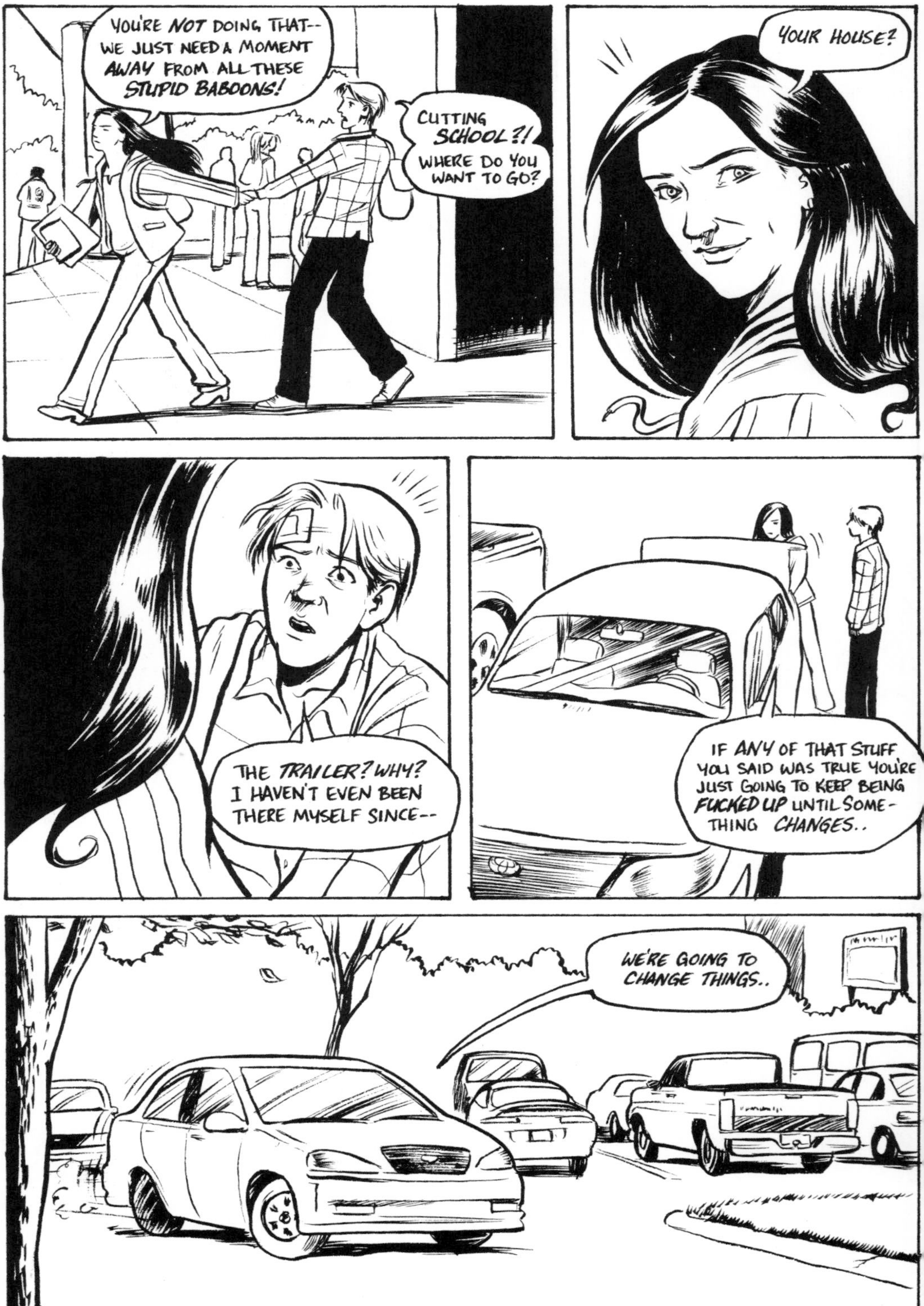
YOU'RE NOT DOING THAT-- WE JUST NEED A MOMENT AWAY FROM ALL THESE STUPID BABOONS!
CUTTING SCHOOL?! WHERE DO YOU WANT TO GO?
YOUR HOUSE?
THE TRAILER? WHY? I HAVEN'T EVEN BEEN THERE MYSELF SINCE--
IF ANY OF THAT STUFF YOU SAID WAS TRUE YOU'RE JUST GOING TO KEEP BEING FUCKED UP UNTIL SOMETHING CHANGES..
WE'RE GOING TO CHANGE THINGS..

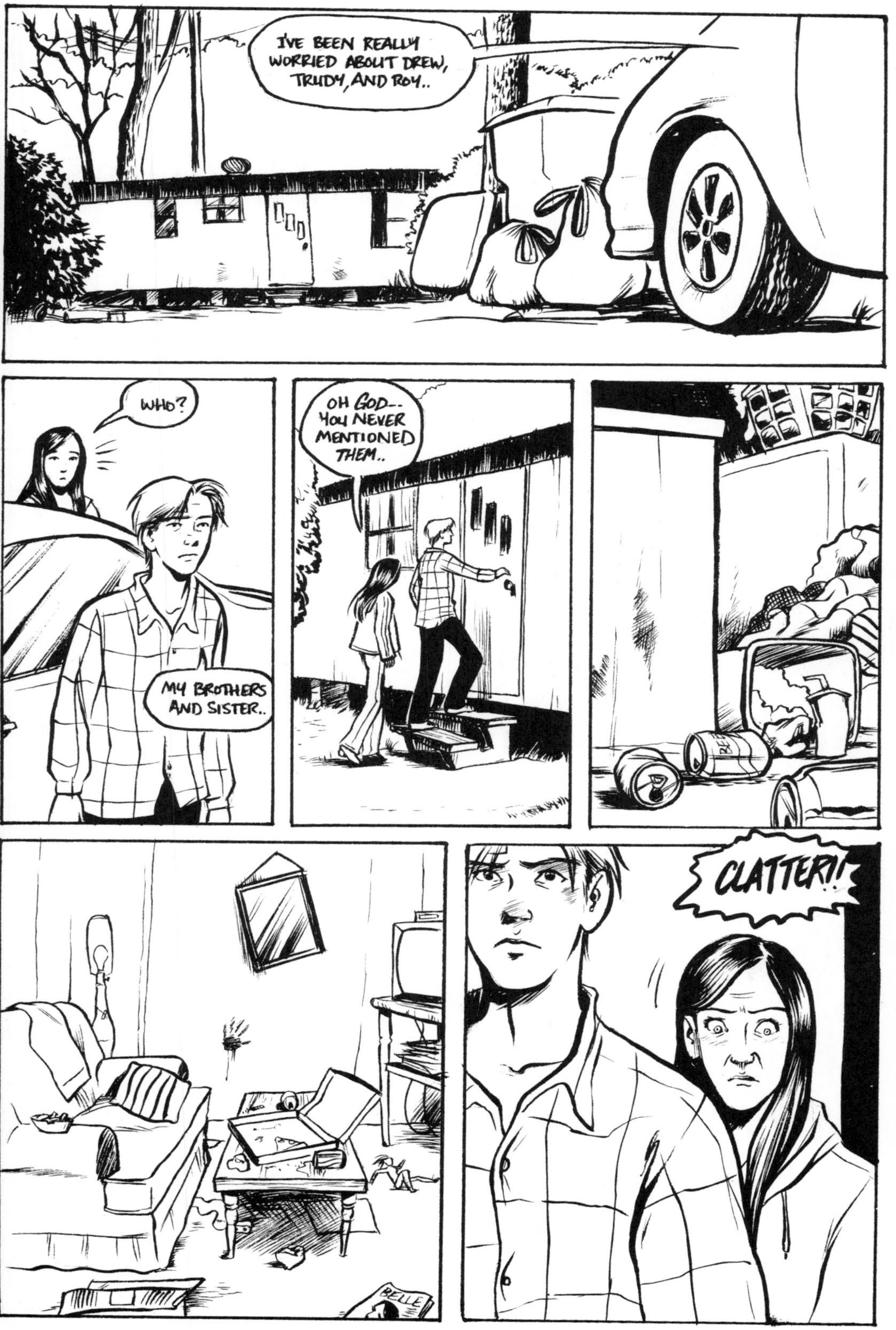
I'VE BEEN REALLY WORRIED ABOUT DREW, TRUDY, AND ROY..
WHO?
MY BROTHERS AND SISTER..
OH GOD-- YOU NEVER MENTIONED THEM..
CLATTER!!
BELLE

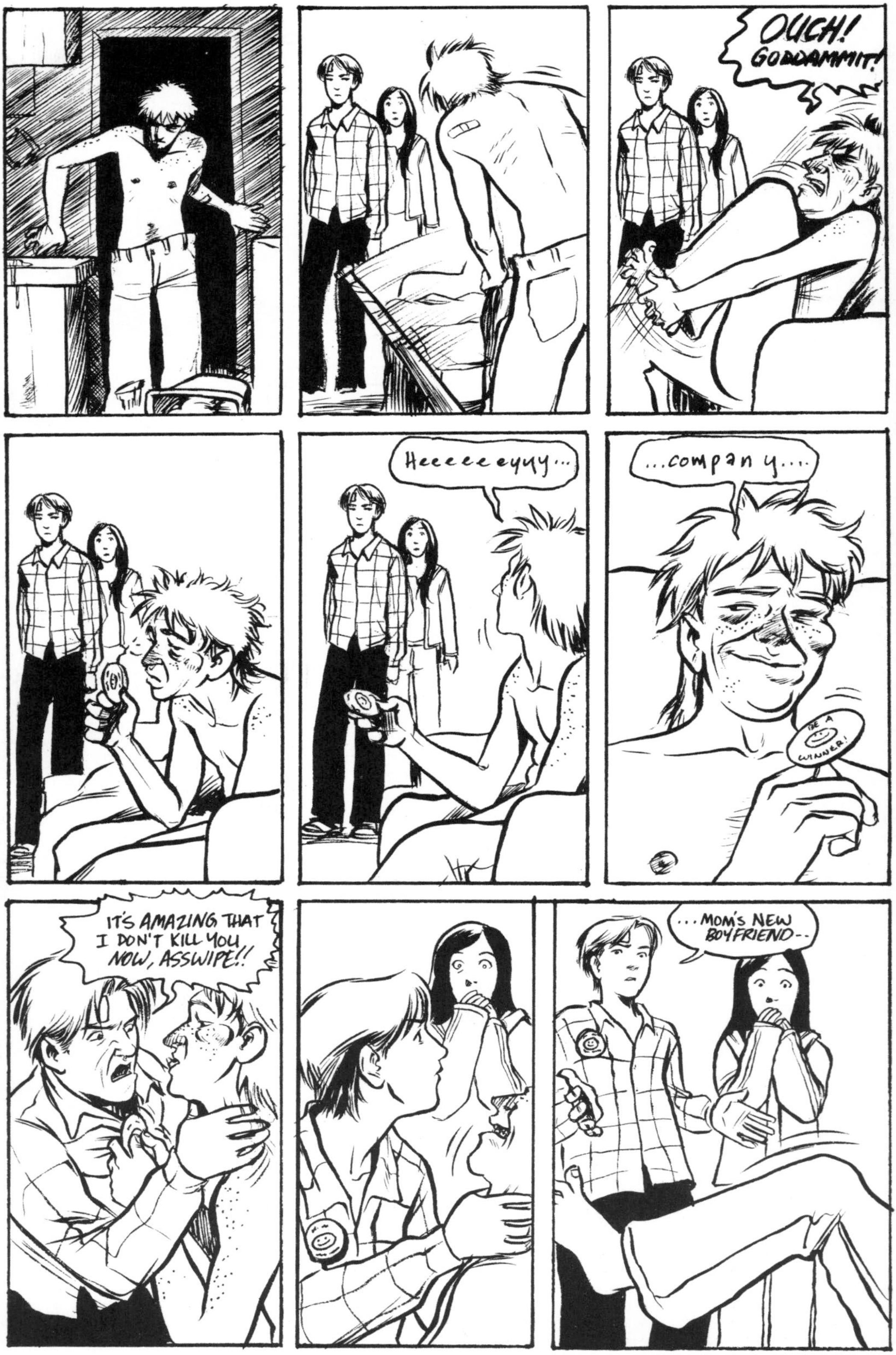
OUCH! GODDAMMIT!
Heeeeeeyyy...
...company...
BE A WINNER!
IT'S AMAZING THAT I DON'T KILL YOU NOW, ASSWIPE!!
...MOM'S NEW BOYFRIEND--

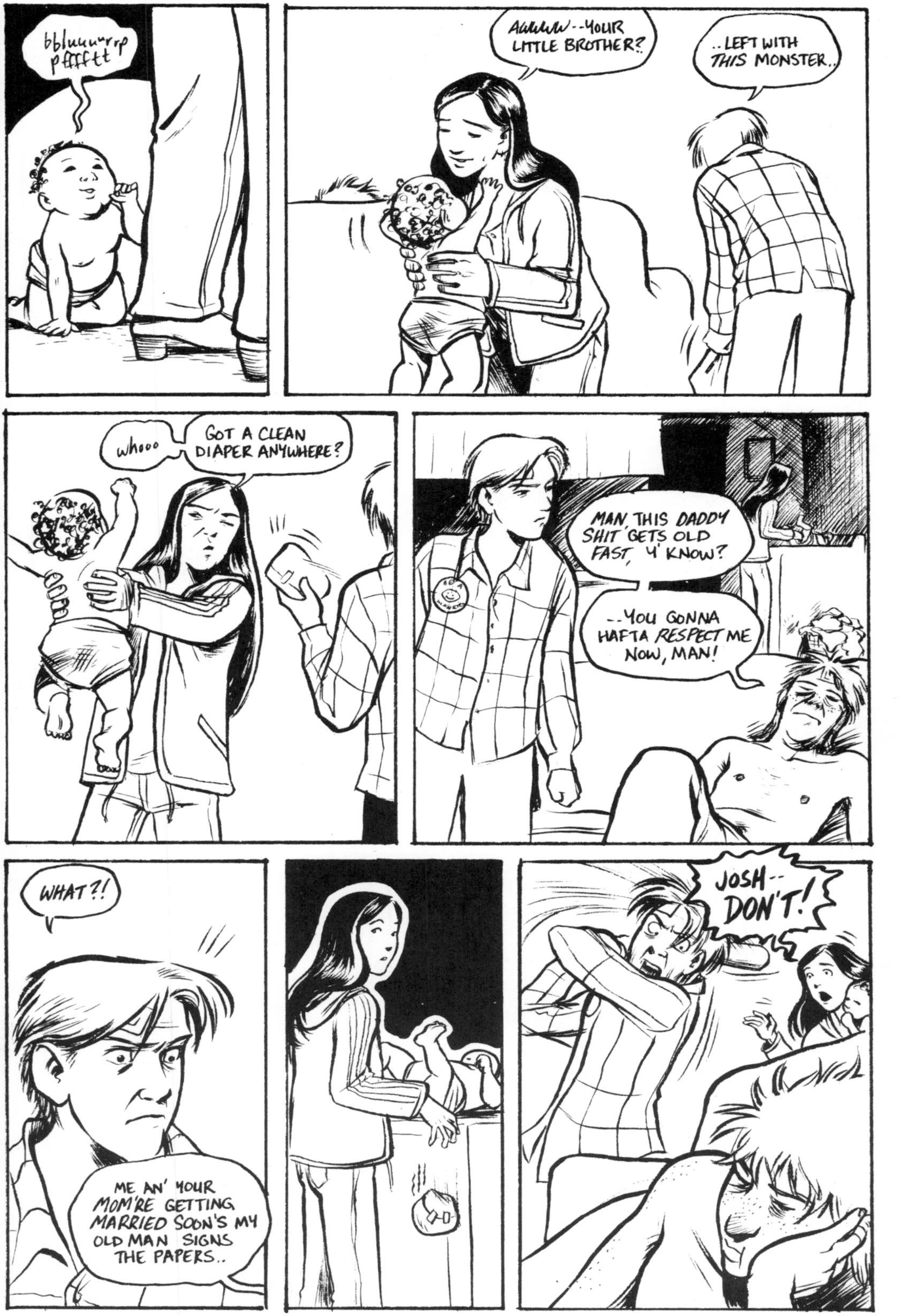
bbluuurrp pffffft
AWWW--YOUR LITTLE BROTHER?
..LEFT WITH *THIS* MONSTER..
whooo
GOT A CLEAN DIAPER ANYWHERE?
MAN, THIS *DADDY SHIT* GETS OLD FAST, Y' KNOW?
--YOU GONNA HAFTA *RESPECT* ME NOW, MAN!
WHAT?!
ME AN' YOUR *MOM'RE* GETTING *MARRIED* SOON'S MY OLD MAN SIGNS THE PAPERS..
JOSH-- DON'T!

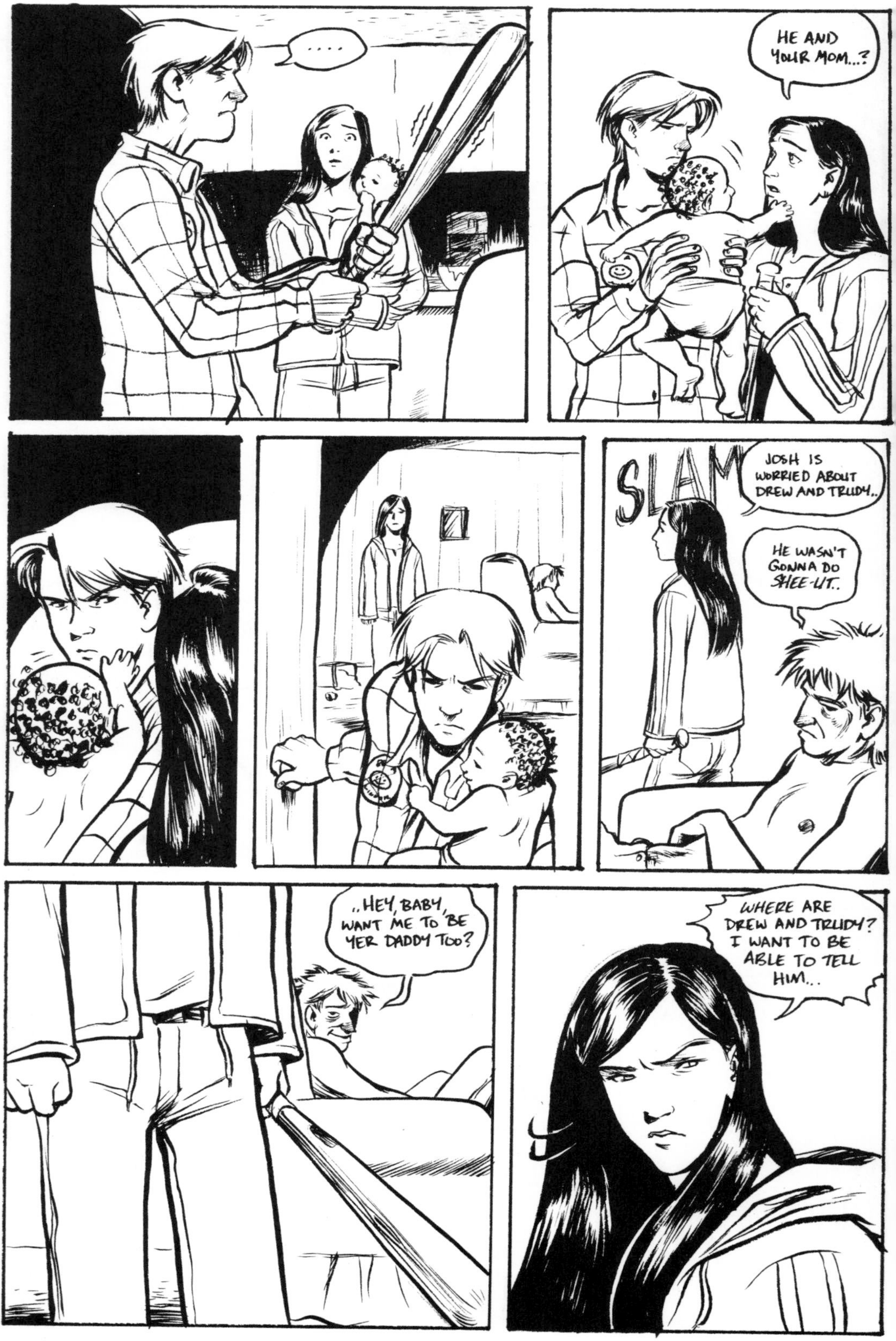
....
HE AND YOUR MOM...?
SLAM
JOSH IS WORRIED ABOUT DREW AND TRUDY..
HE WASN'T GONNA DO SHEE-UT..
..HEY, BABY, WANT ME TO BE YER DADDY TOO?
WHERE ARE DREW AND TRUDY? I WANT TO BE ABLE TO TELL HIM...

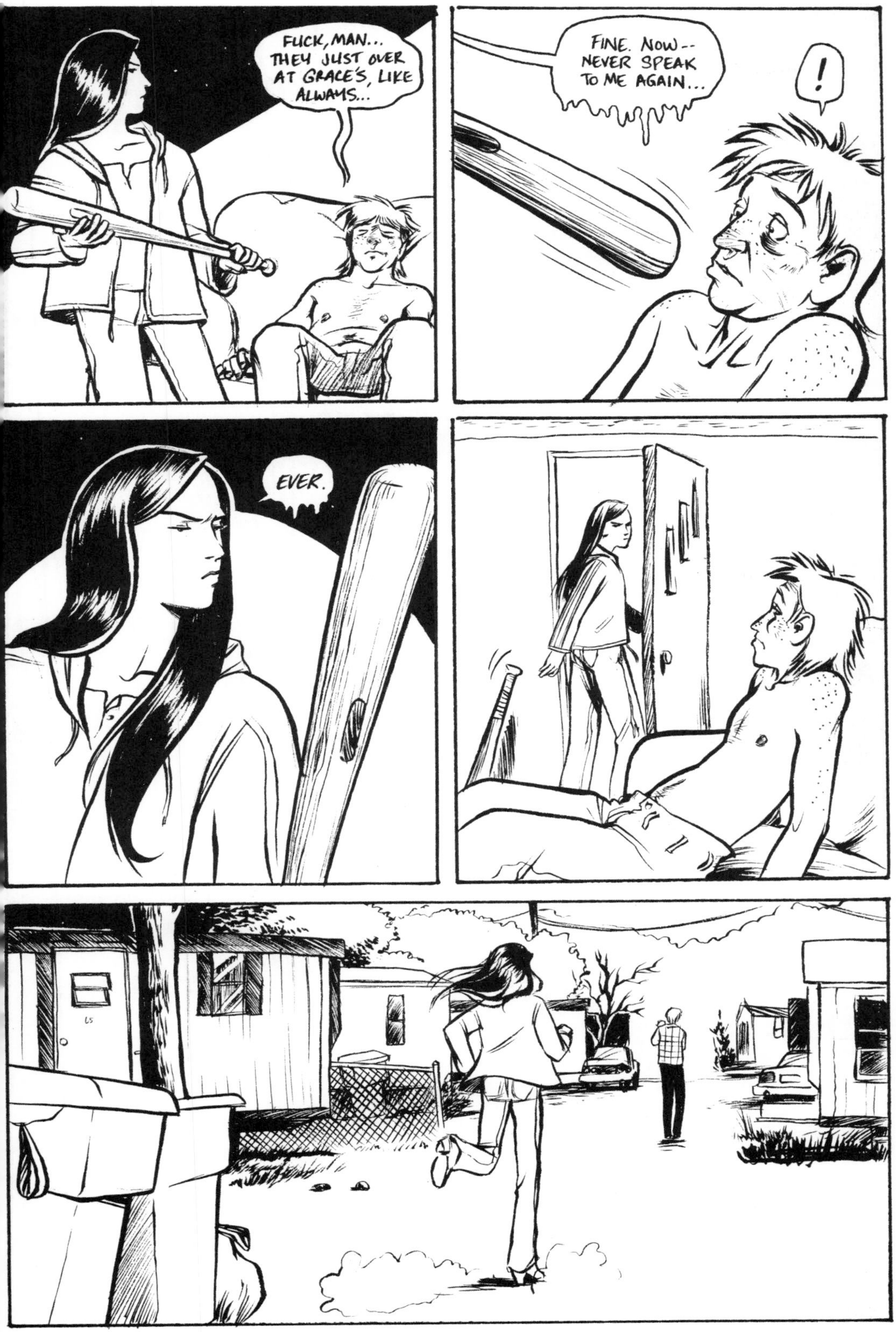
FUCK, MAN... THEY JUST OVER AT GRACE'S, LIKE ALWAYS...
FINE. NOW-- NEVER SPEAK TO ME AGAIN...
!
EVER.

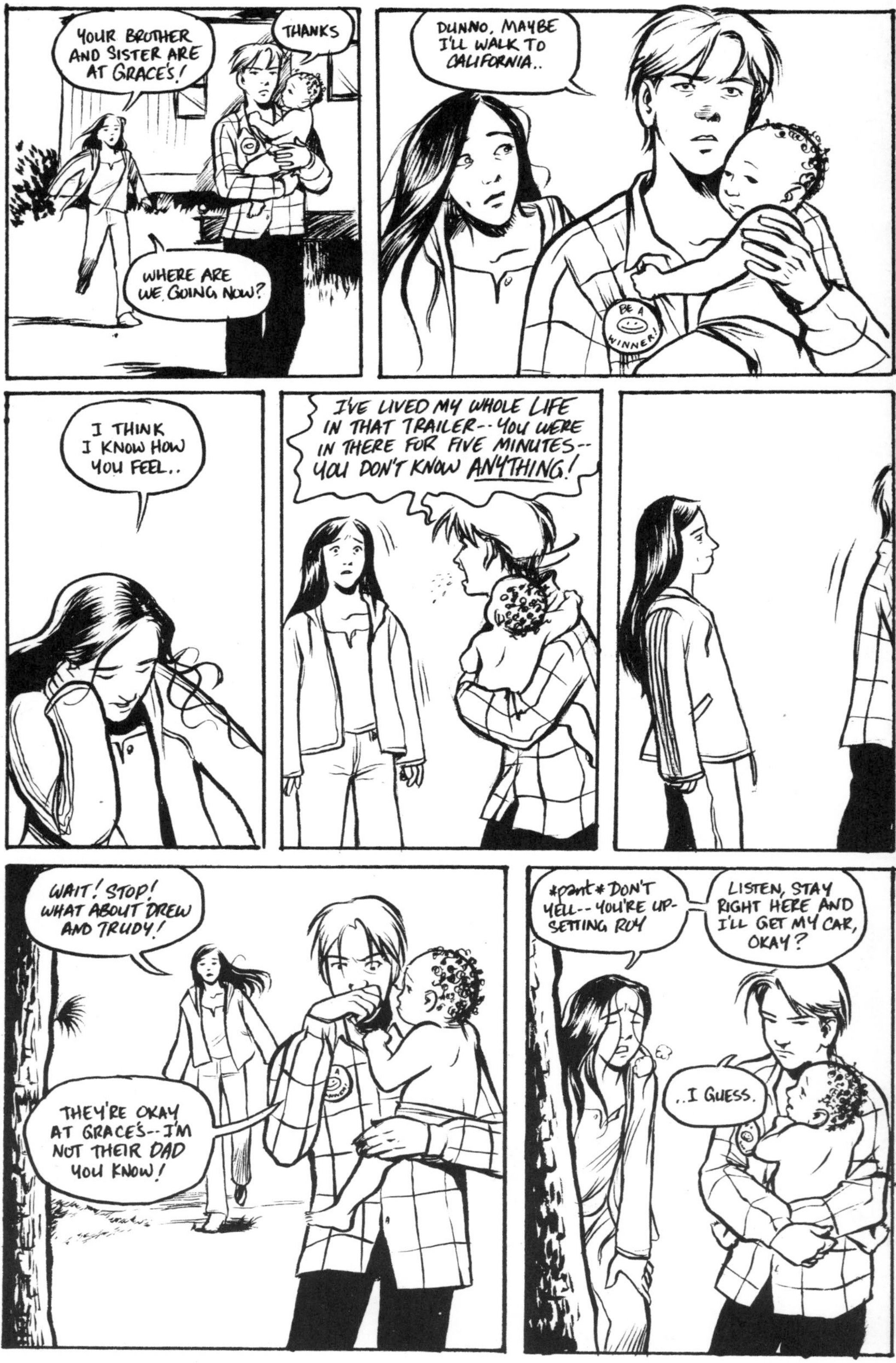

YOUR BROTHER AND SISTER ARE AT GRACE'S!
THANKS
WHERE ARE WE GOING NOW?
DUNNO, MAYBE I'LL WALK TO CALIFORNIA..
BE A WINNER!
I THINK I KNOW HOW YOU FEEL..
I'VE LIVED MY WHOLE LIFE IN THAT TRAILER-- YOU WERE IN THERE FOR FIVE MINUTES-- YOU DON'T KNOW ANYTHING!
WAIT! STOP! WHAT ABOUT DREW AND TRUDY!
THEY'RE OKAY AT GRACE'S-- I'M NOT THEIR DAD YOU KNOW!
pant DON'T YELL-- YOU'RE UPSETTING ROY
LISTEN, STAY RIGHT HERE AND I'LL GET MY CAR, OKAY?
..I GUESS.

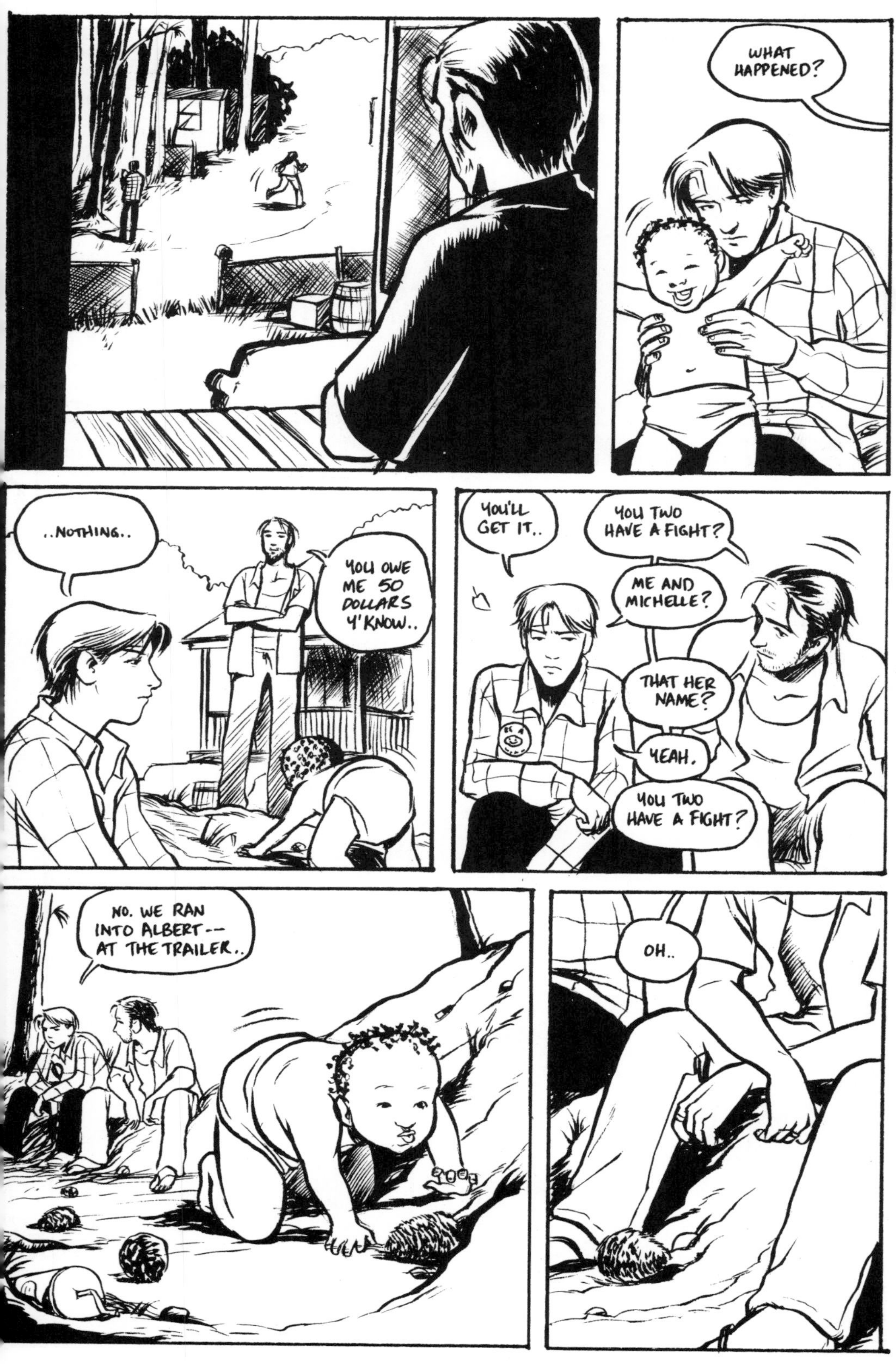
WHAT HAPPENED?
..NOTHING..
YOU OWE ME 50 DOLLARS Y'KNOW..
YOU'LL GET IT..
YOU TWO HAVE A FIGHT?
ME AND MICHELLE?
THAT HER NAME?
YEAH.
YOU TWO HAVE A FIGHT?
NO. WE RAN INTO ALBERT-- AT THE TRAILER..
OH..

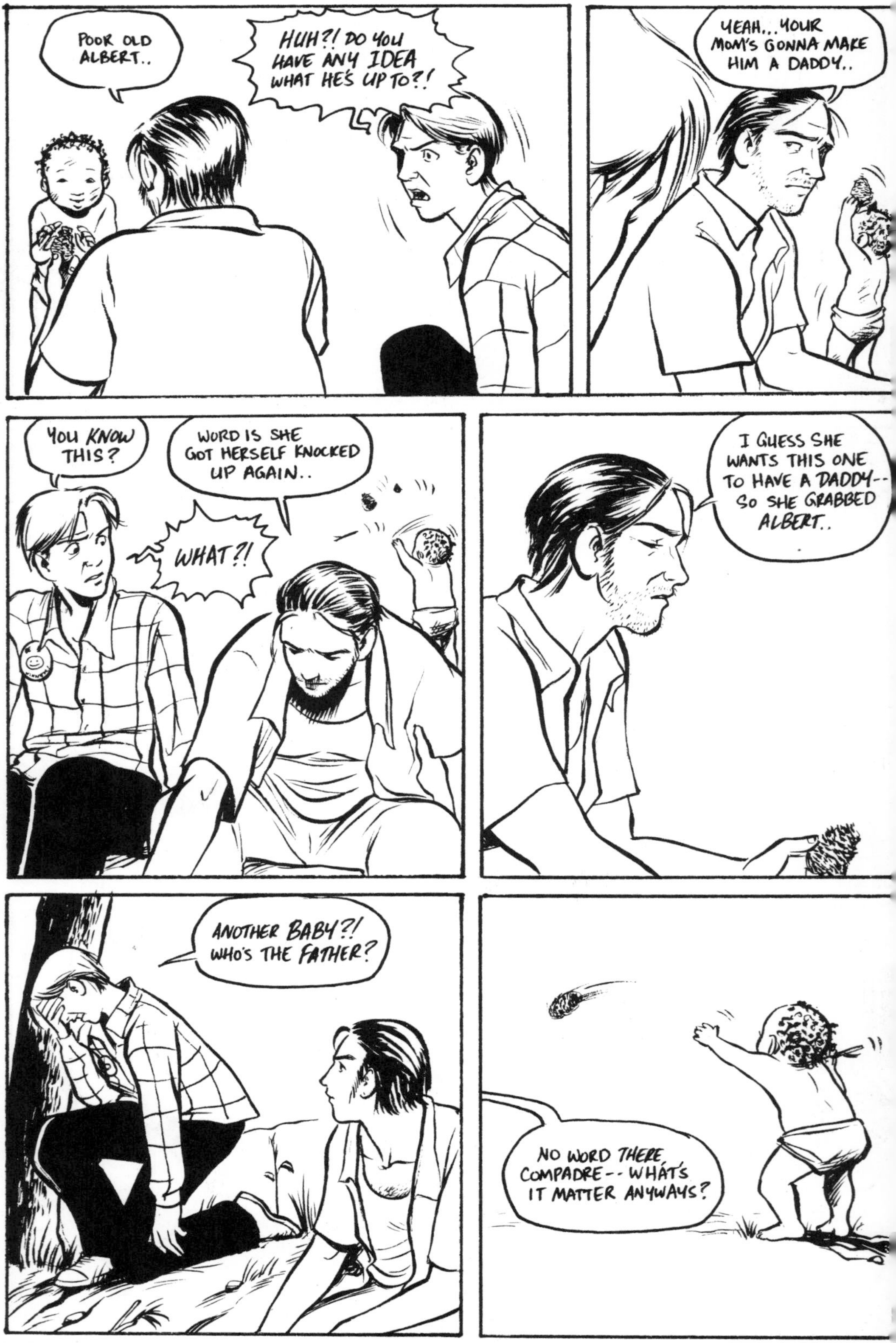
POOR OLD ALBERT..
HUH?! DO YOU HAVE ANY IDEA WHAT HE'S UP TO?!
YEAH...YOUR MOM'S GONNA MAKE HIM A DADDY..
YOU KNOW THIS?
WORD IS SHE GOT HERSELF KNOCKED UP AGAIN..
WHAT?!
I GUESS SHE WANTS THIS ONE TO HAVE A DADDY-- SO SHE GRABBED ALBERT..
ANOTHER BABY?! WHO'S THE FATHER?
NO WORD THERE, COMPADRE-- WHAT'S IT MATTER ANYWAYS?

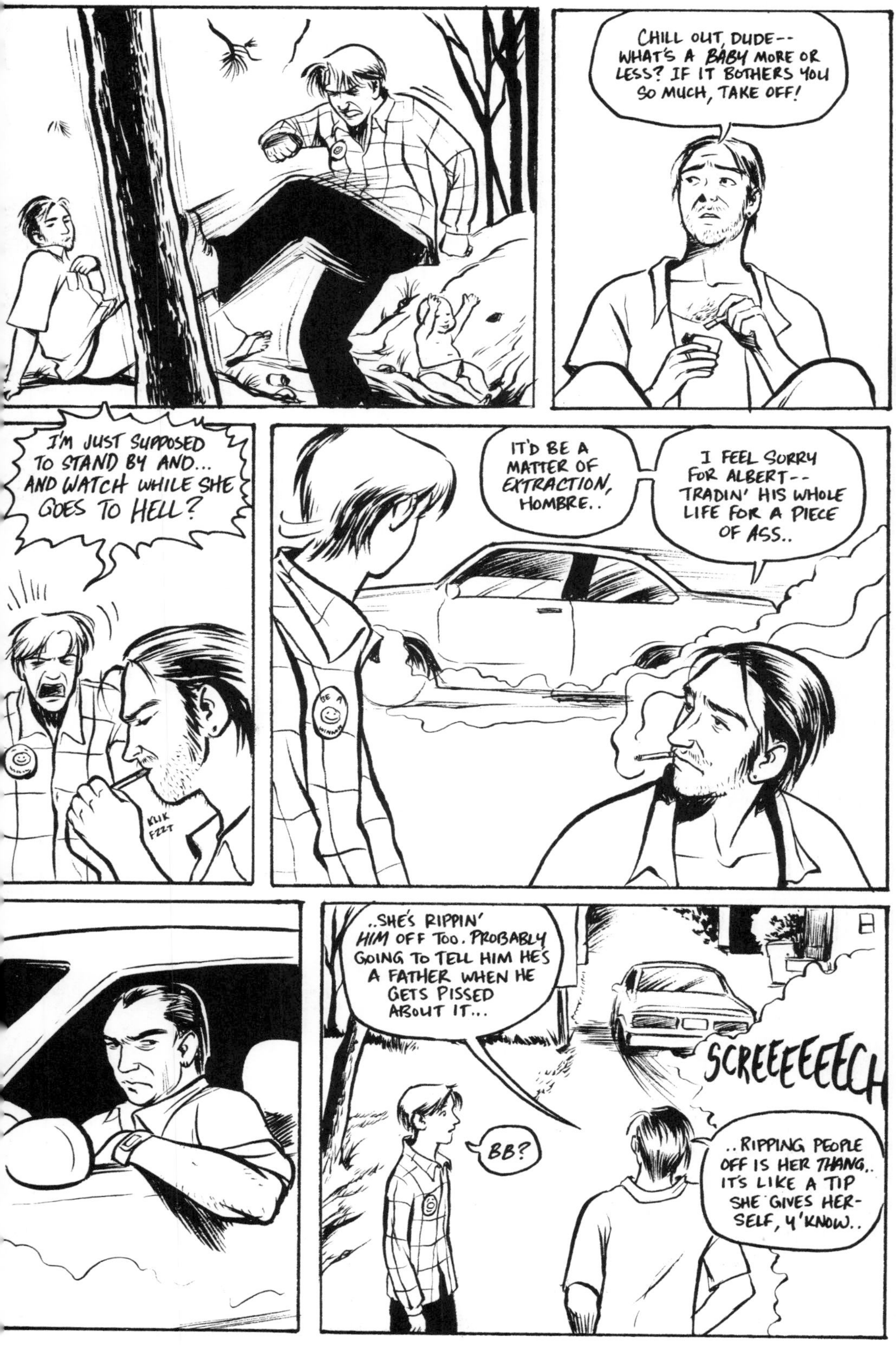
CHILL OUT, DUDE-- WHAT'S A BABY MORE OR LESS? IF IT BOTHERS YOU SO MUCH, TAKE OFF!
I'M JUST SUPPOSED TO STAND BY AND... AND WATCH WHILE SHE GOES TO HELL?
KLIK FZZT
IT'D BE A MATTER OF EXTRACTION, HOMBRE..
I FEEL SORRY FOR ALBERT-- TRADIN' HIS WHOLE LIFE FOR A PIECE OF ASS..
BE A
..SHE'S RIPPIN' HIM OFF TOO. PROBABLY GOING TO TELL HIM HE'S A FATHER WHEN HE GETS PISSED ABOUT IT...
SCREEEEEECH
BB?
..RIPPING PEOPLE OFF IS HER THANG.. IT'S LIKE A TIP SHE GIVES HER-SELF, Y'KNOW..

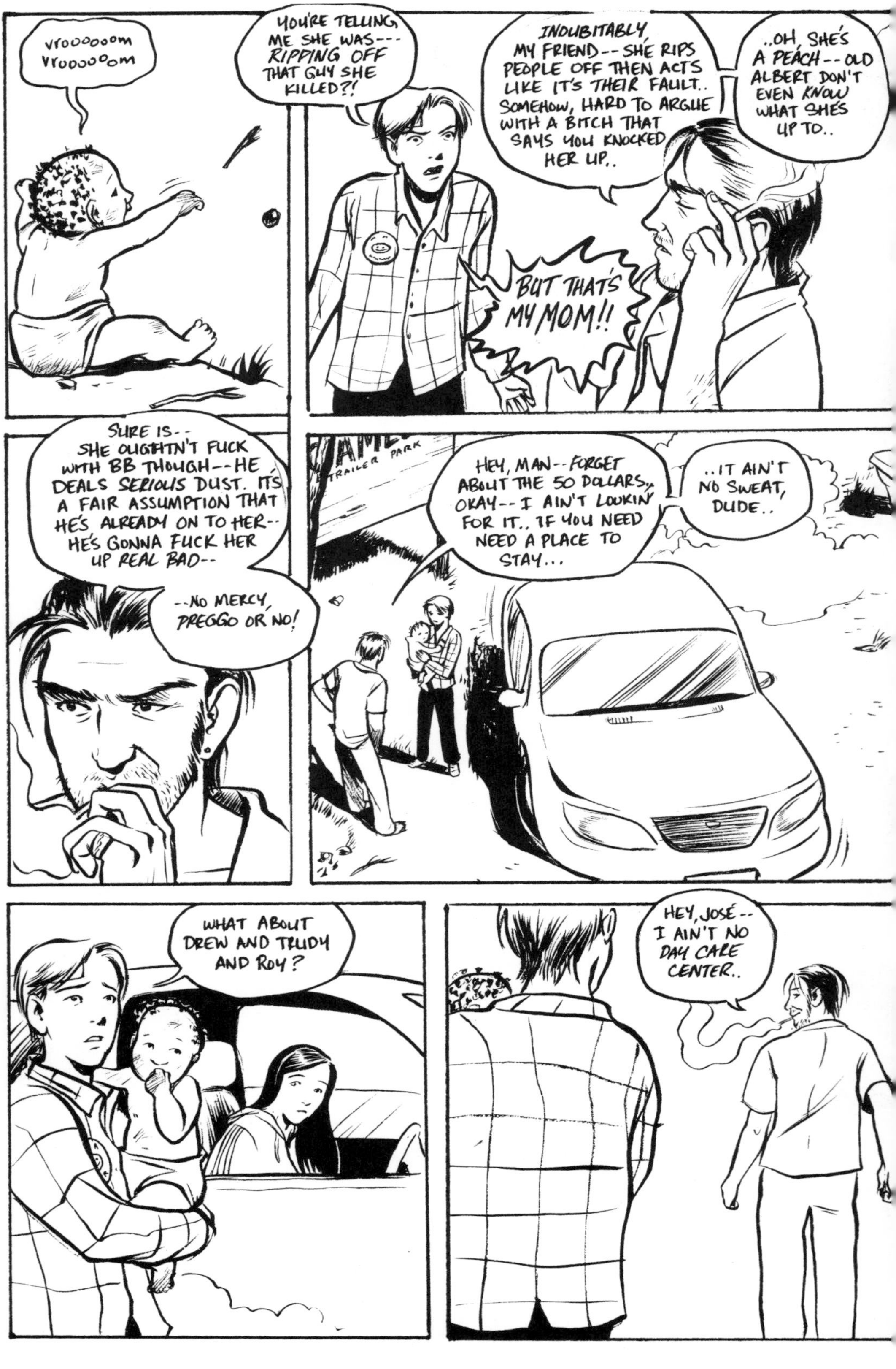
vroooooom vroooooom
YOU'RE TELLING ME SHE WAS--- RIPPING OFF THAT GUY SHE KILLED?!
INDUBITABLY, MY FRIEND-- SHE RIPS PEOPLE OFF THEN ACTS LIKE IT'S THEIR FAULT.. SOMEHOW, HARD TO ARGUE WITH A BITCH THAT SAYS YOU KNOCKED HER UP..
..OH, SHE'S A PEACH--OLD ALBERT DON'T EVEN KNOW WHAT SHE'S UP TO..
BUT THAT'S MY MOM!!
SURE IS-- SHE OUGHTN'T FUCK WITH BB THOUGH--HE DEALS SERIOUS DUST. IT'S A FAIR ASSUMPTION THAT HE'S ALREADY ON TO HER-- HE'S GONNA FUCK HER UP REAL BAD--
--NO MERCY, PREGGO OR NO!
TRAILER PARK
HEY, MAN--FORGET ABOUT THE 50 DOLLARS,, OKAY--I AIN'T LOOKIN' FOR IT.. IF YOU NEED NEED A PLACE TO STAY...
..IT AIN'T NO SWEAT, DUDE..
WHAT ABOUT DREW AND TRUDY AND ROY?
HEY, JOSÉ-- I AIN'T NO DAY CARE CENTER..

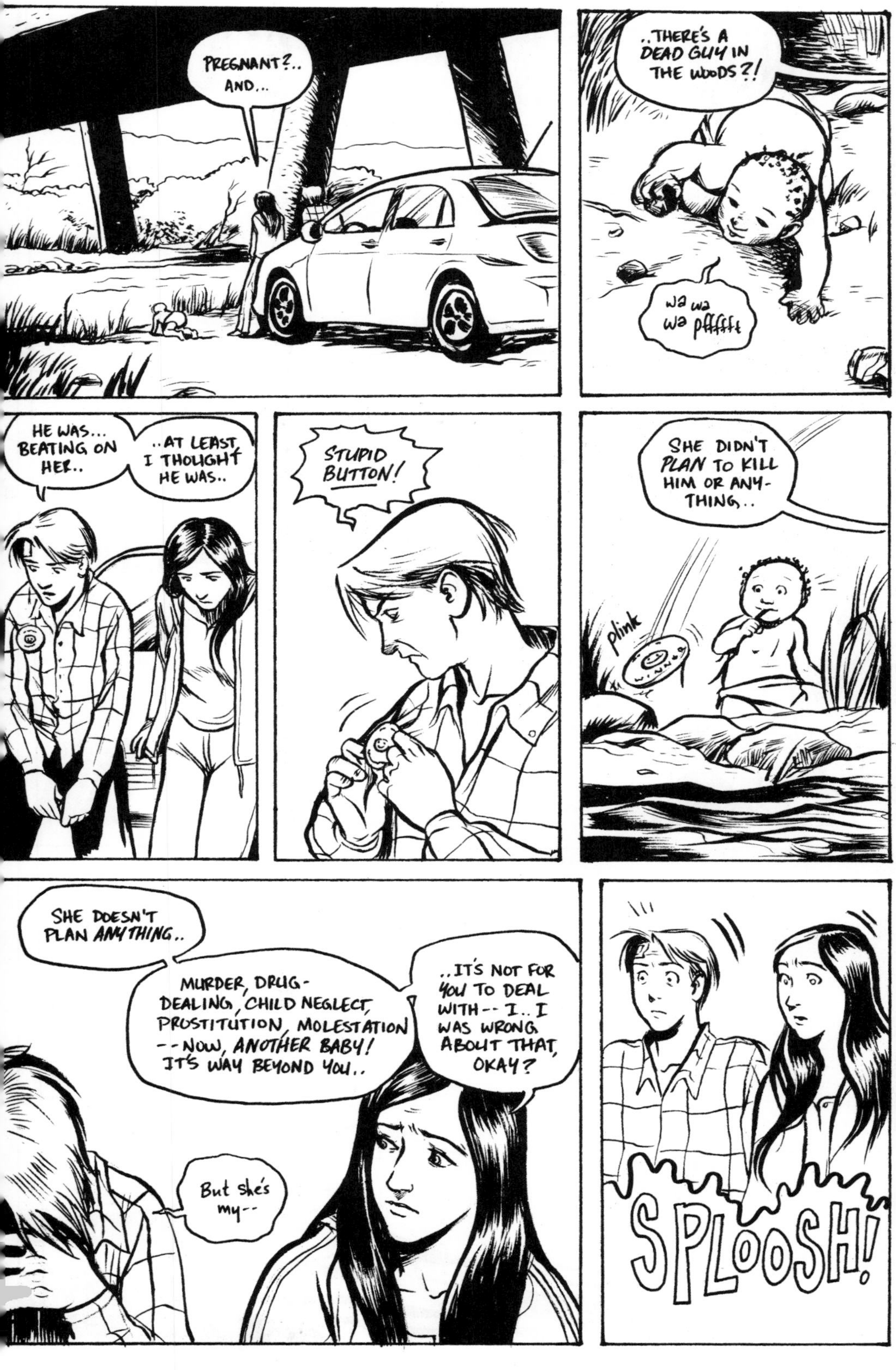
PREGNANT?.. AND...
..THERE'S A DEAD GUY IN THE WOODS?!
wa wa wa pffffft
HE WAS... BEATING ON HER..
..AT LEAST, I THOUGHT HE WAS..
STUPID BUTTON!
SHE DIDN'T PLAN TO KILL HIM OR ANY-THING..
plink
SHE DOESN'T PLAN ANYTHING..
MURDER, DRUG-DEALING, CHILD NEGLECT, PROSTITUTION, MOLESTATION --NOW, ANOTHER BABY! IT'S WAY BEYOND YOU..
..IT'S NOT FOR YOU TO DEAL WITH -- I.. I WAS WRONG ABOUT THAT, OKAY?
But she's my--
SPLOOSH!

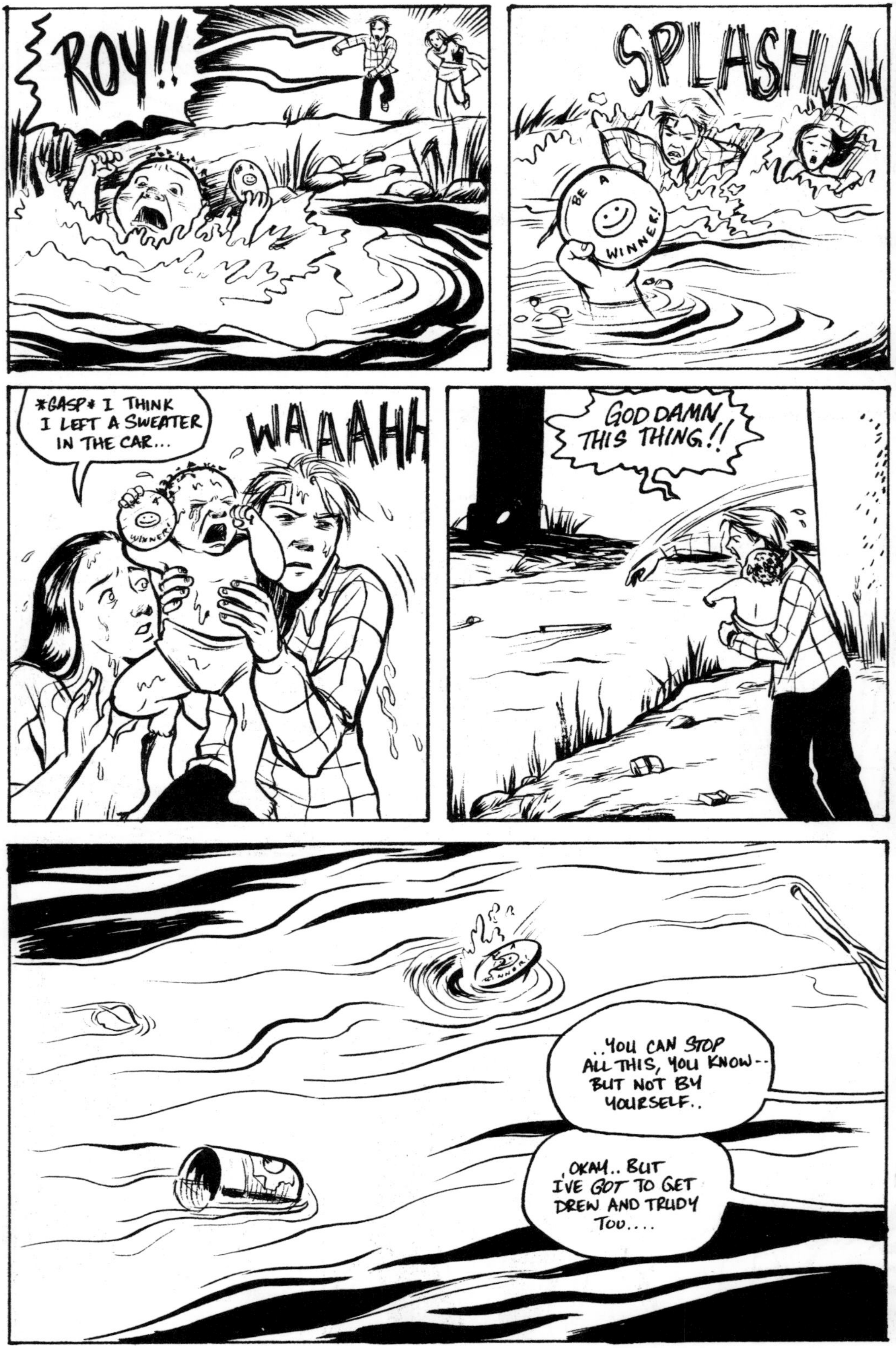
ROY!!
BE A
SPLASH
BE A WINNER!
GASP I THINK I LEFT A SWEATER IN THE CAR...
WAAAHH
WINNER!
GOD DAMN THIS THING!!
..YOU CAN STOP ALL THIS, YOU KNOW-- BUT NOT BY YOURSELF..
OKAY.. BUT I'VE GOT TO GET DREW AND TRUDY TOO....

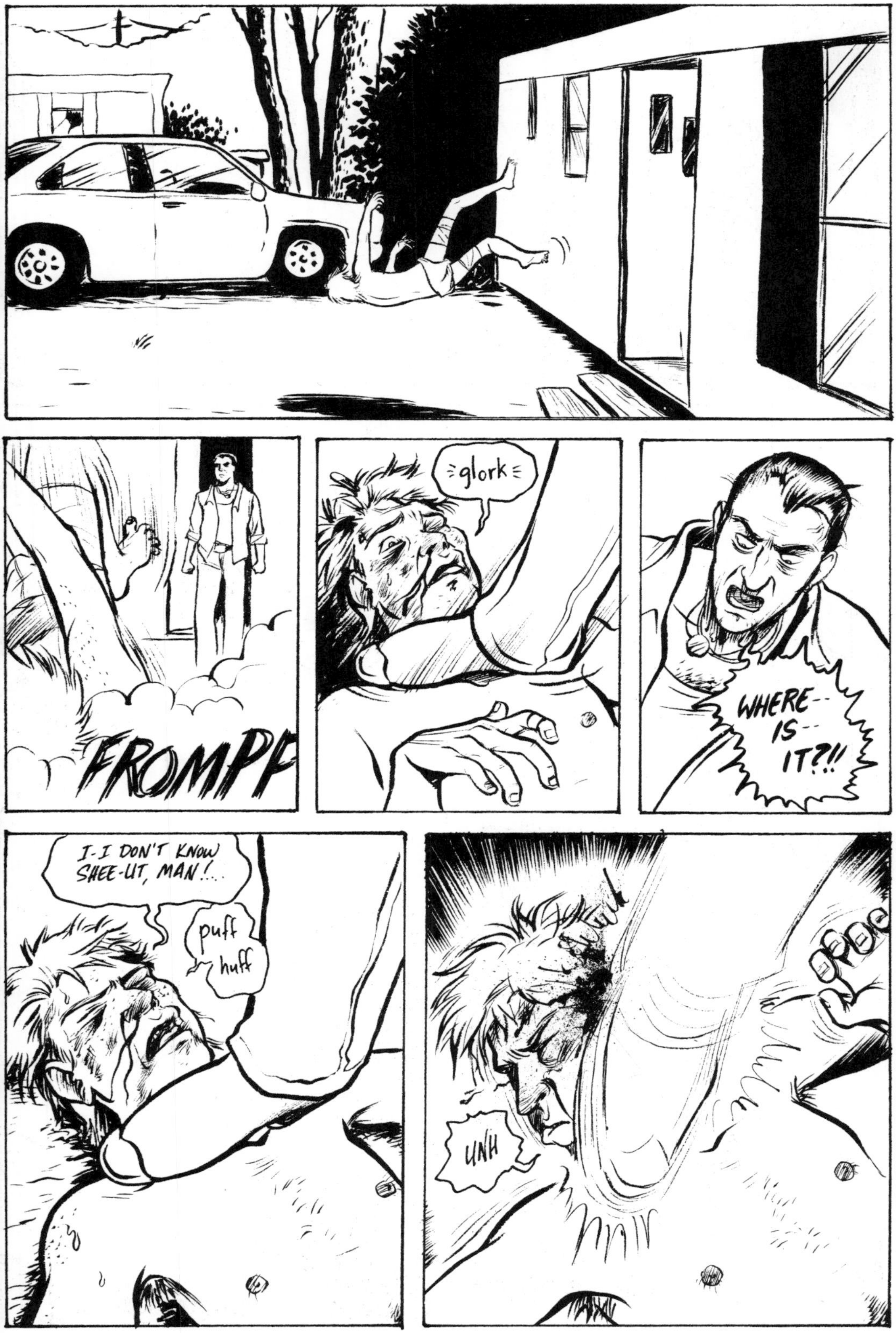
FROMPF
glork
WHERE-- IS-- IT?!!
I-I DON'T KNOW SHEE-UT, MAN!...
puff huff
UNH

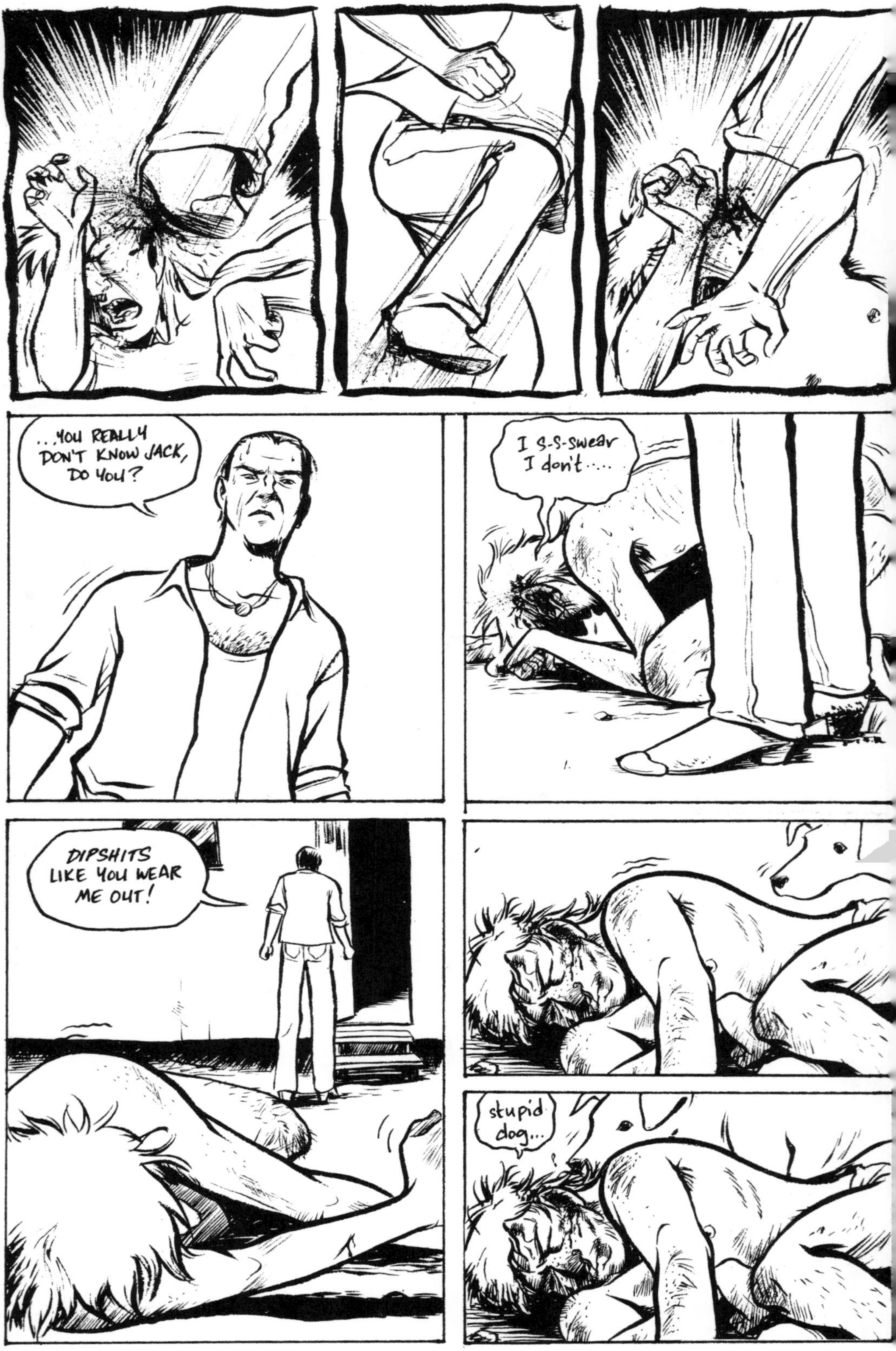
...YOU REALLY DON'T KNOW JACK, DO YOU?
I S-S-swear I don't....
DIPSHITS LIKE YOU WEAR ME OUT!
stupid dog...

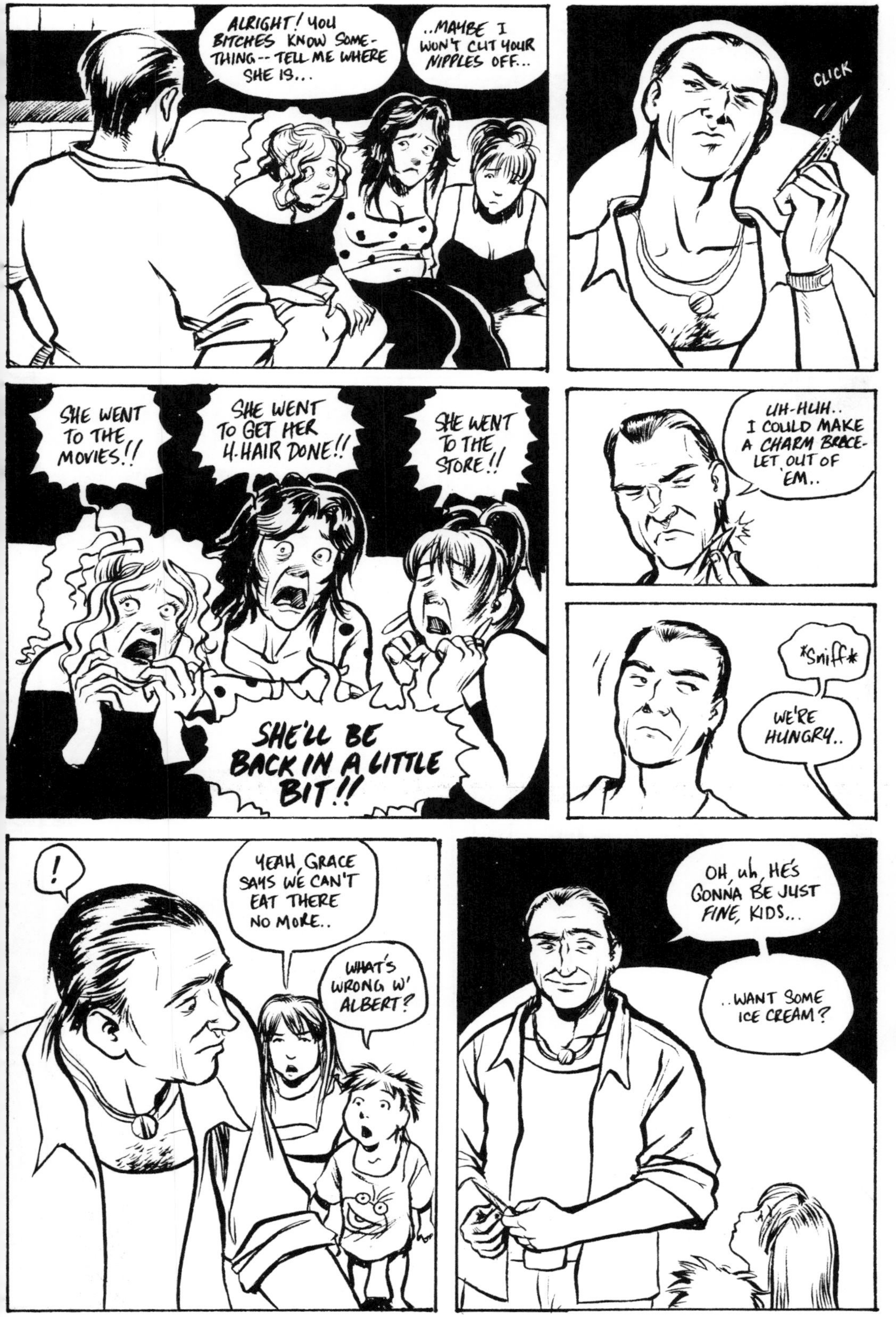
ALRIGHT! YOU BITCHES KNOW SOME-THING -- TELL ME WHERE SHE IS...
..MAYBE I WON'T CUT YOUR NIPPLES OFF...
CLICK
SHE WENT TO THE MOVIES!!
SHE WENT TO GET HER 4-HAIR DONE!!
SHE WENT TO THE STORE!!
SHE'LL BE BACK IN A LITTLE BIT!!
UH-HUH.. I COULD MAKE A CHARM BRACE-LET OUT OF 'EM..
Sniff
WE'RE HUNGRY..
!
YEAH, GRACE SAYS WE CAN'T EAT THERE NO MORE..
WHAT'S WRONG W' ALBERT?
OH, uh, HE'S GONNA BE JUST FINE, KIDS...
..WANT SOME ICE CREAM?

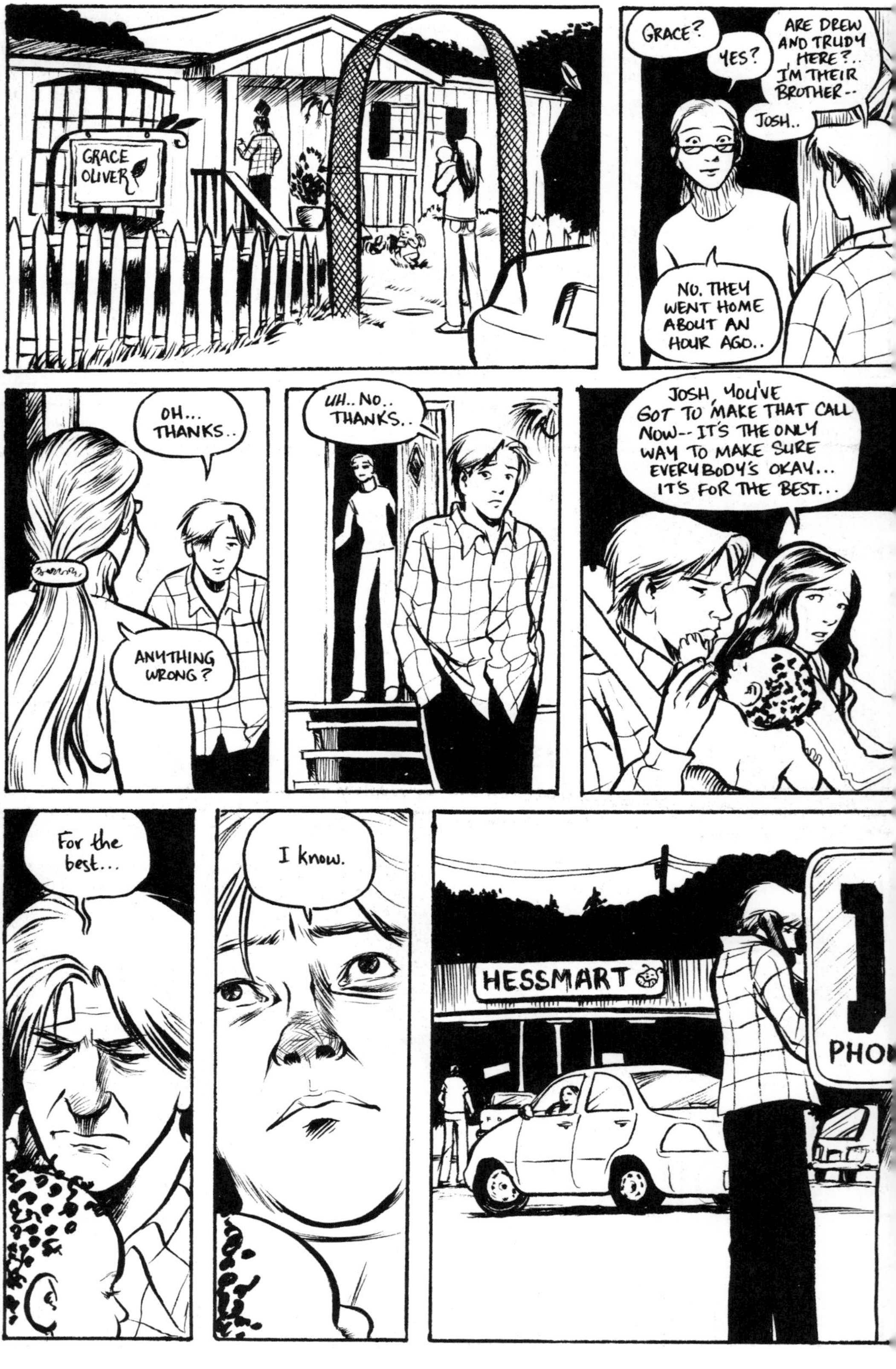
GRACE OLIVER
GRACE?
YES?
ARE DREW AND TRUDY HERE?.. I'M THEIR BROTHER--
JOSH..
NO. THEY WENT HOME ABOUT AN HOUR AGO..
OH... THANKS..
ANYTHING WRONG?
UH.. NO.. THANKS..
JOSH, YOU'VE GOT TO MAKE THAT CALL NOW-- IT'S THE ONLY WAY TO MAKE SURE EVERYBODY'S OKAY... IT'S FOR THE BEST...
For the best...
I know.
HESSMART
PHO

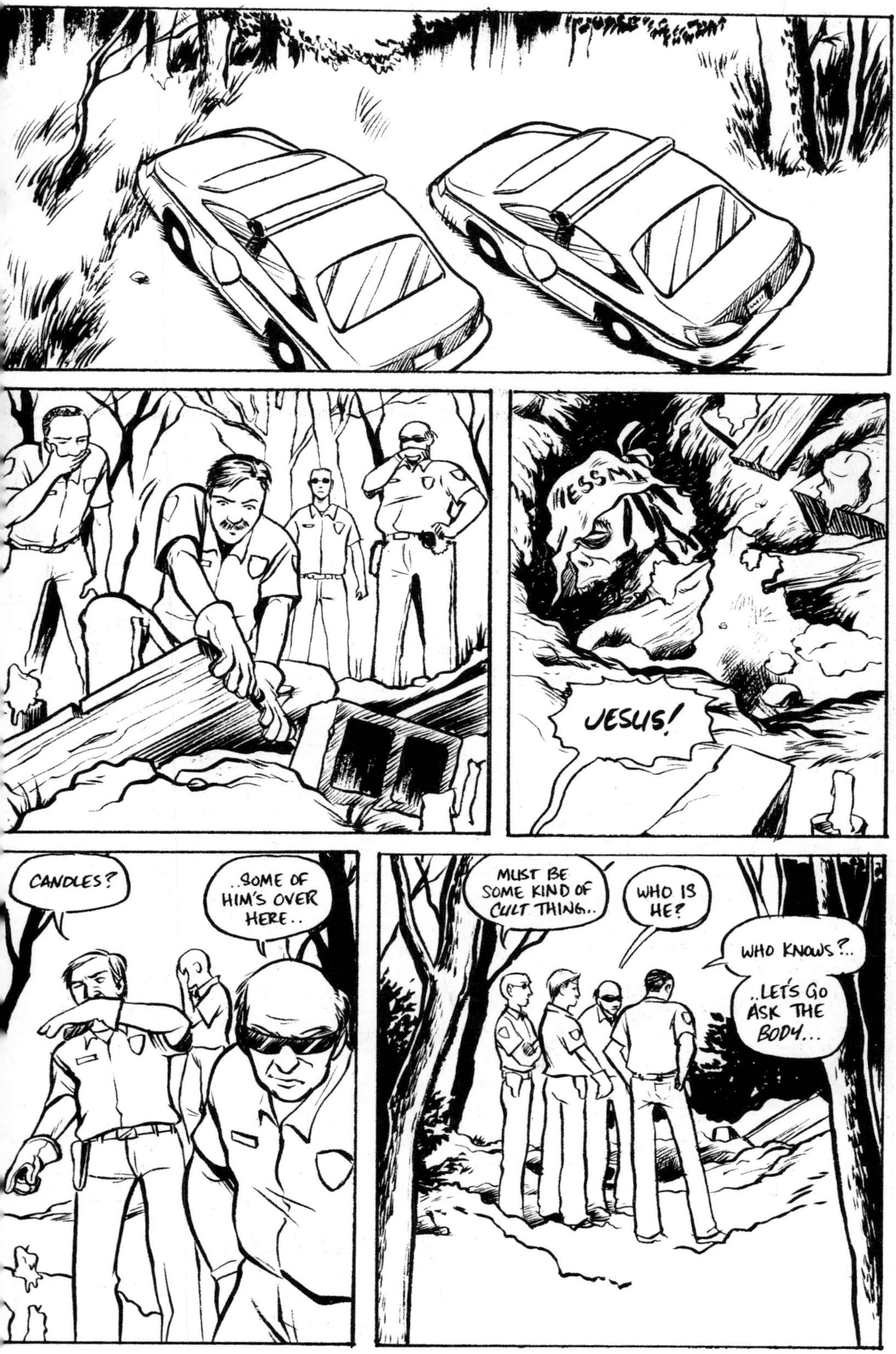
JESUS!
CANDLES?
..SOME OF HIM'S OVER HERE..
MUST BE SOME KIND OF CULT THING..
WHO IS HE?
WHO KNOWS?..
..LET'S GO ASK THE BODY...

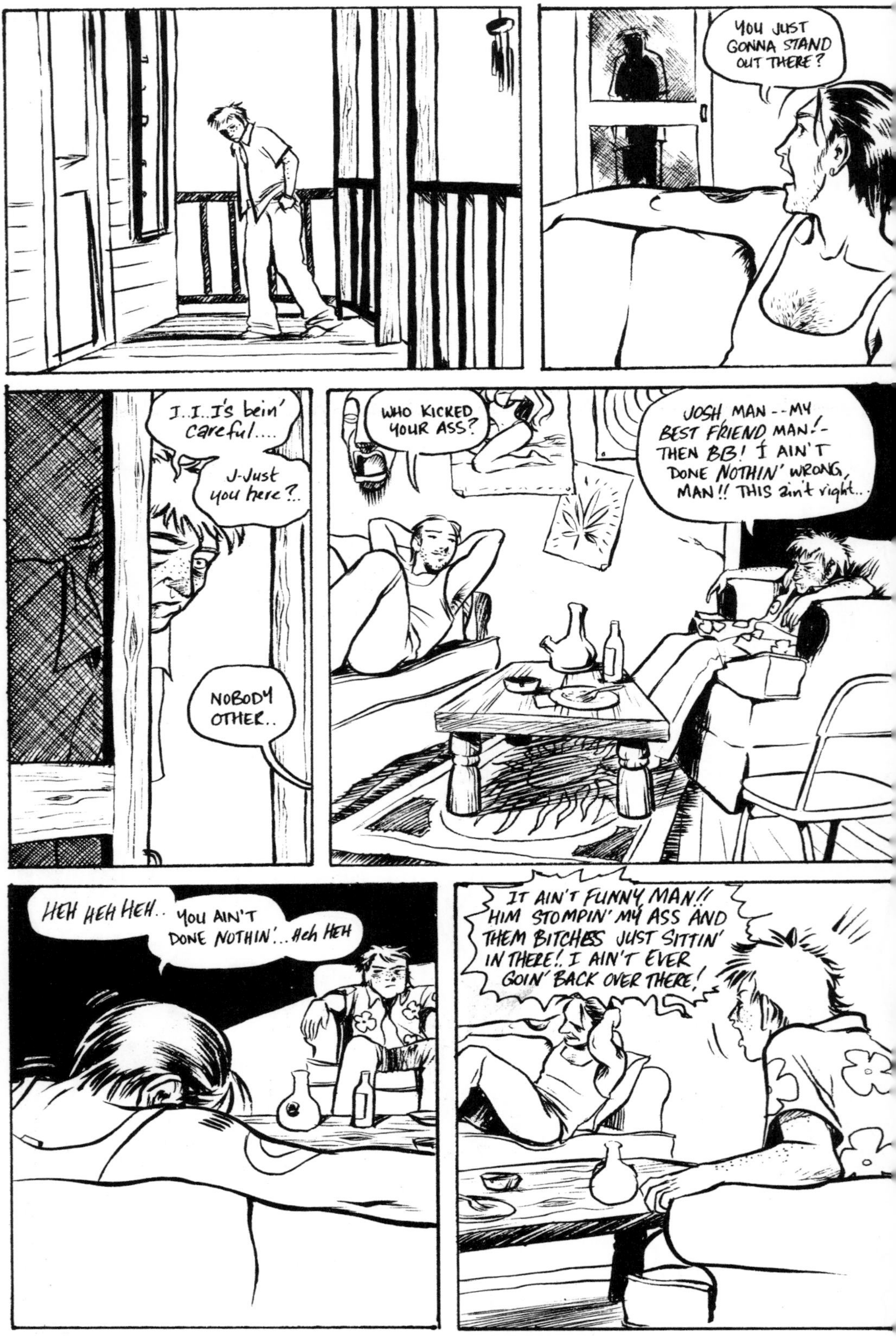
YOU JUST GONNA STAND OUT THERE?
I..I..I's bein' careful....
J-Just you here?..
NOBODY OTHER..
WHO KICKED YOUR ASS?
JOSH MAN--MY BEST FRIEND MAN!- THEN BB! I AIN'T DONE NOTHIN' WRONG, MAN!! THIS ain't right...
HEH HEH HEH..
YOU AIN'T DONE NOTHIN'... Heh HEH
IT AIN'T FUNNY MAN!! HIM STOMPIN' MY ASS AND THEM BITCHES JUST SITTIN' IN THERE!. I AIN'T EVER GOIN' BACK OVER THERE!

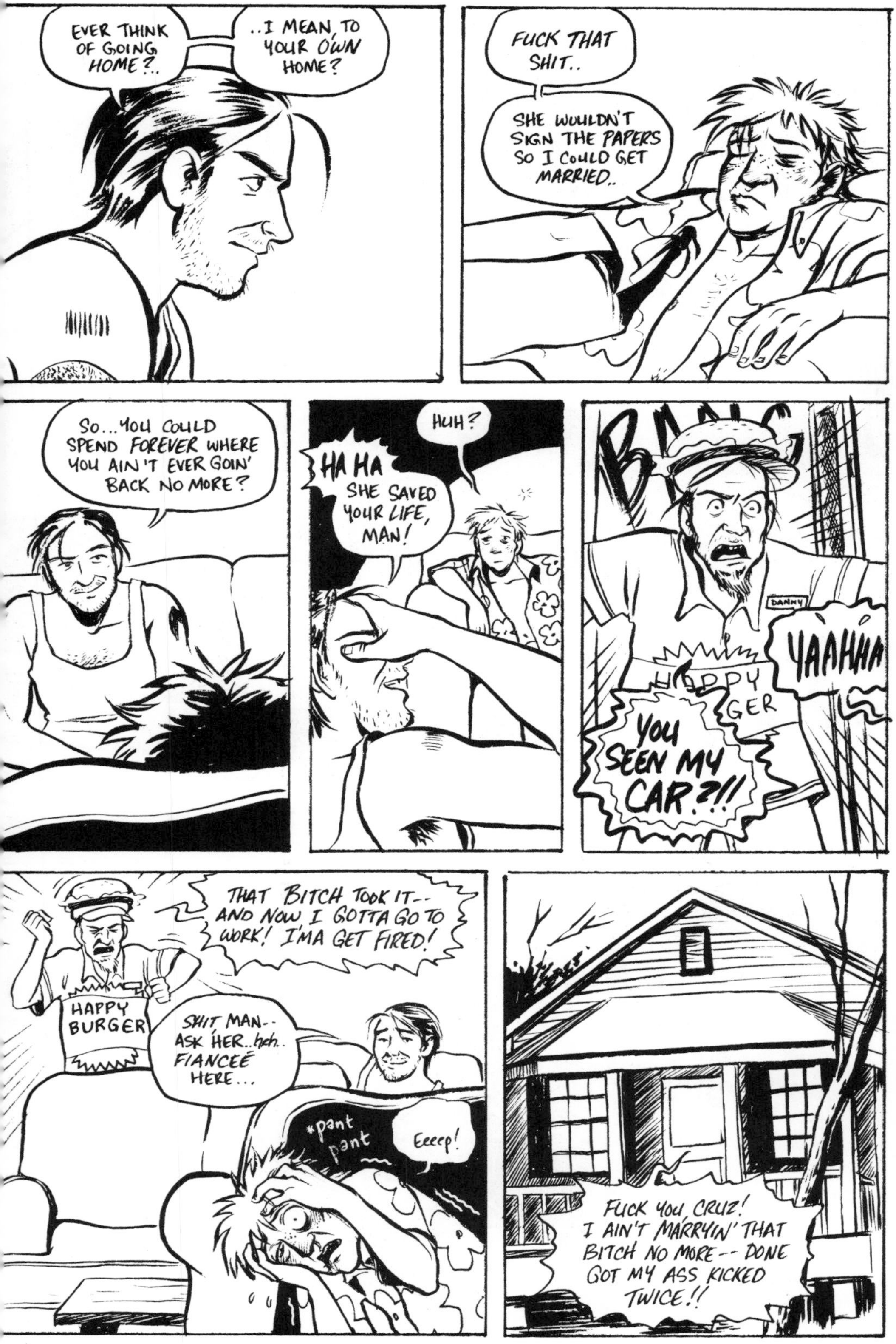
EVER THINK OF GOING HOME?..
..I MEAN, TO YOUR OWN HOME?
FUCK THAT SHIT..
SHE WOULDN'T SIGN THE PAPERS SO I COULD GET MARRIED..
SO... YOU COULD SPEND FOREVER WHERE YOU AIN'T EVER GOIN' BACK NO MORE?
HUH?
HA HA
SHE SAVED YOUR LIFE, MAN!
DANNY
YAAHHA
YOU SEEN MY CAR?!!
THAT BITCH TOOK IT-- AND NOW I GOTTA GO TO WORK! I'MA GET FIRED!
HAPPY BURGER
SHIT MAN-- ASK HER..heh.. FIANCEE HERE...
*pant pant
Eeeep!
FUCK YOU, CRUZ! I AIN'T MARRYIN' THAT BITCH NO MORE-- DONE GOT MY ASS KICKED TWICE!!

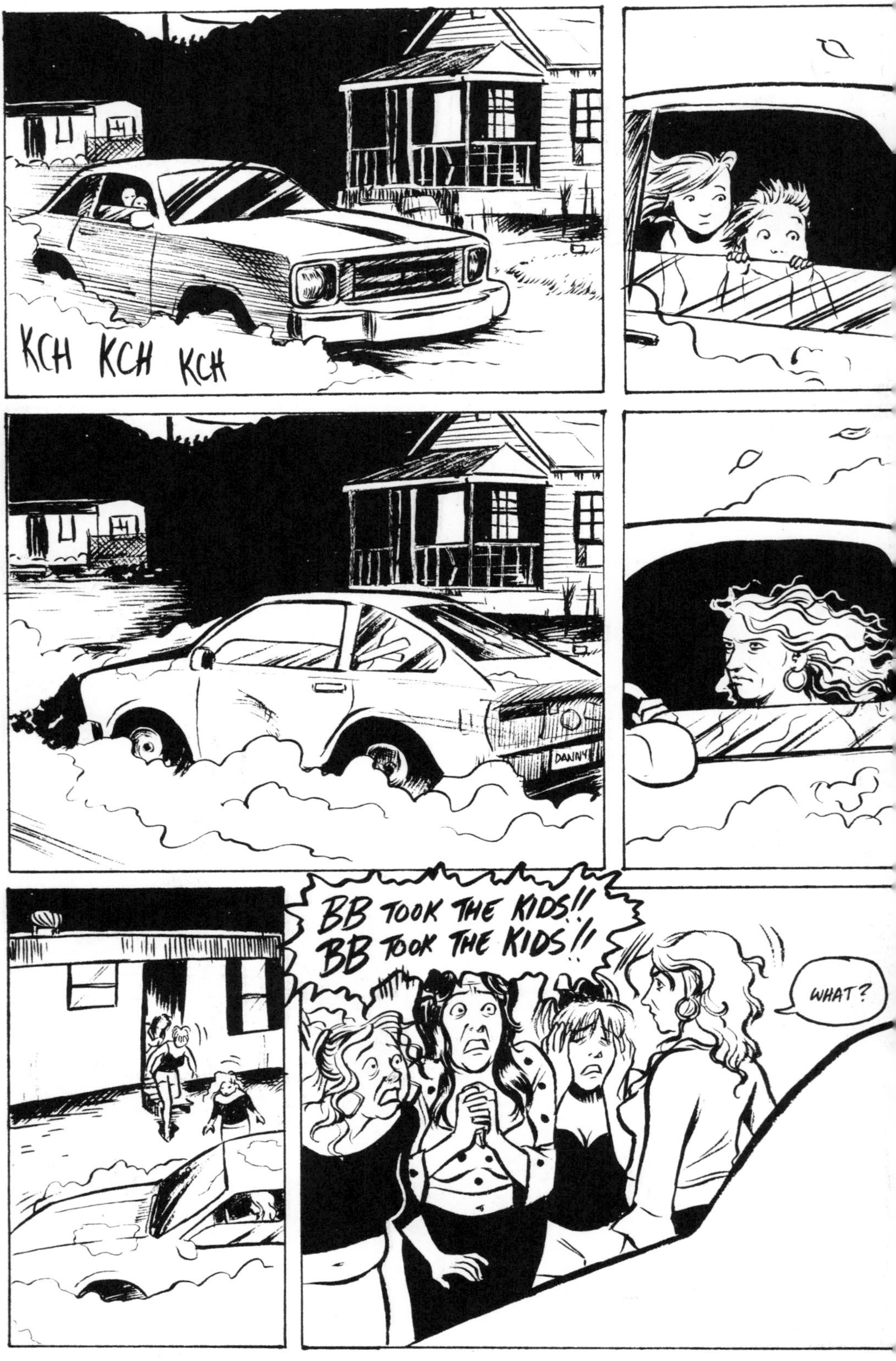
KCH KCH KCH
DANNY
BB TOOK THE KIDS!! BB TOOK THE KIDS!!
WHAT?

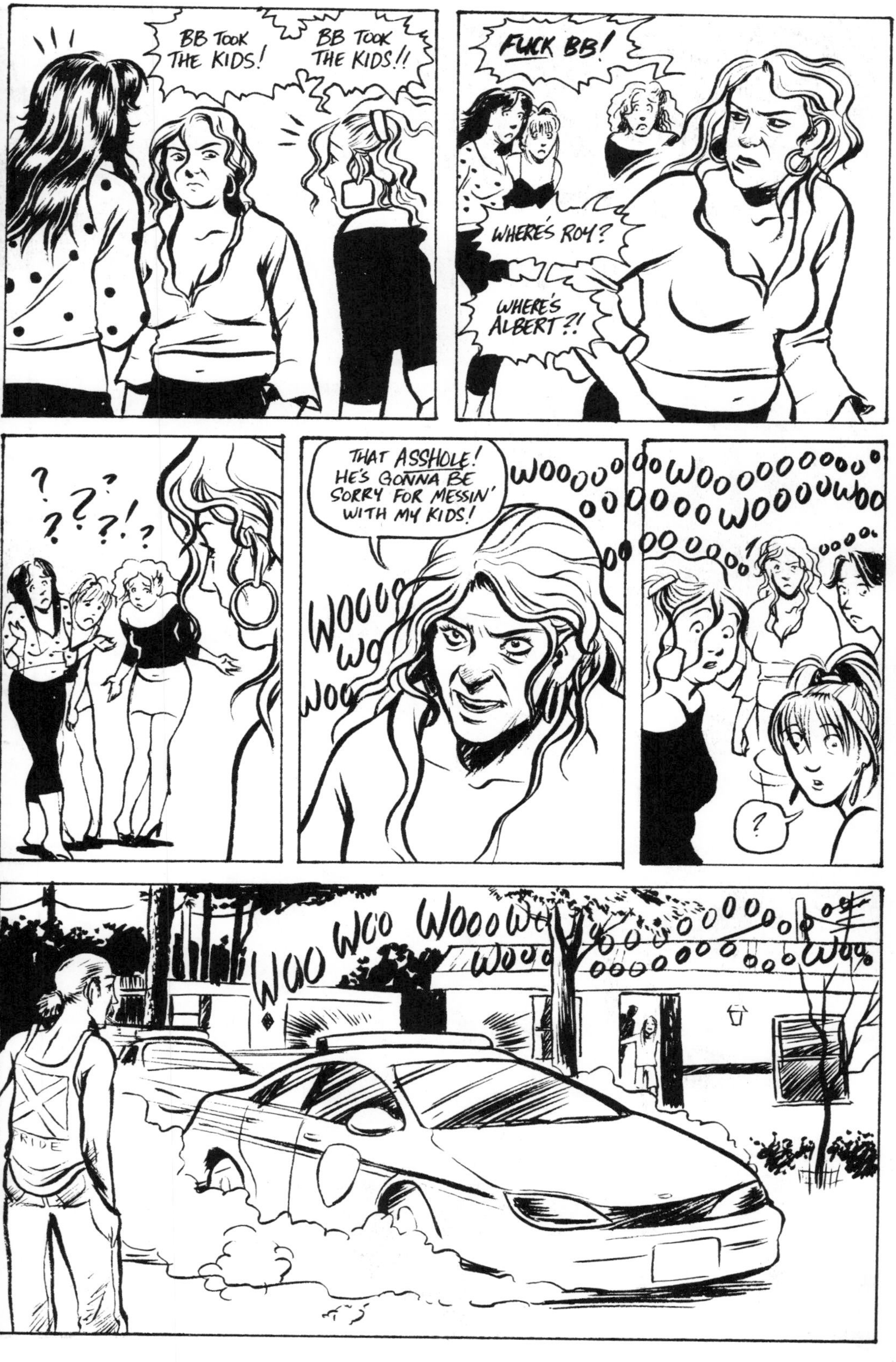
BB TOOK THE KIDS!
BB TOOK THE KIDS!!
FUCK BB!
WHERE'S ROY?
WHERE'S ALBERT?!
?
THAT ASSHOLE! HE'S GONNA BE SORRY FOR MESSIN' WITH MY KIDS!
WOOOO WOO WOO
WOOOOOOOOWOOOOOOOOOOOO
?
WOO WOO WOOO
PRIDE

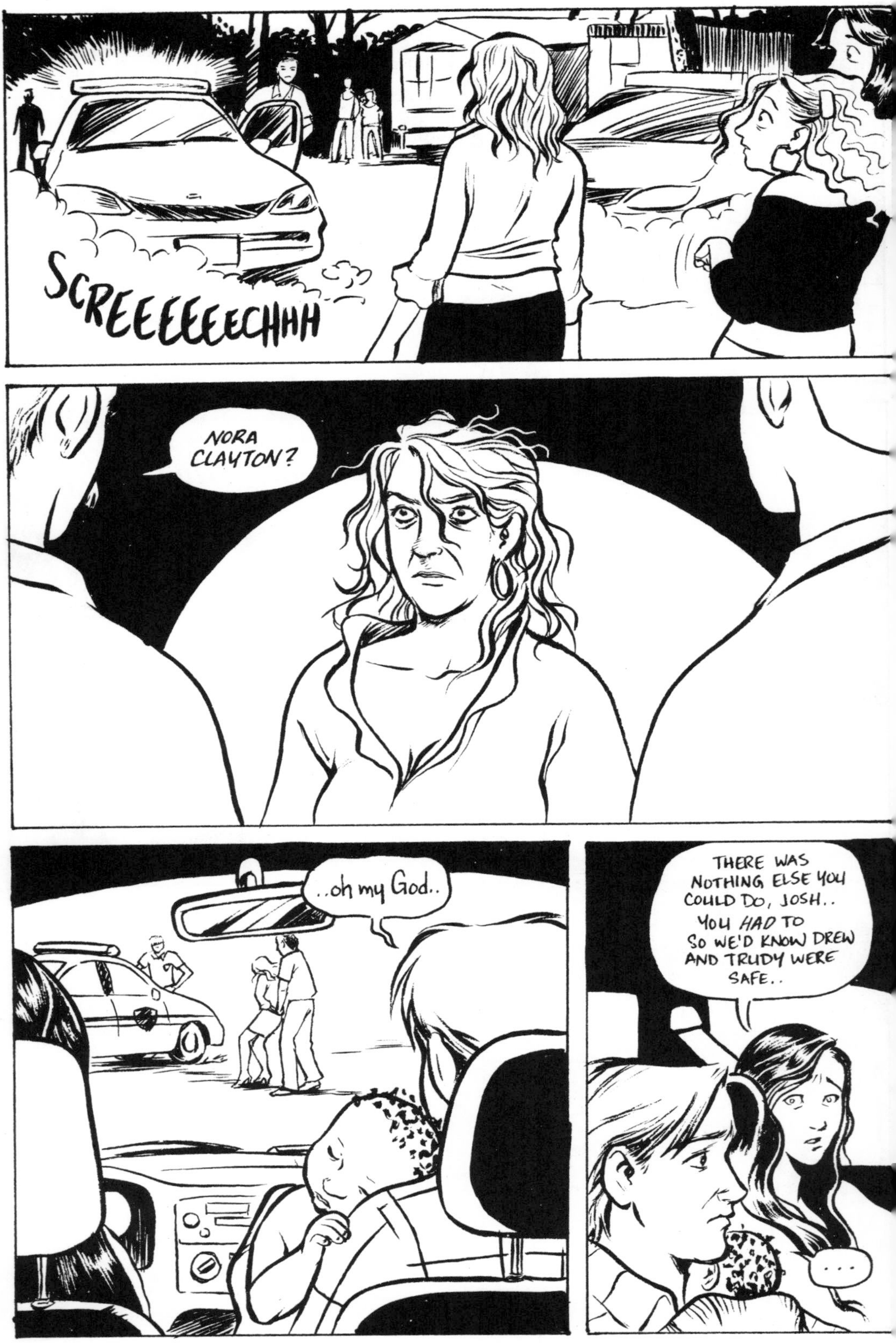
SCREEEEEECHHH
NORA CLAYTON?
..oh my God..
THERE WAS NOTHING ELSE YOU COULD DO, JOSH.. YOU HAD TO SO WE'D KNOW DREW AND TRUDY WERE SAFE..
...

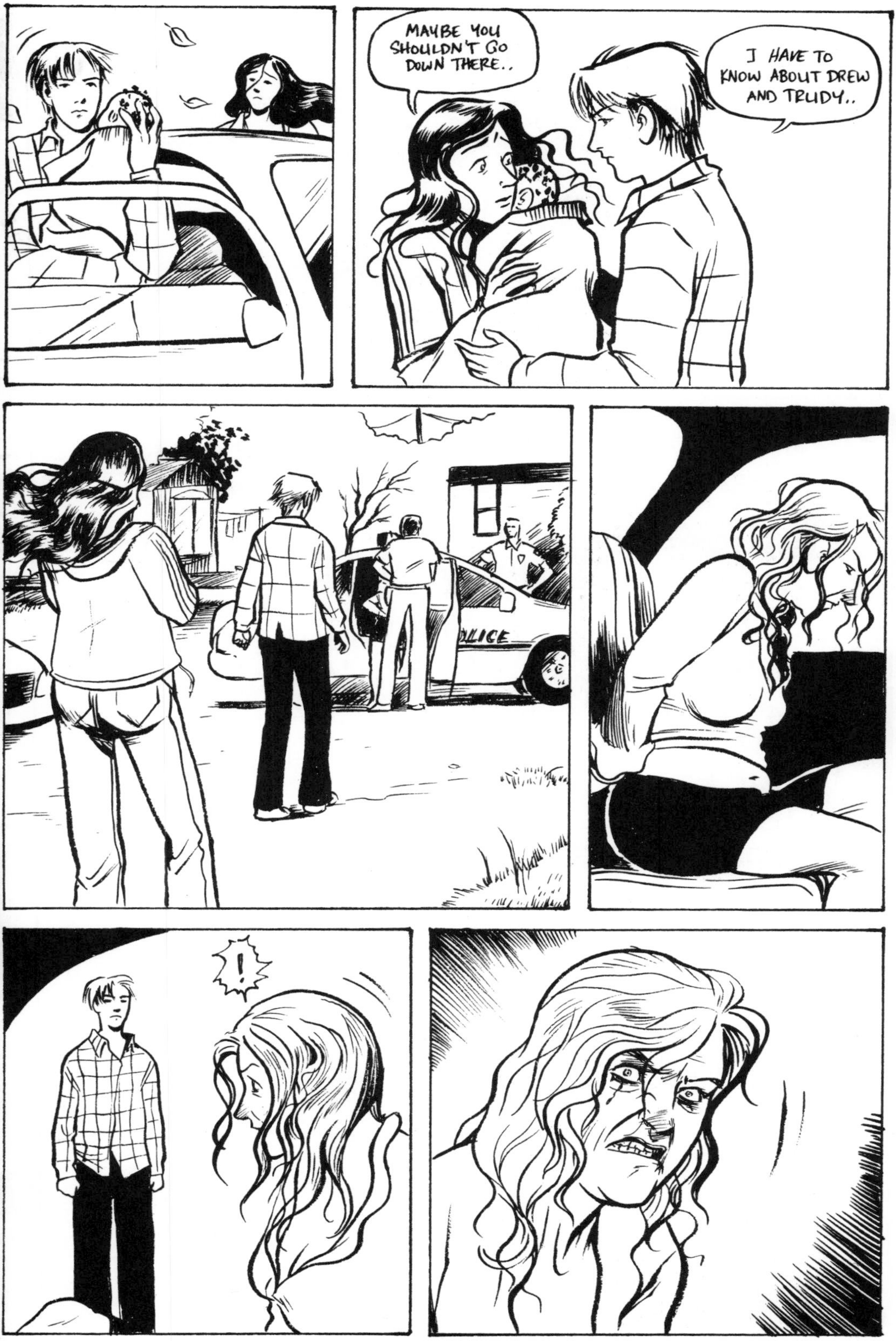
MAYBE YOU SHOULDN'T GO DOWN THERE..
I HAVE TO KNOW ABOUT DREW AND TRUDY..
POLICE
!

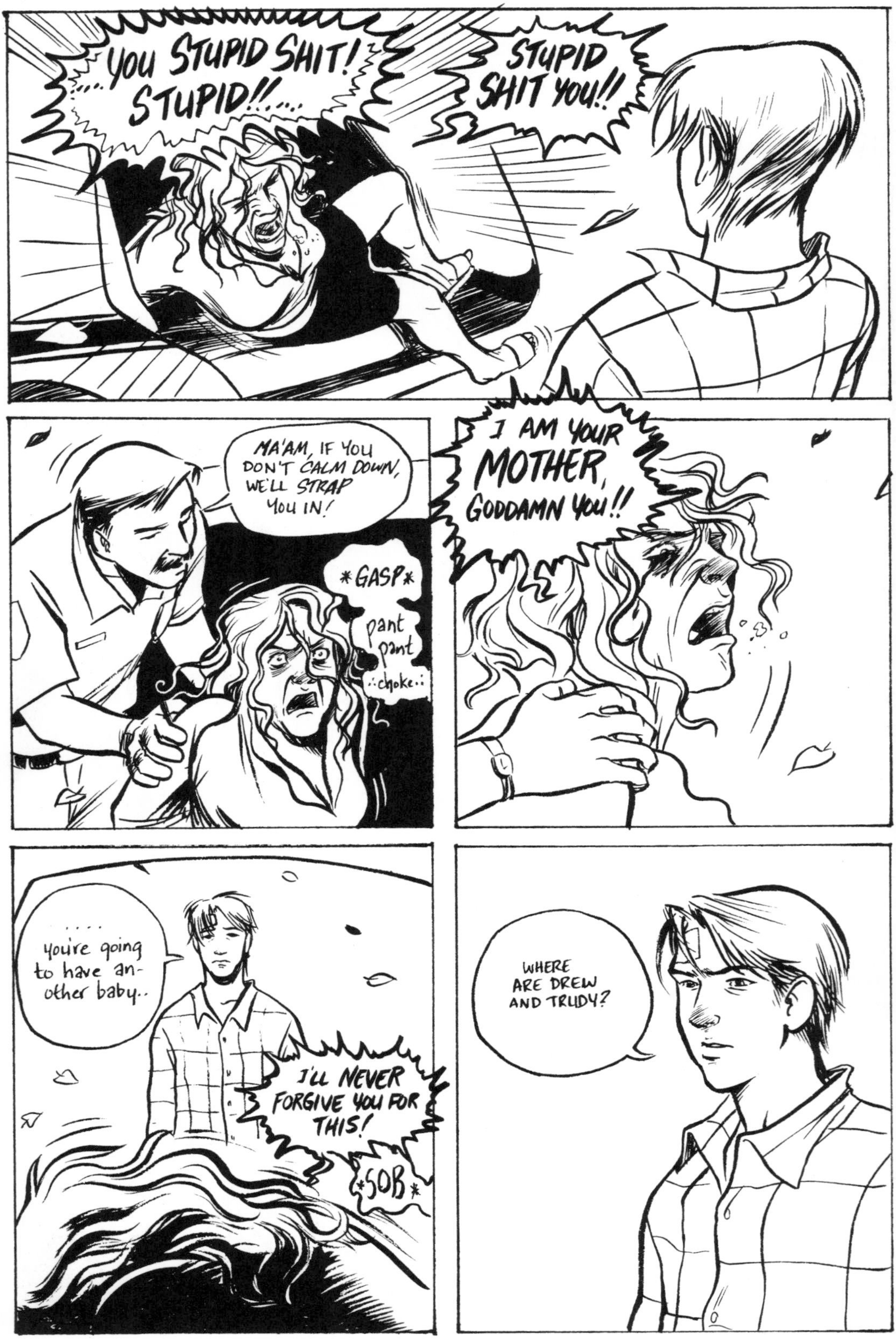
YOU STUPID SHIT! STUPID!!
STUPID SHIT YOU!!
MA'AM, IF YOU DON'T CALM DOWN, WE'LL STRAP YOU IN!
GASP
pant pant
..choke..
I AM YOUR MOTHER, GODDAMN YOU!!
.... you're going to have another baby..
I'LL NEVER FORGIVE YOU FOR THIS!
SOB
WHERE ARE DREW AND TRUDY?

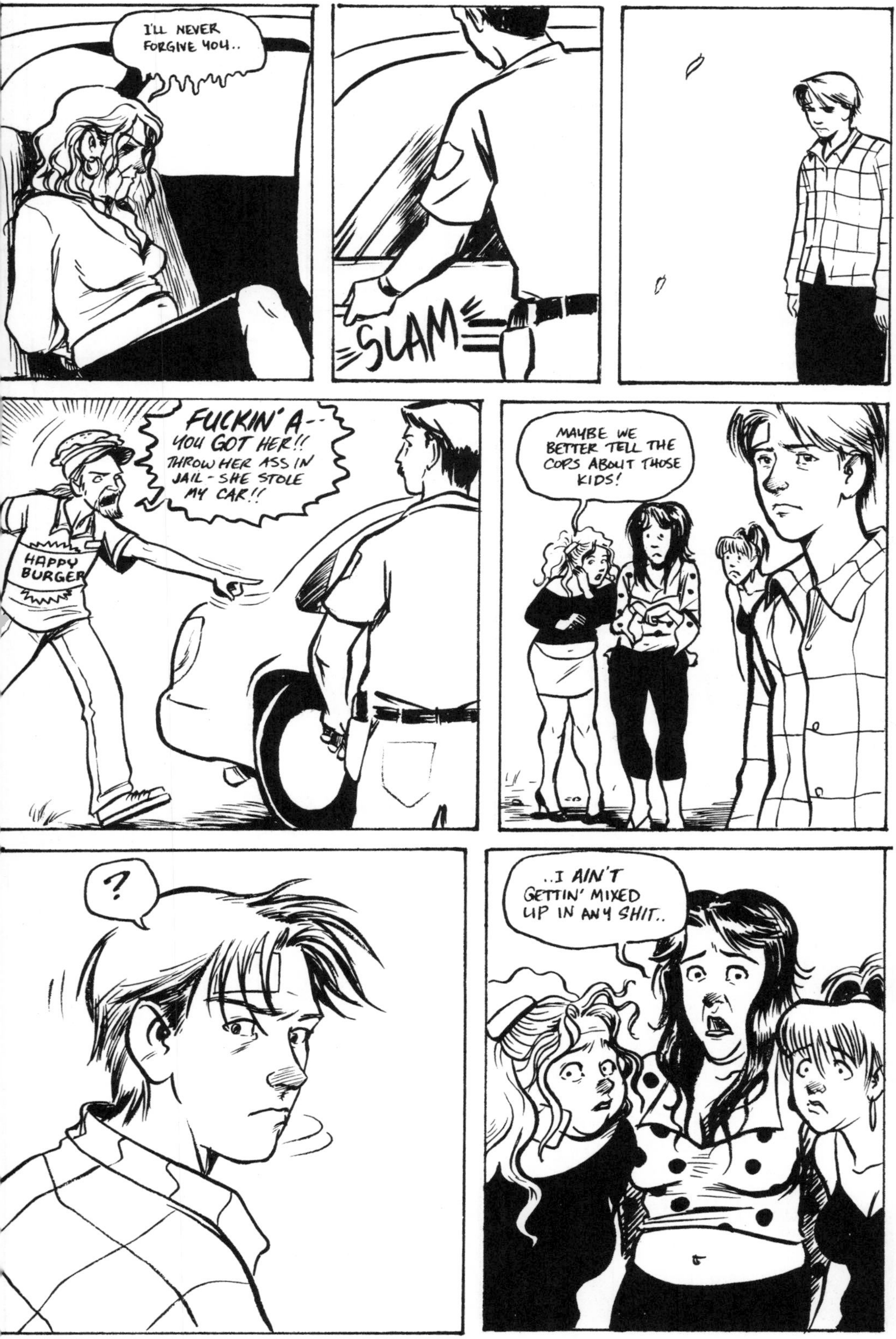
I'LL NEVER FORGIVE YOU..
SLAM
FUCKIN' A-- YOU GOT HER!! THROW HER ASS IN JAIL - SHE STOLE MY CAR!!
HAPPY BURGER
MAYBE WE BETTER TELL THE COPS ABOUT THOSE KIDS!
?
..I AIN'T GETTIN' MIXED UP IN ANY SHIT..

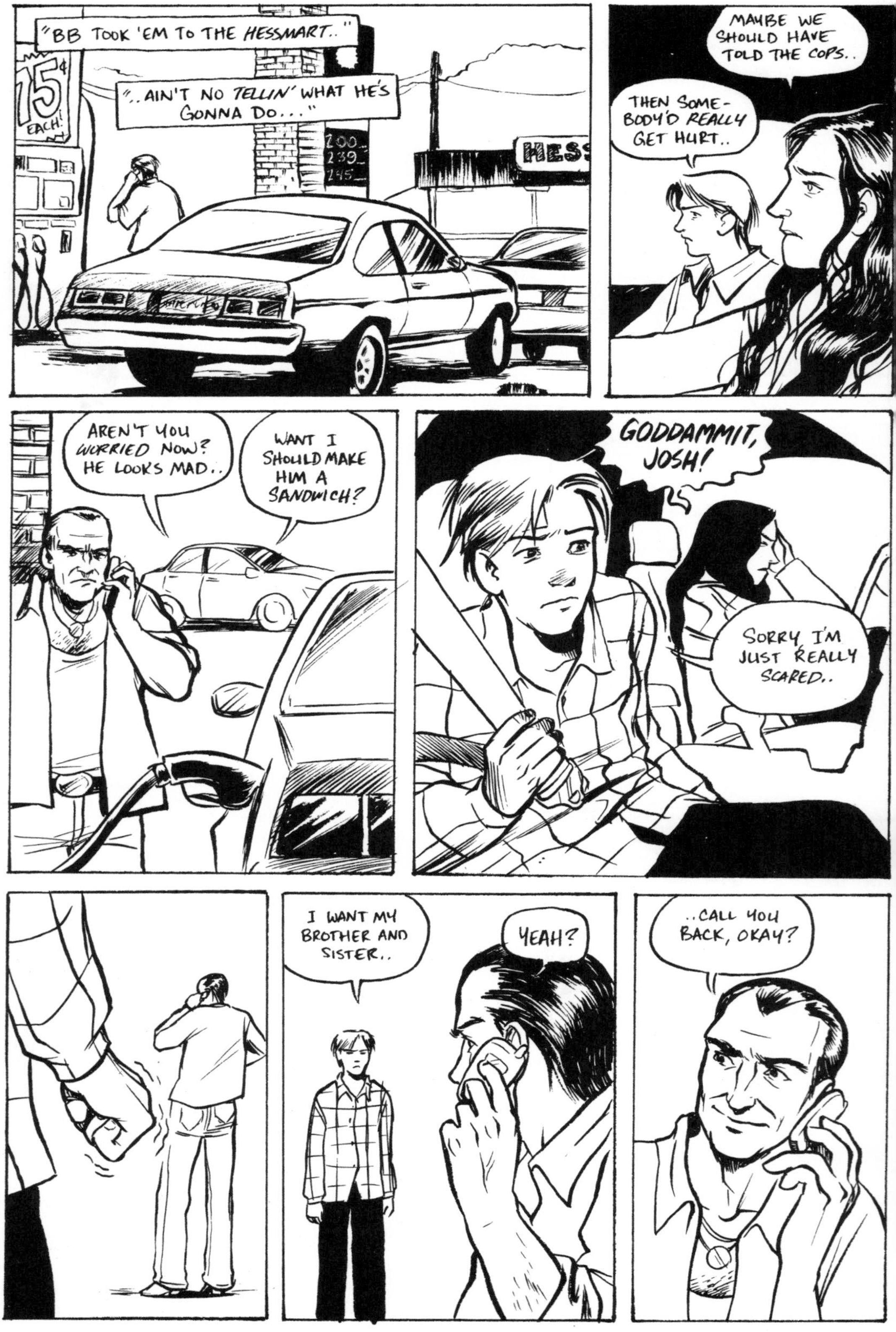
"BB TOOK 'EM TO THE HESSMART.."
"..AIN'T NO TELLIN' WHAT HE'S GONNA DO..."
15¢ EACH!
2.00 2.39 2.45
HESS
MAYBE WE SHOULD HAVE TOLD THE COPS..
THEN SOMEBODY'D REALLY GET HURT..
AREN'T YOU WORRIED NOW? HE LOOKS MAD..
WANT I SHOULD MAKE HIM A SANDWICH?
GODDAMMIT, JOSH!
SORRY I'M JUST REALLY SCARED..
I WANT MY BROTHER AND SISTER..
YEAH?
..CALL YOU BACK, OKAY?

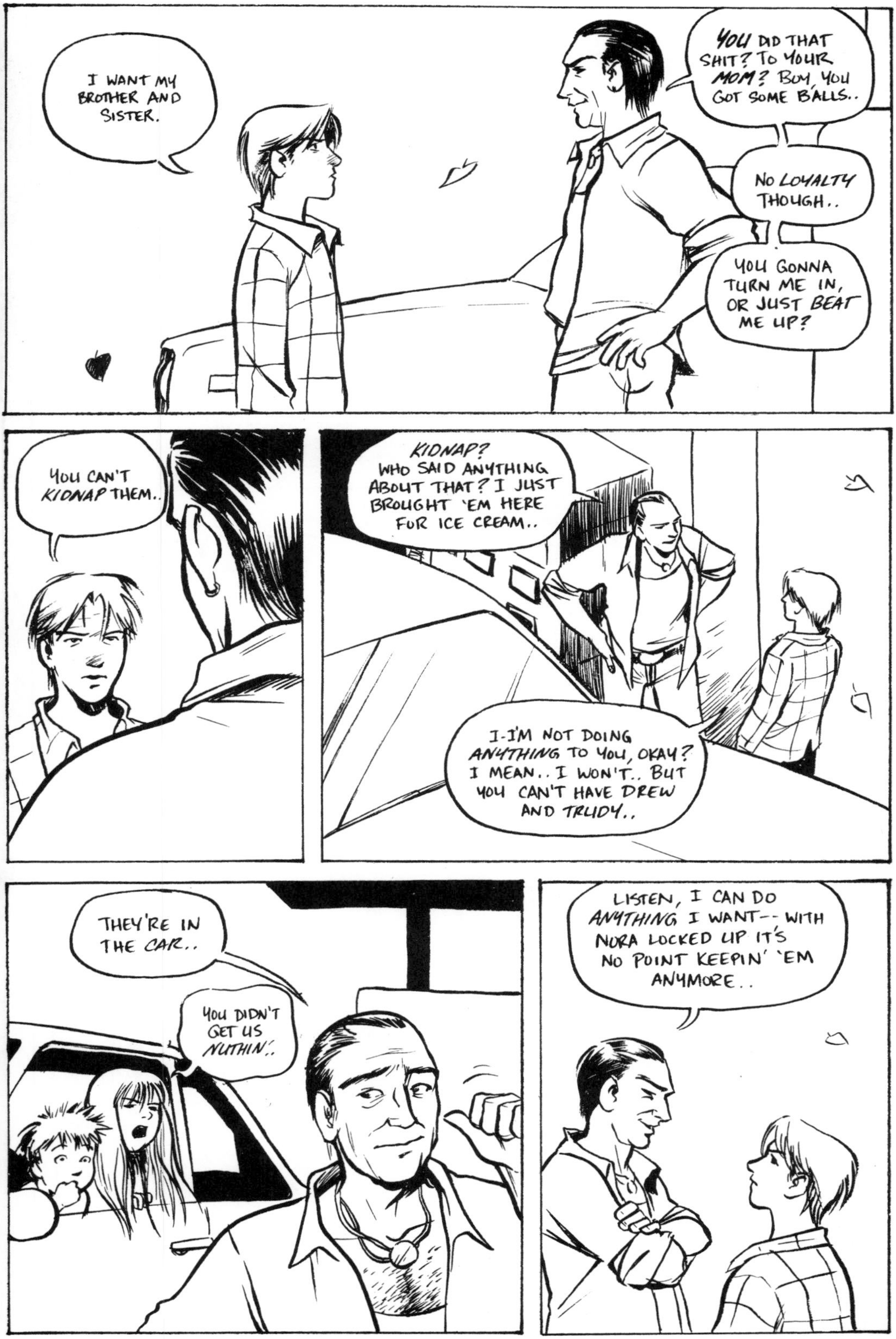
I WANT MY BROTHER AND SISTER.
YOU DID THAT SHIT? TO YOUR MOM? BOY, YOU GOT SOME BALLS..
NO LOYALTY THOUGH..
YOU GONNA TURN ME IN, OR JUST BEAT ME UP?
YOU CAN'T KIDNAP THEM..
KIDNAP? WHO SAID ANYTHING ABOUT THAT? I JUST BROUGHT 'EM HERE FUR ICE CREAM..
I-I'M NOT DOING ANYTHING TO YOU, OKAY? I MEAN.. I WON'T.. BUT YOU CAN'T HAVE DREW AND TRUDY..
THEY'RE IN THE CAR..
YOU DIDN'T GET US NUTHIN'..
LISTEN, I CAN DO ANYTHING I WANT-- WITH NORA LOCKED UP IT'S NO POINT KEEPIN' 'EM ANYMORE..

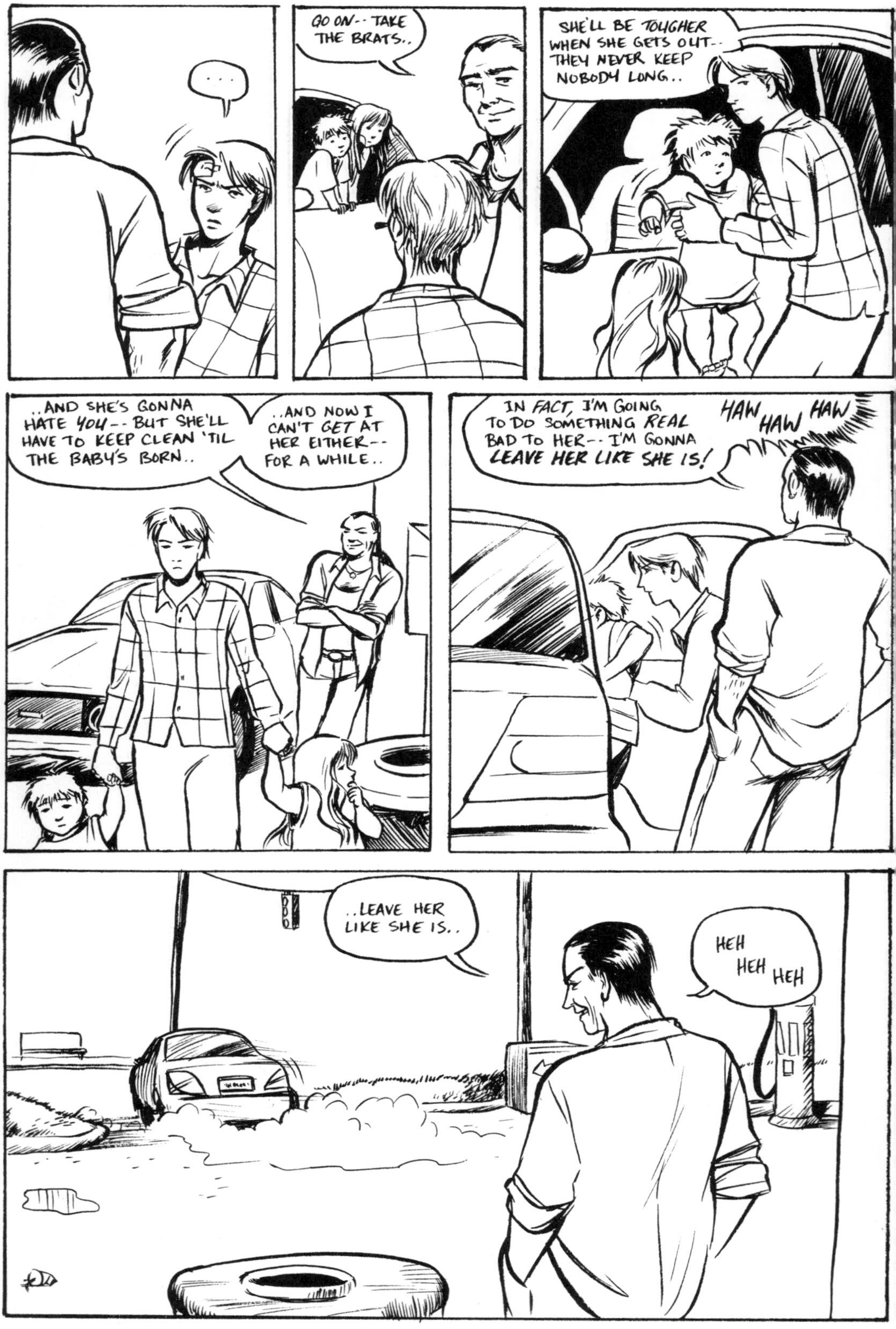
. . .
GO ON-- TAKE THE BRATS..
SHE'LL BE TOUGHER WHEN SHE GETS OUT-- THEY NEVER KEEP NOBODY LONG..
..AND SHE'S GONNA HATE YOU-- BUT SHE'LL HAVE TO KEEP CLEAN 'TIL THE BABY'S BORN..
..AND NOW I CAN'T GET AT HER EITHER-- FOR A WHILE..
IN FACT, I'M GOING TO DO SOMETHING REAL BAD TO HER-- I'M GONNA LEAVE HER LIKE SHE IS!
HAW HAW HAW
..LEAVE HER LIKE SHE IS..
HEH HEH HEH

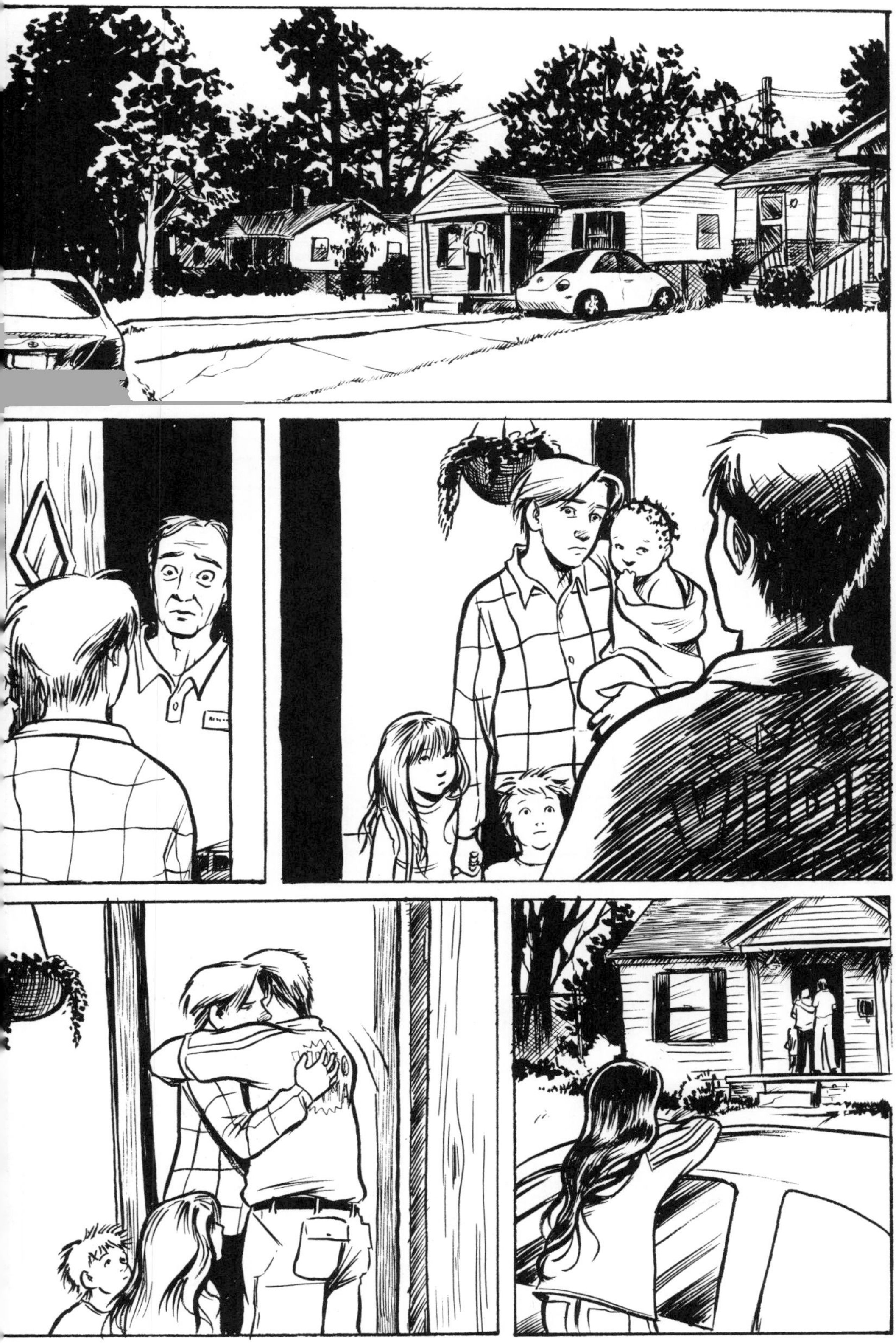

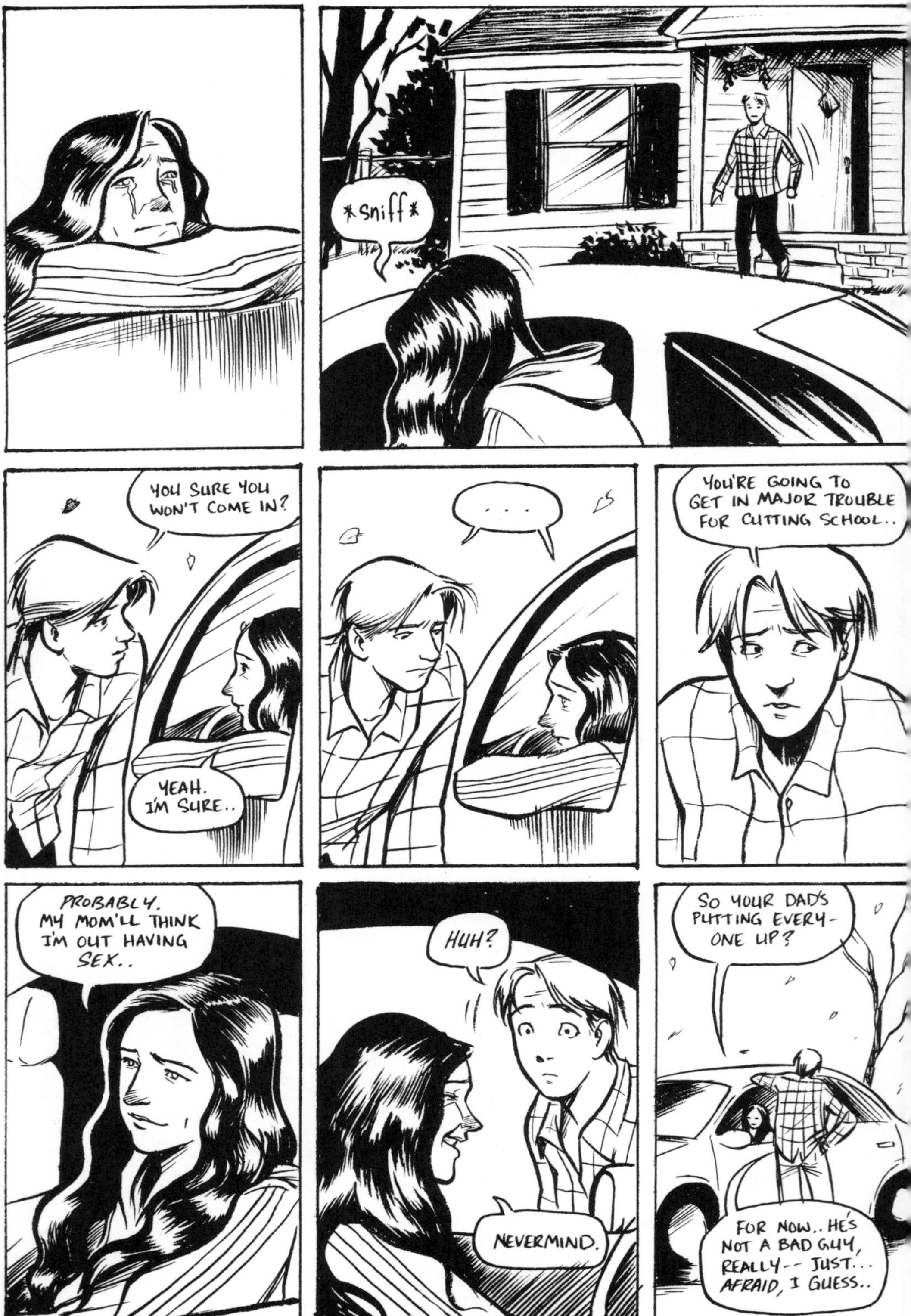
sniff
YOU SURE YOU WON'T COME IN?
YEAH. I'M SURE..
. . .
YOU'RE GOING TO GET IN MAJOR TROUBLE FOR CUTTING SCHOOL..
PROBABLY. MY MOM'LL THINK I'M OUT HAVING SEX..
HUH?
NEVERMIND.
SO YOUR DAD'S PUTTING EVERY-ONE UP?
FOR NOW.. HE'S NOT A BAD GUY, REALLY-- JUST... AFRAID, I GUESS..

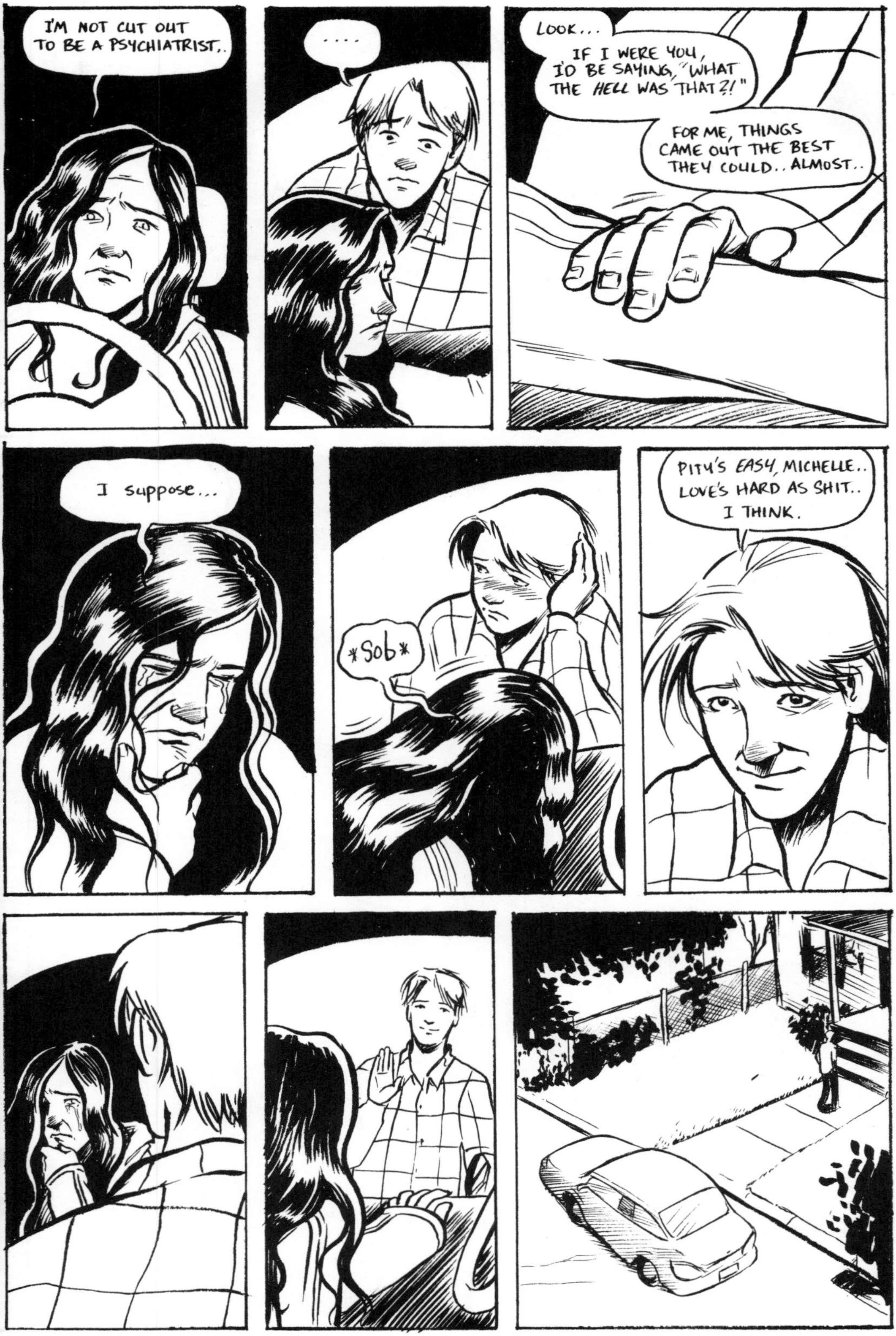
I'M NOT CUT OUT TO BE A PSYCHIATRIST..
....
LOOK...
IF I WERE YOU, I'D BE SAYING, "WHAT THE HELL WAS THAT?!"
FOR ME, THINGS CAME OUT THE BEST THEY COULD.. ALMOST..
I suppose...
Sob
PITY'S EASY, MICHELLE.. LOVE'S HARD AS SHIT.. I THINK.

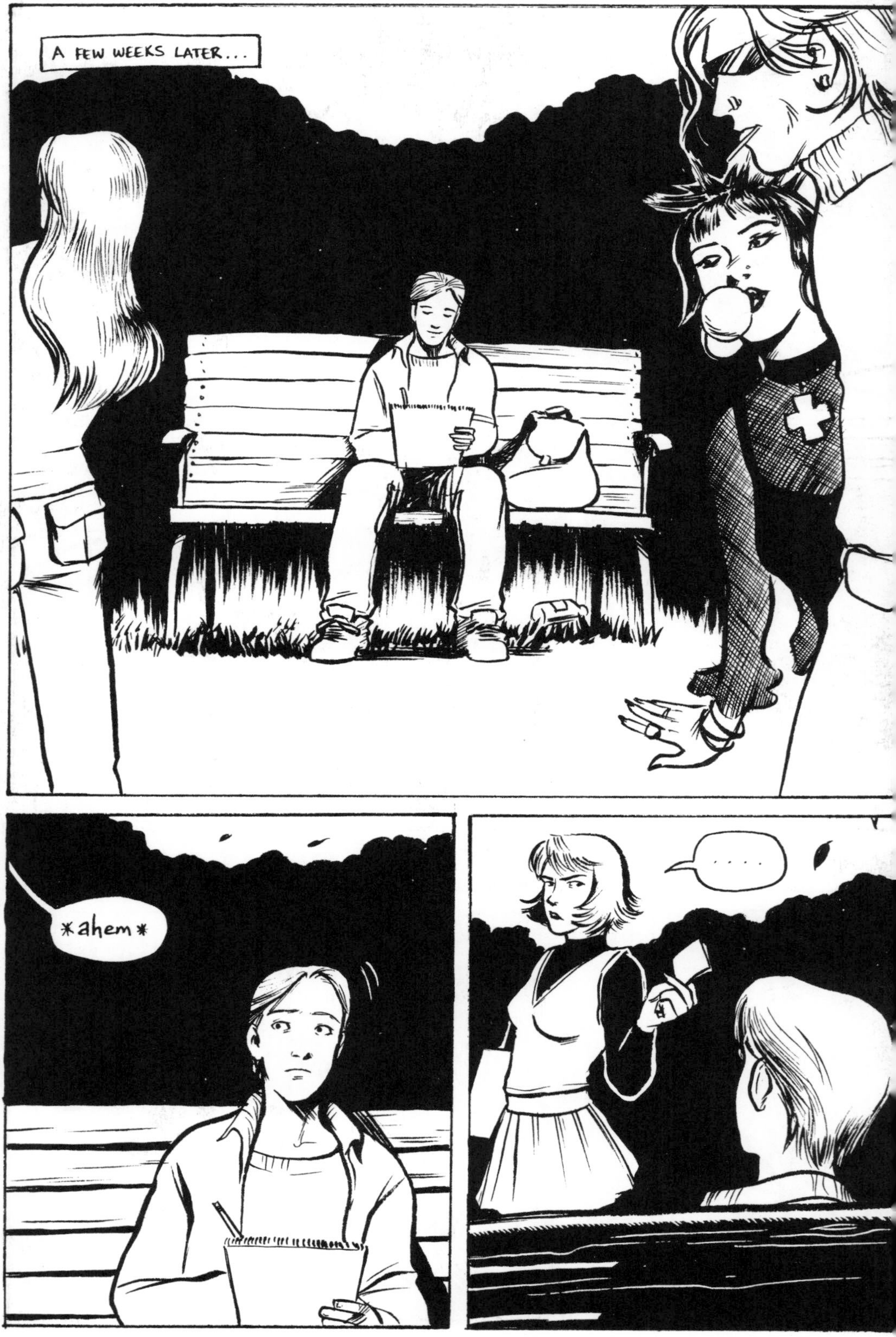
A FEW WEEKS LATER...
ahem
....

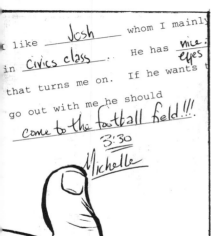

like ___Josh___ whom I mainly
in ___Civics class___ . He has _nice_
eyes
that turns me on. If he wants t
go out with me he should
come to the football field!!!
3:30
Michelle

BRIIIIING

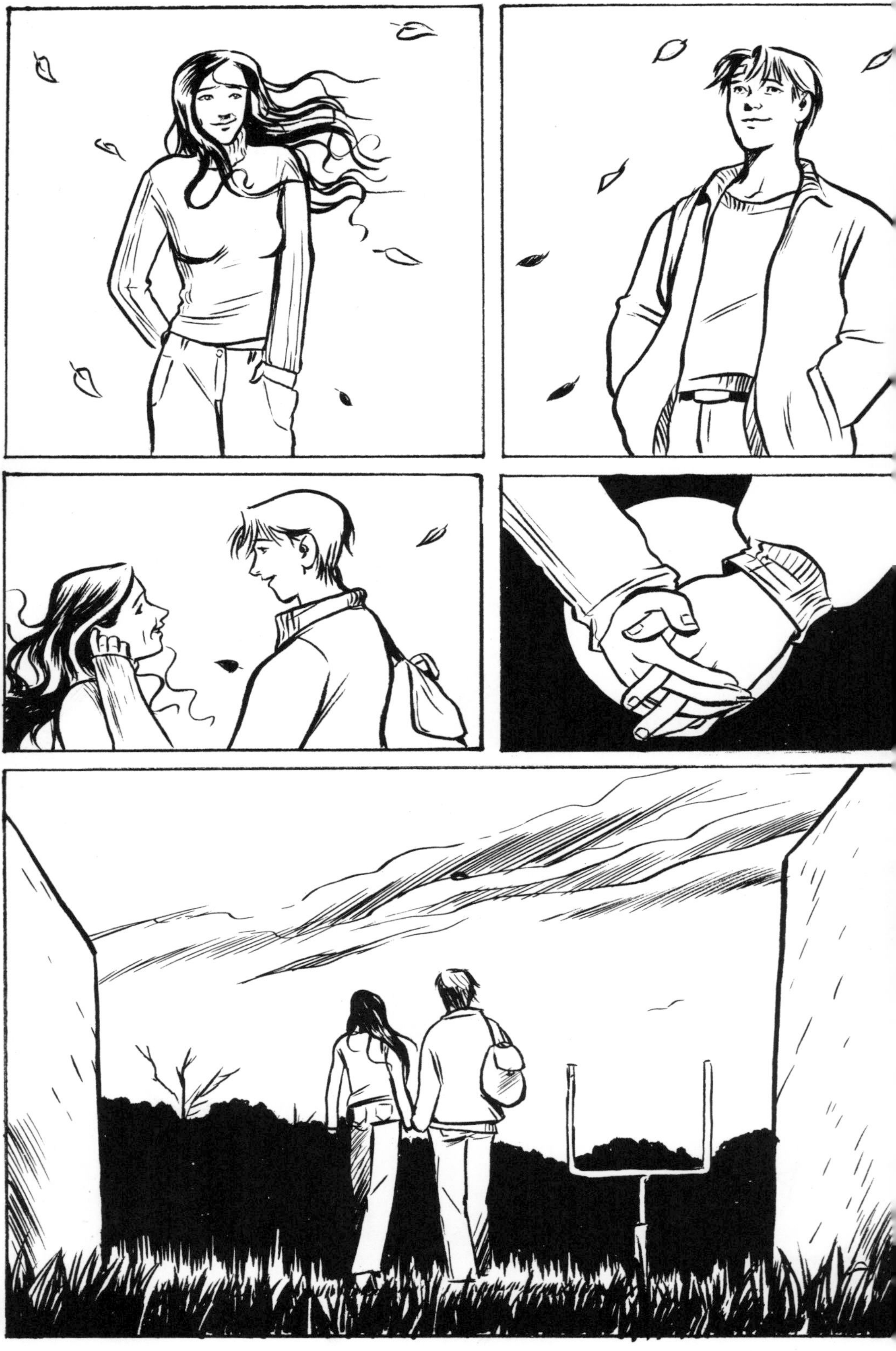

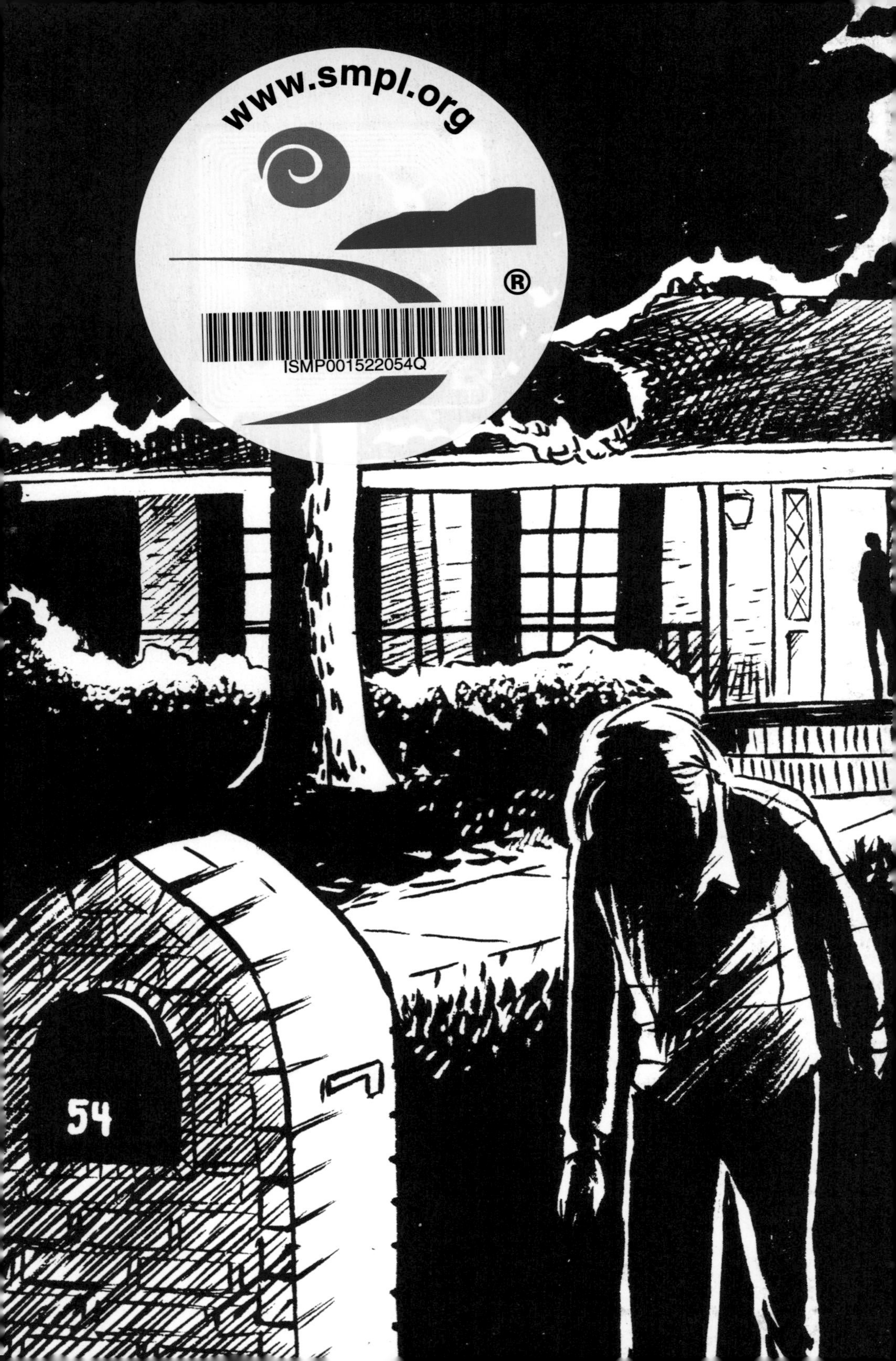
54